THE BLACK WORKER

THE BLACK WORKER

The Negro and the
Labor Movement

STERLING D. SPERO
&
ABRAM L. HARRIS

with a new preface by Herbert G. Gutman

STUDIES IN AMERICAN NEGRO LIFE
August Meier, General Editor

NEW YORK   ATHENEUM   1972

Published by Atheneum
Copyright 1931, 1959 by Columbia University Press
Preface copyright © 1968 by Herbert G. Gutman
All rights reserved
Library of Congress catalog card number 68-16419
Manufactured in the United States of America by
Halliday Lithograph Corporation
West Hanover, Massachusetts
Published in Canada by McClelland & Stewart Ltd.
First Atheneum Printing February 1968
Second Printing September 1969
Third Printing January 1972

TO OUR FRIEND AND TEACHER
THE LATE

HENRY ROGERS SEAGER

PROFESSOR OF POLITICAL ECONOMY
IN COLUMBIA UNIVERSITY

PREFACE TO THE ATHENEUM EDITION

BY HERBERT G. GUTMAN

In the fall of 1930, the authors of two separate works on the same subject prepared their prefaces. One, *The Negro Wage Earner,* was written by Carter G. Woodson and Lorenzo Greene; the other, entitled *The Black Worker: The Negro and the Labor Movement,* had as co-authors Abram L. Harris and Sterling D. Spero. Here we give attention only to *The Black Worker,* but it is of interest to note that both studies appeared at the same time and were, in a sense, a joint summing up of a period in American Negro and labor history that ended with the Great Depression. Each work focused on the Negro worker and the consequences of the massive migration of rural southern Negroes to northern cities and to new modes of employment and living. Spero and Harris gave more attention to the relations between the Negro and organized labor than Greene and Woodson. Republication of *The Black Worker* in 1968 deserves comment for many reasons. Some are obvious—or should be—to people who have been witness to Watts, Newark, and Detroit and to the tense and troubled relations between civil rights advocates and the labor establishment. Other reasons are more subtle and shall be dwelt upon in this brief introduction.

There is no reason to summarize *The Black Worker;* each reader can draw his own meaning from it. But it is important to note that Spero and Harris were not optimistic in their findings. They sensed only a bleak future. So they made it clear in their preface that the study was "neither a good will tract on race relations nor an attempt to offer a program for the solution of a vexing problem." Four general "factors" shaped their study: the interplay between the slave heritage, the structure and policies of craft unions, the recent migration of Negroes from the South, and the influence of the Negro middle class and its ideology within the northern ghetto. Their indictment of most trade unions (a few, such as the United Mine Workers of America and the immigrant garment unions, escaped censure) was severe, as was their scorn for dominant Negro leadership, but what most concerned Spero and Harris was the particular ways in which the Negro lost his place as "an industrial labor reserve" to become "a regular element in the labor force of every basic industry."

Concrete facts in the year or two before their work was published gave Spero and Harris good reason to despair and to write so critical a book. A. Philip Randolph had failed in his early efforts to win recognition for the Brotherhood of Sleeping Car Porters and Maids from the powerful Pullman company. The United Mine Workers suffered a decline, and it, more than any other union, had worked hardest to draw in Negro members. Too many well-established craft unions openly or covertly denied membership and therefore job opportunities to Negro workers. The national American Federation of Labor leadership rebuffed efforts by Negro pressure groups in behalf of trade union reform and against restrictive racial practices. Individual AFL unions left much to be desired. In 1929, for example, the American Federation of Teachers rejected a resolution to devote special attention to organizing Negro teachers and even voted down an effort to censure segregated schools. The Negro middle class dominated ghetto life and largely rejected trade unionism for its less favored brothers and sisters. The ideal of Negro self-sufficiency and an "independent black economy" had come to little, and the promises of white radicals fell on deaf ears (without regard to color). Industrial unionism seemed distant in 1930 and 1931. Spero and Harris therefore despaired. Optimism would have been fatuous and illusory in so dreary a time.

But we read this book for reasons other than its tone. Seen in a comparative perspective, its greatest value is that it is a corrective to the dominant scholarship in American labor history. The point is quite simple. Much has been written about the history of American labor before and since the publication of *The Black Worker*. But the main emphasis has been on institutional trade union history. The central focus on the trade union and the "labor movement" has revealed much. But so narrow a framework has meant the neglect of a central fact (perhaps *the* central fact) that has shaped the very marrow of American social history and especially the history of its lower classes. Unlike any other western industrial nation, the United States drew and continues to draw its labor force from an ethnically and racially mixed population. Not only European, Asian, and Latin American immigrants played a vital role in shaping that history; Negroes were equally important. Together, these groups made for differences in American labor history that separate it from the classic European pattern. We need only remember that for much of its history the American labor force was half-free, or realize that in 1910 southern and eastern European immigrants and American Negroes (to a much lesser degree) made up two thirds of all workers in twenty-one major industries. The focus of much labor history, however, has blurred these and other essential facts. Before 1940, only a small proportion of the nation's labor force belonged to permanent labor unions, so that the excessive attention given to these unions has meant the neglect of the essential interplay between class and ethnicity or race that has so profoundly shaped the nation's history. Spero and Harris chose a subject that broke with this tradition. By making the Negro the central theme of their study, they drew attention to larger aspects of American labor history. And for this reason, among others, their book continues to command attention.

A book such as this one also sheds significant light on the dark disputes that rage in contemporary America. Its findings, for example, help us to understand but do not fully explain the decline of the vital tradition of craftsmanship among southern Negroes. The current arguments over the effects of slavery on Negro personality are illuminated when we realize that of about 120,000 southern craftsmen in 1865 about 100,000 were Negroes, but that over the next forty years this figure declined relatively and absolutely. Much is learned, furthermore, about the historic roots of the current controversy between civil rights organizations and those trade unions that hesitate to share job opportunities and precious skills with Negro workers. Here, however, Spero and Harris should be supplemented by the studies of the post-1930 era by such writers as Herbert Northrup, Horace Cayton and George Mitchell, and F. Ray Marshall.

Every pioneering work has its weaknesses and shortcomings, and *The Black Worker* is no exception. Its greatest strength is in what it tells of the years between 1910 and 1930, formative years that saw the Negro drawn into the national economy and that were a time in which the urban working class began assuming a new shape. In these pages the volume is richest and contains much otherwise inaccessible information. But even here weaknesses occur. In the perspective of forty years, the harsh judgment of A. Philip Randolph's role in the 1920s seems excessive. The role played by large corporations *vis-à-vis* Negro workers in the new mass-production industries is given inadequate attention, and the structure of community life that surrounded the urban Negro worker is treated too sketchily. But these are minor criticisms compared to the weaknesses of the earlier historical sections. Spero and Harris had few scholarly works to guide them through the uncharted history of the nineteenth-century Negro worker and his relations with white workers, the labor market, and the trade union movement. The chapters on the pre-Civil War years and the competition between free and slave labor should be read in light of the recent findings of Leon F. Litwack *(North of Slavery: The Negro in the Free States)* and Richard C. Wade *(Slavery in the Cities: The South, 1820-1860)*. What Spero and Harris wrote of the post-Civil War decades remains more useful, but part of the reason is that little of significance has been written on the Negro worker between 1865 and 1900. That as many as ten percent of the Knights of Labor were Negroes in the mid-1880s is not yet fully understood. Roger Shugg uncovered much evidence of interracial cooperation between workers in his study of the 1892 New Orleans general strike written nearly thirty years ago, and, more recently, Robert Ward and William Rogers *(Labor Revolt in Alabama: The Great Strike of 1894)* hinted at the vast range of materials on southern Negro and white coal miners. But an overview of these formative decades so far as Negro labor is concerned has not yet been written. We turn time and again to Spero and Harris.

Similarly, much concerning the Negro worker in the early decades of the twentieth century (just before and after the great migration) awaits its historians. Spero and Harris offer them dozens of nuggets still to be mined. Labor historians and others have spent much time disputing the intent of the national leaders of the American Federation of Labor *vis-à-vis* the Negro, a dispute that has generated much heat, shed less and less light, and used up unnecessary energy. Much of this talent could have been used more fruitfully to explore in detail the confrontation of the black worker and industrial America in particular settings. Here a great gap still exists. Even the recent superior studies of Gilbert Osofsky *(Harlem: The Making of a Ghetto)* and Allan H. Spear *(Black Chicago: The Making of a Negro Ghetto)* are disappointing in their treatment of the Negro worker between 1890 and 1920 or 1930. Their otherwise valuable work suffers because of such neglect. John Higham's comments on *Beyond the Melting Pot: The Negroes, Puerto Ricans, Jews, Italians, and Irish of New York City* by Nathan Glazer and Daniel P. Moynihan sum up carefully how little is yet known of the urban Negro:

> Only in discussing the Negro does a censorious note become insistent. ...It is perhaps not coincidental that this least sympathetic section of the book is also the least historical, treating the Negro community as if it possesses no density or complexity and almost no past, while the section with the fullest human scale, the section dealing with the Irish, has also the richest historical dimension. But a historian should not carp; for historians have thus far told the sociologists practically nothing of what southern Negroes brought northward with them, what they encountered, or what it was like to be a submerged American in a city of immigrants.

Striking evidence of the rich harvest that awaits the student of American Negro and labor history, however, appears on every page of Elliot M. Rudwick's *Race Riot at East St. Louis, July 2, 1917.* Rudwick is the first to explore fully the complex dimensions of the relations between Negro and white workers and their employers in that violent and tragic town and time. Rudwick picks up where Spero and Harris leave off. Migration and social conflict become concrete: the tragedy becomes more intimate and the quality of the event takes on a more significant meaning.

Rudwick's methods and the nuggets still buried in Spero and Harris offer riches to those concerned with the interplay of class and caste in American social history. Here, we may ask two questions. What did O. H. Underwood, a Negro miner, mean when he wrote in this century's early years: "I believe that the United Mine Workers has done more to erase the word white from the Constitution than the Fourteenth Amendment"? Similarly, what explains the fact that no less than 6,000 of the 20,000 members of the International Longshoremen's Association in 1902 were Negro dockers? Careful study of the Negro miner (especially in Alabama and West Virginia) and of the longshoremen in such cities as New Orleans, Philadelphia, Baltimore, and the Hampton Roads district will answer these questions. And they are small parts of a still unwritten story.

Spero and Harris were honest in their despair and pessimism. "The machine, rather than any concept of working-class unity or industrial brotherhood, will compel the official labor movement to change its structure and policy, if it is not to generate into a mere social relic," they concluded. "An extension of government control" also was suggested, and the authors reminded readers in their last sentence that "the will of the controlling majority" counted most—"and that majority is white." A generation earlier, Mary White Ovington, not yet a co-founder of the National Association for the Advancement of Colored People but already deeply involved in efforts to improve the condition of New York City's rapidly increasing lower-class Negro population and a white woman who Claude Mc-Kay said "radiated a quiet silver shaft of white charm which is lovely when it's real," exuded optimism. "As the Negro gains in productive efficiency," she insisted, "he will become increasingly important to the world of organized labor.... It is only through the solidarity of labor's interests that he can hope to be saved from remaining an exploited class. Every colored man in New York who stands with the organization, working for it in its defeat or its success, gains respect not only for himself but for his race." She reported a story she had heard some days before she penned these words—a story "whose every word I can vouch for." The "story" shifted its focus from the Negro to the white worker:

An Irish friend was talking on trade union matters, and she said: "Do you know, yisterday I dined wid a naygur. Little did I ivir think I wud do sich a thing, but it was this way. You know my man is sicretary of his union, and the min are on strike, and who should come to the door at twelve o'clock but a big black naygur. 'Is Brother O'Neill at home?' says he. 'Brother O'Neill,' thinks I; 'well, if I'm brother to you I'd better have stayed in Ireland.' But I axed him in, and in a minute my man comes and he shakes the naygur by the hand, and says he, 'You must stay and ate wid us.' So I puts the dinner on the table and I sat down and ate wid a naygur." "Well," I said, "how did he seem?" "To tell you the truth," she said, "he seemed just like anybody else."

"Caste lines," Mary White Ovington then believed, "disappear when men are held together by a common interest, and as they feel their interdependence they gain in sympathy and in fraternal spirit." Twenty-five years later, Abram Harris and Sterling Spero detailed aspects of the corrosion of that spirit and reported much else, too. The facts they gathered, together with their interpretation of major changes affecting both Negro and white workers, still retain a chilling import for our times.

PREFACE

This book is neither a good will tract on race relations nor an attempt to offer a program for the solution of a vexing problem. It is an effort to set forth descriptively and analytically the results of a study of the American labor movement in one of its most important aspects, namely, the relation of the dominant section of the working class to the segregated, circumscribed, and restricted Negro minority. Since the Civil War this black minority, by the very fact of the discrimination practiced against it, has been in a position to do great damage to the majority which proscribed it. The recent northward migrations, which brought hundreds of thousands of Negro workers into the industrial centers, dramatically forced the realization of this fact upon the white wage earners. The discrimination which the Negro suffers in industry is a heritage of his previous condition of servitude, kept alive and aggravated within the ranks of organized labor by the structure and politics of American trade unionism. This persistence of the Negro's slave heritage and the exclusive craft structure of the leading labor organizations are, in our opinion, two of four basic factors in the Negro's relation to his white fellow workers. The two others are (*a*) the change in the Negro's fundamental relation to industry resulting from the recent migrations and the absorption into the mills and factories of a substantial part of the reserve of black labor, and (*b*) the rise of a Negro middle class and the consequent spread of middle-class ideals throughout the Negro community.

This study was carried on under a grant of the Columbia University Council for Research in the Social Sciences, made at the instance of Professor Wesley C. Mitchell and Professor Franz Boas. We are deeply grateful to the University for its liberal support. But we appreciate more deeply the generous spirit in which it encouraged us to carry on our work without accounting, without supervision, without unsought advice or interference. The members of our advisory committee, Professor Henry R. Seager, Professor Robert E. Chaddock, and Professor Paul F. Brissenden, as well as Professor James C. Bonbright, Secretary of the Council for Research in the Social Sciences, were always ready to help us when we called upon them, and we thank them for their coöperation and assistance. To the late Professor Seager, in particular, we owe a debt of gratitude for wise counsel and generous aid for which no formal acknowledgment is adequate. We are also indebted to Mr. David J. Saposs, Dr. W. E. B. Du Bois, Mr. Elmer A. Carter, Mr. Louis M. Hacker, Miss Irma Rittenhouse, and Mrs. Edna Brand Mann for their valuable criticisms and suggestions, and to Miss Gertrude C. Smith for her expert assistance. The most important element in the conduct of this study has been the active coöperation of those with whom we came in contact in the field: employers, labor leaders, and white and Negro workers of the rank and file.

The substance out of which this book was made has come not merely out of other books and published sources. A large part of it was drawn from first hand investigation and observation in the field. This work is in every essential respect the joint product of both of us, although Sterling Spero was primarily responsible for the writing of Chapters I, VI, VII, VIII, IX, XI, XII, XIII, XVI, and XX, and Abram Harris for II, III, IV, V, X, XIV, XV, XVII, XVIII and XIX. We each read, criticized, and suggested changes in the other's work. For every statement and every conclusion — in fact, for everything in this book, we take joint responsibility.

STERLING D. SPERO
ABRAM L. HARRIS

COLUMBIA UNIVERSITY
September 7, 1930

CONTENTS

CONTENTS

PART V. NEGRO LABOR SINCE THE WAR

APPENDICES

PART I

THE HERITAGE OF SLAVERY

CHAPTER I

THE SLAVE REGIME: COMPETITION BETWEEN NEGRO AND WHITE LABOR

THE position of the Negro in America today is conditioned by the fact that he was brought here as a slave. He lived here as a slave through eight generations. He has been a free man for barely three. It is hardly strange, therefore, that the habits and attitudes of the years of bondage should still influence the relations of black men and white. All the outstanding characteristics of those relations — the doctrine of the Negro's racial and social inferiority, the aloof and condescending paternalism of the southern gentlefolk, the missionary spirit of northern philanthropy, and the mutual suspicions of the black and white working classes — have their roots in slavery.

Southern society at the outbreak of the Civil War was made up not of two classes, white masters and Negro slaves, but of four classes. These were: first, the slave-holding families, about 350,000 in number, representing about 1,750,000 individuals; second, the Negro slaves, nearly 4,000,000 in number; third, the free Negroes who numbered about 500,000 throughout the whole country and about 260,000 in the South; and fourth, the "poor white" small farmers, artisans, laborers, and tradesmen, who numbered more than 5,250,000.

The last not only had no stake in the slave system, but were actually its victims. With most of the choice lands in the possession of the great plantation families, the poor white farmers were obliged to take what was left and to depend for their credit upon the slave holders who owned most of the wealth of the section. The economic position of many of these poor whites was often worse than that of the slave, for the slave had to be clothed, fed, cared for, and sheltered in order to remain an asset to his master. The poor white, who represented no

3

one's investment, was obliged to feed, clothe, shelter, and care for himself and his family on his own meager resources. Had the poor white class been educated and alert, it might have developed a leadership which would have seen that its interests were at one with those of the slaves. But the plantation masters kept their poor white neighbors in ignorance hardly less dense than that of their black chattels.

The poor white envied the slave's security and hated him for his material advantages, while the slave envied the white man's freedom and hated him for the advantages of his whiteness. Each group, in an effort to exalt itself, looked down upon the other with all the contempt which the planter aristocracy showed to both. The slave was a "nigger" and the poor white was "po' white trash."

This mutual animosity was strikingly revealed in an audience between President Andrew Johnson, leader of the poor whites, and Frederick Douglass, leader of the Negroes:

THE PRESIDENT: When you would look over and see a man who had a large family, struggling hard upon a poor piece of land, you thought a great deal less of him than you did of your own master's Negro, didn't you? . . .

Well, I know such was the case with a large number of you in those sections. When such is the case, we know there is an enmity, we know there is hate. The poor white man on the other hand was opposed to the slave and his master; for the colored man and his master kept him in slavery by depriving him of fair participation in the labor and productions of the rich land of the country.

Don't you know that a colored man in going to hunt a master (as they call it) for the next year, preferred hiring to a man who owned slaves rather than to a man who did not? I know the fact at all events. They did not consider it quite as respectable to hire to a man who did not own Negroes as to one who did.

DOUGLASS: Because he wouldn't be treated as well.

THE PRESIDENT: Then that is another argument in favor of what I am going to say. It shows that the colored man appreciated the slave owner more highly than the man who didn't own slaves. Hence the enmity between the colored man and the non-slave holders.

To this Douglass and the Negro delegates replied:

The hostility between the whites and blacks is easily explained. It has its root and sap in the relation of slavery and was incited on both sides by the cunning of the slave masters. Those masters secured their ascendency over the poor whites and the blacks by putting enmity between them.

They divided both to conquer each. There was no earthly reason why the blacks should not hate and dread the poor whites when in a state of slavery; it was from this class that their masters received their slave catchers, slave drivers and overseers.[1]

This hatred was further aggravated by competition between black and white craftsmen in the towns. For though slavery in the South was primarily a system of agricultural labor, slaves were used as domestics and artisans as well as plantation hands. In fact, the ablest and most promising slaves who were not assigned to service in the great house were trained in the skilled crafts. The plantations were to a large extent self-sustaining units which did practically all their own repairing and made a large proportion of their own supplies. The masters found it easier and cheaper to have their slaves trained in carpentry, masonry, blacksmithing, and the other mechanical trades than to depend upon outside free white labor.[2]

The Negro slave artisan was valuable property, worth considerably more than the ordinary plantation hand. It was not unusual for well-trained mechanics to sell for two thousand dollars, while able bodied field hands brought eight hundred to one thousand dollars.[3] Many masters regarded their skilled slaves as a profitable source of income, and instead of keeping them on the plantation to serve the mechanical needs of the establishment, sent them to practice their trades in the cities. There the owner sometimes hired them out to master crafts-

[1] Edward C. McPherson, *The Political History of the United States of America during the Period of Reconstruction* (1875), pp. 53-56.

[2] Charles Nordhoff, *How Slavery Injures the Free Workingman* (1865), pp. 8-10.

[3] Booker T. Washington, *The Story of the Negro* (1909), Vol. II, p. 63.

men or sometimes contracted out their labor directly to the
public. There were also many masters who permitted their
slave mechanics to hire out on their own time in return either
for a fixed sum of money or for a certain percentage of the
slave's earnings. The Negro mechanics in the cities were
usually better trained and more competent workmen than the
slave artisans on the plantations. Frequently they learned their
trades from white master mechanics to whom they were ap-
prenticed in boyhood by their owners.[4]

Advertisements for colored apprentices appeared frequently in the southern papers. One blacksmith in Georgia
advertised that he "would willingly receive three Negro fellows as apprentices," declaring, "The owners may confidently
rely that every necessary attention will be given to their in-
struction."[5] Another blacksmith advertised as follows:

Wanted immediately, as an apprentice to the blacksmith's business,
a smart, active boy, of from 12 to 15 years of age, who can come well
recommended. A black boy of this description will be taken. Wanted also
a journeyman who understands his business, and has good recommendations for honesty, industry and sobriety. A black man would not be
rejected.[6]

Much of the work of the slave artisan on the plantations
was rough and crude though sufficient for their needs.[7] Yet
some of it was of the highest quality as the beautiful southern
mansions, built by Negro labor, still testify. In the towns
where colored craftsmen were obliged to compete with white
and where black artisans had as good training as their white
rivals, the quality of work was equal. Yet slave labor had decided advantages in the struggle for trade. The poor white
artisan was not competing with the black slave artisan any

[4] Ulrich B. Phillips, *American Negro Slavery* (1918), Chapter XX.

[5] From the Augusta, Ga., *Chronicle*, March 2, 1811. See *Documentary History of American Industrial Society* (1910), Vol II, pp. 348-49.

[6] Nashville, Tennessee, *Gazette and Mers District Advertiser*, Oct. 24, 1804,
Documentary History, Vol. II, p. 349.

[7] W. E. B. Du Bois and August G. Dill, *The Negro American Artisan*
(1912), p. 28.

more than the independent storekeeper of the present is competing with the manager of the chain store in his territory. The white mechanic was competing with the slave owner whose cheap slave labor, financial resources, and political power gave him every advantage. In some places slave labor practically monopolized the field, driving white labor out of town. "I am aware," said a citizen of Athens, Georgia, in an open letter to the local contractors,

> . . . that most of you have too strong antipathy to encourage the masonry and carpentry trades of your poor white brothers, that your predilections for giving employment in your line of business to ebony workers have either so cheapened the white man's labor, or expatriated hence with but a few solitary exceptions, all the white masons and carpenters of this town. [8]

The writer ended his complaint, declaring,

> As masters of the polls in a majority, carrying all before them, I am surprised the poor do not elect faithful members to the Legislature, who will make it penal to prefer Negro mechanic labor to white men's. [9]

Though more alert and independent than the poor whites on the land, the white mechanics in the towns were able to make but little headway in politics in the face of the slave power. Tradition, property qualifications for the suffrage, the counting of the slave population for purposes of legislative apportionment, the gerrymandering of legislative districts to the detriment of the poor whites, or, as in South Carolina, qualifications which barred office to all but slave-holders made it easy for the master class to control the state and block all unfavorable legislation. [10]

There were exceptions, however, as when the legislature of Georgia in 1845 by a small majority passed a law providing:

[8] An open letter printed in the *Southern Banner*, Athens, Ga., Jan. 13, 1838, *Documentary History*, Vol. II, p. 360.

[9] *Ibid.* p. 361.

[10] Nordhoff, *op. cit.*, pp. 17-19. See also William E. Dodd, *The Cotton Kingdom* (1919), pp. 118-46. See also Hinton Rowen Helper, *The Impending Crisis* (1857, edition of 1860), p. 42.

That from and after the first day of February, next, each and every white person who shall hereafter contract or bargain with any slave, mechanic or mason, or free person of color, being a mechanic or mason, shall be liable to be indicted for a misdemeanor; and on conviction, to be fined, at the discretion of the Court, not exceeding two hundred dollars.

A following clause imposed like penalties upon the owners of slaves or guardians of free persons of color who authorized contracts prohibited by the statute.[11]

But even this attempt to protect the white mechanic from Negro competition curbed only certain classes of colored labor, namely, free Negroes and slaves who hired out on their own time and were to all intents and purposes as free as the legally free Negroes.[12] Slave labor used by white contractors was not affected. Charles Lyell, commenting on this law which he characterized as "disgraceful," declared that it proved "that not a few of the Negro race have got on so well in the world in reputation and fortune and in skill in certain arts that it was worth while to legislate against them in order to keep them down and prevent them from entering into successful rivalry with the whites." [13]

The legislation does not seem to have achieved its purpose, for about twelve years after it became effective two hundred mechanics and laborers in Atlanta petitioned the city council to relieve them of the very competition at which the law was aimed. "We, the undersigned," the petition read,

would respectfully represent to your honorable body that there exists in the city of Atlanta a number of men who, in the opinion of your memorialists, are of no benefit to the city. We refer to Negro mechanics whose masters reside in other places and who pay nothing toward the support of the city government, whose Negro mechanics can afford to underbid the regular resident citizen mechanics of your city to their great injury and without benefit to the city in any way. We most respect-

---

[11] Du Bois and Dill, *op. cit.*, pp. 32-33.

[12] *Ibid.*, p. 31.

[13] Quoted in *Documentary History*, Vol. II. p. 361, from Charles Lyell, *A Second Visit to the United States* (1849).

fully request your honorable body to take the matter in hand, and by your action in the premises afford such protection to the resident mechanics of your city as your honorable body may deem meet in the premises, and in duty bound your petitioners will ever pray.[14]

White mechanics in Virginia petitioned the legislature to forbid the apprenticing of slaves to learn any trade or craft. In North Carolina they protested against the use of slave artisans to underbid them in contracts and take away "business that belonged to white laborers." [15] But all their protests had little effect.

Competition between free labor and slave was not confined to the handicrafts and building trades but extended to nearly every branch of manual labor. As the following advertisement indicates, slaves who for the time being were not needed on the plantations were frequently hired out for construction work and other unskilled jobs to firms which required their labor for but a short time.

Five Hundred Laborers Wanted. We will employ the above number of laborers to work on the Muscle Shoals Canal, etc., at the rates of fifteen dollars per month, for twenty six working days, or we will employ Negroes by the year, or for a less time, as may suit the convenience of the planters. We will also be responsible to slave holders who hire their Negroes to us, for any injury or damages that may hereafter happen in the progress of blasting rock or of caving in of banks. For information in regard to the health of the men, the fare, etc., we would refer, etc.

HENRY AND KIBB [16]

May 24, 1883

Negro slaves were employed in foundries as forgemen, blacksmiths, and founders. They were used to mine both coal and ore. They worked along the water front as longshoremen. With the exception of conductors, they worked on the railroads in every capacity including that of locomotive engineer, and they piloted the steamboats that plied on southern waters.

---

[14] *Documentary History*, Vol. II, pp. 367-68.
[15] Charles H. Wesley, *Negro Labor in the United States* (1927), pp. 71-72.
[16] *Documentary History*, Vol. II, p. 348.

They were even used to some extent as hands in the textile mills and formed a large portion of the workers in the tobacco factories. In all these employments they came into competition with white labor. Sometimes, as in a mill in Athens, Georgia, slave labor was on a hired basis, the slave owner receiving rent for each slave.[17] Sometimes the mill owner owned the slaves himself. A factory near Columbia, South Carolina, reported the average cost per annum of its slave operatives at $75 and that of its free white operatives at a minimum of $106.[18] Whether the slave was rented or owned, slave labor was cheap and operated to depress the wages of white labor. It is significant that in all these employments free white and black slave labor worked side by side without apparent difficulty.[19]

Apart from the Georgia legislation in 1845 and the unsuccessful petitions of white craftsmen in a few cities, the white workers accepted their lot, blaming and hating the Negro for their plight. Such attempts as were made to check slave competition aimed only at superficial regulation or control and left the root of the evil, slavery, untouched. Helper's famous book, *The Impending Crisis*, appearing in 1857, telling the poor whites that their only hope was abolition, had no effect upon the group whose cause it espoused. Three years later Robert C. Tharin, an Alabama lawyer, set up a paper called the *Non-Slaveholder* which he hoped to make the organ of the white working class in towns. His program was legislation forbidding the employment of slaves except in agriculture and as servants. But the Alabama slave power would stand for no agitation for the restriction of the "peculiar institution," and Tharin was driven from the state.[20]

The master class insisted on employing its slaves in whatever manner it found profitable. If they were not needed on the plantations they were rented out to dig ditches. If they

[17] J. S. Buckingham, *Slave States of America* (1842). See *Documentary History*, Vol. II, p. 357.
[18] Nordhoff, *op. cit.*, p. 10.
[19] *Documentary History*, Vol. II, p. 357.
[20] Nordhoff, *op. cit.*, pp. 5-6.

were too weak to stand the strain of working in the fields, they were sent to the cotton mills to "attend to the looms and spindles." [21] The slave owner demanded a steady income on his investment. Furthermore, what there was of southern industry and enterprise was owned by the slave-holding class.

Aside from a few restrictions by municipal ordinance on the right of slaves to hire out on their own time,[22] the only group of colored workers on whose activities effective restrictions were placed were the free Negroes. Their freedom of movement, their right to reside in given places and their right to engage in certain occupations were limited by law and custom.[23] Their competition was resented alike by white workers and slave holders and they were obliged to submit to whatever restrictions the white community cared to impose on them. Nearly half of these people lived in the free states. Those who remained in the slave states, with the exception of a few who became planters and a few others who achieved success in business or the professions, lived on the land in much the same manner as the poor whites, or in the towns in much the same manner as the slaves or white workers. Their distribution in the various town occupations was much the same as that of the slaves.[24]

In the North, the presence of the free Negro workman was resented even more sharply than in the South. Several of the states as well as many local communities prohibited their residence. Even where the law permitted them to come and go and do as they pleased, the hostility of the white population made life hard for them. Thus, a New Jersey paper in 1834 declared that a portion of the state was "literally overrun with blacks, driven by the violence of an infuriated mob from their homes and property in Philadelphia to seek shelter and protection among the farmers of our county. Their numbers

[21] *Ibid.*, p. 10.

[22] *Documentary History*, Vol. II, p. 147.

[23] U. B. Phillips, *op. cit.*, pp. 440-41, 448. Also Phillips, *Life and Labor in the Old South* (1929), pp. 171-72.

[24] Charles H. Wesley, *op. cit.*, pp. 29-50.

previous to this influx," the paper went on to say, "had become in some places troublesome — in others a burden and a nuisance. A temporary sojourn among us, considering the circumstances of the case, may be borne with, but the first indication of a permanent residence should, and we feel confident will, call forth rigid enforcement of the statute against the admission of blacks into our boundaries." [25] Even in Massachusetts, the center of abolitionist agitation, the legislature seriously considered, but finally rejected, the passage of legislation barring the immigration and residence of Negroes.[26]

In Philadelphia, Cincinnati, New York, and many smaller cities of Illinois, Indiana, Ohio, New Jersey, and Pennsylvania the white workers seriously objected to Negro competition. In a number of places, but particularly in Pennsylvania, many violent anti-Negro demonstrations took place.[27] Philadelphia had always had a large Negro population and it is probable, according to W. E. B. Du Bois, that, up to about 1820,[28] a very large proportion, if not a decided majority of the artisans of the city, were colored. After that, however, the influx of foreign immigrants "and the demand for new sorts of skilled labor of which the Negro was ignorant, and not allowed to learn, pushed the black artisans more and more to the wall," so that in 1837 only about 350 out of the 10,500 Negroes in the city were engaged in skilled trades.[29] Relations between the races throughout this period were marked by a series of bitter riots. The effect of this violence and loss of economic position drove so many Negroes from the city that the colored population actually showed a decrease at the census of 1850.

In New York City, although no violence comparable to that in Philadelphia took place until the importation of Negro strike breakers in 1863,[30] anti-Negro feeling ran high. This

[25] From the *American Sentinel*, reprinted in the *Federal Union* (Milledgeville, Ga.), Sept. 17, 1834. See *Documentary History*, Vol. II, p. 159.

[26] John Daniels, *In Freedom's Birthplace* (1914), pp. 25-29.

[27] E. R. Turner, *The Negro in Pennsylvania* (1911), pp. 143-68, 195-205.

[28] W. E. B. Du Bois, *The Philadelphia Negro* (1896), p. 33.

[29] *Ibid.*

[30] See below, pp. 197-198.

was particularly true among the Irish, the Negro workers' closest competitors. Prior to the coming of the Irish, most of the personal service and much of the common labor was done by Negro men and women whose wages for such work were comparatively high. The new immigrants undercut the Negro scale and pushed the black workers out of their jobs. A deadly hatred resulted which constantly manifested itself in quarreling and fighting between the two groups.[31]

The fear of Negro competition among certain groups of white workmen in the North was so great as to lead them to oppose emancipation. In Pennsylvania race prejudice ran so high that the legislature was urged in 1860, on the very eve of the Civil War, to reënact the laws permitting Negro slavery. A union meeting held in Philadelphia the next year, 1861, protested against anti-slavery legislation and urged the repeal of all state laws which put obstacles in the way of the enforcement of the federal Fugitive Slave Act.[32] In New York City the Democratic party, dominated by the Irish and supported by the unskilled Germans and other immigrant groups, purported to represent the working class. It opposed the freeing of slaves on the ground that emancipation would result in the migration of thousands of blacks to northern states, increasing competition for jobs and reducing wages even below the level to which an oversupplied labor market had already sent them.[33] Herein is found part of the explanation of the alliance between the Democratic party in the South and Tammany Hall and the other Democratic machines in the northern cities.

On the other hand, there were throughout the North groups of workers schooled in socialist theory and the doctrines of labor solidarity who constituted a substantial section of the anti-slavery movement. This was especially true of the organizations of German workers whose members not only had a socialistic background but were also for the most part

[31] John Finch, *Notes on Travel in the United States* (1843). See *Documentary History*, Vol. VII, p. 60.

[32] Turner, *op. cit.*, p. 247.

[33] *Documentary History*, Vol. VII, pp. 60-61.

highly skilled mechanics. Unlike their unskilled compatriots
and the Irish common laborers, they came into little competition with the Negro. Among the native American workers
anti-slavery sentiment was strongest in the New England
workingmen's associations. These, like the German organizations, opposed not only Negro slavery but the "white slavery"
of the wage system as well.[34] They were interested in the overthrow of the capitalistic exploitation of the working class of
which the southern slave system was regarded as but a phase.

Emancipation resulted in the decline of the planters' political monopoly and in a corresponding increase in the political
importance of the white workers. This new power was used
largely to keep the Negro down in the name of racial purity
and the "white South." The planters' South, the slave-holding
aristocrats' South, gave way to the "white South." The southern democracy so long despised by the slave-holding aristocracy
now considered itself the inheritor of the great white planter
tradition. Every southern person became in his own eyes an
aristocrat holding the Negro in contempt.

Freedom at first left relations between the races on the
land essentially unchanged. Likewise, the Negro domestics
and those engaged in personal-service trades, such as barbers,
waiters, or porters, continued much as before, for their work,
looked down upon as "black" jobs, was beneath the aspiration
of the whites. The Negro monopoly of personal-service work
has now been broken, but the distinction born in slavery between "white" and "black" jobs remains. While its meaning
has become rather elusive and its application inconsistent and
differing from place to place, the idea of jobs belonging to one
race or another is an important characteristic of southern
economic life. It has even to some degree penetrated to the
North. It is part of the general policy of racial separation and
it means, with certain exceptions, that where white persons
and black persons work together the latter occupy a position
of inferiority.

[34] Herman Schlüter, *Lincoln, Labor and Slavery* (1913), pp. 34-84.

Emancipation had its most immediate and profound effect among the mechanics and artisans. Here competition between white and black workers was greatly accentuated. Gradually the colored artisans, thrown on their own resources without the support of the master class, gave way under the pressure of the better equipped whites. The rise of craft unionism with its apprentice system helped to consolidate the white artisan's position. Industrial changes and the introduction of machinery made much of the Negro's skill and training obsolete. Opportunities to learn trades outside the unions were more limited than under slavery since the Negro's training, no longer redounding to the profit of the master, had to depend upon good will and philanthropy.

Such philanthropy came from two sources. Some of it came in the form of help to individual colored men and women from members of the old master class who still retained their sentimental attachment to the Negro even after the law had changed the latter's status. But most of it came from the North from the spiritual descendants of the abolitionists who sought to better the freedman's lot through the establishment of agencies for his relief, education, moral, religious, and material improvement. The doctrine of racial separation which the white South imposed upon the black decreed that these institutions should be separate and distinct from similar agencies of the white world. Thus white northern philanthropy by accepting the southern doctrine of racial separation became a powerful instrument for fortifying "white supremacy" and "keeping the Negro in his place."

Meantime the white employing class continued to employ the free black man in one capacity or another. The white man and black man continued to compete for jobs. The old suspicion and distrust which they acquired for each other under slavery persisted. The black man, who as a slave looked to his master for protection and found it, because it was to the master's interest to block the white workman's competition, now looked to his new master, his employer, when the pressure of white labor's competition pushed him back.

CHAPTER II

THE AFTERMATH OF SLAVERY

WITH the dissolution of the slave regime the commercial and industrial life to which the late fifties gave birth in the northern and middle western states took on fresh energy. The striking growth of corporate wealth that took place in these states in the twenty-five years that followed the liberation of the slaves, and the corresponding reflection of its power in iron and steel, oil, rail transportation, and in banking and finance laid the foundation of the present business economy. Equally important was the parallel development of the labor movement, which, after suffering recurring setbacks from the death of local and national trade unions in the sixties, from the futile attempts at federating the rising but weak national unions, and from experimentation with greenbackism, coöperation and socialism, finally emerged as a confederation of "pure and simple" trade unions whose leaders were as determined to monopolize the job and the labor market as the new captains of industry were to monopolize the productive processes and the commodity market. This was the changing state of affairs when the 4,000,000 blacks were freed. Largely illiterate and, except for the few artisans among them, undisciplined in sustained and free labor, the emancipated Negroes were not looked upon as a wholly dependable source of labor for industry. But it has been estimated that in 1865 there were 100,000 Negro mechanics in the South, as compared to 20,000 white ones.[1] The occupations in which Negroes were found included blacksmiths, gunsmiths, cabinetmakers, plasterers, painters, shipbuilders, stone and brickmasons, pilots, and engineers.[2]

[1] Charles H. Wesley, *Negro Labor in the United States*, p. 142.
[2] *Ibid.*

The competition of the Negro was most seriously felt in the crafts in which his employment was a tradition from slavery. These were the building and allied crafts. He was also a competitor in the heavy unskilled occupations, such as dock work, and in the southern iron mills and coal mines.

The first economic result of the emancipation was the entrance of the Negro into the labor market as a free man and direct competitor with white labor. In 1863 [3] bloody fights occurred at New York, Buffalo and other eastern cities, between striking white longshoremen and Negro strike breakers; [4] and in 1867 colored ship caulkers were imported from Portsmouth, Virginia, to Boston to defeat the white workers' struggle for the eight-hour day. This entrance of the emancipated slave into the free labor market and his use as a strike breaker elicited various responses from the labor movement. The benevolent leaders and the socialistic workingmen's societies [5] looked upon Negro competition and the frequent racial clashes resulting from it with distress, regretting that racial strife prevented resistance to a common exploitation by the new "money power." [6] The trade unions, dominated as they were by the skilled workers, were less conscious of class interests. They met competition or sought to forestall it by excluding Negroes from the workshops and membership in the unions. The attitude of the trade unions, however, was not the same in every case. In many instances, Negroes were admitted to locals in northern cities. But the efforts of the more progressive elements in the craft unions to bring about a general admission of Negroes or their organization into separate

[3] Negroes had been used as early as 1855 to break strikes along the New York water front. See Chapter VII and Chapter IX.

[4] *Fincher's Trades' Review*, July 11, 1863.

[5] *Protokoll des Kommunistischen Klubs in New York, 1857-1867.* The constitution said that the members "recognize that all men are created equal regardless of colour or sect — and that they therefore aspire to abolish the so-called bourgeois property," etc. (MS in library of the Rand School of Social Science in New York. Courtesy Mr. Algernon Lee.)

[6] See William H. Sylvis' "Travels in the South" in James C. Sylvis, *Life, Speeches, Labors and Essays of Wm. H. Sylvis* (1872), p. 337.

unions met the opposition of southern locals under the aegis of "local autonomy."

In 1865, the white caulkers of Canton, Ohio, struck "to maintain the superiority of white men," which was threatened by the employment of a Negro foreman.[7] The bricklayers at Washington, D. C., were similarly disposed toward the Negro and the local union there forbade its members to work beside a colored man. When four white members were found working with Negroes on a government job in 1869, they were expelled from the union by unanimous decision.[8] As this was a purely local affair the national union was powerless to act. The question of Negro affiliation presented itself to the national bricklayers' union only when a local refused to recognize the travelling card of a Negro bricklayer who had been admitted to some less racially hostile local, or when attempts were made to charter separate Negro locals.

The violation of the card system with respect to the Negro bricklayer continued as long as the national union acquiesced by remaining silent. A resolution at the 1870 convention, however, proposed to empower the national union to organize separate Negro locals. It failed to pass. It was not until 1881 that the national union became sufficiently strong to demand that local bodies recognize travelling cards held by Negro bricklayers. About four years later the national board was empowered to charter separate Negro unions.[9] This still left the local bodies free to refuse Negro applicants.

The policy of organizing Negro craftsmen separately was also accepted by the coopers' union, one of whose three locals in New Orleans in 1871 was composed exclusively of Negro coopers.[10] Other trade unions when brought face to face with the race prejudice of their local constituencies accepted separation as the easiest way out.

[7] *Fincher's Trades' Review*, Nov. 4, 1865.

[8] H. G. Lee, *The History of the Negro in Organized Labor to 1872* (MS Thesis, University of Wisconsin, 1914).

[9] F. E. Wolfe, *Admission to American Trade Unions* (1912), p. 119.

[10] *Coopers' Monthly Journal*, Sept. 1871, p. 352.

In 1866, the carpenters and joiners of Boston had admitted two Negro carpenters to the union.[11] But twenty years passed before the United Brotherhood of Carpenters and Joiners was able to modify its rules so that Negro carpenters could be chartered in separate locals wherever existing unions refused to admit them. Even then the policy was to be followed only when "the existing union offered no reasonable objection." [12]

Negro cigar-makers had been debarred in 1865 by the Cigar-Makers' International Union,[13] but the national convention of 1879 removed the racial qualification for membership. However, the power of locals to refuse Negro applicants, or to block attempts of the national executives to form Negro locals was not disturbed by the new legislation. Almost a decade and a half passed before the national board was given the power to form locals wherever it saw fit.[14]

The question of admitting Negroes to membership in the Typographical Union arose at the 1869 national convention. The application of Lewis H. Douglass, a Negro printer, had so disturbed the Columbia Typographical Union of Washington that it presented the case to the national body. The resolution presented by the local union read:

Resolved that the wanton attempt of the congressional printer to force upon Columbia Typographical Union, No. 101, L. H. Douglass, an avowed rat, meets our unqualified condemnation.[15]

The resolution was passed. But the convention refused to go into the question because it considered it a local affair and, therefore, beyond the jurisdiction of the national officers. From the way the case was presented to the national convention one would judge that Douglass' race was not the important issue. According to Tracy [16] no mention was made of race,

[11] H. G. Lee, *op. cit.*

[12] Wolfe, *op. cit.*, p. 128.

[13] MS proceedings of the Cigar-Makers' International Union, 1865, p. 60. Quoted by Wolfe, *op. cit.*, p. 128.

[14] Wolfe, *op. cit.*, p. 128.

[15] George Tracy, *History of the Typographical Union* (1913), pp. 239-40.

[16] *Ibid.* Also, see Wesley, *op. cit.*, p. 167.

although it was known that Douglass was a Negro. The story as recorded in the newspapers of the period is told differently by another writer.[17] According to this account Douglass had been employed in Denver, Colorado, where a chapter of the typographical union existed. Upon going to Washington, he secured employment in the Government Printing Office, and later applied for admission to the local union, which refused to admit him and referred the case to the national convention with the following objections:

1. That he came from a place within the jurisdiction of a union, and had no card of membership;
2. That he was rejected as an improper person to become a member of the Denver Typographical Union;
3. That he worked in an unfair or "rat" office; and
4. That he was a colored man.[18]

Which of the interpretations is correct is uncertain. However, the fact that the Washington local requested the 1871 convention to expunge all reference to the affair from the minutes [19] might indicate that Douglass was finally admitted. If Douglass was never admitted, two other Negroes were.

The question of Negro affiliation came up again at the 1870 convention when a considerable part of the president's annual report was devoted to the subject. The special committee to which the subject was referred reported that it regretted the introduction of the race issue; and that any legislation by the international on the admission of colored printers to subordinate bodies would be an assumption of arbitrary power.[20] The acceptance of the committee's report left the local unions free to decide the matter as they saw fit. But the question as to whether all locals were obliged to recognize the travelling card of a Negro from some other local was

[17] H. G. Lee, *op. cit.*
[18] Quoted by Lee, *op. cit.*, from Washington *Daily Morning Chronicle*, June 19, 1869.
[19] Tracy, *op. cit.*, p. 258.
[20] *Ibid.*, p. 248.

still unsettled. At the 1879 convention it was reported that locals in Memphis, Tennessee, and Little Rock, Arkansas, refused to recognize travelling cards presented by colored members of Columbia Typographical Union, No. 101, Washington, D. C. The convention ruled that no subordinate unions should thereafter refuse to accept properly accredited travelling cards.[21] Thenceforth, Negro affiliation ceased to be an issue in the typographical union. As time passed the Negro cut an increasingly insignificant figure in the printing trades. By 1920, there were hardly 2,000 [22] Negro printers and compositors in the United States; and these were mostly employed in non-union shops owned by themselves or other Negroes.

The manner in which the question of Negro affiliation was disposed of by the organized crafts that felt Negro competition in the Reconstruction period reflects the characteristics that trade unionism was adopting. At that time the national unions were almost powerless. The local unions, fearing centralization, refused to delegate much authority to distant national executives. In this stage of trade-union development, the doctrines of local autonomy and decentralization — which grew to be cardinal principles in trade-union government — were becoming increasingly dominant. Idealistic craftsmen, always in the minority at national conventions, might strenuously oppose the exclusion of a fellow worker on racial grounds. They might even go so far as to insist upon the admission of the Negro mechanic on equal terms with the white. But the conventions would not risk the future of the national unions by attempting to force the idealism of the few upon the intolerant and apathetic many. To do so was to violate the autonomy of the local unions which insisted that it was their right to determine membership eligibility. The national officers felt

[21] *Ibid.*, p. 307-8.

[22] In 1920, there were about 5,000 Negroes employed in the printing trades in the United States, but only about 1,800 were printers, engravers and compositors, etc. See Table IV, Chapter IV. See also Chapter VIII, Table VII and footnote 16.

that the only way Negro competition could be met without offending local unions or usurping their power was to establish separate Negro locals.[23] In some cases, separate organization was frustrated for a long time by the local union's refusal to consent to the creation of another local in its territory. At any rate, the issuing of separate charters to Negro craftsmen wherever existing locals debarred them had become the accepted policy in the coopers' union by the seventies, and in the cigar-makers', the bricklayers', the carpenters', and the steel workers' unions [24] by the middle and late eighties. The Typographical Union refrained from declaring a national policy, while the rising aristocracy of labor — the Brotherhood of Locomotive Engineers, the Brotherhood of Railway Conductors, and the Brotherhood of Locomotive Firemen and Enginemen — made belonging to the white race the supreme test of eligibility to membership in their organizations. The Brotherhood of Railroad Trainmen, which was not organized until 1883, adopted the racial restrictions of the older railroad transportation unions.

In contradistinction to the oscillations of craft unionism between the extremes of outright exclusion and compromise, which were due to its impatience of idealism and a growing practical-mindedness, labor reformism sought an alignment of "white and black toilers" against a "non-producing aristocracy." Typical of the reformers was William Sylvis whose journeys through the southern states in 1868 led him to prophesy: " . . . Careful management, and a vigorous campaign,

[23] The national union became powerful to the degree that its officers usurped local power, or to the degree that the necessity for strong national organization paralleling the national expansion of industry forced the local union to yield to some centralization and to give up some of its autonomy. Constant usurpation by national officers brought protests from aggrieved locals, yet it continued, sometimes frankly and at other times surreptitiously. But forcing local unions to accept as members all persons, irrespective of race, if otherwise qualified was not the kind of usurpation of local power that appealed to the national officers. See Theodore H. Glocker, *The Government of American Trade Unions* (1913).

[24] See above, pp. 18-19.

will unite the whole laboring population of the South, white and black, upon our platform. The people down here will be a unit on the great money question, because everybody is poor, and ours is a war of poverty against a moneyed aristocracy." [25] The platform upon which Sylvis wished to align the Negro and white workers was that of the newly organized National Labor Union.

The National Labor Union was organized in 1866 at Baltimore, Maryland. It was a delegate body in which the existing trade unions, eight-hour leagues, and trades assemblies had representation. It followed the short-lived and uneventful International Industrial Assembly of North America of 1864 and was the first national federation of labor to secure some permanence in this country. Thus it was the lineal ancestor of the Knights of Labor and the American Federation of Labor. It proposed coöperation, greenbackism and homesteadism as the workers' escape from the abuses of the rapidly expanding industrial system and financial power. These reforms were to be secured through agitation and independent political action. The eight-hour day was one of the more practical reforms in which the National Labor Union was interested. Shortly after the first convention in Baltimore, A. C. Cameron, of the Chicago Trades' Assembly, issued an *Address to the Workingmen of the United States* on behalf of the National Union.[26] In addition to discussions of coöperation, trade unions, the apprentice system, female labor, the public domain and political action, the address called attention to the position of Negro labor. It recited the importation of colored caulkers from Portsmouth, Virginia, to Boston to take the places of white men who were striking for an eight-hour day. From this the address concluded that:

The systematic organization and consolidation of labor must henceforth become the watchword of the true reformer. To accomplish this

---

[25] *Life, Speeches, Labors and Essays of William H. Sylvis*, p. 341.

[26] See the "National Labor Union," *Documentary History of American Industrial Society*, Vol. IX, p. 141.

the coöperation of the African race in America must be secured. . . .
What is wanted then, is for every union to help inculcate the grand,
ennobling idea that the interests of labor are one . . . that there is but
one dividing line — that which separates mankind into two great
classes, the class that labors and the class that lives by others' labors. . . .
But aside from all this, the workingmen of the United States have a
special interest in seeking their coöperation. . . . Their moral influence,
and their strength at the ballot box would be of incalculable value to
the cause of labor. Can we afford to reject their proffered coöperation
and make them enemies? By committing such an act of folly we would
inflict greater injury upon the cause of Labor Reform than the combined
efforts of capital could accomplish. Their cherished idea of an antagonism between white and black labor would be realized, and as the
Austrian despotism makes use of the hostility between the different
races . . . to maintain her existence and her balance, so capitalists, north
and south, would foment discord between the whites and blacks, and
hurl the one against the other . . . to maintain their ascendancy and
continue the reign of oppression.[27]

The address concluded by requesting the formation of trades'
unions, and eight-hour leagues among the colored race that
they might be instructed in the true principles of labor reform,
and invited to coöperate in the general labor movement.[28]

At the 1867 congress of the National Labor Union, President Whaley emphasized the subject of Negro labor. A
special committee was appointed to handle the question. But
the committee reported "that, while we feel the importance of
the subject, and realize the danger in the future competition
of mechanical Negro labor, yet we find the subject involved
in so much mystery, and upon it so wide diversity of opinion
amongst our members, that we believe that it is inexpedient
to take action on the subject in this National Labor Congress." [29] The report aroused intense debate between those who
thought unqualified Negro admission was the duty of common
brotherhood, and those who wanted to temporize or to meet

[27] *Ibid.*, Vol. IX, p. 157-60.
[28] *Ibid.*, p. 160.
[29] *Ibid.*, p. 185.

the issue by organizing Negro workingmen separately.[30] William Sylvis, true to the spirit of reformism, protested against delay and maintained that unless the workers of the two races were consolidated the antagonism created by whites striking against blacks would kill off the trade unions. "There is no concealing the fact," he said, "that the time will come when the Negro will take possession of the shops if we have not taken possession of the Negro. If the workingmen of the white race do not conciliate the blacks, the black vote will be cast against them." [31] The report was recommitted. Afterwards the committee reported that the constitution as adopted precluded the necessity of reporting on the subject. Here the question rested until the 1869 Congress, when, as is explained below, action was forced by the appearance of four Negro delegates from a convention of Negro labor held shortly before.

In the interim between the 1868 and 1869 Congresses of the National Labor Union, state and local conventions of Negro workingmen began to appear. The proceedings of these conventions are veiled in such obscurity that it is impossible to know their exact composition and accomplishments. From the available records it seems that they were both political and economic and aimed at free education without racial discrimination. Out of them grew the first national convention of colored labor in the United States,[32] which met in Union League Hall, Washington, D. C., on January 13, 1869. The credentials committee reported 161 accredited delegates from the various states. Several resolutions on political reform, equal citizenship rights and free land were introduced, but none of them was acted upon.

[30] *Ibid.*, p. 186.

[31] *Ibid.*, p. 187. Also see above reference to Sylvis' activities in the South. His report on Public Lands and Agriculture as adopted by the 1867 convention requested the Congress of the United States to appropriate $25,000,000 to aid in establishing the eight-hour system, coöperation and the removal of such poor as wish to go to the public domain, and for the general benefit of laborers, without distinction of sex, color or locality. *Ibid.*, p. 188. p. 188.

[32] Washington *Daily Morning Chronicle*, Jan. 12-16, 1869.

The convention appears to have split on the question of the relations of white and Negro labor. G. T. Downing of Rhode Island said the impression had gone out that the colored workingmen had decided to disconnect themselves from other organizations. He strongly protested against the convention's sanctioning such a move because, in his opinion, it would prove detrimental to the Negro. The matter was tabled, and the convention adjourned *sine die*. But in the following July another state convention was held in Baltimore looking toward a thorough organization of different departments of colored labor throughout the country. The convention issued a call for another national labor convention to be held in Washington in December. Delegates were to be admitted without distinction of race or color.[33]

Although admittedly bitter toward white unions that excluded the Negro, the Maryland convention, unlike the first national meeting at Washington, showed no inclination to side-step the question of fraternizing with white labor. This attitude was responsible for the election of Isaac Myers, James Weare, Ignatius Gross, Squire Fisher, and Robert H. Butler as delegates to the white National Labor Union which, as noted above, was to meet the following month in Philadelphia.

When the Philadelphia congress convened, a resolution was passed stating that "the National Labor Union knows no north, no south, no east, no west, neither color nor sex, on the question of rights of labor," and urges "our colored fellow members to form organizations . . . and send their delegates from every state in the union to the next Congress." [34] Robert H. Butler, of Maryland, on behalf of the colored delegates, returned thanks for the reception. He said that they "did not come seeking . . . parlor sociabilities, but for the rights of manhood." [35] The convention appointed Butler and four of the white delegates as a committee to organize the colored

[33] *Ibid.*, July 13, 1869.
[34] *Documentary History*, Vol. IX, p. 239
[35] *Ibid.*, p. 239-40.

workingmen of Pennsylvania into labor unions and to report their progress to the president of the International Labor Congress at its next session.

The appointment of this committee clearly indicates that the National Labor Union, while desirous of uniting Negro and white labor, did not wish to alienate the support of the delegates from trade unions that excluded Negro workingmen by continually harping upon racial discrimination, for the loss of trade-union support meant the downfall of the National Labor Union. But separate trade-union organization did not mean that Negro delegates were to be excluded from the succeeding congresses. Far from excluding the Negro from the congresses, the National Labor Union welcomed him. What the National Labor Union wished to do was to create a single congress of representatives of white and black labor even though trade-union organization had in many cases to be separate. But this proffered fellowship of the National Labor Union merely marked the racial discord which made coöperation impossible after 1870.

It has already been noted that the first National Convention of Negro Labor which met in January, 1869, in Washington, did not decide whether it would maintain an independent position or identify itself with the white National Labor Union. Many of the delegates to the convention were strongly opposed to separation. After the futile and indecisive January convention had adjourned, a state convention held in Baltimore sent representatives to the white National Labor Union's August congress at Philadelphia, and issued a call for another national convention of Negro labor to be held in December at Washington. The Negro delegates, although well received at the Philadelphia congress, showed no inclination to abandon their projected December convention.

When the Negro convention met, several white representatives of the National Labor Union were present. Richard Trevellick, president of the National Labor Union, delivered the opening address, and Samuel P. Cummings, a leading Knight of St. Crispin, recorded the proceedings.[36] If Trevellick and Cummings hoped that their presence would convince the Negroes of the brotherhood of the labor reformer and lead to the abandonment of future separate congresses, the resolutions adopted by the convention clearly showed them that this was not the mind of the Negro brethren. The resolutions set forth the purpose of the convention as being "to consolidate the colored workingmen of the several states to act in coöperation with our white fellow workingmen . . . who are opposed to distinction in the apprenticeship laws on account of color, and to so act coöperatively until the necessity for separate organization shall be deemed unnecessary." Thus, while willing to fraternize with friendly whites through an interchange of delegates, the Negro wage earners decided to organize separately. Several causes were responsible for this attitude. The most obvious was "the exclusion of colored men and apprentices from the right to labor in . . . industry or workshops . . . by what is known as Trades' Unions." [37] Other points of disagreement are revealed by the platforms adopted by the Negro and white workingmen respectively.

The Negro convention deprecated class conflict and urged the study of political economy as the means of teaching capital and labor their respective rights and duties so as to eliminate the wholly unnecessary strife between them. It advocated free public education irrespective of race and color; the establishment of coöperative workshops as the remedy against trade-union discrimination and exclusion from workshops, and as the means of acquiring homesteads; and finally, it admonished faithful obedience to the laws of the United States.[38] On the other hand, the white National Labor Union emphasized greenbackism, taxation of the rich for war purposes, the question of competition with prison labor, the eight-hour day, the

[36] *Ibid.*, p. 250.
[37] H. G. Lee, *op. cit.*
[38] *Ibid.*

restoration of civic rights to southerners, and independent political action for labor. Both platforms were in agreement on coöperation, the futility of strikes, and the exclusion of Chinese contract labor. But the white workers, in demanding monetary and taxation reforms and the creation of a labor party, evinced a social philosophy that the Negroes did not share. These differences instead of being lessened by separation, were actually accentuated by it. The discord was further augmented by the conflicting political outlooks and ambitions of the leaders.

The leaders of the National Labor Union were populist. To them the Republican party was the political expression of a huge money and land monopoly. John M. Langston, lawyer and later United States congressman from Virginia, and P. B. S. Pinchback, lieutenant governor of Louisiana, the ablest Negro representatives, stressed equal citizenship rights and civil liberties, and persuaded the Negro to the belief that these rights were attainable only through the Republican party. Pinchback and Langston were more interested in keeping the Negro loyal to Republican politicians than they were in his problems as a workingman, or in labor reform, or in bridging the gap between the white and black labor classes. These were the elements of the discord that broke loose at the 1870 convention to which Langston and Pinchback went as representatives of the Negro Labor Congress.

The convention refused to seat Pinchback and Langston, both of whom were charged with being Republican party politicians and office-holders. The charge against Pinchback was withdrawn and he was seated, but Langston was not. Cameron, a leading St. Crispin and Massachusetts Democrat, accused Langston of stirring up race prejudice at the recent Negro convention and of attempting to use the congress for furthering his political ambitions.[39] The tension thus created

---

[39] Langston had warned the Negro Labor Congress against Cameron, who, according to Langston, was an emissary of the Democratic party. See Commons and Associates, *History of Labor in the United States* (1918), Vol. II, p. 137.

was intensified when the proposals to divide the National
Labor Union into industrial and political divisions and to form
the National Labor Reform party came up. Weare, another
member of the Negro delegation, protested that Negro sentiment was opposed to the formation of a new political party.
Myers, president of the Negro Labor Congress, held that the
Republican party was the source of all reforms and that independent political action was, therefore, unnecessary. Some of
the trade unionists were likewise opposed to the measure but
for reasons different from those held by the Negro delegates.
However, the resolution was carried by a large majority. The
resolutions committee offered a measure designed to prevent
the withdrawal of the Negro delegates. This had little effect.
Thereafter no Negro delegates appeared at the National
Labor Union. When the Negro Labor Congress assembled at
New Orleans in 1872, it repudiated the white National Labor
Union, declared unflagging loyalty to the Republican party,
and passed into oblivion.

Divergent as were the interests and political outlook of
the Negro and white wage earners, these interests were not
so irreconcilable that statesmanship might not have har-
monized them. It was true that equal suffrage, education, and
politics were foremost among the ambitions of the freedmen,
and that they looked to the Republican party as their savior
and the guardian of their rights. Still it is also true that their
political ambitions were closely tied up with a less well artic-
ulated desire for economic emancipation and protection which
led to the founding of organizations for that purpose. These
organizations, springing up immediately after the Civil War
and often originating in the hostility of white labor to the
Negro workingman, took on the coöperative character of the
contemporary labor movement. In Baltimore, Maryland, for
example, shortlived coöperative grocery stores and coal yards
sprang up all over the city.[40] The outstanding coöperative ven-

[40] See W. E. B. Du Bois, *Atlanta University Studies*, Vols. 8-12, 1903-1907.

ture was the Chesapeake and Marine Railway and Dry Dock Company of which Isaac Myers, the first president of the National Negro Labor Congress, was secretary. The company was capitalized at $40,000 and the stock was divided into 8,000 shares. It lived from 1865 to 1883. Efforts at producers' and consumers' coöperation continued into the nineties with little success.[41] The freedman also took some steps toward independent unionism. By 1868, the Negro caulkers of Baltimore and Canton, Ohio, and the engineers, the bricklayers, the butchers, the hod carriers, and draymen of Baltimore had formed unions.[42] In New York Negro labor, encouraged by the Workingmen's Assembly, had formed three organizations in 1870 — the Saloon Men's Protective and Benevolent Union, the Colored Waiters' Association, and the First Combined Labor Institute.[43] The constituencies represented by the delegates to a New York convention of colored workers, held on November 11, 1869, for the purpose of sending representatives to the first convention of the National Negro Labor Congress, give some idea of the widespread realization among Negro mechanics of the necessity for organization. The groups that sent these delegates comprised fifty engineers, four hundred waiters, seven basket-makers, thirty-two tobacco twisters, fifty barbers, twenty-two cabinetmakers and carpenters, fourteen masons and bricklayers, fifteen smelters and refiners, two rollers, six moulders, five hundred longshoremen, and twenty-four printers.[44] And in Norfolk, Virginia, Negro workingmen were strongly in favor of Sylvis' proposed colored labor union.[45]

These efforts of Negro working-class action did not materialize for four reasons: (1) the decreasing importance of the Negro in industry; (2) the growth of craft unionism, which excluded the Negro mechanic; (3) the mutual antag-

[41] *Ibid.* [42] See Wesley, *op. cit.*, p. 174.
[43] See Glocker, *op. cit.*, p. 26.
[44] See Wesley, *op. cit.*, p. 175.
[45] See Sylvis, *op. cit.*, p. 337.

onism between the white and black laboring classes; and (4) the social outlook of Negro leadership.

Under the leadership of ambitious politicians these movements were foredoomed to uselessness and early extinction. Had there been in these organizations fewer politicians like Langston and Pinchback and more labor leaders like George Downing, Sella Martin,[46] and Wesley Howard, they might have become the spearhead of Negro labor organization. Instead their energies were dissipated by political agitation and bickering.

Although the first effect of emancipation was to subject the white worker to the competitive menace of a large supply of black labor, several forces diverted much of this new labor away from industrial employment and the labor movement into the less remunerative, menial, and what later became known as the unorganizable occupations. The Civil War had left the South, where most Negroes were found at the close of the war, weak and prostrate. The persistence of its old economic habits rendered it insensible to the country's new industrial vigor. Shorn of its chief form of wealth, human chattels, the South continued to rely upon cotton farming as its chief economic activity, and looked to the free Negro, long familiar with the system, for labor. Cotton culture thus continued its traditional hold on the labor of black men, reducing them to a rural proletariat whose entrance into the trades and industries or whose migration to the centers of industry was forestalled by the Negro's habituation to a rather easy economic existence under southern paternalism, and to the slowly rising condition of peonage. The active competition of the freedmen was further reduced by two other factors: first, the hostility of the southern white worker who, to protect limited job opportunities, debarred Negro craftsmen from the trade

[46] The Reverend Sella Martin was appointed to represent the National Negro Labor Congress at the 1870 Paris World's Labor Congress. Martin was selected because of his knowledge of the French language and his broad views on the labor problem. Wesley, *op. cit.*, p. 166.

unions and refused to accept Negro apprentices; and second, the opinion, rather prevalent in the industrial community, that because the Negro's nature was not amenable to the "laws of political economy" he was a workman good only for rough, heavy or agricultural work.[47] Nevertheless all of these factors even when combined did not completely eliminate the Negro competitor from the trades and industries in the South. What happened was that the Negro rural workers, the numerically most important part of the Negro labor supply, became an industrial reserve, while the more alert city Negro who entered industry was forced to underbid his white competitor.

The emancipation of the slaves in the perspective of the labor movement produced the following results. The major portion of the Negro labor supply was shunted away from the labor movement and industrial employment into agriculture and domestic service as a result of the Negro's industrial inexperience, and the social habits, racial traditions, and the economic backwardness of the southern community. The Negro artisan, previously trained and contracted out by his master, and the Negro laborer were projected into the free labor market as competitors with white men. Negro competition was intensified by the fact that Negro labor was forced to accept lower wages than white and was frequently drawn upon for strike breaking by northern industrialists. This unfortunate rôle that Negro labor was called upon to play threatened the progress of the then impotent labor movement; and in the South competition widened the social distance that the slave regime had put between the Negro and the poor whites who grew increasingly apathetic when not actually hostile to each other's welfare. The divergence in interest was widened by the spiritual forces of the Reconstruction — education and philanthropy, and politics and equal citizenship.

Northern philanthropy, in equipping the former slave for

[47] See A. A. Taylor, *The Negro in the Reconstruction of Virginia* (1926), Chapter V, p. 85.

freedom, made education the footstool of religious and moral discipline. The products of its missionary zeal were the preacher and the educated middle-class Negro. The preacher rationalized the other-worldly predilections of the masses. The educated Negro sought the professions or settled in the class-room where he perpetuated the traditions of the church school. Both looked to heaven and the philanthropy of benevolent whites for Negro economic salvation. When they actually came to grips with economic reality they established fraternal, ben-efit, and insurance societies, and later banks — institutions which were projected as the basis of the material advancement of the masses, but which were nothing more than the lever by which a Negro middle-class was to elevate itself. The labor movement was foreign to these sources of enlightenment. Nor was the economic vision of the reconstruction politicians clearer than that of the preacher and the Negro of the profes-sional classes. Political equality and equal citizenship rights were to them the touchstone of freedom and advancement. Even the ablest of the reconstruction leaders, Frederick Doug-lass, who cannot be accused of failing to understand the labor movement and the problem of Negro workers, based Negro advancement almost wholly upon the attainment of political rights.[48] The prestige of men like Douglass, Langston, and Pinchback was so great among the masses, that their counsel — the attainment of equal citizenship and education, through loyalty to Republican politicians — prevailed against the judg-ment of those like Wesley Howard who told the 1869 state convention of colored labor at Baltimore that the franchise without the organization of labor would be of little benefit.[49] The politician looked upon the labor movement as inimical to

[48] Douglass' famous slogan was "ultimate assimilation through self-assertion and on no other terms." See W. E. B. Du Bois, *The Souls of Black Folk* (1903), p. 49. Also see, *Life and Times of Frederick Douglass*, an autobiography, for Douglass' early proposal of a manual college for Negroes to meet trade-union exclusion and apprenticeship discrimination. Note his views on subjects like: Negro and white competition, Negro agricultural labor, and communism.

[49] See Wesley, *op. cit.*, p. 173.

Negro welfare because he saw it as a contrivance for the elevation of poor white men, Democrats in political faith, and, therefore, the traditional enemies of the Negro. This was the attitude of John Langston, whose activity in the National Negro Labor Congress has been described. The attitude of the southern white workers to Negro political equality lent authenticity to the conviction of the politician. They were as bitterly opposed to "manhood rights" for the Negro as were the former slave-holders. In vain did John R. Lynch, Negro congressman from Mississippi, plead with the leaders of the Democratic party to change its racial policy so that Negroes who differed with the Republican party on economic issues might join.[50] And toward the close of the seventies when the southern white workers joined the aristocracy in Negro disfranchisement, the Negro leaders had no other choice, even if they had desired it, than that of redoubling their efforts to keep the Negro solidly aligned with the Republican party. In the face of the white worker's racial hostility, the Republican party was, indeed, what it was proclaimed, "the ship, while all else the sea"— a dictum which continued to rule Negro political sentiment sixty years after freedom. The flow of these events to fulfillment was arrested, however, in the eighties when, with the rise of the Noble Order of the Knights of Labor, the Negro workingman was again brought into the labor movement.

[50] See John R. Lynch, "Some Historical errors of James Ford Rhodes," *Journal of Negro History*, Oct., 1917, p. 345.

PART II

THE NEGRO WORKER AND THE RISE OF TRADE UNIONISM

CHAPTER III

INDUSTRIAL BROTHERHOOD AND INDUSTRIAL EDUCATION

SHORTLY after the disintegration of the National Labor Union fresh attempts were made toward a revival of national federation. The initiative came from the trade unions which withdrew from the National Labor Union when it entered politics. On account of the domination by the trade unions the newly created Industrial Congress, organized a few months before the panic of 1873, vowed to remain "a purely Industrial Association, having for its sole and only object the securing to the producer his full share of all he produces."[1] The Industrial Congress was non-political. The trade unionists wished not only to keep it so but to exclude as far as possible all non-trades-union elements such as had figured in previous national federations. This attempt to create a wage-conscious labor movement foreshadowed the not distant conflict between Knights of Labor idealism and trade-union wage-consciousness. The Industrial Congress was thus the harbinger of trade separatism and the American Federation of Labor, but the trade unions were still too weak to maintain it. It was nipped in the bud by the business depression that followed the panic of 1873, the last Industrial Congress being held in 1875.

No Negro delegate appeared at either the 1873 or the 1875 Industrial Congress. Nor do the proceedings reveal that any reference was made to the question of the affiliation and organization of Negro labor. But the Noble Order of the Knights of Labor, the next federation, faced the issue resolutely.

[1] See J. R. Commons and Associates, *History of Labor in the United States,* Vol. II, p. 158.

The Knights of Labor was founded as a secret working-class brotherhood by Uriah Smith Stephens in 1869.[2] In 1878 it threw off secrecy and in 1880 found itself an aggressive national organization with a steadily growing popularity and membership.[3] The Knights, even though composed to a large degree of craft unions, looked upon these as being effective only in "regulating purely trade-union matters," and cautioned them that their influence "upon all questions appertaining to the welfare of the masses as a whole" must prove comparatively futile without a closer union.[4] The Order was thus the antithesis of trade unionism in philosophy and structure.

The trade unions were becoming increasingly wage-conscious and limited their functions to the organization of the skilled worker and bargaining with the employers. The Order was more idealistic. It sought to consolidate all labor, the unskilled and semi-skilled as well as the trade unionists, in an offensive against "unjust accumulation of wealth."[5] To overcome the "pauperization and hopeless degrading of the toiling masses" it proposed education, mutual aid, the establishment of coöperative worshops, and consumers' coöperation. The difference between the structure of the Knights of Labor and that of the trade unions was also striking. The trade unions, in restricting membership to the skilled crafts, could organize only a limited proportion of the working class. The ambition of the Order was to organize all workers, skilled and unskilled. As the trade unions were unable to organize the latter, the Order organized them in the Local Assembly[6] which was

[2] See Commons and Associates, *op. cit.*, Vol. II, p. 197.

[3] The membership was 20,151 in 1879; 28,136 in 1880; 42,517 in 1882; 51,914 in 1883; and 700,000 in 1886. Commons and Associates, *op. cit.*, Vol. II, pp. 343 and 396.

[4] *Ibid.*, Vol. II, p. 336.

[5] *Ibid.*, p. 335.

[6] "A Local Assembly of the Order of the Knights of Labor shall be composed of not less than ten members, at least three-fourths of whom must be wage-workers or farmers, and this proportion shall be maintained for all time." Article 1, Section 1. Constitution for Local Assemblies of the Order of Knights of Labor of America, *Convention Proceedings*, 1886, p. 780. For further descrip-

proclaimed to be "not a mere Trade Union, or beneficial society," but something "more and higher." ". . . While it retains and fosters all the fraternal characteristics and protection of the single trade union, it also, by multiplied power of union, protects and assists all. It gathers into one fold all branches of honorable toil, without regard to nationality, sex or color." [7]

The policies and attitudes of the early trade unions on Negro organization and affiliation were the subject of the preceding chapter. There it was noted that although the trade unions differed on the subject, there was a rather well defined tendency among them to avoid it. Many unions did not exclude the Negro mechanics. Others organized them into separate locals. But even if the trade unions had organized all of the Negro mechanics, a tremendous volume of unskilled Negroes would still have remained unabsorbed by the labor movement.[8] At the close of the Civil War over 97 per cent of the Negro working class was unskilled and, therefore, excluded from the trade unions. The restriction of apprenticeship to whites and the exclusion of the Negro mechanic from the union further increased the number that could not be organized. These the Knights of Labor sought to bring into the labor movement by way of the local assembly.

At the 1885 convention the proposal "that a colored organizer be appointed for each of the old slave states" [9] was referred to the executive board. The resolution was approved, but the proceedings reveal no further action. At the next convention the general secretary-treasurer reported that "rapid strides have been made in the South, especially in Virginia, the Carolinas, Georgia, and Alabama. The colored people of the South are flocking to us, being eager for organization and

---

tion of the structure of the Knights, see Commons and Associates, *op. cit.*, Vol. II, Chapter VIII.

[7] *Ibid.*

[8] This of course was equally true of the unskilled and semi-skilled whites.

[9] Knights of Labor, *Convention Proceedings*, 1885, p. 125.

education, and when thoroughly imbued with our principles are answering in their fidelity." [10]

This report followed the organization of two district assemblies at Richmond, Virginia, one of which was composed entirely of colored members.[11] The latter, District Assembly 92, had 13 local assemblies of Negro workers in Manchester (South Richmond) and Richmond with a paid up membership of 1,285.[12] Likewise at Durham, North Carolina, a local assembly with more than a hundred Negro members had been formed.[13] At one time or another Negro local assemblies were formed at Harrisburg, Texas,[14] Birmingham, Alabama,[15] and Nashville, Tennessee.[16] Prosperity Assembly, Wheeling, West Virginia, included both Negro and white hod carriers,[17] but Progress Assembly was composed exclusively of Negroes.[18] It is impossible to tell from the available records how many Negro assemblies the Knights established, or how many Negroes became members of the Order.[19] John W. Hayes, once general secretary, and one of the few surviving Knights, estimated that in 1886 there were no less than 60,000 Negroes in the Knights of Labor. This, of course, is only an estimate. But in view of the reports that "Negroes were flocking to us," it is safe to say that the Order had a much larger Negro membership than

[10] Knights of Labor, *Convention Proceedings*, Vol. IV, 1886, p. 44.

[11] Report of John R. Ray, organizer at the ninth regular session of the General Assembly, Hamilton, Ontario. *Convention Proceedings*, 1885, p. 31.

[12] *Ibid.*, p. 174. The locals were Nos. 3564, 3572, 3619, 3620, 3626, 3637, 3675, 3732, 3808, 3821, 3822, 3895, and 3912.

[13] *Ibid.*, p. 32.

[14] Local Assembly 4250, Doc. 423, *Convention Proceedings*, 1887, p. 1316.

[15] Local Assembly 8059, *Ibid.*, p. 1316.

[16] Local Assembly 3378, Doc. 224, *Convention Proceedings*, p. 1296.

[17] Wesley, *op. cit.*, p. 258.

[18] *Ibid.*

[19] The *Proceedings* do not distinguish between white and colored assemblies. The assemblies mentioned in the text were distinguished as colored by some casual reference in the *Proceedings*. For example, L. A. 3378, Nashville, Tennessee, petitioned the 1887 convention for aid to go to Liberia, Africa. *Convention Proceedings*, 1887, p. 1296.

is indicated by the few assemblies we have mentioned. This view is supported by the fact that a resolution was introduced at the 1886 convention empowering the general secretary-treasurer to "have published in book form and numerically every six months a directory of Master Workmen and Recording Secretaries of every Assembly in the United States, stating . . . whether they are white or colored. . . ." [20] The Proceedings fail to show the action taken upon the proposal, and Mr. Hayes, who is our authority for the fact that such a directory was published, was unable to locate it after a diligent search.

It was in 1885, when the labor movement was in "great upheaval," that the Negroes "flocked" to the Knights. Then it was that the Order reached its maximum power and began to disintegrate, and when "the trades unions increased their membership and powers as never before. . . . The skilled and the unskilled, the high paid and the low paid, all joined hands. The color line had been broken, and black and white workers were found working together in the same cause." [21]

To say that the Knights had broken down the color line in the labor movement is to exaggerate their power, for the trade unions, many of which still excluded Negro mechanics, were beyond the control of the Order. But the democratic spirit which the Knights sought to create among the laboring classes was a powerful influence toward creating solidarity between Negro and white workingmen and bringing the former into the labor movement. The cigar-makers, the brick-layers, and the carpenters were organizing Negro craftsmen into separate locals where it was otherwise impossible to admit them. The Brotherhood of Carpenters and Joiners had 14 local unions of Negro carpenters scattered through the South in 1886.[22] Negro and white longshoremen, draymen, yardmen, cotton classers, screw-men, and so forth were admitted equally to the federations of dock workers in the cotton-exporting

[20] Doc. 83, *Convention Proceedings*, 1886, p. 186.
[21] George McNeill, *The Labor Movement* (1887), pp. 170 and 171.
[22] Wesley, *op. cit.*, p. 255.

ports of Savannah, New Orleans, and Galveston. In New Orleans Negro organization was quickened by the Central Trades and Labor Assembly. "The formation of this association of trades and labor unions is confessed to have done more to break the color line in New Orleans than any other thing . . . since emancipation of the slaves; and today the white and colored laborers of that city are as fraternal in their relations as they are in any part of the country — the Negroes, especially, taking great pride in their loyalty to their organizations." [23] At New Orleans, the employers' refusal to negotiate with a union of Negro draymen was met by a sympathetic strike of organized labor until recognition was secured for the union.[24] These examples of Negro unionization seem to mark an unprecedented era of good feeling between Negro and white workingmen and should be credited to the spirit of solidarity with which the labor movement, under the guidance of the Knights of Labor, was infused. This spirit was manifested on several occasions when a declaration of racial policy became imperative.

When the General Assembly convened at Richmond, Virginia, in 1886, a Negro, Frank J. Ferrell,[25] of District Assembly 49, New York City, was selected to introduce Terrence V. Powderly, General Master Workman. In concluding his address Mr. Powderly turned toward Delegate Ferrell and said:

When it became necessary to seek quarters for a delegation to this city, and when it became known that there was a man among them of a darker hue than the rest, it became evident that some of these men could not find a place in the hotels in this city, which is in accordance with long and established customs, and customs are not readily vanquished. Therefore, when one that happened to be of a dark skin of

[23] McNeill, *op. cit.*, p. 168.

[24] Wesley, *op. cit.*, p. 258. See also below Chapter IX, p. 184.

[25] Ferrell was a machinist who was very active in socialist and labor politics. In 1886 he ran for chairman of the United Labor party. He was defeated by Louis F. Post, the right-hand man of Henry George, the single taxer, by a vote of 91 to 61. See Nathan Fine, *Labor and Farmer Parties in the United States* (1928), p. 47. Also see Ferrell's speech presenting Mr. Powderly to the Richmond Convention, Appendix IA, p. 473, below.

a delegation of some sixty or seventy men, could not gain admission to the hotel where accommodations for the delegation had been engaged, rather than separate from that brother, they stood by the principles of our organization, which recognized no color or creed in the division of men. The majority of these men went with their colored brother. I made the selection of that man from that delegation to introduce me during the address of his Excellency, Governor Lee, so that it may go forth from here to the entire world that "we practice what we preach." [26]

The prominent rôle assigned to Ferrell and the fact that a party of delegates had refused to accept seats in one of the theaters because Ferrell was not admitted brought severe criticism from the press which accused the Order of attempting to disturb southern customs in race relations. In replying to the criticism, Mr. Powderly said that while he did not wish to interfere with the social relations between the races in the South, he strongly desired the "education of the black man" and the elevation of labor irrespective of race and color.[27] Two other instances of the display of this working-class fellowship may be cited. One was the Order's recommendation to District Assembly 41, Maryland, that it admit Negro apprentices into the mechanical department.[28] The other was the Order's notification to local assemblies in Texas that "they must treat . . . colored members with respect." [29]

While the Knights of Labor never succeeded in destroying race prejudice in the labor movement, it did attack the problem with greater determination than any of its predecessors, or its successor the American Federation of Labor. Its persistence in the organization of Negroes should be attributed to an idealism of industrial brotherhood which knew neither race, creed, nor color. But this very idealism precipitated a conflict between the Order and the trade unions, from which it emerged shattered and irretrievably beaten.

[26] *Convention Proceedings*, 1886, p. 12.
[27] See Excerpts from Mr. Powderly's letter to the *Richmond Press*. Appendices IA and IB, below, pp. 473-74.
[28] Doc. 116, *Convention Proceedings*, 1886, p. 194.
[29] Doc. 423, *Convention Proceedings*, 1887, p. 1316.

The principles upon which the Order and the trade unions were founded were essentially different. The principle cherished by the Knights that "an injury to one is an injury to all" contradicted that upon which the craft unions predicated their power and future existence — trade separatism. The Knights attempted to use the power of the skilled workers as leverage in raising the status of the unskilled, while the skilled workers wished to use their bargaining strength to obtain privileges for themselves. As the skilled crafts increased in number and in bargaining power with employers, they grew less sympathetic with the Order's zeal for solidarity. The numerous unsuccessful strikes led by the Knights in the eighties, the period of its most formidable expansion, portrayed the ineptitude of the leaders and gave impetus to the craft-union movement. The Order was shown to be impotent when unaided by the skilled workers, and above all, ill-equipped to battle on the new industrial frontier of corporate wealth and financial power. Just as the new combinations of wealth were desirous of establishing control over the commodity market and production, the craft unions wished to do likewise with the labor market. In order to do this, the craft unions, instead of attempting to supplant capitalism by establishing the coöperative commonwealth, accepted the wage system. Instead of seeking to organize the whole body of laborers, they limited their scope and functions to the few and easily organized skilled workmen. This was the economic spirit in which the trade unions, while still identified wth the Knights of Labor, launched the Federation of Organized Trades and Labor Unions of the United States and Canada at Pittsburgh in 1881.

At the first convention the committee on organization, of which Samuel Gompers was chairman, "reported in favor of a purely trade federation under the name 'Federation of Organized Trades' Unions of the United States and Canada,' to be composed of 'trades' unions' only." [30] Several delegates

---

[30] Norman J. Ware, *The Labor Movement in the United States, 1860-1895* (1929), p. 247.

opposed the plan because it excluded the unskilled laborer. One of the dissenters, a Negro named Grandeson, said:

We have in the city of Pittsburgh many men in our organization who have no particular trade, but should not be excluded from the Federation. Our object is, as I understand it, to federate the whole laboring element of America. I speak more particularly with a knowledge of my own people, and declare to you that it would be dangerous to skilled mechanics to exclude from this organization the common laborers, who might, in an emergency, be employed in positions they could readily qualify themselves to fill.[31]

Because of the row over the exclusion of the laborer the name was changed to the Federation of Organized Trades and Labor Unions in the United States and Canada. But this change in front did not alter the truth that had been uttered by Grandeson and others.

In 1886 the trade unions in the new federation withdrew from the Knights of Labor, joined hands with other elements and formed the American Federation of Labor. The new federation soon superseded the Knights. Having gained mastery over the labor movement, the American Federation of Labor stripped the latter of its ideal of inclusive industrial brotherhood and gave it the business ethics of job-conscious trade unionism. Thus the rising unionism of the late nineteenth century, based primarily upon skill, automatically excluded the laborers, white and black, whose welfare had been the chief concern of the Knights of Labor. The change struck the Negro with greater force than it did the white worker. At that time the Negro was engaged in the unskilled occupations to an even greater degree than now. Consequently the number of Negroes who were automatically excluded from the labor movement because of a lack of skill was relatively greater than the number of whites who were similarly excluded. Where the Negro was not excluded by his inability to meet the industrial qualifications for union membership, clauses in many unions'

[31] A. J. James, *The First Convention of the A. F. of L.*, pp. 35, 36, and 37. (Reprint from *Western Pennsylvania Historical Magazine*, March 3, 1924.)

constitutions, admitting only "white men," further restricted the Negro trade-union membership.

With the disintegration of the Knights of Labor and the rise of pure and simple trade unionism, the masses of Negroes, increasingly excluded on racial grounds, were placed psychologically at a great distance from the white working classes. Meanwhile, the Negroes were being turned to the program which Samuel C. Armstrong inaugurated in the sixties at Hampton Institute, and which his disciple, Booker T. Washington, placed before the country in 1895 as the Negro's economic and industrial emancipation.

In his memorable Atlanta Exposition address of 1895 Washington said: "Ignorant and inexperienced, it is not strange that in the first years of our new life we began at the top instead of at the bottom; that a seat in Congress or the state legislature was more sought than real estate or indusrial skill; that the political convention or stump speaking had more attractions than starting a dairy farm or truck garden." He admonished the Negro: "Cast down your bucket where you are — cast it down in making friends in every manly way of the people of all races by whom we are surrounded. Cast it down in agriculture, mechanics, in commerce, in domestic service, and in the professions." [32] The conciliatory nature of Washington's speech and his strictures on the Negro's political ambitions coincided with the best opinion of the "new South." But above all, the speech met with the approval of the northern industrial and financial leaders, who, now that the war was over and their dominance unquestioned, desired internal peace and harmony. In this atmosphere the sentiments uttered by Booker T. Washington won him the confidence of the influential whites of both North and South. Thenceforth he was proclaimed the economic emancipator of the Negro.

The picture which Washington drew of the Negro during Reconstruction was not historically accurate. If Negroes had been more interested in politics than in their economic advance-

[32] Booker T. Washington, *Up from Slavery* (1913), p. 218.

ment, it is not likely that thousands would have entered the labor movement from 1869 to the collapse of the Knights of Labor in 1890. Nor would they, during these years, have established producers' and consumers' coöperative societies. If they placed undue emphasis upon political equality and the right of suffrage and were often the pawns of unscrupulous white and black politicians, it was because they, like the working classes throughout history, dimly saw the relation between political and economic power. If they began "at the top" they were not unlike white American workers who in the early nineteenth century sought to escape economic inequality through the acquisition of "equal citizenship" and the right of suffrage. But however faulty his interpretation of history and the Negro's political aspirations, it would be incorrect to attribute Booker T. Washington's fame only to his "repudiation" of Negro political rights. His nationally accepted leadership of Negroes partly rests upon the counsel he gave them on their economic welfare.

When Washington delivered the Atlanta address, the skilled Negro worker was being eliminated by more advantageously situated white men supported by all-white trade unions. The greatest losses were suffered between 1865 and 1890, and even in 1900 the proportion of Negroes in eight major skilled occupations showed little sign of increasing.[33]

To meet the competition of white workers and at the same time to raise Negro economic standards and to achieve the respect of the white man, he sought to make Negroes into efficient workers through industrial education. He encouraged them to become economically independent through farming and land ownership and, above all, through the establishment of Negro business and trade.

Negro workers were to be made efficient in such schools as Hampton and Tuskegee. To the proponents of Negro industrial education, an efficient worker was one who was reliable, capable of giving the maximum return for his wages,

---

[33] See Tables VII and IX, Chapter VIII, pp. 159, 160, below.

and loyal to his employer. Enlightenment on the problems peculiar to the wage earner in modern industry had no part in the education which the industrial schools gave to the future black workers. This was so: first, because the emphasis of these schools was upon those branches of learning whose practical ends were demonstrable; and, second, because the industrial schools tacitly accepted and perpetuated the master-servant tradition that lingered from a vanished age. The acceptance of this tradition was implicit in Washington's remark, in a discussion of the Negro's relation to trade unionism, that the average Negro had found the friendship and confidence of a good white man a valuable asset in time of trouble and therefore "does not like an organization which seems to be founded on a sort of personal enmity to the man by whom he is employed." [34] Because the leaders of industrial education directed their efforts toward cultivating the good will of the wealthy whites, they avoided utterances or deeds that might lead to subversiveness among the black workers who, in Washington's words, had "without strikes and labour wars," tilled the fields, cleared the forests and built the railroads and cities of the South.[35]

As Hampton and Tuskegee were to develop skilled and efficient workers, so the Negro Business League, founded by Booker T. Washington in 1900, was to foster business and industry. The spirit that animated the League was described as being based upon the belief that "if you can make a better article than anybody else, and sell it cheaper than anybody else, you can command the markets of the world. Produce something that somebody else wants . . . and the purchaser . . . will not trouble himself to ask who the seller is. . . . Recognize this fundamental law of trade; add to it tact, good manners, a resolute will, a tireless capacity for hard work, and you will succeed in business." [36] These maxims by which Negroes were

[34] Booker T. Washington, "The Negro and the Labor Unions," *Atlantic Monthly*, June 1913, pp. 756-57. See also Chapter VII, p. 129.

[35] Booker T. Washington, *Up from Slavery*, p. 221.

[36] Booker T. Washington, "The National Business League," *World's Work*, Oct. 1902, p. 2671.

to make themselves into capitalists were an adaptation of the theories of free competition and economic individualism taught by classical political economy. If there ever existed the competitive economic order of classical theory in which merit received its just reward and the rationality of consumers and producers brought about a perfect distribution of goods and income, it is significant that its meliorative trend did not encompass the economic aspirations of black men. Or why should there be a league for fostering Negro business? If purchasers are not concerned about the maker or seller of goods, what has forced the Negro business men to restrict their dealings to Negroes? Why have they not entered the general competitive market as merchants, bankers, and industrialists?

In 1900, when the Negro Business League was organized, the economic philosophy in which it placed its faith was becoming more fictitious than ever. The prevailing notion of the eighteenth and nineteenth centuries, that a man of small capital could raise himself to affluence and power through hard work and thrift, was being discredited by the spread of vertical and horizontal combinations capitalized in hundreds of millions and interlocked in the financial domain by common directorates and ties of mutual interest. While the law sought to prevent the new combines of wealth and industrial power from completely monopolizing the markets, it never sought to prevent them from raising the plane of competition from small to giant enterprise under the spur of greater profits and productive efficiency. And in the years that followed, the man of small capital, although a persisting and ubiquitous phenomenon, was reduced to petty trade and to a much diminished social prestige. These realities of the economic world were not faced by the Negro Business League, because its founder showed little understanding of them. He had seen white men of an earlier period rise to great economic stature through individual initiative, sagacity, and by what the moralists of today would call not too scrupulous practices, and he concluded that Negroes could do likewise. At heart he was a

small capitalist, an eighteenth-century individualist, in an era
of corporate wealth and industrial integration. He therefore
urged Negroes to emulate essentially individualistic virtues,
the virtues of the white middle classes — thrift, enterprise,
and efficiency.

The individualistic economics of Booker T. Washington
and his theory of education for practical ends widely influenced
the Negro world. Even if the industrial schools failed as training grounds for Negro industrial workers because their philosophy and curriculum were based upon the needs of the pre-
machine age, they have nevertheless served as models for
Negro schools throughout the South, while their graduates
have played a tremendous rôle in the education of Negro
youth. But widespread as was the influence of Washington and
the Hampton and Tuskegee Schools, their doctrines did not go
unchallenged. Almost as soon as they were enunciated they
gave rise to the well-known controversy between the proponents of industrial and higher education.[37] This controversy,
though ostensibly a conflict over educational theory, had its
roots in divergent social and racial philosophies. The opposition, led by W. E. B. Du Bois, militantly demanded full social
and political equality. "I hold these truths to be self-evident,"
declared Du Bois, explaining his position in 1928,[38] "that a
disfranchised working class in modern industrial civilization
is worse than helpless. It is a menace not simply to itself but
to every other group in the community. It will be diseased, it
will be criminal, it will be ignorant, it will be the plaything of
mobs, and it will be insulted by caste restrictions."

[37] See Du Bois, *Souls of Black Folk* (1903).
[38] Paper read at the National Interracial Conference, Washington, D. C., 1928.

CHAPTER IV

CRAFT UNIONISM AND EXCLUSION

THE ascendancy of the American Federation of Labor marked the triumph of craft individualism over industrial brotherhood and of business unionism over equalitarianism. It substituted a job-conscious labor movement for a coöperative anti-monopolistic one. The ideology of the nineteenth century unionism reflected the structural and functional transformation of the labor movement. Structurally the new unionism was a confederation of autonomous and self-sustaining national and international craft unions. Such power as came to be possessed by the confederation, i.e., the American Federation of Labor, was delegated to it by the sovereign constituents, the national and international unions.[1] Between conventions this power resides in an advisory body of officials, the Executive Council, elected by the Federation. Because the unions that made up the Federation were autonomous, they were left to manage their internal affairs without outside interference. Craft autonomy became so sacred a doctrine in the Federation that a union might judge a whole class of workers ineligible for membership without the Federation interfering. This was the structure of the new unionism. Its functions were closely consonant with the structure. As the expression of the dominant forces of organized labor, the skilled workers, the Federation functioned primarily in their behalf.

[1] "All power and final authority within the A. F. of L. resides in its conventions, held annually. All international unions, city and state federations of labor and local and federated unions are entitled to send delegates to these annual meetings." See David J. Saposs, *Readings in Trade Unionism* (1925) p. 107. Between conventions the Executive Council acts on behalf of the American Federation of Labor. Its acts are subject to review and its decisions are not final.

The trade unions that formed the Federation were wage conscious. Their attention was centered upon establishing "group control" over limited "job opportunities." [2] The effectiveness of job control was expressed in the wage contract, a result of bargaining with the employer. As bargaining power and "job control" were inseparable, the union confined its operations to those callings in which an *esprit de corps* was easily built up as a protective wall around the job. This meant narrowing the outlook of the trade union to interest in the skilled mechanic. And, like the medieval guild, the modern craft union came to look upon the skilled mechanics' competence and reliability as a kind of good will which it could capitalize through the employers' acceptance of the work of craft members in preference to outsiders. The apprentice system was the means whereby organized skilled workers protected the good name of their craft. At the same time it was a means of preserving the "mysteries" of the craft from general knowledge, thereby lessening future competition and maintaining control over the job. It was this spirit which characterized the opposition of the blacksmiths', boilermakers', the iron molders', the machinists', printing pressmen's, plumbers', potters', sheet metal workers', steam fitters', and tile layers' unions to the white helper.[3] As put by Ashworth:[4]

Craft pride, together with the belief that recognition of the helper as a member would impair a vested right, was no doubt of considerable force in causing skilled artisans of many unions to refuse their less

[2] According to Dr. Selig Perlman, the ideology of the American Federation of Labor grew out of the consciousness of limited opportunities, a situation which required that the individual, both in his own interest and in that of a group to which he immediately belonged, should not be permitted to occupy any job opportunity except on observing the "common rule" laid down by his union. The safest way to assure this group control over opportunity was for the union to become the virtual owner and administrator of the job without displacing the employer as the owner of his business and risk taker. See Selig Perlman, *A Theory of the Labor Movement* (1928), p. 199.

[3] John H. Ashworth, *The Helper and American Trade Unions* (1915), p. 32.

[4] *Ibid.*, p. 79.

skilled associates admission into their organizations. Evidences of this can be found in the convention proceedings of almost any union in which there has been an attempt to provide for the organization of auxiliary workmen. For instance, when the machinists were contemplating a change in their constitution so as to make handymen eligible for membership, there were many objections, some of which were wholly the result of craft pride. One delegate said: "If you are in favor of taking in the handymen you must remember that the general feeling in our organization is opposed to being put on an equal basis with the handymen." Another said: "We do not want to lose sight of the fact that we belong to the International Association of Machinists, not of handymen. If we take in these men we will have to change our name to the International Association of Machinists and Handymen." [5]

The craft-union leaders attributed the "disintegration and overcrowding" of the trade to the helper. Thus the helper system, poor mechanics, and craft disintegration were looked upon as inseparable.[6] Various measures for eliminating the helper were initiated by the union. Where no attempt was made to eliminate him, effort centered upon making permanent his status as a helper. But when specialization began to strike away the skill of the mechanic, the tactics of the unions changed from opposition and elimination to control and organization.

What is the relevance of these changes in trade-union outlook and structure to the Negro's position in the labor movement? If the spirit of "job control," "craft pride," and fear of competition of the newcomers caused the exclusion of white labor from the trade unions, should one expect it to operate differently where Negro workers are concerned? Hardly. In the first place the Negro has been almost entirely engaged in the unskilled and agricultural occupations. The workers in these occupations, irrespective of race, receive scant attention from craft unionism. Because it is employed in so-called unorganizable occupations, the major proportion of Negro labor, like the white, is in the nature of things excluded. In the second

[5] *Ibid.*
[6] *Ibid.*, pp. 50, 53, 58, 59, 60 and 63.

place, the Negro was customarily believed to be unfitted by racial temperament for skilled mechanical work.[7] For this reason the competence and reliability of Negro craftsmen were usually doubted. By refusing to accept apprentices from a class of workers which social tradition has stamped as inferior, or by withholding membership in the union from reputed craftsmen of this class, the union accomplishes two things simultaneously. It protects its good name. It eliminates a whole class of future competitors. While race prejudice is a very fundamental fact in the exclusion of the Negro, the desire to restrict competition so as to safeguard job monopoly and to control wages is inextricably interwoven with it. Which is more important would be difficult to say. But one can say with some degree of certainty that the exclusion of white men is due largely to the psychology of craft unionism while that of the Negro is due to an interplay of craft-union psychology with the psychology of race prejudice.

It has already been seen that the craft unions of the sixties and seventies encountered the Negro problem. Some of them, like the cigar-makers and the carpenters, eventually took a rather progressive stand on the question. Others, like the Brotherhoods of Engineers, Firemen, and Conductors, accepted the theory of inescapable racial differences. In the eighties these older craft unions were showing signs of stability and permanence. One evidence of this permanence was the attempt to form national organizations which pooled their common trade interest in the American Federation of Labor. In the nineties a new crop of national unions appeared, and they, too, became affiliated to the Federation. Some of the latter at their founding limited eligibility to membership white persons. This

[7] The Journeymen Tailors' Union attributes its small Negro membership to the fact that few Negroes are found capable of making coat, vest, and trousers of a suit. — Charles S. Johnson, secretary, *Abstracts of the Report of the Research Committee to the National Interracial Conference*, 1928. Part IV. The same thing has been said about the Typographical and other unions which call for a fairly high degree of manual dexterity or academic discipline.

was accomplished by placing a clause to that effect either in the constitution or in the ritual.

The unions whose constitutions limited membership to white men were the Brotherhood of Railway Carmen, the Switchmen of North America, the Brotherhood of Railway and Steamship Clerks and Freight Handlers, the Order of Sleeping Car Conductors, the Order of Railway Telegraphers, the National Organization of Masters, Mates and Pilots of North America, the Railway Mail Association, the Wire Weavers' Protective Association, and the Commercial Telegraphers.[8] The Boilermakers, Iron Shipbuilders and Helpers Union and the International Association of Machinists excluded Negroes by ritual.[9] All of the foregoing unions were affiliated with the American Federation of Labor in 1929.[10] In addition to the foregoing, the constitutions of several unaffiliated unions continued to debar Negroes as late as 1926. These are the Brotherhood of Dining Car Conductors, the Order of Railway Expressmen,[11] the American Federation of Express Workers,[12] the American Federation of Railroad Workers,[13] the Brotherhood of Railroad Station Employees,[14] the Train Dispatchers,[15] the Railroad Yard Masters of America,[16] the Railroad Yard Masters of North America,[17] the Neptune Association,[18] and the four railroad transportation

---

[8] See United States Department of Labor, Bureau of Labor Statistics, *Handbook of American Trade Unions*, 1929 edition, Bulletin No. 506, pp. 79, 80, 82, 94, 96, 104, 189, 208 and 215.

[9] At first the Machinists' constitution contained a clause limiting membership to whites. A controversy with the A. F. of L. when the union applied for affiliation led to its removal from the constitution. See Chapter V.

[10] *Handbook*, 1926 edition, p. 69.

[11] *Ibid.*, p. 73.

[12] *Ibid.*, p. 74.

[13] Debars Negroes by constitutional provision but organizes them into separate unions. *Ibid.*, p. 79.

[14] *Ibid.*, p. 81.

[15] *Ibid.*, p. 86.

[16] *Ibid.*, p. 90.

[17] *Ibid.*, pp. 90-91.

[18] *Ibid.*, p. 94.

Brotherhoods. Thus in 1926 the constitutions [19] or rituals of eleven unions affiliated with the American Federation of Labor and of thirteen unaffiliated unions limited membership to white persons. Since 1926 a few changes have somewhat reduced the number. The Order of Railway Expressmen and the American Federation of Express Workers have returned to the Brotherhood of Railway and Steamship Clerks from which they seceded.[20] It is also interesting to note that membership in the white race is not listed in 1929 as a qualification for membership in the Brotherhood of Railroad Station Employees.[21] Thus in 1930 there are nine unions affiliated with the Federation and ten unaffiliated unions whose constitutions debar Negro members.

The absence of such constitutional clauses does not mean that Negroes are admitted. The constitutions of the granite workers', the electrical workers', the flint glass workers', the plumbers' and the structural iron workers' unions do not specify membership in the white race as a prerequisite to membership in the union, but Negro workers have been kept out of these unions by tacit agreement. Granite-cutting in the South, where most of the few Negro granite cutters are to be found, is a white man's trade.[22] The Flint Glass Workers' Union, it has been reported, objects to Negroes "universally on the ground that the pipe on which the glass is blown passes from mouth to mouth and no one would use it after a Negro." [23] The editor of the electrical workers' journal wrote in 1903: "We do not want the Negro in the International Brotherhood of Electrical Workers, but we think they should be organized in locals of their own, affiliated with the American Federation of Labor,

[19] An example of this clause reads: "Any railroad-station employee born of white parents who is sober, moral and otherwise of good character . . . is eligible to membership." Brotherhood of Railroad Station Employees and Clerks. See *Handbook*, 1926 edition, p. 81.

[20] *Handbook*, 1929 Edition, p. 1.

[21] *Ibid.*, p. 92.

[22] Booker T. Washington, "The Negro and the Labor Unions," *Atlantic Monthly*, June, 1913, p. 762.

[23] Charles S. Johnson, *op. cit.*, Part IV.

as the organization knows no creed or color." [24] This opinion is still the prevailing sentiment in the Electrical Workers' Union.

It is generally understood that Negroes are not admitted to the Plumbers' and Steamfitters' Union. One of the plans for disqualifying them is the license law. It requires that every person wishing to practice the plumbing trade must pass an examination given under municipal authority. Some idea of the operation of the plumbers' license law is obtained from a bill introduced in the Virginia State Legislature.[25] The bill provided, among other things, that members from the local plumbers' union should be included on the board of examiners that passes upon the competency of applicants. A Norfolk plumber recommended the plan to the national union as a means of disqualifying Negroes.[26] The Virginia bill was patterned after the Kansas regulation, which is typical of the plumbers' license laws found in twenty-four states and Porto Rico in 1925. These states are Arkansas, Colorado, Delaware, District of Columbia, Illinois, Kansas, Kentucky, Louisiana, Maine, Montana, Nebraska, New Hampshire, New York, Oklahoma, Oregon, Pennsylvania, South Carolina, Tennessee, Texas, and Wisconsin.[27] Virginia has not appeared in the foregoing list since 1914. According to a statement from the plumbers' secretary-treasurer, the union seeks to have such laws adopted in every state: "When state laws are written up and enacted the personnel and qualifications of administration committees are definitely arranged and the union, in all cases, has a representative, so have the contractors in our trade, and the third party is an outstanding citizen of the particular locality." [28] But the national union has never taken any stand on the question of admitting Negroes. "Competency determined

[24] *Electrical Worker*, April, 1903, p. 102.
[25] See Appendix III B.
[26] *Plumbers' Official Journal*, March, 1905, p. 16.
[27] United States Department of Labor, *Labor Laws in the United States*, Bulletin No. 370, 1925, p. 26.
[28] Correspondence with Thomas E. Burke, general secretary-treasurer.

by examination" is the only qualification mentioned.[29] Yet in a city like Philadelphia the licensing board will not grant a Negro a license. "If a Negro is in some way able to set himself up as a plumber, when he goes to buy fixtures from a plumber's outfitter they refuse to sell to him. When certain plumbers' outfitters have sold fixtures to Negro plumbers the plumbers' organizations have boycotted these firms." [30] And in Chicago the Negro plumbers have failed to gain admission after six years of effort.[31] The plumbers have not been alone in their attempt to exclude Negroes through license requirements. In 1909 a bill requiring the licensing of locomotive firemen, frankly aimed at the Negro, was introduced in the Georgia legislature,[32] while similar provisions affecting barbers, which the Negroes claim are aimed at the members of their race, have also been proposed in a number of states. In this discussion of the plumbers it should be noted that the union has been strenuously opposed to the employment and promotion of white helpers.[33] And it seems that opposition to the Negro is just a little greater in intensity than that exhibited toward the white helper.[34]

Some of the unions that do not exclude Negroes from membership have established most onerous conditions as the only terms under which they can be admitted. The terms of admission to these unions show both race prejudice and the desire of white unionists to confine Negro competition within certain limits. For example, the Negro motion picture operators in New York attempted to obtain a charter from the national union some years ago. In 1926 the secretary of the union in-

[29] *Handbook*, 1926 edition, p. 37.

[30] Forrester Washington, executive secretary of Armstrong Association, Philadelphia, Pennsylvania, before the National Interracial Conference held by Federal Council of Churches, Cincinnati, Ohio, March 25-27, 1925. *Proceedings*, p. 123.

[31] Charles S. Johnson, *op. cit.*

[32] See Appendix IV.

[33] See Ashworth, *op. cit.*, p. 79.

[34] See Appendices III A, B, C, D, and E.

formed the Negro operators that only on the following conditions could they be admitted to the union:

1. The Negro operators admitted to this auxiliary must pay the prevailing initiation fee upon admittance. They must pay the same dues as the white members of this local, as well as any assessments levied by our assembly;

2. The Negro operators shall be entitled to all of the privileges enjoyed under our prevailing wage scale and conditions, excepting as follows: the Negro operators shall be confined as far as is physically possible to working in the colored belt under the jurisdiction of Local 306;

3. The Negro operators shall be subject to the provisions of our Constitution and By-Laws with the following exceptions: the Negro operators will not be permitted to attend the regular meetings of Local 306. The President shall appoint a member of Local 306 to represent .the Negro operators at our regular meetings, said appointment to be approved by the auxiliary members to Local 306 for Negro operators. The member so appointed shall also act as the representative of local at all caucuses of the Auxiliary and the local which he may call at the discretion of the Executive Board of the local. He shall also act as the representative of the auxiliary members to Local 306 for Negro operators in all their grievances;

4. The above rules as set forth are made for an indefinite period. After these rules are in effect for a reasonable length of time upon petition properly made to the local and upon the will of our body, the auxiliary members to Local 306 may become full-fledged members to Local 306 with the following exceptions: they shall not attend the regular meetings of the Union; and

5. The above rules as laid down are subject to change at any time at the discretion of the Executive Board of Local 306, I. A. T. S. E.

Fortunately the Negro operators did not accept these terms. The theater owners preferred to employ them because the patronage of the Harlem theaters is made up mostly of Negroes. Because of this power the Negro operators insisted upon a local charter and won it. When this sort of strategic advantage is wanting the Negroes take what is given them, as in the cases of the Blacksmiths, Drop Forgers and Helpers', the National Rural Letter Carriers', the National Federation of Rural Letter Carriers', and the Maintenance-of-Way Employees' Unions.

The constitutions of the National Rural Letter Carriers' Association and the National Federation of Rural Letter Carriers, the latter affiliated with the American Federation of Labor, provide that "only white members are eligible to serve as delegates to conventions or to hold office." [35] That of the Maintenance-of-Way Employees provides that "colored workers shall be entitled to all the benefits and protection guaranteed by the constitution to members and shall be represented in the lodge by delegates of their own choosing selected from any white lodge on the system division where they are employed. Nothing in this section operates to prevent colored employees from maintaining a separate lodge for social purposes." [36] A variation of this attitude is exhibited by the Sheet Metal Workers' Alliance which holds that "where there are a sufficient number of Negro sheet metal workers, they may be organized as an Auxiliary Local and shall come under the jurisdiction of the white Local Union having jurisdiction over said locality. Members of Auxiliary Locals composed of colored sheet metal workers shall not transfer except to another Auxiliary Local composed of colored members." [37] Severe as the above limitations are, the impositions of the International Brotherhood of Blacksmiths, Drop Forgers and Helpers are more restrictive. Article XVII of the latter's constitution reads:

Sec. 1. Where there are a sufficient number of colored helpers, they may be organized as an auxiliary local; and shall be under the jurisdiction of the white local union, having jurisdiction over that locality; and minutes of said auxiliary local must be submitted to duly authorized officers of said white local for their approval;

Sec. 2. In shops where there is a grievance committee of the white

---

[35] *Handbook of American Trade Unions*, 1929 edition, pp. 177 and 178.
[36] *Ibid.*, p. 77.
[37] Article IV, Section 1, Constitution of the Amalgamated Sheet Metal Workers' International Alliance, 1918, p. 8. See 1926 and later.

local, grievances of members of said auxiliary local will be handled by that committee;

Sec. 3. Members of auxiliary locals composed of colored helpers shall not transfer, except to another auxiliary local composed of colored members, and colored helpers will not be promoted to blacksmiths or helper apprentices; and will not be admitted to shops where white helpers are now employed; and

Sec. 4. Auxiliary locals will be represented in all conventions by delegates elected from the white local in that locality.[38]

These provisions look more like a contrivance for eliminating Negro mechanics from the craft than a means of admitting them to the union. Section 3, by prohibiting Negro helpers from becoming blacksmiths or apprentices, seems designed to thwart the ambition of Negro union members who wish to advance in skill. And section 4 reduces the Negro auxiliary to a dues-paying entity regulated by the white local in order to safeguard itself against undercutting competition of unorganized Negro helpers. Membership in a union under such provisions is obviously more disadvantageous to the Negroes who join than non-unionism, under which many Negroes have advanced from the unskilled to the semi-skilled and skilled occupations. The same industrial forces which gradually forced the blacksmiths' union to change its attitude toward the white helper,[39] whose encroachments upon the mechanic's position was paralleled by mechanization and specialization, may cause the union to grant a greater equality to the Negro whose competition has recently become a positive factor in the organized labor movement.

The position taken by the Brotherhood of Railway Carmen was analogous to that of the blacksmiths. At the 1921 convention the railway carmen's constitution was amended

[38] Constitution and By-Laws of the International Brotherhood of Blacksmiths, Drop-Forgers and Helpers. Correspondence with Henry Carlson, secretary, Blacksmiths Local No. 205, Minneapolis, Minnesota.

[39] "The Blacksmiths, the Machinists, and the Boilermakers tried in every conceivable manner to check the encroachment of the helpers, both in work and in numbers before reaching the conclusion that it is good policy to have the helpers connected with their respective organizations." Ashworth, op. cit., p. 92.

so as to organize Negroes. The amendment states that:

> On railroads where the employment of colored persons has become a permanent institution they shall be admitted to membership in separate lodges. Where these separate lodges of Negroes are organized they shall be under the jurisdiction of the nearest white local and shall be represented in any meeting of Joint Protective Board, Federation meeting or convention where delegates may be seated by white men.[40]

According to this legislation Negroes within the jurisdiction of the carmen's union are not to become members of white lodges and are to be organized only where their employment has become permanent. In other words, new Negro workers or strike breakers would have to work in a shop for considerable time before they would be eligible for membership. The probable result of the amendment is to leave unorganized such new Negro workers as might obtain jobs as a result of railroad expansion or the advance of white men to higher occupations. Practical and cautious men may have dictated the plan as the only possible solution. Yet it is plain that unionism blunders when it adopts the policy of a closed fraternity with respect to particular classes of workers.

The boilermakers did not get as far as the carmen on the question of Negro admission. Heeding the appeal of the American Federation of Labor, the boilermakers considered the question at their 1920 convention. There was substantial agreement on the necessity of taking steps toward caring for the rapid introduction of Negro mechanics and helpers in new territory. It was proposed that since almost all the Negroes eligible to membership in the boilermakers' union were in the South, a conference should be called between southern leaders and the international officers. This conference was to recommend the procedure.[41] The conference was not held. At the 1925 convention a new proposal was offered. It called for a

---

[40] American Federation of Labor, *Proceedings*, 1922, p. 118.

[41] Fourteenth Consolidated Convention of the International Brotherhood of Boilermakers, Iron Shipbuilders and Helpers Union, *Proceedings*, 1925, Resolution 236, pp. 60-61.

removal of restrictions on the admission of Negroes and a militant campaign for Negro members.[42] The resolutions committee reported unfavorably on the proposal; it called for a reaffirmation of the action of the 1920 convention, which had merely proposed a conference to consider the subject. Was the committee trying to circumvent the organization of the Negro? Or did it actually believe a conference necessary because it knew that the admission of Negroes under any condition except one of racial separation, in which white men were recognized as superior, would be interpreted as social equality by the majority of members? This latter consideration seems to have determined the committee's action, for notwithstanding its denial that the contemplated admission of Negroes was on a basis of social equality,[43] and its expressed recognition of the necessity of organization, it rejected the only straightforward method presented to the union and recommended a measure which for five years after its adoption has failed of results.

The question of admitting Negroes to the carmen's union was discussed for the first time at the special session on amalgamation which met in Buffalo in 1905. Some doubt was expressed in the convention on the possibility of the carmen's union being admitted to the American Federation of Labor as long as its constitution contained a clause limiting membership to white persons. A national officer asked the chairman of the convention if Mr. Gompers would issue "a charter discriminating on the nigger." [44] The chairman replied that the retention of the word "white" would not cause the Federation to deny the union's application for affiliation.[45] A resolution in favor of admitting the Negro provoked much debate. The chief obstacle to its passage was the belief that admission of Negroes on equal terms of membership with white men was racial equality. One of the typical arguments along this line

[42] *Ibid.*, p. 345.

[43] *Ibid.*, p. 345. Committee's Report on Resolution 236.

[44] International Car Workers, *Proceedings*, Special Session, Sept. 1905, pp. 31-85.

[45] *Ibid.*, p. 31.

was made by one Delegate Dennis: "I do not think," he said, "there is a member in this room that believes in taking the Negro in with him on social equality. I believe that God in his infinite mercy made the Negro but he never made him to be a car worker. I do not believe the time will ever come when he should come into a union along with carmen. . . . I want to tell you that I am a northern man. . . . I was born with an abolitionist father; but when the time does come that I must sit down in social equality with the Negro. . . . I want to be carried to the nearest insane asylum." [46]

Something of the same point of view on race relations led to opposition to the appointment of a Negro organizer in the carpenters' union in 1902. Numerous communications were directed to the president. Some of them expressed opposition to the appointment of a Negro under any circumstance. Others cautioned against a Negro's attempting to organize white men.[47] The appointment was not rescinded, however, and the organizers' success took the sting out of the opposition. In a period of ten years Negro organizers in the carpenters' union had organized in southern states twenty-five locals composed exclusively of Negro carpenters.[48] Here the policy of racial separation was accompanied by that of parity between white and Negro locals. But in the carmen's union and the others mentioned, the plan providing for Negro organization was framed so as to avoid antagonizing those elements in the union that were opposed to Negro admission. The 1905 convention of the carmen's union abandoned the question of Negro admission because it was construed to mean the social equality of the races. The acceptance of this racial theory in the labor movement causes either the complete exclusion of Negroes by constitutional and other methods, or the segregation of them in a union under the paternalistic guidance of their white brothers. This psychology of white superiority and competence

[46] *Ibid.*, p. 34.

[47] *Carpenter*, Jan., 1903, p. 3; Feb., 1903; and April, 1902, pp. 6 and 7.

[48] Booker T. Washington, "The Negro and the Labor Unions," *Atlantic Monthly*, June, 1913, p. 757.

is particularly strong among labor aristocracies like the "big four" railway brotherhoods[49] and in what Professor R. F. Hoxie called the uplift unions[50] that combine benevolence and fraternalism with business strategy.

Uplift unionism is characterized by a feeling of brotherhood of the kind customarily found in the secret society and lodge. For example, included among the purposes of the Maintenance-of-Way Employees is the ambition "to alleviate distress and suffering caused by sickness . . . among our members; to assist the widows and orphans of deceased members; to allow no person to remain a member of the brotherhood unless he lives a sober, moral and honest life." The social and moral features are quite as much in evidence as the economic. Because of these features the union is as much justified in eliminating the Negro from membership as the Elks, Masons, Odd Fellows or any other fraternal group. But the Maintenance-of-Way Employees' Brotherhood attempts to separate its economic from its social or moral functions. It provides that colored workers are to be protected in the economic sense by the union, but that they are to be represented in the union by white delegates. They may maintain a separate lodge for social purposes if they desire.[51] Similarly, the fraternal purpose is fundamental in the Railway Mail Association which limits membership to male railway clerks of the Caucasian race.[52] "The object of this association is to conduct the business of a fraternal beneficiary association for the sole benefit of its members and beneficiaries and not for profit; to provide closer social relations among railway postal clerks; to enable them to perfect any movement that may be for their benefit as a class . . . and [to] make provision for the payment of benefits to its members and their beneficiaries in case of death. . . ."[53]

[49] See Chapter XII, pp. 287-88.

[50] See R. F. Hoxie, *Trade Unionism in the United States* (1921), p. 47.

[51] See Maintenance-of-Way Employees. *Handbook of American Trade Unions* (1926), p. 77.

[52] *Ibid.*, p. 173.

[53] *Ibid.*

In other words the Association is a non-commercial insurance society as well as a union of workers affiliated with the Federation.[54] Negroes were at one time admitted to this union, but in 1911 the constitution was amended so as to exclude them. The reason for the change was the fact that the Negro members were found to be a poor insurance risk.[55] Only a few of the large commercial insurance companies exclude Negro risks completely, but because Negro mortality is higher than white many of them charge a Negro policyholder a higher premium rate than is paid by a white man holding the same type of policy. The Metropolitan Life Insurance Company follows a different method. It includes among its preferred risks classes of Negroes who can obtain the same type of policy at the rate open to similar white risks. As a non-commercial insurance society the policy of the Railway Mail Association with respect to Negro membership is more drastic than that of many commercial insurance companies.

It appears from the following resolution, adopted by the Illinois branch of the Railway Mail Association, protesting against the appointment of a Negro clerk-in-charge at the Terminal Railway Post Office in Chicago, that the "high mortality rate among Negro Members" was only a pretext for excluding others in the future:

WHEREAS, a colored clerk has been appointed in the Chicago, Illinois, Terminal R. P. O., and

WHEREAS, said clerk-in-charge has direct supervision over thirty-three clerks of Caucasian birth; and

WHEREAS, this does not create harmonious relations between clerks and clerks-in-charge, nor would it in any other case similar in character, nor can the best interests of the service be obtained under such condition; and

WHEREAS, we believe that no colored clerk-in-charge can supervise the work of clerks of Caucasian birth to best advantage, nor to the best welfare of the employees, therefore be it

---

[54] Letter from H. W. Strickland, industrial secretary, Railway Mail Association, May 15, 1929.   [55] *Ibid.*

Resolved, That the Illinois Branch Sixth Division R. M. A., in regular session assembled vigorously protest this assignment or any future assignment of a [Negro] clerk-in-charge who will have direct supervision over a crew any of whom are of Caucasian birth.[56]

This branch was not unique in its stand. Other branches protested similar appointments.[57]

Some unions have organized Negroes as a matter of self-defence. Particularly is this true in the trades, like building, where Negro employment is traditional. A few of such unions have passed laws prohibiting the practice of racial discrimination on the job. Having committed themselves to Negro organization, these unions have been forced to establish white and Negro locals because of race feeling.

The constitution of the Bricklayers' and Masons' Union imposes a fine of $100 upon any member found guilty of color discrimination on the job.[58] That of the Operative Plasterers' and Cement Finishers' Union is somewhat analogous. It provides that "any member or members that refuse to work with any other member in good standing in this association on account of his race, creed or nationality, thereby causing him to lose his job when such charges can be proven to the satisfaction of the Executive Board, he or they shall be fined the sum of One Hundred Dollars." [59] Others, like the Broom and Whisk Makers' International, the International Ladies Garment Workers', the Wood, Wire and Metal Workers', and the Lathers' Unions, either declare that "no one shall be discriminated against because of race, creed or color," or state as one of their objects "the organization of all workers regardless of race . . ." But the race psychology of a local union often counteracts the wholesome effect of the international union's stand. It is reported that white bricklayers in parts of the

[56] *Railway Post Office*, Feb., 1929, p. 59.

[57] Interview with secretary, National Alliance of Postal Employees, April, 1929.

[58] Article XVI, Section 2, No. 11, Constitution and By-Laws, Bricklayers, Masons and Plasterers, 1905, p. 52 (See 1922 and later).

[59] Constitution Operative Plasterers and Cement Finishers. Sec. 64, p. 15.

South refuse to work with Negroes even though the latter are union members.[60] Negro bricklayers, members of the union in Pittsburgh, contend that their white associates have refused to work with them, the union's law to the contrary notwithstanding.[61] White bricklayers have been known to leave the scaffold without a word of protest as soon as a Negro bricklayer comes upon the job. In cases of this kind racial discrimination cannot be proven. The Negro bricklayer is slow to report discrimination because he fears he will not be able to prove his charge. If he makes a complaint and fails to prove it he can be disciplined by the union. The constitution provides that "any member bringing a charge against a fellow member which proves unfounded shall be punished as may be deemed proper." [62]

The experience of other unions with the race issue has also been disappointing. The bakery and confectionery workers could never organize permanent mixed locals in the South. The whites refused to remain in locals into which Negroes were admitted on a basis of equality. They even refused to belong to the same international union. Strife between the two groups of workers broke up every bakery worker's local established in the South. Finding themselves unable to effect "harmony" by means of interracial education, the executives of the union decided to issue separate charters to white and Negro locals, respectively.[63]

Two resolutions affecting Negroes were presented to the thirteenth convention of the American Federation of Teachers in Chicago in July, 1929. The first urged the abolition of Jim-Crow schools, the providing of equal facilities for black and

[60] Thomas Dabney, "The Conquest of Bread," *Southern Workman*, Oct., 1928, p. 421.

[61] Abram L. Harris, *The New Negro Worker in Pittsburgh* (Master's Essay, University of Pittsburgh, 1924).

[62] Article 3, Section 3, Constitution and Rules, Bricklayers Union, p. 58.

[63] Bakery and Confectionery Workers' International Union of America, *Proceedings of the 7th Convention*, Sept. 1920, p. 8.

white children and equal expenditure for education per child, equal pay for Negro and white teachers doing the same grade of work, and the selection and promotion of teachers on an equal basis regardless of race. The second resolution called upon the American Federation of Teachers to endorse a special campaign for the unionization of Negro teachers, and declared that Negro and white teachers should be organized in the same locals. Both resolutions were defeated by the opposition of delegates from southern locals.[64]

Similarly, resolutions providing for the admission of Negroes which were introduced at the convention of the Switchmen's Union of North America in June, 1930, with the approval of the union administration, were defeated by the southern delegates. Concessions to southern prejudice in the shape of great restrictions upon the colored workers were of no avail. "We do not come preaching social equality with the Negro, for he himself does not want that," said the sponsors of the resolutions. "Neither do we advocate industrial equality, for we have provided in our recommendations provisions that if adopted will segregate the Negro, as he wants to be, yet this union will have jurisdiction over his numerical strength." The southern delegates contended that the Negroes would demand "social equality" if given a chance to join the organization, that they would "overrun the whites" and "wreck the union in the South."[65]

The difficulties of organizing Negroes and whites in the Seamen's Union has been stated by its president, Andrew Furuseth: "We found . . . that having common clubrooms for both, they would not mix. Sailing together in the same vessel would cause eternal trouble, and the Negro was as impossible as the white, if not more so. . . . Our organization was never hostile to Negroes, and is not now. The employment on the same vessel, in the same department, has, however, been found

[64] *Opportunity*, August 1929, pp. 257-58.
[65] *Labor's News*, June 28, 1928, p. 8.

impossible for two reasons. The Negroes protest and the white protest and we do not know which . . . protests the louder and the more effectively." [66]

Similar antagonism also prevails among the letter carriers in the southern states. The constitution of the National Association of Letter Carriers permits the existence of no more than one local branch under the jurisdiction of a postmaster. The branches are in control of either the white or colored group. Where the whites are in control the Negroes do not join and where the Negroes are in control the whites do not join. President Gainor of the National Association estimated in 1919 that the race issue kept 1,500 possible members out of the organization.[67] To meet this situation the National Association in 1917, on its president's recommendation, amended its constitution to permit the chartering of white and colored branches in states where segregation was practiced.[68] Due to opposition from the colored membership, and from outside politicians, particularly Congressman Martin B. Madden of Illinois, representative from the Chicago Negro district, authority conferred by the amendment was never exercised. Two years later the action of the 1917 convention was rescinded.[69]

One argument advanced in support of the separation of white and black trade unionists is that the latter prefer to be by themselves.[70] Another is that race consciousness makes it necessary. Certain differences should be noted, however, between various forms of separation. One form is voluntary and unofficial. It is practiced for political reasons — usually that of obtaining offices. In the Baltimore and Hampton Roads shipping districts several locals of longshoremen are composed exclusively of Negroes. Here separation is not forced by the

[66] Quoted by Thomas L. Dabney, "Organized Labor's Attitude Toward Negro Workers," *Southern Workman*, August, 1928, p. 323.

[67] *Postal Record*, October, 1919, p. 332.

[68] *Ibid.*, October, 1917, pp. 294-95 and 329.

[69] *Ibid.*, October, 1919, pp. 331-32.

[70] Testimony of Victor Orlander before the Chicago Commission on Race Relations, August 16, 1920, pp. 6 and 7.

international. Negroes in these locals state that they prefer
separation. It gives them an experience in union government
and office-holding that they claim they cannot obtain in a mixed
local. In both sections they are as numerous as the whites.
Through concerted action the Negro longshoremen in the
Hampton Roads district have been able to cause the selection of
one of their number as business representative for the district.
This man, George Millner, is also third vice-president of the
International Longshoremen's Union.[71] The district council is
composed of both white and black longshoremen.

Separation of this kind is the means employed by a minority group to obtain recognition and status in the union. It is
possible for the motive back of it to lead to a greater emphasis
upon race consciousness than upon working-class consciousness.
In this respect it contains the seeds of disruption and antagonism.

A second type of separation is involuntary, and official only
in the sense that the international adopts it as a matter of
racial expediency. The white and colored locals are usually
permitted to function independently and on parity. This is the
policy followed in the South by some unions like the bakery
and confectionery workers, the carpenters, and the bricklayers,
whose official attitude is non-discriminatory. On the other
hand, a union like the Hotel and Restaurant Employees' International Alliance makes separation the rule, but in practice
follows an opportunistic policy by permitting locals to accept
Negro members if they choose. According to its constitution,
"If a member of a colored local moves to a city where no local
of his craft or race exists, he shall remain a member of a local
of the city from which he came. . . . If a colored worker at our
craft shall desire to enter a local in a city where only a white
local exists he may be accepted in the International Union as
a member-at-large." [72] This regulation does not exclude Ne-

[71] See Chapter IX, p. 196.
[72] Constitution of the Hotel and Restaurant Employees' International Alliance, p. 7.

groes from local organizations that are willing to accept them. Negroes are to be found in Local 34 of Boston, but the bulk of the Negro membership is found in locals of an entirely Negro composition. In Chicago 150 of approximately 3,500 Negro hotel men are in Local 444. The cooks and pastry-men who were once members of their craft local are now members of the Negro waiters' local, and an international organizer claims that the cooks formed their own local because they preferred to be by themselves.

When the international union attempted to organize the Negro waiters in Philadelphia, Baltimore and Minneapolis, its plan of organization was racial separation. In Philadelphia the Negroes refused to join on the basis of separation. In Minneapolis the Negro local was short-lived. As the result of his experience with organizing the Negro waiters of Minneapolis one labor leader concluded:

1. [The Negro workers] depend too much on leadership which our experience has proven of a questionable type;

2. They are too timid and distrustful of white officers for assistance to organization;

3. [They have a] fear of losing the job on account of color;

4. The [Negro] emissary of employers instills them with fear that the colored workers will be replaced with whites if they attempt to organize;

5. [There is] a lack of education along trade union lines, hence lack of stability.[73]

Distrust of white men and the ignorance of the labor movement among the Negro cannot be overcome by separating the Negro from the main current of the labor movement. Separation of white and colored workers may be a necessary expedient in the South, but there is less justification for it in most northern communities. Even when adopted as a matter of expediency, it hinders the development of trade-union consciousness among a class of workers whose industrial traditions are agricultural and servile.

[73] J. E. Spielman, Bookbinders' Local Union, No. 12. Minneapolis, Minnesota. See Abram L. Harris, *The Negro Population in Minneapolis* (1926), p. 38.

The third type of segregation is that which is enforced by the national union as its official policy in organizing Negroes. It makes use of one or all of the following discriminations: (1) Negroes are organized in auxiliary locals usually in subordination to the nearest white local; (2) they may not transfer to white locals; (3) they are not eligible for promotion to skilled work; (4) they may not hold office; and (5) they are represented in conventions or conferences only by white men. This type of separation characterizes the organization of Negroes in the Carmen's, the Blacksmiths,' the Maintenance-of-Way Employees,' the National Rural Letter Carriers' Unions and the National Federation of Rural Letter Carriers. This third type of separation lends validity to the Negro's belief that organized labor means organized white labor. It vitiates solidarity. Race consciousness is so accentuated by it that the union finds it difficult to organize Negroes when strikes, industrial expansion, or the lowering of old skill requirements by technological changes make their employment possible and their organization, even though difficult, a matter of the union's self-protection. When this form of separation is accepted, as is done by Negro carmen and maintenance-of-way employees, it is accepted as a business proposition to which the only alternative is exclusion from the union.

It would be strange indeed if racial antipathy and restrictions upon Negro membership did not keep the Negro trade-union membership low. The extent to which exclusion imposes serious economic disadvantages is demonstrated negatively and positively, first by the fact that in view of patent discrimination by such unions as the carmen and the blacksmiths, Negroes contribute memberships of 500 and 300 respectively to these unions out of total memberships of 56,000 and 15,000; and, secondly, by the attempt of Negro workers to overcome the weakness of individual bargaining by the organization of "their own unions" [74] in crafts where they are excluded from the regular trade union. Both of these situations are shown in the following tables.

[74] See Chapter VI, "Independent Negro Unionism."

TABLE I

NEGRO MEMBERSHIP IN INTERNATIONAL AND NATIONAL UNIONS
AND LOCAL UNIONS DIRECTLY AFFILIATED WITH THE
AMERICAN FEDERATION OF LABOR FROM 1900-1928

		Number 1900[a]	Number 1910[b]	Number 1928[c]
1.	Actors and Artists	——	——	12
2.	Bakery and Confectionery Workers	——	——	190[d]
			(as of 1903)	
3.	Barbers, Journeymen	800	1,000	239[d]
4.	Blacksmith, Drop Forgers and Helpers	——	——	300
5.	Boot and Shoeworkers	50	50	——
6.	Brewery, Flour and Cereal Workers	——	10	——
7.	Bricklayers, Masons and Plasterers	——	——	1,117
8.	Brick and Clay Workers	200	——	3
9.	Broom and Whisk Makers	——	6	50
10.	Carmen, Railway	——	——	500
11.	Carpenters and Joiners	1,000	2,500	933[d]
12.	Carriage and Wagon Makers	500	——	——
13.	Carvers, Wood	——	——	——
14.	Cigar-Makers	——	5,000	110[d]
15.	Clerks, Post Office	——	——	356[d]
16.	Cloth, Hat, Cap, and Millinery Workers	——	——	300[d]
17.	Coopers	200	——	——
18.	Elevator Constructors	——	(a few)	10[d]
19.	Engineers, Operating	——	——	1,200
20.	Engravers, Photo	——	——	2[d]
21.	Federal Employees	——	——	2,008[d]
22.	Firemen and Oilers	2,700	——	150
23.	Fire Fighters	——	——	18
24.	Foundry Employees	——	——	150
25.	Fur Workers	——	——	11
26.	Garment Workers, International Ladies'	——	——	519[d]
27.	Garment Workers, United	——	——	30[d]

TABLE I — (Continued)

		Number 1900[a]	Number 1910[b]	Number 1928[c]
28.	Glove Workers	——	——	2
29.	Granite Cutters	——	4	2
30.	Hod Carriers, Building and Common Laborers	——	——	5,131[d]
31.	Hotel and Restaurant Employees	——	2,500	1,000
32.	Iron, Steel, and Tin Workers	——	——	24[d]
33.	Jewelry Workers	——	——	50[d]
34.	Lathers, Wood, Wire, and Metal	——	——	23[d]
35.	Laundry Workers	——	——	111[d]
36.	Leather Workers	——	——	8[d]
37.	Letter Carriers, National Association	——	——	376[d]
38.	Lithographers	——	1	1[d]
39.	Longshoremen	6,000	——	5,381[d]
40.	Maintenance-of-Way Employees	——	——	10,000
41.	Meat Cutters and Butcher Workmen	——	——	1
42.	Metal Workers, Sheet	——	——	4
43.	Mine Workers	20,000	40,000	5,000
44.	Molders	——	12	12[d]
45.	Musicians	——	——	3,000
46.	Painters, Decorators and Paperhangers	169	——	418[d]
47.	Paving Cutters	——	——	310[d]
48.	Piano and Organ Workers	——	1	——
49.	Plasterers, Operative	——	——	782[d]
50.	Printing Pressmen and Assistants	——	6	43[d]
51.	Railway Employees, Street and Electric	——	——	16[d]
52.	Roofers, Damp and Water Proof Workers	——	——	19[d]
53.	Seamen	——	——	8[d]
54.	Signalmen, Railway	——	——	2
55.	Stage Employees, Theatrical	——	4	100[d]
56.	Stereotypers and Electrotypers	——	——	12

TABLE I — (CONTINUED)

	Number 1900[a]	Number 1910[b]	Number 1928[c]
57. Stone Cutters	——	——	2
58. Tailors, Journeymen	——	——	17[d]
59. Teachers, American Federation of....	——	——	11[d]
60. Teamsters, Chauffeurs, Stablemen, etc.	——	6,000	313[d]
61. Textile Workers	——	——	4
62. Tobacco Workers	1,000	——	100[e]
63. Tunnel, Subway Workers	——	——	600
64. Typographical Union	——	250	128[d]
Total for National and International Unions	32,619	68,353[f]	41,219
65. Negro Locals Directly Affiliated with American Federation of Labor [75]	——	400	3,197
Total for all Unions	32,619	68,753	44,416

[a] Taken from Eric W. Hardy, *The Relation of the Negro to Trade Unionism* (Master's Essay, University of Chicago, 1911), p. 11.

[b] Estimates obtained by Wolfe, *Admission to American Trade Unions*, pp. 122 and 124.

[c] Unpublished findings of National Urban League, Courtesy Ira DeA. Reid, director, Research and Investigations.

[d] Obtained from locals in which Negroes were members. It may or may not represent the entire number in the International Union. See Note *c* above.

[e] In the 1916-1920 period there were 3,000 Negroes in the Tobacco Workers Union. See discussion of tobacco workers, Chapter XIV, pp. 322-23.

[f] As explained in the text this total is too high, by perhaps 36,000, since the number in the United Mine Workers is greatly overweighted.

[75] See Chapter V, p. 103.

TABLE II

INDEPENDENT NEGRO UNIONS

	Locals	Reported Membership
1. Association of Train Porters, Brakemen and Switchmen (Richmond, Va.)..	14	1,700[a]
2. Association of Colored Railway Trainmen (Memphis, Tenn.)........	60	3,000[b]
3. National Alliance of Postal Employees (Washington, D.C.)....		2,470[c]
4. Electricians' Union (Chicago)............		200[d]
5. Plumbers' Union (Chicago)...............		200[d]
6. Plasterers' Union (Chicago)...............		200[d]
7. Interstate Order of Colored Locomotive Firemen, Enginemen, etc. (Chicago).........................		
8. Train Porters, Brakemen (St. Louis)		
9. International Order of Colored Locomotive Firemen (Savannah, Ga.)[e]		
10. Dining Car Cooks and Waiters, (New York City)............		2,700
11. Brotherhood of Dining and Sleeping Car Employees (Minneapolis, Minn.)		260[f]
12. Protective Order of Railroad Trainmen (Council Bluff, Ark.)		1,000
	74	11,730

[a] *Handbook of American Trade Unions*, 1929 edition, p. 89.

[b] *Ibid.*, p. 98.

[c] *Postal Alliance*, March, 1929, p. 12.

[d] *The Negro Industrial Proletariat* (July 1928), p. 19. (Published by Trade Union Educational League of America.)

[e] Disbanded in 1929.

[f] Operates mainly on Great Northern Railroad. Formerly Local No. 548, American Federation of Labor.

The reader should be warned against making comparisons between Negro and white membership on the basis of these figures. The 1900 and 1910 figures were obtained through correspondence with union officials. The total membership as given for 1910 is undoubtedly wide of the mark. There could not have been 40,000 Negroes in the United Mine Workers' Union in 1910, as reported by Wolfe, since there were only 40,000 Negroes in the whole industry. According to the Coal Commission's report there were 43,000 Negroes engaged in mining coal in 1920. In 1926 only 5,000 Negroes were reported as members of the United Mine Workers' Union. Probably the 1910 membership was 4,000 instead of 40,000. The 1926 figures were given in some cases by the national unions and in others by locals which probably contained the greatest numbers of Negroes in the national union. By this method 44,416 Negroes were found in the national unions affiliated with the American Federation of Labor in 1926. If the membership in the independent Negro unions and the Negro locals directly affiliated with the Federation is added to the total membership in the national unions, the total known Negro trade-union membership would be about 56,000. But it should be remembered that many of the 11,000 members in the independent Negro unions exist only on paper.

A comparison of the total membership for 1900, 1910, and 1926 is admissible only if we bear in mind that the figures are mere approximations. If the 1910 Negro membership of the United Mine Workers was 4,000 instead of 40,000 the total membership for the reporting unions was about 33,000. This is almost the same as it was in 1900. In 1926, the known Negro membership in trade unions was around 45,000 or about 36 per cent over the approximated Negro membership in the unions that reported in 1910. When membership in the Negro local unions directly affiliated with the American Federation of Labor and the independent Negro unions is included, the total membership for 1926 is 70 per cent higher than it was in 1910. While the membership of the Federation's directly affiliated Negro locals should be included in the total

Negro trade-union membership, the national trade unions should not be credited with the increase. The Federation's Negro locals owe their existence to the neglect of the national unions rather than to their vigilance. It should also be noted that about 3,000 Pullman porters are included in the Negro federal labor and local union membership. Since the Pullman porters' organization began as an independent union, neither the Federation nor the national unions can be credited with any increase in membership due to Pullman porter affiliation.

Any attempt to trace the growth of Negro membership in specific trade unions is fraught with difficulty, since figures for the same unions were unobtainable for the three dates 1900, 1910, and 1926. Some idea of the degree of organization may be gained by comparing the number gainfully employed with the known trade-union membership.

TABLE III

NEGROES GAINFULLY EMPLOYED IN CHIEF INDUSTRIAL GROUPS, 10 YEARS OF AGE AND OVER, IN 1920 [76]

Division of Industry	Number	Per Cent
1. Agriculture, Forestry and Animal Husbandry	2,178,888	45.2
2. Extraction of Minerals	73,229	1.5
3. Manufacturing and Mechanical	886,810	18.4
4. Transportation	312,421	6.5
5. Trade	140,467	2.9
6. Public Service	50,552	1.0
7. Professional Service	80,183	1.7
8. Domestic and Personal Service	1,064,590	22.0
9. Clerical Occupations	37,011	.8
All Occupations	4,824,151	100.0

In order to secure a fairly accurate basis for estimating the ratio between Negro trade-union membership and the number

[76] Adapted from Table 4, Vol. IV, *Fourteenth Census of the United States* (1920).

employed in the industries that are considered organizable, we shall exclude all industrial divisions in the above table except extraction of minerals, manufacturing, and transportation. In these divisions 1,272,460 Negroes were employed in 1920. If there were not more than 56,000 Negro members of trade unions in 1926, Negro workers were about 4.2 per cent organized in these divisions. If there were 100,000 Negro trade-union members, as Mr. Charles S. Johnson estimated,[77] Negro wage earners were about 7.6 per cent organized. But in 1923 it was estimated that only 20.8 per cent of all American wage earners, excluding agricultural workers, were in the trade unions.[78] If this estimate held good in 1926, the Negro worker on the basis of our figures was about one-fifth, and on the basis of Mr. Johnson's calculations about one-third, as well organized as the total number of wage earners. The same ratio does not hold good for certain specific industries. The wage earners in the extraction of minerals, for example, were about 41 per cent organized in 1920.[79] The Negroes in this division were chiefly bituminous coal miners, who were less than 12 per cent organized, while the whole bituminous coal industry was nearly 50 per cent organized.[80] Transportation was 37.2 per cent organized in 1920.[81] But almost 100,000 of the Negroes employed on the railroads, which was about a third of those in transportation, could not join the union because they were laborers or because of barriers against Negro membership in the railroad unions.

The assumption of the above analysis is that all the Negro wage earners in all industries are available for trade-union membership. But this is not true. Some of the gainfully em-

[77] Charles S. Johnson, *op. cit.*, Part IV, p. 33.

[78] Leo Wolman, *The Growth of American Trade Unions, 1880-1923* (1924), p. 85. An estimate of 20.8 per cent is probably too high for both years. Mr. David J. Saposs puts the figure at a little over 12 per cent which is probably too low.

[79] *Ibid.*, p. 86.

[80] *Ibid.*, p. 87.

[81] *Ibid.*, p. 86.

ployed are under age and a greater number are unskilled workers, as is shown in the following table.

TABLE IV

NEGROES GAINFULLY EMPLOYED IN THE CHIEF MANUFACTURING INDUSTRIES, 10 YEARS OF AGE AND OVER, AT THE 1920 CENSUS. CLASSIFIED AS SKILLED, SEMI-SKILLED AND LABORERS

Industry, Occupation, or Service Group Skilled:	Number in each group	Total	Per Cent
Bakers	3,164		
Blacksmiths	8,521		
Boilermakers	1,398		
Brick and Stone Masons	10,609		
Cabinetmakers	456		
Carpenters	34,243		
Compositors, Linotypers and Typesetters	1,540		
Coopers	2,191		
Electricians	1,342		
Engineers (Stationary) Cranemen, Hoistmen, etc.	6,353		
Engravers	45		
Filers, Grinders, Buffers and Polishers	936		
Furnacemen, Smelters, etc.	3,236		
Glass-Blowers	45		
Dyers	299		
Electrotypers, Stereotypers, and Lithographers	78		
Forgemen, Hammermen and Welders	365		
Jewelers, Watchmakers, Goldsmiths and Silversmiths	524		
Machinists	9,753		
Millwrights	375		
Mechanics (Not Otherwise Specified)	9,290		
Millers (Flour, Grain, Feed, etc)	367		
Molders, Founders and Casters (Metal)	6,634		
Oilers of Machinery	1,027		

TABLE IV — (Continued)

Industry, Occupation, or Service Group

Skilled:	Number in each group	Total	Per Cent
Painters, Glaziers, Varnishers, etc.	9,234		
Paper Hangers	954		
Pattern and Model Makers	48		
Plasterers	5,814		
Cement Finishers	1,265		
Plumbers and Gas Fitters	3,516		
Pressmen, Printing and Plate Printers	101		
Rollers and Roll Hands (Metal)	736		
Roofers and Slaters	609		
Sawyers	2,755		
Piano and Organ Tuners	77		
Annealers and Temperers	51		
Tinsmiths, and Coppersmiths	970		
Tailors and Tailoresses	6,892		
Loom Fixers	29		
Stone Cutters	280		
Structural Iron Workers (Building)	196		
Wood Carvers	9		
Other Skilled Occupations	101	136,626	16.6

Semi-Skilled:

Total Number in Principal Industries:

Chemical and Allied Industries	2,253	
Cigar and Tobaco Factories	19,849	
Clay, Glass and Stone Industries	3,551	
Clothing Industries	13,888	
Food Industries	15,792	
Harness and Saddle Industries	255	
Iron and Steel Industries	23,616	
Other Metal Industries	1,234	
Lumber and Furniture Industries	9,598	
Paper and Pulp Mills	845	
Printing and Publishing	1,595	
Shoe Factories	1,306	
Tanneries	971	

TABLE IV — (CONTINUED)

Industry, Occupation, or Service Group		
Semi-Skilled: *Number in each group*	*Total*	*Per Cent*
Textile Industries 7,687		
Apprentices 2,326		
Other Industries 22,757	127,523	15.5

Laborers:
Total Number in Principal Industries:

Building, General and Not Specified............134,828		
Chemical and Allied Industries...................... 17,486		
Cigar and Tobacco Factories.......................... 21,334		
Clay, Glass and Stone Industries................... 18,753		
Clothing Industries 1,407		
Harness and Saddle Industries...................... 150		
Food Industries 27,730		
Helpers in Building and Hand Trades........ 13,223		
Iron and Steel Industries...............................105,641		
Other Metal Industries 3,996		
Lumber and Furniture Industries 106,276		
Paper and Pulp Mills 2,926		
Printing and Publishing 1,244		
Shoe Factories 344		
Tanneries 2,503		
Textile Industries 17,047		
Other Industries 86,284	561,172	67.9

| Total Skilled, Semi-Skilled and Laborers | 825,321 | 100.0 |

There were 825,321 Negroes employed in manufacturing industries in 1920. Only 16.6 per cent of them were skilled workers; 67.9 per cent of them were laborers; and 15.5 per cent were semi-skilled. The percentages for the white workers were 32.4 for the skilled, 19.1 for the semi-skilled, and 48.5 for the laborers. In other words, if skill is made a prerequisite to trade-union membership not more than 32 per cent of the Negroes in mechanical industry and 51.5 per cent of the whites are available for organization.[82] As has already been noted, the whole range of industry is not more than 20.8 per cent organized. In other words four-fifths of the American workers are unorganized. Since this is true of American workers in general, is it surprising that so few Negroes are in trade unions? While the white worker is not organized because he is unskilled, or because trade-union leaders are too lethargic to tackle such open-shop industries as tobacco, automobiles, packing, steel, and rubber, the Negro is excluded for these same reasons plus an additional one, racial antipathy.

[82] Assuming that the semi-skilled are organized as helpers, etc., in the craft bodies.

CHAPTER V

THE OFFICIAL POSITION OF THE AMERICAN
FEDERATION OF LABOR

FOUR years after its formation, the American Federation of Labor declared that it "looks with disfavor upon trade unions having provisions which exclude from membership persons on account of race or color." [1] At the convention of 1893 the Federation resolved: "We here and now re-affirm as one of the cardinal principles of the labor movement that the working people must unite and organize irrespective of creed, color, sex, nationality or politics." [2] For a time one of the conditions of affiliation with the American Federation of Labor was the taking of an oath not to discriminate against a fellow workman because of race. One of the early pamphlets [3] published by the Executive Council contained this statement: "The American Federation of Labor does not draw the color line nor do its affiliated national and international unions. A union that does cannot be admitted into affiliation with this body. A portion of the pledge taken by every candidate for membership reads: 'I promise never to discriminate against a fellow worker on account of color, creed or nationality.' " Such were the sentiments prevailing in the Federation of Labor when the ideal of solidarity irrespective of race, which had been characteristic of the old Knights of Labor, still exerted an influence on the former's leaders. Before long, however, the heads of the Federation came to realize that this ideal was standing in the way of its expansion. It was presented with the

[1] American Federation of Labor, *Proceedings*, 1890, p. 31.

[2] Correspondence with Frank Morrison, secretary, American Federation of Labor, April 23, 1929.

[3] This pamphlet was found in the New York Public Library. It was captioned "An Open Letter to Ministers of the Gospel." (Undated.)

choice of remaining a militant body true to its ideals, or of compromising for the sake of increased membership. Without very great struggle it chose the latter course.

The first test of the consciousness of the Federation's determination to insist upon the observance of its declared ideals by its constituent unions came in 1890, when a resolution was presented to the convention requesting that an organizer be furnished the machinists. The convention was advised that a group known as the National Machinists' Union already existed, but that the constitution of this organization limited membership to white persons.[4] The convention thereupon directed the Executive Council to request the union "to strike out their color line discrimination." [5] This the organization promised, but failed to do. Then the Executive Council called a convention of machinists' unions having no connection with the existing National Machinists' Union. Out of this convention there grew a new organization named the International Machinists' Union of America. The sole purpose of the establishment of this new union was to compel the old organization to change its anti-Negro policy. The new union declared that as soon as this end was achieved it would be pleased to amalgamate with the old organization "upon an honorable basis." [6] The amalgamation was effected shortly afterwards and the resulting body, under the name of the International Association of Machinists, was admitted to the American Federation of Labor in 1895.[7]

While it is true that the new union eliminated the white clause from its constitution under the terms of the "honorable basis" of amalgamation, this did not mean that the policy of Negro exclusion for which the original union had been denied admission to the American Federation of Labor, had been

---

[4] A similar clause in the Constitution of the Brotherhood of Locomotive Firemen was the chief obstacle, it has been said, to its affiliation with the American Federation. Report of the Industrial Commission, 1901, Vol. XVII, p. 36.

[5] American Federation of Labor, *Proceedings*, 1891, p. 12.

[6] *Ibid.*

[7] Theodore H. Glocker, *The Government of American Trade Unions*, p. 27.

abandoned. The method of discrimination was merely changed. A pledge binding each member to propose only white men for membership was placed in the ritual.[8] A similar method of excluding Negroes was employed by the Boiler-makers and Iron Ship Builders' Union,[9] which became an international in 1896, the Federation having organized it out of the former directly chartered locals.[10]

The admission of the machinists marked the abandonment of the Federation's rule of requiring prospective member unions to pledge not to discriminate against a fellow worker because of race. In 1909, the Brotherhood of Railway Steam-ship Clerks and Freight Handlers, and the Brotherhood of Railway Carmen, whose constitutions debarred Negroes from membership, were admitted. The Railway Mail Association was admitted in 1917, although its constitution had debarred Negroes since 1911. The available records fail to show that the Executive Council of the Federation opposed the affiliation of any of these unions because of their membership policy. Presumably the belief had come to prevail that it was wiser to attempt to purge a union of racial antipathy after admitting it to fellowship, than to risk its loss by demanding repentance as a condition of affiliation. This compromise was satisfactory as long as the problem of organizing the Negro lay dormant. But when the war-time migrations brought Negroes into in-dustry by thousands, the Federation was forced to beg the very unions which it had admitted under the compromise to find some way of organizing the black newcomers.

At the 1920 and 1921 conventions of the American Fed-eration of Labor the question of Negro membership in the Brotherhood of Railway Carmen, the Boilermakers and the Railway Clerks stimulated considerable discussion. The Negro freight-handlers, express and station employees whose work fell under the jurisdiction of the Brotherhood of Railway

8 F. E. Wolfe, *Admission to American Trade Unions*, p. 120.
9 *Ibid.*
10 American Federation of Labor, *Proceedings*, 1917, p. 28.

Clerks, which debarred Negroes by constitutional provision, petitioned the 1920 convention of the Federation to use its power to have the words "only white" struck from the clerks' constitution so that Negroes could be admitted to full membership. If the Federation failed in this the clerks were to relinquish jurisdiction over the Negro freight-handlers and permit the latter to establish a brotherhood of their own.[11] This resolution resulted from the failure of the clerks to adjust certain grievances, presently to be discussed, for which the freight-handlers had been promised relief in 1919.[12] The following year, 1921, the Negro railway-coach cleaners in Local No. 16088 of St. Louis, Missouri, requested the American Federation of Labor to have the word "white" removed from the constitutions of all affiliated bodies. Upon the failure of a union to comply with the request, its charter should be revoked. This resolution was directed at the Brotherhood of Railway Carmen under whose jurisdiction the coach cleaners came.[13] A similar resolution emanated from the Negro boilermakers' helpers of Columbia, South Carolina.[14] They complained that the boilermakers' union which did not admit them also barred them from certain types of work for which they were qualified. After considerable debate the resolution involving the clerks was carried. But the resolutions relating to the boilermakers and carmen, for the reasons discussed hereafter, were referred to the committee on law. The report of this committee recommended that the Executive Council call a conference of representatives of the parties affected.[15]

Before the proposed conferences could be held, the carmen's union had amended its constitution so as to provide for Negro organization without changing its policy of racial separation and discrimination. In explaining why the confer-

[11] American Federation of Labor, *Proceedings*, 1920, Resolution No. 5.
[12] For discussion see below, pp. 98-99.
[13] American Federation of Labor, *Proceedings*, 1921, Resolution No. 72, pp. 299-300.
[14] *Ibid.*, Resolution No. 83, p. 300.
[15] *Ibid.*, Report of Committee on Law, p. 432.

ence with the carmen was never held, the Executive Council said that in view of the amendment adopted by the carmen "President Ryan of the Brotherhood expressed the belief that the suggested conference would be barren of results because he and his fellow officers would have no authority to go beyond the amended constitution." [16] Nothing was reported on the boilermakers as the Council had not heard from them. But this organization had already appointed at its 1920 convention a committee to investigate the problem. There the question remained unsettled until 1925 when the 1920 action was reaffirmed.

The recommendation of the 1920 convention that the Brotherhood of Railway Carmen remove the "white clause" from their constitution was deliberately ignored by the Executive Council of the Federation. The Council's report to the 1922 convention does not even mention this recommendation, but merely refers to the resolution adopted at the 1921 convention directing it to call a conference for working out a "plan to handle the grievances of colored railway employees directly affiliated with the American Federation of Labor," until the Brotherhood of Railway Clerks could hold a convention. Although this conference resulted in the creation of temporary adjustment machinery, the clerks never removed the "white clause" from their constitution.

The negotiations and discussions which followed from the aforementioned resolutions showed a decided inclination on the part of the Executive Council to avoid the real issue, namely, the removal of the "white clause" from the constitutions of some of its affiliated bodies. It will be remembered that in the nineties the Council opposed the admission of unions that discriminated against Negroes. But as early as 1900 circumvention and opportunism were fast supplanting the courageous stand of the previous decade. In reporting to the 1900 convention the refusal of southern central bodies to seat Negro delegates, President Gompers pointed out that "to

---

[16] American Federation of Labor, *Proceedings*, 1922, p. 119.

insist . . . upon a delegation . . . of colored workers being accorded representation in a central body would have meant the dissolution of that organization. . . ." [17] The problem was met by the formation of central bodies composed of representatives from unions of Negro and white central bodies on matters of local or general importance to labor.[18] In addition to this measure the Executive Council was equipped with the means for circumventing the obstacles to Negro membership in the national unions. It was authorized to issue separate charters to local and federal labor unions of Negro workers. Article 12, Section 6, of the constitution as revised in 1900 reads, "Separate charters may be issued to central labor unions, local unions or federated labor unions, composed exclusively of colored workers where in the judgment of the Executive Council it appears advisable. . . ." [19] Thus was inaugurated the policy of organizing colored workers under charter issued directly by the American Federation when admission was denied them by the union of their craft.

The adoption of this policy was the Federation's tacit admission of its impotence in the face of trade autonomy, craft separatism, and exclusiveness. The Executive Council knew that its power was limited to moral suasion,[20] backed up by the voluntary support of the national and international unions that comprise the Federation. A proposal by the Council to revoke the charter of a union because it refused admission to Negroes would surely not have received the necessary two-thirds vote of the convention. The general adherence of the unions to the doctrine of trade autonomy makes any one of them very reluctant to pass upon the eligibility of applicants

[17] American Federation of Labor, *Proceedings*, 1900, Presidential Address.
[18] *Ibid.*
[19] *Ibid.*, 1919, Committee's Report on Resolution No. 18, p. 263.
[20] The supreme power of the Federation is the Annual Convention. The Executive Council acts between conventions. "The American Federation of Labor is without power to enforce its decision other than suspend or revoke the charter of an affiliated recalcitrant international union. This can be done only by a two-thirds vote of the convention. . . ." David J. Saposs, *Readings in Trade Unionism*, pp. 106-7.

to some other union. And trade-union leaders contend that, should the Federation attempt to force a union to admit Negroes, it would violate its cardinal principle of craft sovereignty. On the basis of this doctrine the committee on organization opposed the resolutions which demanded that the 1920 convention request the railway clerks and freight-handlers to remove the white clause from their constitution and to admit Negroes to membership.

The chairman of the committee maintained that the resolution asked "that we decide who is eligible and who is not eligible to admission to a national organization with the A. F. of L. The committee has not that authority, the Executive Council has not that authority. That authority rests only with the national and international unions. The committee and Executive Council wish to see the colored men organized. We reaffirm the action taken in the last convention that if a national or international union refuses to accept colored workers, the A. F. of L. will grant them charters." [21] Naturally enough the viewpoint expressed by the committee coincided with that of the representative of the clerks. The delegate from the clerks raised no objection to a conference on the admission of Negroes. What roused his opposition was the notion that the Federation had power even to suggest a change in a national union's constitution. According to this delegate, although the Federation at the previous convention had requested the clerks to remove the word "white" from their constitution, it "has no power to dictate to any international union the class of men they shall or shall not take in. That autonomy and that right belong to the international unions themselves." [22]

When resolutions 72 and 83 providing for the revocation of the charters of nationals that refused to strike out the word "white" in their constitutions was referred to the committee on law for judicial review, the decision handed down by the

[21] American Federation of Labor, *Proceedings*, 1920, p. 309.
[22] *Ibid.*, 1921, pp. 431-32.

committee was in substantial agreement with the above opinion. The committee reported "that the American Federation of Labor cannot interfere with the trade autonomy of affiliated national or international unions. The Atlantic City Convention . . . authorized the organizing of colored workers under charters from the American Federation of Labor, if affiliated . . . unions refuse to accept them." [23] It recommended a conference between the aggrieved parties and the boilermakers and the carmen with the results noted, thus giving to the tradition of craft sovereignty, the sanction of the Federation's constitutional law.

This theory of trade autonomy is part and parcel of a decentralized confederation of independent wage-conscious and business unions. But it is probable that any attempt of a more highly centralized organization to force racial equality upon its affiliated bodies would cause them to rebel. Gomper's anticipation of disruption of membership as between whites and Negroes in the various nationals was revealed in his 1900 report on the attitude of southern local bodies toward seating Negro delegates. From 1900 on the Federation skirted the issue of full and complete admission of Negro workers into the national unions. By chartering locals composed exclusively of Negroes where the national union denied them admission, Federation leaders came to believe that the disparity between the theory of organizing all workers irrespective of race, and the practice followed by many unions of debarring some workers because of race, had disappeared. This achievement was considered all the more significant because it was accomplished without encroaching upon the autonomy of the national unions. Yet to Negroes outside of the unions and to many Negroes organized directly by the Federation, the disparity has never ceased to exist. The former have never understood the structure of the Federation and the limits of its powers. The latter recognized that the Federa-

[23] *Ibid.*

tion's policy was a compromise, and, in some instances, protested against its ineffectiveness.[24]

The Federation's policy of organizing groups into directly affiliated local and federal labor unions was not originally designed for the purpose of solving the problem of the Negro unionist. It was first designed to care for the white helper and laborer,[25] who were excluded from the unions of their crafts, and for the white craftsmen whenever they were too few in numbers to organize separate locals of the national unions of their respective crafts. The differences between the directly affiliated Negro and the white bodies should be noted. White craftsmen who have been organized in locals directly affiliated with the A. F. of L. are turned over to their respective international or national unions as soon as they are sufficient in number to form an independent local of their craft. Not so with the Negro craftsmen. When the Federation charters a local of Negro craftsmen it is because the union of the craft debars them, which means that members of these Negro bodies must always remain outside the union if it does not see fit to take them in.

Since the Federation's directly chartered locals of Negro craftsmen are likely to remain under its jurisdiction their status is almost analogous to that of the locals of white or Negro laborers affiliated with the Federation, as the latter must likewise remain under the jurisdiction of the Federation. The position of a local of Negro craftsmen chartered by the Federation is decidedly weaker from the standpoint of bargaining power than that of a local of white craftsmen who are ultimately absorbed by the national union, or that of the white helpers' local over which the Federation relinquishes jurisdiction whenever the national union desires, or whenever the Federation itself forms a national union out of such local

[24] See protest of Negro freight-handlers against separation and their elimination from the clerks' union. American Federation of Labor, *Proceedings*, 1920, p. 309.

[25] Ashworth, *op. cit.*, p. 85.

unions. This bargaining weakness of the Federation's directly affiliated locals of skilled Negroes is manifested in the wage agreement, and in the Negro members' uncertainty of receiving the wage rate established by the craft. Once the Federation charters a local of Negroes who are debarred from the union of their craft, there arises the difficulty of determining whether such a union falls under the direct jurisdiction of the Federation or under that of the national union from which the Negroes are excluded. One viewpoint is that the Federation itself is the national union of its directly affiliated Negro locals.[26]

If this be the correct interpretation of the relationship between the Federation and its directly affiliated Negro locals, it should follow that the Federation, i.e., the Executive Council, is responsible for representing these directly affiliated locals at wage negotiations and for seeing that the wage scale is observed. In other words, according to this interpretation, the responsibility of negotiating and administering a wage scale for the coach cleaners, let us say, belongs to the Federation by whom they were directly chartered instead of to the Brotherhood of Railway Carmen, whose jurisdiction covers coach cleaning but whose constitution limits membership to white persons. Now let us suppose that in the town of X, there are several Negro machinists, boilermakers, etc., who cannot become members of the unions of their crafts. If possible, the Federation would organize all of them into a federal labor union until an increase of numbers in each craft warranted their separation into different locals. What is the status of the members of this federal labor union with respect to the wage scale? Who is responsible for representing them when the scale is negotiated? Who sees to it that they

[26] "When the Federation of Labor grants charters to the colored workers no matter of what trade or calling, the A. F. of L. becomes the national or international union of those men. It is the duty of the A. F. of L. then to take up the grievances of those workers." This statement was made by the chairman of the committee on organization during the discussion of the railway clerks' failure to handle the grievances of the Negro freight-handlers. See American Federation of Labor, *Proceedings*, 1920, Resolution No. 5, p. 309.

receive the rate of wages agreed upon? The answer, according to the authority cited above, is that the responsibility rests with the Executive Council of the American Federation of Labor. But does it? Obviously, the recognition of a union by an employer establishes bargaining relations with the union and not with the Executive Council or the Federation. Where collective bargaining exists the wage scale and other conditions of employment are determined by negotiations between representatives of the union and management. The members of the Executive Council have a voice in these negotiations only when it is given to them by the union. This is seldom if ever done. There is no evidence to show that the Executive Council was ever given the right of representing the Federation's directly chartered Negro locals in wage conferences, or that it ever attempted to establish a precedent for such representation by arbitrarily exercising the power. The assumption of such a right is inconsistent with the federal theory on which the American Federation of Labor rests.

Since the Council has no voice in negotiating the wage agreement in any given craft, it is therefore not a party to the terms of the agreement. And assuming that it has the power to enforce the agreement, it has no authority to do so. It is meaningless then to say that where unions refuse to admit Negroes and the Executive Council charters them in locals directly affiliated to the Federation, the Federation becomes the national union of those local Negro unions. It is clear that the Federation is powerless to protect them as they would be protected by the national union of their craft. In the final analysis then the responsibility of insuring the economic protection of the Federation's directly affiliated Negro locals can only rest with the union that negotiates the wage scale for the craft. The Federation's recognition of this accounts for its "acquiescence" (to use the words of Secretary Morrison)[27] in the Brotherhood of Railway Clerks' claim to jurisdiction over the Negro freight-handlers whom the Federation had organ-

[27] American Federation of Labor, *Proceedings*, 1920, p. 308.

ized into locals for the reason that the clerks' constitution prohibits Negro membership. Should an employer refuse to pay the members of a local Negro union at the agreed rate for the craft and the latter appeal to the Federation, about the only thing the Executive Council would do would be to request the union of the particular craft or crafts to take up the Negroes' grievances, or seek some adjustment through conference with the aggrieved party and the members of the union.

This is exactly what happened in the case of the freight-handlers and the Brotherhood of Railway Clerks. In 1919, the Negro Freight Handlers' Union, No. 16220, of Richmond, Virginia, explained their anomalous situation. "Owing to the peculiar position of the Colored Freight Handlers and Station Employees in the C. and O., S. A. L., and R. F. and P. Ry. systems and on the American Railway Express Company ... under the jurisdiction of the Brotherhood of Railway Clerks and chartered direct from the American Federation of Labor and having no representative or grievance man in the Brotherhood of Railway Clerks, we are receiving little or no assistance from them." The Negro representatives asked the Federation to organize the freight-handlers and station employees into a system organization for mutual protection. They appealed to the Council to help them obtain a contract from the respective companies since the clerks' agreement covered only the freight-handlers on one system, the C. and O.[28] Fully two years elapsed before the freight-handlers' grievances were taken care of. At the 1922 convention, the Executive Council reported the results obtained from the conference with the colored freight-handlers. The conference had agreed:

That a plan should be developed by the Brotherhood of Railway Clerks that will admit to the Brotherhood the colored railway employees, whose work belongs to the jurisdiction of the Brotherhood of Railway Clerks; that in the interim of their admission ... the representatives of [the latter] would take up the reduction in wages enforced upon the

[28] *Ibid.*, 1919, Resolution No. 118.

colored freight handlers and other station employees; [and] that the colored local union should form system boards of adjustment for each railroad system or group of systems to act in coöperation with one or more representatives selected by the Brotherhood of Railway Clerks in protecting the rights and interests of the colored workers.[29]

According to one of the provisions of the plan, six system boards of adjustment were organized among the colored freight-handlers with the assistance of A. F. of L. organizers. The colored freight-handlers on some of the divisions did obtain the increases demanded. But from the very beginning the clerks' locals had shown little interest. The Federation's plan for protecting the Negro freight-handlers shifted responsibility for making it effective to the clerks.

While a union is morally obligated to execute the Federation's request, is it likely that one which debars Negro workers from membership will use the full force of its bargaining power in the protection of these workers if, in spite of their membership in Federation locals, the employer persists in refusing to pay them at the union scale? Under these conditions should the Negroes strike, their places could easily be filled with unorganized Negroes or organized white men. Herein lies the weakness of the Federation's Negro organization policy. Where the unions refuse to admit Negroes, it can organize them into directly affiliated bodies; but the economic protection of these bodies must, in the nature of the circumstances, rest with the unions to whose racial proscription they owe their existence. At best this method of organizing affords uncertain protection, as the protests from some of the Federation's directly affiliated Negro locals suggest.

The Railroad Shopworkers' Union, No. 16,797, of Houston, Texas, composed of machinists, boilermakers, carmen, blacksmiths, sheet-metal workers, pointers, and others, petitioned the 1920 convention of the Federation to see to it that Negro workers in the federal and local unions are included in agreements negotiated by unions that do not admit them. The

[29] *Ibid.*, 1922, Executive Council's Report.

colored union also asked for assistance in getting the railroads to recognize its status as a bona fide labor organization.[30] The committee on local and federal bodies dismissed the resolution with the statement that the Negro shopworkers were "already protected in agreements with the R. R. crafts . . . and other actions taken by the conventions." [31] It seems strange and inconsistent that these Negro machinists, boilermakers, and blacksmiths were protected by the agreements made by the unions of their respective crafts, and yet requested the Federation to assist them in getting the employers to recognize their union status. If they were recognized and given the consideration to which they were entitled, it must have been only after considerable difficulty. Or why present such a resolution? Again the action to which the committee referred as affording protection was the result of resolutions 5 and 37. What action was taken on these resolutions? And in what way did it amount to a defense of the petitioners?

Resolution 37, it should be recalled, directed the Federation to prohibit the creation of racial barriers by an international union. The railway-coach cleaners who introduced the resolution were aiming at the Brotherhood of Railway Carmen, who claimed jurisdiction over coach cleaning, and likewise at the boilermakers, blacksmiths, and machinists.[32] The committee on organization in reporting Resolution 37 stated "that many of the statements in it were incorrect." [33] It pointed out that although the carmen claimed jurisdiction over coach and car cleaners, and did not admit Negroes, the president of the international had assured them that the carmen would either admit colored coach cleaners to membership or, upon failing to do so, surrender its jurisdiction over them. The committee further maintained that the boilermakers had "no law in their constitution prohibiting the admission of colored workers following the trade"; that "the Blacksmiths

[30] *Ibid.*, 1920, Resolution No. 9, p. 264.
[31] *Ibid.*, Committee's Reports, p. 433.
[32] *Ibid.*, p. 359.
[33] *Ibid.*, p. 351.

issue charters to colored workers of the trade and have no law denying admission to colored workers"; and that "the Machinists have nothing in their constitution prohibiting the admission of colored men of the trade." [34] These statements are only partly true. The committee was correct in saying that neither the boilermakers' nor the machinists' constitutions prohibit Negro membership. It ignored the fact, however, that Negroes are kept out of both unions by the ritual. There are no known Negroes in either organization. The organization of Negroes in the blacksmiths' union portrayed in the last chapter appears to be a method of "keeping the Negro in his place" rather than an honest attempt to organize competing labor.[35] The committee concluded that the only thing to do was to request the carmen to remove the discriminating clause from their constitution. The same action followed the committee's consideration of Resolution 5 which was similar to Resolution 37 in intent, but which was aimed at the Brotherhood of Railway Clerks. How the committee could claim that this action protected the Negro machinists, blacksmiths, boilermakers and carmen in the Houston shopworkers' union is a mystery.

Instead of regarding these protests as symptoms of underlying weakness in the Federation's organization policy, or as an opportunity for critical examination of its effectiveness, the committee evaded the issue by resorting to subterfuge and hid its timidity in ambiguous statements. Because of inertia and self-deceiving satisfaction, the Federation leaders have demonstrated that they are psychologically unequipped to prosecute a vigorous program of unionization among Negroes. Moreover, the initiation of such a program would be in the nature of a radical transformation of old methods and policies, and seldom has a well-intrenched old guard willingly assumed such a task. Not until after the Negro migrations of 1912-1917 began, did the Federation leaders show much realization of

[34] *Ibid.*, p. 351.
[35] See Chapter IV, pp. 62-63. Also see above discussion on Resolution No. 83, in 1921. *Ibid.*, 1921, p. 300.

the necessity of quickening union activity among Negroes. Even then the organization of them into federal and local unions was not as vigorous as it might have been. Criticisms by outsiders of the Federation's lethargy or the attempts of insiders to have machinery developed for facilitating a greater degree of Negro organization were usually met with fine phrases, such as the declaration of a desire to organize all workers or the re-iteration of the principle of organization inaugurated at the 1900 convention.

The first great impact of southern Negro labor upon the organized labor movement provoked much concern. The echo of it resounded in the conventions of the Federation. In the 1916 convention at Baltimore, the representatives of the Ohio State Federation of Labor and the Cleveland Federation of Labor, respectively, called attention to the menace of the migration of southern Negro labor to northern industry. The convention was asked to instruct the president and the Executive Council to inaugurate a movement for the organization of Negroes in southern states, educating them as to the purpose of trade unions so as to eliminate the menace to organized northern workers.[36] The subject was referred to the Executive Council which at its meeting in November decided "that all matters pertaining to special organizers be referred to President Gompers to take such action as the funds permitted." [37]

Some organizers were appointed. This alone does not account, however, for the extraordinary increase of Negro local trade and federal labor unions between 1918 and 1922. It was not accidental that most of these unions were composed of railroad employees, for the years covered included the period of federal control of the railroads when unionization was made almost compulsory by the administration's policy of dealing with employees only through organization. But the Negro local and federal labor unions declined as rapidly as

[36] *Ibid.*, 1916, Resolution No. 3.
[37] Correspondence with Secretary Frank Morrison.

they sprang up. In 1919 there were 92; in 1921, 141; in 1922, 136; in 1923, 79; in 1925, 67; in 1926, 38; and in 1927, 21. In 1929, the Federation reported 36 local unions and five central labor unions composed exclusively of Negroes. But thirteen of these local unions had been organized by the Brotherhood of Sleeping Car Porters and the Federation had nothing whatsoever to do with their organization.[38] The Pullman porters' locals have a book membership of about 3,000 while the remaining 23 locals affiliated with the Federation have hardly more than 500 members. Of these 23 locals only 8 replied to our query on membership. The locals with their memberships are as follows:

Local	Craft	Location	Membership
17165	Freights-Handlers	Cleveland, Ohio	48
17603	Boilermakers, Pipe Fitters and Machinists	Jacksonville, Fla.	30
16665	Freight-Handlers	Brunswick, Md.	15
17803	Station Porters	Savannah, Ga.	15
17985	Freight-Handlers	Columbia, S. C.	41
17980	Freight-Handlers	Tampa, Fla.	24
17766	Navy Yard Helpers	Portsmouth, Va.	14
17919	Federal Labor Union	Newark, N. J.	10
	Pullman Porters	New York City, etc.	3,000
Total			3,197

Had the rapid decline of the Negro locals affiliated with the Federation resulted from absorption by international unions, it would have signalized great progress. But this did not take place. The majority of the Negro locals organized by the Federation from 1919 to 1929 were freight-handlers who were debarred from the Brotherhood of Railway Clerks, the union of their craft, by constitutional proscription. Obviously, the Federation's directly affiliated Negro locals could be absorbed by the national unions only if the latter chose to do so

[38] See Chapter XX, p. 456.

by lowering their bars or by devising special provisions for Negro organization. Some unions, like the carmen's, the maintenance-of-way employees', and the blacksmiths', followed the latter policy. Others, like the machinists,' boilermakers,' and clerks,' crafts in which the number of A. F. of L. Negro locals predominated, have persisted in pursuing a policy of rigorous exclusion. And the Negroes in these crafts soon realized that organization into local A. F. of L. unions was but a means of masking the international's policy of exclusion and, at the same time, one which afforded little protection to those who joined such locals, since the internationals which did the excluding were the only groups in a position to bargain with the employers. The decline in the number of Negro locals, a sad commentary on the effectiveness of the Federation's policy, caused slight perturbation among the old guard. No one knew the weaknesses of the Federation's policy better than the members of the Negro locals. Their petitions against these weaknesses may often have been ill-formulated, but they showed a desire for an improvement in the policy of the Federation with respect to Negro wage earners.

The habitual theme of the petitions from the Negro delegates to the conventions was the appointment of colored organizers. At almost every convention, beginning with 1917, Negro organizers were requested. In 1917, two resolutions were presented.[39] One requested that Negro organizers be appointed for industrially strategic cities in Virginia, North Carolina, and Florida. The other resolution requested the appointment of a colored railroad man to organize Negro laborers on fifteen southeastern railroads. The petitioners based their request upon the need of awakening the Negro's interest in the labor movement. Both resolutions were approved and referred to the Executive Council. The Council referred the question of appointing Negro organizers to President Gompers and Secretary Morrison. The Council also

[39] American Federation of Labor, *Proceedings*, 1917, Resolutions Nos. 58 and 166.

requested Mr. Gompers to appoint a committee t
plan of organization of the Negro workers on
eastern railroads.[40] But the records do not show
plan was worked out.

At the 1918 and 1919 conventions six resolution
question of organizing Negro workers were presen
of them showed lack of understanding of the pow
Federation. However mistaken these resolutions we
phasis, they showed dissatisfaction among Negro wor
the failure of the Federation's methods to achieve
organization. One resolution requested an inte
charter for colored workers. One asked for the
of organizers from the Federation. Another asked
colored organizer be appointed in every state in the union
since white organizers in the South have difficulty in organizing
Negroes. Another asked that a man, preferably a colored man,
be stationed at Washington to look after the interests of
colored workers. Another called attention to the difficulty Negroes had in becoming members of unions in the Metal Trades
Department of the Federation and requested that where Negroes were debarred from joining the union they be organized
into national unions of their own. The recommendations were
adopted and referred to the Executive Council which was in
turn advised to give special attention to organizing colored
workers everywhere. Similar resolutions had been presented in
1902 and 1907 with little action resulting. One of the petitions [42] presented to the 1918 convention by representatives of
the Central Labor Council of Tacoma, Washington, recommended the organization of colored Pullman porters, dining
car cooks and waiters, train porters, firemen, switchmen, yard
engineers, boilermakers and assistants, machinists and helpers,
headlight tinkers, coach cleaners, laundry workers, shop and

[40] Correspondence with Secretary Morrison.

[41] American Federation of Labor, *Proceedings*, 1919, Resolutions Nos. 76,
101, 118, 120, 122, pp. 304-6.

[42] *Ibid.*, 1918, Resolution 18, p. 263.

track laborers and section men into a separate colored railway department. The resolution read:

WHEREAS, the influence of world affairs on the present and future conditions of the mass of laborers is such as to make necessary a closer and more kindred feeling of sympathy and purpose on the part of all labor; and

WHEREAS, this spirit of oneness of purpose can and will only be most completely achieved when the benefits derived by the efforts of organized labor are not predicated on race or creed, or sex or color, but rather shall be the common lot and heritage of all; and

WHEREAS, in the past because of a lack of realization on the part of the organized white laborers that to keep the unorganized colored laborers out of the field of organization has only made it easily possible for the unscrupulous employer to exploit one against the other to the mutual disadvantage of each, resulting always in creating that undemocratic and un-Christian thing — race prejudice and its foul by-products, riot and mob rule, as during the mine trouble in the Pacific Northwest in the early nineties, as more recently on Puget Sound during the Longshoremen's strike, and at East St. Louis; and

WHEREAS, it is the duty and should be the privilege of every man or woman to labor under such conditions and at such times . . . as will be conducive to his or her contributing such strength as to effectively aid our common country and successfully wage the battles of war, and to meet the problems of peace; be it

Resolved, that we the undersigned colored railway employees being typical colored laborers, do hereby petition the Central Labor Council of Tacoma, Washington, to give its endorsement to the plea for a plain square deal for the colored American laborers; and be it further

Resolved, that the Central Labor Council . . . be and is hereby petitioned to instruct its delegates to the forthcoming convention of the American Federation of Labor to give us support in applying for international charter to organize colored railway workers.

A lengthy hearing was held on the subject. The representatives of the hod carriers and building laborers, which admitted Negroes, and the boilermakers, which did not, opposed the adoption of the resolution. The committee on resolutions reported that acceptance and execution of the aims of the proposal would contravene the jurisdiction of unions of trades represented in the proposed colored railway department. It said: "It is not the policy of the American Federation of Labor to grant charters along racial lines. We know that many international organizations affiliated with the American Federation of Labor admit colored workers to membership and in these organizations their interests can best be protected and taken care of. There are other organizations that have not as yet opened their doors to colored workers but we hope to see the day in the near future when these organizations will take a broader view of this matter. Until that time we urge the Executive Council to organize the colored workers under charters of the American Federation of Labor." The committee's statement that the Federation does not issue charters on the basis of race, while technically true, evaded rather than faced the conditions that prompted the proposal for a colored railroad international. The contemplated international of colored railway workers was an unconscious and crudely expressed desire for greater effectiveness in Negro organization. The probable conflict in jurisdiction with some of the railway shop crafts and a colored railway international was small excuse for dismissing the subject. A possible amelioration of the whole problem of Negro organization might have been found in the construction of some definitive machinery for handling it. Something of the kind was sponsored by the Negro delegates, with the assistance of Abraham Lefkowitz of the teachers' union, at the 1920 convention. And two years before this the conference with Negro leaders and welfare workers might have worked out in a similar fashion. But the Federation leaders dismissed both summarily.

The first attempt to bring about greater organization of Negroes through the Federation came in 1918 when John R. Shillady, secretary to the National Association for the Advancement of Colored People; Fred Moore, editor of the New York *Age*; Emmett J. Scott, special assistant to the Secretary of War; Thomas Jesse Jones, educational director,

Phelps Stokes Fund; and Eugene Kinckle Jones, secretary to the National Urban League, conferred with the Council on plans for organizing Negro workers. The first meeting was merely consultative. But six months later Mr. Jones of the National Urban League wrote to President Gompers in behalf of the committee:

We write to present suggestions for further coöperation between our committee and the American Federation of Labor as growing out of our recent conference in Washington.

First we wish to place before you our understanding of your statement to us at the conclusion of the meeting. We quote you as follows, and will be glad to have you make any changes in the text as will make the statement more nearly conform to the ideas which you have in mind relative to the connections that should be established between white and Negro workingmen:

"We the American Federation of Labor welcome the Negro workingmen to the ranks of organized labor. We should like to see more of them join us. The interests of workingmen white and black are common. Together we must fight unfair wages, unfair hours, and bad conditions of labor. At times it is difficult for the National organization to control the actions of local unions in difficulties arising within the trades inasmuch as the National body is made possible by the delegates appointed by the locals, but we can and will use our influence to break down prejudice on account of race, color or previous condition of servitude, and hope that you will use your influence to show Negro workingmen the advantages of collective bargaining and the value of affiliation with the American Federation of Labor. But few people who are not thoroughly acquainted with the rapid growth of the American Federation of Labor know of the large numbers of colored people who are already members of our organization. The unpleasant incidents in connection with efforts of colored men to get recognition in trades controlled by the American Federation of Labor have been aired and the good efforts of wholesome and healthy relationship have not been given publicity; and for that reason a general attitude of suspicion has developed toward union labor on the part of colored working people; but I hope that out of this conference will spring a more cordial feeling of confidence in each other on the part of men who must work for a living."

We are willing to coöperate with the American Federation of Labor in bringing about the results of the recent conference and would make the following suggestions and recommendations which, with your approval, we shall proceed to carry out to the best of our ability.

First, we suggest that you prepare a statement along the lines of the quotation from you given above, and send it to us for approval and that it be given to the Negro press throughout the country as expressing your position along matters connected with the relationship between Negro and white workingmen.

This statement in our judgment should contain a clear exposition of the reasons why certain internationals may exclude colored men as they do by constitutional provision and still be affiliated with the American Federation of Labor whose declared principles are opposed to such discrimination. This we think necessary because the stated facts above alluded to will be familiar to the leaders among the colored people, particularly the editors and ministers whose coöperation it is essential to secure if best results are to be obtained. We would suggest that you consider the expediency of recommending to such internationals as still exclude colored men that their constitutions be revised in this respect.

Second, that a qualified colored man to handle men and organize them be selected for employment as an organizer of the American Federation of Labor, his salary and expenses, of course, to be paid by the American Federation of Labor.

Third, that for the present we meet at least once a quarter to check on the results of our coöperative activities and to plan for further extension of the work, if satisfactorily conducted.

Fourth, that you carry out your agreement to have your Executive Council voice its advanced position in its attitude toward the organization of Negro workingmen and have these sentiments endorsed by your St. Paul convention in June and this action be given the widest possible publicity throughout the country. We shall be glad to hear from you at your earliest convenience as to the action taken by your Council on these recommendations with such other suggestions or recommendations as may occur to you.

Sincerely yours,
Eugene Kinckle Jones

The Council reported that it was pleased with the report of these race leaders but it could find no fault with the past work of the Federation. It agreed that with the coöperation of these leaders it could do much better in the future. No further action was taken upon the proposition.

At the 1920 convention the other proposal which was presented by Negro delegates from some of the Federation's directly affiliated bodies and by Abraham Lefkowitz of the American Federation of Teachers was no more effective than the Jones' letter in shaking the Federation's complacency. The resolution [43] read:

WHEREAS, the American Federation of Labor has taken a firm position on the claims of negro labor to fair and impartial sharing of the benefits of organized labor; and

WHEREAS, despite this attitude of the American Federation of Labor, encouraging results have not followed; and millions of negro working-men continue ignorant of the benefits of collective bargaining, thus militating against the successful operation of the Federation in its fight for a square deal for labor; therefore, be it

Resolved, That the American Federation of Labor enter upon a campaign of education among both white and colored workingmen to convince them of the necessity of bringing into the ranks of labor all men who work, regardless of race, creed or color; and be it further

Resolved, That, with this end in view, there be called into periodical conference with the Executive Council of the American Federation of Labor white and colored leaders who can suitably represent and express the point of view of negro workingmen, and can convey to the negro workingmen the good will and sympathy felt by the American Federation of Labor towards them; and be it further

Resolved, That there be employed in headquarters at Washington a competent negro agent, taken from the ranks of labor, who will express the hopes and yearnings of negro workingmen to the American Federation of Labor, and in turn be the mouthpiece of the Federation for such messages and information as the Federation may from time to time wish to convey to the negro workers throughout the country; said agent to be the executive secretary and official representative in the interim of meetings of said special committee on negro workers; and be it further

Resolved, That this Convention endorse the appointment of negro

---

[43] American Federation of Labor, *Proceedings*, 1920, Resolution No. 48, p. 311.

organizers in all states and for all crafts in which negroes are or may be employed, whose duty will be to build up negro membership.

The committee on resolutions recommended that the "second and third resolves" be struck out and that the fourth be amended to read: "Negro organizers be appointed where necessary to organize negro workers under the banner of the American Federation of Labor." The committee's report was unanimously adopted. Why did the committee emasculate these proposals? Why did it reject one of the best plans for enhancing the Federation's significance to Negro labor? Why did it reject the proposed periodical conference with white and Negro leaders? About the only answer which can be made to these questions is that the Federation officials, having organized a few Negro locals, looked upon their work with supreme satisfaction even though these locals were short-lived. The report of the Executive Council on its conference with Negro leaders in 1918, as noted, stated that it could find little fault with its past work among Negro workers. Had the aims of this 1918 conference been taken seriously by the Federation, or had the Negro delegates' resolution of 1920 been put into operation, the Federation's Negro policy would have undergone considerable revamping.

These proposals and the Federation's rejection of them, occurred, it should be remembered, during the first wave of Negro migrations to northern industry. In such a period, when the adjustment of a large supply of essentially inexperienced and low standard workers was threatening the position of organized labor, the self-satisfaction of the Federation leaders was a great impediment to vigorous organization of this new labor. Had a greater degree of organization taken place among the Negro migrant it is likely that some of the consequences that followed the migration would not have occurred.

The widespread introduction of southern Negro labor into northern industries during 1916 and 1920 was resented by both organized and unorganized white labor. The resentment of white workers at having to compete in the labor market with low-standard Negroes was augmented by the general community feeling against an undesirable racial element. In one industrial center, East St. Louis, the Central Trade and Labor Union issued an appeal for action to curb the "growing menace" of Negro labor and "also to devise a way to get rid of certain portions of those who are already here." [44] This manifesto was issued in the late spring of 1917 after more than 10,000 Negroes had migrated to the East St. Louis industrial districts.[45] Some of the Negroes were imported to break a strike at the Aluminum Ore Company.[46] In July, 1917, East St. Louis was the scene of the most bitter race riot in the history of the nation. Two years later another racial clash broke out in Chicago where thousands of southern Negroes had been induced to go by the offer of high wages and jobs in the Calumet steel district and the packing and slaughtering industry. Organized labor was not directly responsible for the outbreak in Chicago because the leaders of the Chicago Federation of Labor did try to avoid the catastrophe. But in the Chicago race riot as well as in the East St. Louis affair, competition between white and Negro labor, and organized labor's failure to bring the Negro into the unions stimulated latent racial antipathy.[47] Racial antagonism made it possible for employers to play one racial group off against the other. The ease with which the packers were able to pit Negro against white workers and the effect of this policy upon the efforts to organize the stockyards during 1917-1920 are related in Chapter XII. It should be noted here, however, that although the Amalgamated Meat Cutters and Butcher Workers' Union admitted Negroes on equality with white members, many of the other twelve crafts in the packing in-

[44] Quoted from Thomas Dabney, "Organized Labor's Attitude Towards Negro Workers," *Southern Workman*, August 1928, p. 323.

[45] Report of the Special Committee Authorized by Congress to Investigate the East St. Louis Riots, 65th Congress, 2d Session, House Document No. 1231.

[46] *Ibid.*

[47] See below, pp. 162-63 and 276-77.

dustry excluded them. The Stock Yards Labor Council on advice of the Executive Council of the Federation organized the Negro workers who were not admitted to some of the unions into a federal labor union chartered by the Federation. If the Negroes so organized did not look upon the method as discriminatory it was played up as such by anti-union and race-conscious groups. There was no reason why the unions could not lower their barriers to Negro affiliation. Resorting to a subterfuge in the form of the federal labor union did not efface the unions' obduracy in refusing Negroes admission. Their refusal could only serve to make coöperation between Negroes and whites impossible. Had this coöperation been effected these racial conflicts might possibly not have occurred. But up to the migrations the organization of Negroes received little more than verbal recognition by the Federation.

Negro labor was employed in the South where its unionization was retarded by race feeling or disregarded because it was unskilled or non-industrial. The agricultural and unskilled Negro workers and the skilled Negro mechanics whom the unions debarred formed an industrial reserve for northern industries. The first impact of this reserve upon the forces of organized labor was heard in the 1916 convention of the American Federation of Labor when it was called upon to organize southern Negroes so as to protect white organized labor in the North. In view of this one wonders why the Federation leaders had not foreseen the uses to which the Negro reserve could be put. Moreover, the occasional use of Negroes in previous industrial conflicts furnished some basis for premonition of their future employment. Of course to the extent that the Negro reserve was made up of non-industrial workers, it could not have been effectively organized prior to the migrations. But a large number of the early Negro migrants were from the urban South where they had been employed in the unskilled branches of industry and in some of the skilled branches.

The skilled Negro was kept out of the unions in the South

or was segregated. The unskilled Negro could not be organized by craft unionism. As compensation for the inadequacy of craft unionism and exclusion, the Federation organized the unskilled Negro into federal labor unions and the skilled Negro who could not join the union of his craft into directly affiliated locals. This policy did not greatly facilitate Negro organization because the Executive Council was complacent and satisfied with meager results. Even if it had been more energetic about building up the Negro membership in the federal labor and local unions, disillusionment would soon have followed the inevitable realization of the economic ineffectiveness of these organizations. On the other hand, organization in federal and local unions pushed by a vigorous campaign of trade-union education might have changed the Negro's class and labor outlook. These shortcomings of the Federation and its leaders played into the hands of the northern industrialist who desired to win a strike or to render the union more submissive. Spurred on by the prospects of wages far beyond their accustomed standard but somewhat below that of the northern white workers, Negroes, undisciplined in the traditions of trade unionism and in the art of collective bargaining, left the South. The terms and conditions of employment were dictated by the employers and accepted by Negro workers as a golden opportunity. They took the places of strikers while the leaders of labor looked on helplessly. They entered the heavy industries like iron and steel, packing, and automobiles where specialization and the machine had robbed craftsmanship of its ancient importance and where company unionism, welfare capitalism, or the open shop had pushed trade unionism out of the picture.

There is every indication that the march of the machine, and with it the reduction of old skills, will continue. If the American Federation of Labor is really interested in becoming the representative of all the industrial workers and not just the spokesman of a decreasingly important skilled group of them, it must turn its energies in earnest to those very industries where large numbers of unskilled Negroes are found. But this is the very job which in recent years it has shown little disposition to tackle. In the first place its very nature as a federation of autonomous groups of skilled craftsmen renders it indifferent to the organization of the unskilled rank and file who constitute the majority of the employees. In the second place the leaders of a number of those of its constituent unions which would have to bear the brunt of the burden of organizing the industries in question seem content to remain the comfortable heads of small dues-paying groups, such as the International Union of Tobacco Workers[48] or the Amalgamated Association of Iron, Steel and Tin Workers,[49] in control of a few small plants. These unions are large enough to support their leaders in the style to which they have become accustomed; and the leaders, satisfied with their position, will take no chances at losing what they have. The successful organization of these industries as a whole must wait for a more courageous leadership and a type of unionism which will embrace all workers, skilled and unskilled, black and white.

[48] See below, pp. 322-23.
[49] See below, pp. 254-57.

Chapter VI

INDEPENDENT NEGRO UNIONISM

IN THOSE occupations where Negroes have won a substantial place but where the unions have excluded them from membership, independent Negro unions have arisen. This is especially true on the railroads where Negroes have been employed in almost every capacity since the days of slavery, but where they are barred from membership in practically every recognized union.[1] These independent unions are intended to serve the double purpose of protecting the black worker in his dealings with his employer and of helping to counteract the discriminatory policies of the white groups.

Prior to the World War, independent Negro unions made little headway. Aside from the attempts on the railroads, the most important colored labor organization was a short-lived group of stationary engineers and firemen in Pittsburgh, known as the National Association of Afro-American Steam and Gas Engineers and Skilled Laborers. For a time this union promised to become an important factor in the Pittsburgh labor world. Shortly after its formation in 1903, it had three locals in Pittsburgh and received recognition from the central labor body and sent representatives to its meetings. But it was unable to make further headway and soon disappeared.

In 1919, when interest in the organization of Negro workers was becoming widespread, a resolution was introduced at the American Federation of Labor convention proposing the organization under an international charter of a union of Negro railway workers covering every branch of railroad service. After extended hearings at which all interested groups

[1] For discussion of independent Negro railway unions, see Chapter XIII, pp. 311-15, and Chapter XX, "The Pullman Porters."

were represented, the resolutions committee brought in an adverse report which was accepted by the convention. The committee declared that the terms of the proposed charter were so broad that they trespassed "upon the jurisdictional rights and claims of several organizations affiliated with American Federation of Labor."[2] It recommended that where international organizations refused to admit Negroes the American Federation of Labor organize the excluded workers in federal labor unions directly affiliated with it. But, as has been shown above in the chapter dealing with the policy of the American Federation of Labor,[3] such independent locals without the support of the international of the craft can neither protect the interests of their members in their relations with employers nor bring sufficient pressure on the discriminating international to force it to change its policy. There is no more effective illustration of this than the very short life of colored federal unions. There were 169 such locals in 1919 when the American Federation of Labor was urging their formation as a solution for its Negro problem. In September 1929 there were but 23, exclusive of thirteen locals of Pullman porters.

While the liberals and social workers, white and black, were urging the American Federation of Labor to take the Negro worker seriously, a group of Negro workingmen in 1919 under the leadership of T. J. Pree and R. T. Sims[4] formed an organization called the National Brotherhood Workers of America, a body, according to its supporters, built upon "sound union principles" and following "militant revolutionary methods."[5] This organization planned to do for the colored worker what the United Hebrew Trades had done for the Jews, namely, to federate all the Negro unions and serve as an agency for organizing those Negroes who did not belong to a union. The initial strength of the National Brotherhood Workers came from the Negroes employed in the

[2] American Federation of Labor, *Proceedings*, 1919, p. 305.

[3] See above, pp. 102-4.

[4] See Chapter XV, p. 328, below.

[5] *Messenger*, Aug., 1919, p. 10.

shipyards and on the docks at Newport News, Norfolk, and Portsmouth, Virginia. Since many of these workers belonged to American Federation of Labor unions, their affiliation with the National Brotherhood Workers gave the latter considerable power in the councils of the Virginia State Federation of Labor. Shortly after its formation, the new organization was strong enough to be able to influence the selection of the president of the state federation and to secure representation on its executive board.[6] At the same time the Brotherhood Workers gained the support of the then socialist magazine, the *Messenger*, in New York. The editors of the *Messenger*, A. Philip Randolph and Chandler Owen, became members of the Brotherhood Workers' board of directors while the magazine served as the organization's official mouthpiece. Though the Randolph-Owen influence was noticeable in the resolutions of the first convention dealing with Russia, Mexico, political prisoners, coöperation, and the unionization of the Negro, this influence soon died down and the new union went its own way. Wherever the Botherhood Workers succeeded in winning the adherence of successful locals, American Federation of Labor pressure became heavy upon workers concerned to change their affiliation. The growing strength of the International Longshoremen's Association among the Negro dock workers in the Virginia tidewater area cut heavily into the Brotherhood Workers' strength, while the reductions of force in the shipyards weakened it still further. When its third convention met at Philadelphia in September 1920, the National Brotherhood Workers' financial statement showed a balance on hand of but $1,296.85.[7]

The organization managed to go on for another year. During this time its attitude toward the American Federation of Labor became increasingly hostile. In the spring of 1921, shortly before its dissolution, it made a final effort to win the

[6] *Ibid.*, p. 7.

[7] National Brotherhood Workers of America, *Convention Proceedings*, 1920, p. 44.

colored workman to its side. It issued a magazine, the *National Brotherhood Worker*, which carried a challenging article entitled, "To the American Federation of Labor — Our Answer." The American Federation of Labor, the article contended, had failed to help the black worker. This failure was due not alone to bad faith and lack of interest, but largely to the fact that the Federation made no attempt to organize the Negro where his economic power was greatest, that is, in the cotton fields. The Brotherhood Workers' "answer" to the American Federation of Labor was to offer itself to the Negro worker as an alternative. Here are its words:

The Negroes of the National Brotherhood Workers of America are now organized and intend to keep on organizing the members of the race in the Cotton Fields and every branch of industry for the purpose of securing to the Negroes those rights that justly belong to them. It is this great organization composed of Negro workers to whom we can look as a savior of our race. We do not intend to affiliate with the American Federation of Labor or any other economic organization that does not stand for a fifty-fifty break in every industrial, political and social requirement. . . .

The organizations that heretofore have been used to keep the Negro divided in the industrial area, must be brushed aside. . . . If you are not with us, you are against us, white or black. . . . We stand uncompromisingly for the complete emancipation of the "working class" from "class conditions," which is the only means of salvation for the Negro. How long are we to wait for justice at the white man's hands? [8]

A few months later the National Brotherhood Workers disappeared.

Though the Brotherhood Workers failed as a national federation of Negro labor, independent Negro unions continued to rise and fall in this trade and that. This was especially true in the building trades where Negroes were employed in considerable numbers, but barred or subordinated in many of the unions. One group, the Association of Colored Engineers and Electricians of Philadelphia, was sufficiently successful for

[8] *National Brotherhood Worker*, May, 1921, pp. 6, 7.

a time to attract the attention of the American Federation
of Labor, which sent representatives to its meetings urging
affiliation. Opinion within the association was so sharply
divided on the question that it was considered wise to reject
the Federation's invitation. But this decision, made to hold
the group together, proved to be its undoing, for half the membership, believing the organization useless unless affiliated with
organized labor, withdrew.[9]

In Chicago, where the building trades are highly unionized,
a number of colored workers got into the industry on open-
shop jobs carried on under the supervision of the Landis
Award Committee. This committee was set up to administer
the award of Judge Landis of the federal court who sat as
arbitrator in the building trades dispute of 1921.[10] The Landis
Award Committee organized trade classes which were attended by many of the Negroes who came into the industry.
The result was the establishment of a considerable body of
proficient non-union building-trades workers. When the unions
again gained control of the situation, most of the white men
trained under the Landis Award Committee were taken into
the organizations, but the Negroes were unable to gain admission to several important unions, particularly the plumbers', gas fitters', electricians', and tinners'. As a first step
toward correcting the situation, the Negro electricians organized a local of their own and received a federal charter from
the American Federation of Labor as Colored Electricians'
Union No. 9,632. The formation of a number of other colored
unions followed. These were federated into an organization
known as the American Trades Council. This body soon broad-
ened its scope to include groups of colored employees outside
of the building trades, such as bell boys and motion picture
operators.

The attitude of the white organizations towards these new

[9] *Ibid.*, p. 3.
[10] Royal E. Montgomery, *Industrial Relations in the Chicago Building
Trades* (1927), Chapters XII and XIII.

colored bodies differed from trade to trade. Some were coöperative, some were competitive, some were openly hostile,
and some were treacherous. When the colored motion picture
operators' union was formed, the established union which had
excluded Negroes decided to change its policy and invite them
into its ranks. The Negroes, thinking they had accomplished
their purpose, accepted the move in good faith and surrendered their charter. Then the white local decided to admit
no more Negroes. The colored operators who had failed to
get in in time were left without a union and were unable to
get another charter because the white group no longer drew
the color line. With this example before them other colored
organizations were exceedingly wary about accepting overtures to amalgamate with the established white union.

In a few cases the colored local union has really afforded
its members efficient protection. One such instance involved a
group of colored lathers who got work on a building under an
agreement with the contractor. The leader of the white
lathers' union, which also had an agreement with the contractor, ordered his men off the job. But when the contractor
showed that the black lathers were regular union men and
had a right to be employed under his agreement with the
unions, the white leader was obliged to send his men back to
work in order to avoid a law suit.

On the other hand, a number of colored unions gave their
members no protection whatever. In the case of plumbers, and
to a less extent of the electricians, city inspectors, who usually
got their jobs through the influence or at least with the approval of the white union, refused to put their stamp of
approval on the work of colored men. White craftsmen were
called in and did no more than cover up the black man's jobs.
The inspectors then declared the work satisfactory. The situation became so bad among the Negro plumbers that a number
of them, feeling that their organization could give them no
protection, left it and joined the communists.

Negro unions such as these must at best concern themselves with matters of detail. They are obliged to accept the standards set by the dominant white group and they are completely dependent upon the latter's support in all important negotiations or controversies. In some occupations, however, such as the government services where the political power of the employees counts quite as much as their economic strength, independent Negro organizations have played a rôle of some importance. This is particularly true of the postal service where the Negro is an important factor in most of the large northern offices. The entire postal service employed 25,390 Negroes in 1928, about 9 per cent of the total force.[11] In Detroit Negroes constitute about 16.4 per cent of the postal staff.[12] In Chicago they constitute 31 per cent;[13] in New York 16 per cent.[14] They are thus unmistakably a factor to be reckoned with. Though the regular unions of postal workers such as the clerks and letter carriers have large colored memberships, the Negro workers have felt that their interests could be served best by supplementing the work of the regular organizations with associations of their own. Almost every city where Negroes are employed in significant numbers has a colored postal employees' benefit society or club, purely local in scope, which aims to consolidate the political power of the Negro worker and to guard his interests before the local postal officials. These groups do not pretend to take the place of the regular postal unions but merely aim to supplement their work.

In the railway mail service, which also employs a large number of Negroes, a very different situation prevails. There, the Railway Mail Association — the regular union of the craft, affiliated with the American Federation of Labor — bars Negroes by constitutional provision. It is, in fact, one

[11] United States Department of Labor, Office of the Secretary Release Sept. 8, 1928.

[12] Files of the survey of the Negro in Detroit, 1926.

[13] *Congressional Record*, Vol. 69, Feb. 2, 1928, p. 2483.

[14] From the Post Office Department, Sept. 3, 1930.

of the nine national or international unions in the American Federation of Labor which exclude black members in this direct fashion.[15] In 1913, two years after the adoption of this exclusion policy by the Railway Mail Association, a group of railway postal clerks formed the National Alliance of Postal Employees. The Alliance soon extended its jurisdiction to colored employees in every branch of the postal service. Its membership in March, 1929, according to an unofficial list in its journal, was 2,453.[16] These included not only railway mail clerks but employees in every branch of the postal service.

In 1927 a resolution was presented to the convention of the National Association of Letter Carriers endorsing the National Alliance and urging all Negro carriers to join it. The resolution, vigorously opposed by the Negro delegates to the convention as a move to force the colored carriers out of the Association, was overwhelmingly defeated. At the same time the convention went on record as "being utterly opposed to the organization of any group within the membership of the National Association of Letter Carriers, and especially a group known as the Postal Alliance." [17]

Largely through the efforts of the Alliance a Negro official was assigned to the Postmaster-General's office to handle matters affecting the colored personnel. Yet the Alliance has never received the same official recognition in Washington which has been accorded to the white unions. It never appears before committees of Congress or makes any effort to secure legislation affecting working conditions. That is left entirely to the regular unions, perhaps for reasons of political expediency. But even in departmental matters the Alliance has not played a very forward rôle. It is both interesting and significant that when the Postmaster-General organized a national service-relations council in 1921 composed of representatives of all national postal organizations, the Alliance sent no dele-

---

[15] See above, p. 57.
[16] *Postal Alliance*, March, 1929, p. 12.
[17] *Postal Record*, October, 1927, pp. 408-9.

gates and it has never since taken any part in the affairs of this body.[18]

The only independent Negro unions which have really been effective have been those in occupations in which the personnel has been predominantly or entirely colored. The most significant of such groups are the dining car employees and the sleeping car porters. Both of these groups began to organize during the period of federal control of the railroads. At the time they were probably the worst paid employees in the railroad service. The entrance wages of dining car waiters and sleeping car porters in 1917 were $25 and $30 a month respectively, while the pay of dining car cooks averaged about $65 to $70.

Organizations grew up among these employees in several places at the same time. The Railway Men's International Benevolent Industrial Association organized a large number.[19] It was instrumental in bringing about an increase in dining car waiters' wages to $45 a month in January, 1918, and to $55 a month in May, 1919, based upon a 240 hour month with payment for overtime. The Association also brought about a substantial increase in the wages of cooks. First cooks now receive a minimum of $125 a month. On some roads they get up to $150 a month, while overtime frequently brings their earnings up as high as $250. Several roads formally recognized the Railway Men's International as the official spokesman of their dining car employees. Contracts regulating working conditions were entered into with the Association by the Michigan Central, Lake Shore, Chicago and Alton, Chicago Northwestern, Rock Island, Chicago Great Western, and the Pennsylvania lines west of Pittsburgh. Recently some of these contracts expired, but Robert L. Mays, the head of the Railway Men's International, renewed them in the name of the organization, even though it had for some time past actually ceased to function.

[18] Sterling D. Spero, *The Labor Movement in a Government Industry* (1924), pp. 297-98.

[19] See below, p. 312.

While Mays was bringing large numbers of dining car men into his union in 1918, another organization, known as the Brotherhood of Dining Car Employees, was begun among the cooks and waiters of the New England railroads and the New York Central. At the same time a group called the Dining Car Cooks' and Waiters' Association was formed among the men on the Pennsylvania east of Pittsburgh, the Baltimore and Ohio, Erie, and Lackawanna Railroads. In 1920, under the leadership of Rienzi B. Lemus, these two unions were amalgamated into the present Brotherhood of Dining Car Employees. This organization claims a membership of 2,700, or about half of the colored dining car cooks and waiters east of the Mississippi, and has contracts on the most important roads in the area.

The Brotherhood won recognition on most roads with very little trouble. Three important lines at first resisted its claims but finally yielded. On the Pennsylvania the union won recognition by carrying its case to the general manager, and it has held its ground ever since. Even the road's employee-representation plan has not disturbed it. The Brotherhood continues to nominate its own officers while the company provides the election machinery.

The Southern Railroad and the Atlantic Coast Line also resisted the Brotherhood's claims to speak for their employees. The latter finally yielded on the question of recognition but carried the organization's wage claims to the Railway Labor Board. The Southern went to the Board with its entire controversy. The Board ordered a secret ballot among the employees who in turn designated the Brotherhood as their representative by an overwhelming majority.

A few years after the Brotherhood of Dining Car Employees was established, another group was formed among the employees of the Chicago, Milwaukee and St. Paul, and the Northern Pacific Railroads. This organization included sleeping car porters as well as dining car workers, but these porters, unlike the vast majority of sleeping car porters, were employees of the railroads rather than of the Pullman Company. This organization called itself the Brotherhood of Sleeping and Dining Car Employees' Union. Shortly after its organization it affiliated with the American Federation of Labor as a federal labor union, but before long it grew disappointed with the results of its affiliation and surrendered its charter.

The sleeping car porters employed by the Pullman Company, having already received substantial improvements in working conditions through the agency of the Railway Men's International, sought still further improvement. These workers had been talking about organized effort since the investigation of the Pullman service by the United States Commission on Industrial Relations in 1915, but it was not until the International Association took them into its ranks during federal control that they took any serious steps to help themselves. Between 1921 and 1925 a number of attempts were made to organize the Pullman porters, the most important of which were the Order of Sleeping Car Employees, headed by a man named Warfield in Kansas City, and the Sleeping Car Porters' Protective Union, headed by S. J. Freeman in New York. However the efforts of these workers did not assume significant proportions until the organization of the spectacular Brotherhood of Sleeping Car Porters and Maids under the leadership of A. Philip Randolph in 1925.[20] But in spite of the great promise which this organization first gave, it has, like the other independent Negro unions, shown no capacity to deal effectively with the employer.

The Negro's experience with unions of his own, though apparently discouraging, is not unlike that of new immigrant groups. Like the Negro, these groups were for the most part neglected by the established labor unions, and because of this neglect were forced to form organizations of their own.[21] Despite ups and downs the formation of such groups con-

[20] See Chapter XX.
[21] David J. Saposs, *Left Wing Unionism* (1926), pp. 102-3.

tinued, until in time stable and effective organization was evolved. It is probable that the Negro's experience with independent unions will produce similar results, training him in the methods and tactics of trade unionism and producing a labor-conscious leadership which will eventually break down the indifference of the official labor movement.

Chapter VII

STRIKE BREAKING AND RACE CONSCIOUSNESS

The use of Negroes for strike breaking has increased friction between the races and led the white trade unionist to regard the black worker as an enemy of the labor movement. Such hostility has been further increased by the fact that many race leaders condone, if they do not actually urge, strike breaking as a method of gaining entrance into industry. It is, they argue, the Negro's one chance to prove his competence as an industrial worker and to win the good will of employers. It is, too, a way of showing the white worker, and especially the organized white worker who excludes the Negro from his ranks, that colored labor can not be perpetually ignored with impunity. While the Negro has indeed gained some footing in industry via the strike-breaking road, such gain has on the whole been slight. Negroes taken on in a strike have usually been let out as soon as the old workers returned. Even the few who proved satisfactory and were retained at the end of the strike were in most cases eventually replaced by whites. But the race leaders think even small gains worth while.

"Members of my race," said a Negro professional man in St. Louis, prominent in the affairs of the Urban League of that city, "had never been able to get jobs as locomotive engineers in the steel plants of St. Louis. Some years ago the locomotive engineers in one large plant went on strike. The company put Negroes in their places and has been running its engines with Negroes ever since." [1] This, according to the speaker, opened up oppportunities for the Negro which he would not otherwise have had, and justified the manner of his entrance into the jobs.

[1] Interview, Dec., 1926.

Discussing the peculiar steadiness and loyalty of their Negro force, an official of this company declared, "We were the first company in this vicinity to employ Negroes as molders, cranemen or locomotive engineers. The better class of Negroes recognize this and have shown a peculiar loyalty to our company and have always felt that they could get a fair deal and justice in every way." [2]

The Negro's willingness to break the white man's strike is partly traceable to his slave time distrust of white labor and his dependence on the white master class. Primarily, however, the Negro's availability as a strike breaker has been due to his complete ignorance not only as to what a strike or a union was, but even of what a factory was. Most of the colored labor used to break strikes came straight from the farms without any previous industrial contacts. When these ignorant farm hands heard the leaders of their own group, such as the minister or politician whom they were accustomed to respect, counsel them to beware of the white man's union and remain loyal to the employer, the word naturally carried more weight than that of the white unionist asking them to quit their jobs.

According to Booker T. Washington, "the average Negro who comes to town does not understand the necessity or advantage of a labor organization which stands between him and his employer and aims apparently to make a monopoly of the opportunity for labor." He is "more accustomed to work for persons than for wages. When he gets a job, therefore, he is inclined to consider the source from which it comes." He looks upon his employer as his friend and "does not understand and does not like an organization which seems to be founded on a sort of impersonal enmity to the man by whom he is employed." [3]

Such attitudes were prevalent among the Negroes who

[2] Correspondence, Feb. 23, 1927.

[3] Booker T. Washington, "The Negro and the Labor Unions," *Atlantic Monthly*, June, 1913, pp. 756-57.

came North in the recent migrations, and organizers for unions which did not discriminate against the Negro and wanted his membership testify that they were a powerful obstacle to his organization. Miss Mary McDowell tells a story of a Negro recently employed in the stockyards who was approached by a union organizer and told the advantages of union membership. "It all sounds pretty good to me," said the Negro, "but what does Mr. Armour think about it?"

Unaccustomed to the complexities of modern large-scale industry, the colored worker still regards his relationship to his employer as a personal one. His grievances are his own affair. If he can take them up with the employer and settle them, well and good. If he cannot settle them he does not go back to the plant and raise the issue with his fellows. He just quits his job. Employers in every kind of industry have called attention to this, citing it as one of the Negro's most desirable qualities. "The Negro is no trouble maker. When he is dissatisfied he quits," was the well-nigh universal comment.

"Scarcely has there been a complaint by employers against these people on the ground of their being trouble makers," said a report on the Negro in Cleveland's industries. "On the other hand, it is said that these workers are loyal to their northern employers to the best of their ability. They come here understanding our American language and having a knowledge of our basic ideals. They do not bring with them any of the communistic or socialistic spirit to be found among some immigrants from certain portions of Europe." [4]

In a similar vein but not quite so outspokenly, Mr. Eugene K. Jones, executive secretary of the National Urban League, the leading Negro social-work organization, declared in 1919: ". . . Sufficient testimony is available to prove conclusively that Negro labor on the whole was found to be extremely promising. They were loyal to their employers. In fact, they took proprietary interests in their employers' plants. They were American to the core, and their great advantage was their

---

[4] John B. Abell, "Negro in Industry," *Trade Winds*, March, 1924, p. 17.

ability to speak and understand English. They were not easily inflamed against their employers for imagined grievances." [5]

These attitudes which made the Negro an obedient, uncomplaining, docile worker, grateful for his job, naturally made it exceedingly difficult for the unions to organize him and almost impossible for them to induce him to strike.[6] The Negro has thus played the part of a strike breaker in two ways. He has stayed at work when the other employees walked out, and he has come in from outside to take the place of workers on strike.

Negroes were brought in to take the places of white strikers on the New York docks as long ago as 1855; and again in 1863 they were used against the longshoremen in half a dozen eastern cities.[7] Since that date there has hardly been an important industry in which colored labor has not at one time or another been used for the same purpose.

But when all is said and done, the number of strikes broken by black labor have been few as compared with the number broken by white labor. What is more, the Negro has seldom been the only or even the most important strike-breaking element. Employers in emergencies take whatever labor they can get and the Negro is only one of many groups involved. But the bitterness of American race prejudice has always made his presence an especially sore point and not infrequently a signal for exceptional disorder.

"Strikers seem to consider it a much greater crime," said Booker T. Washington, "for a Negro who had been denied an opportunity to work at his trade to take the place of a striking employee than for a white man to do the same thing. Not only have Negro strike breakers been savagely beaten and mobbed by strikers and their sympathizers, but in some instances every

[5] Speech of E. K. Jones before the National Conference of Social Work, 1919, *Proceedings*, p. 439.

[6] See Chapters XI and XII.

[7] Charles H. Wesley, *Negro Labor in the United States*, pp. 79-80. Also see below, pp. 197-98.

Negro, no matter what his occupation, who lived in the vicinity of the strike has found himself in danger." [8]

Union exclusion may serve as moral justification for the Negro's breaking the white man's strike, but so far as the white unionist is concerned, it serves to intensify anti-Negro feeling. The union excludes the Negro to keep him out of the trade and it is but natural that, when he forces his way into the trade at a time when the union is fighting for certain objectives, the members should be doubly enraged, first, at the opposition to their aims, and second, at the circumvention of their membership policy.

The Negro always stands out in the crowd. His color makes this inevitable. The presence of a dozen black men in a force of strike breakers appears to the strikers like a hundred. During the celebrated teamsters' strike of 1905 in Chicago, it was estimated that 5,800 strike breakers were used throughout the summer to fill the places of 5,000 strikers. Of these 5,800 strike breakers, 5,000 were white.[9] Yet the Negro was singled out for special violence and abuse. The papers printed exaggerated accounts of imported Negroes taking the places of white men, and aroused the public to a fever pitch of racial feeling. As a matter of fact, the white strike breakers brought into Chicago from outside during this dispute outnumbered the Negro by more than seven to one.[10]

Even where Negro unionists have struck side by side with white, the introduction of Negro strike breakers has stirred up the same racial antipathies among white strikers as if they alone had been carrying on the strike. In strike after strike, in the coal mines, in the packing houses, in the needle trades, and elsewhere, Negroes have fought on both sides. Yet organized labor regards the Negro unionist as an exception. He and his few fellows are lone individuals. The "race," through its leaders and official organs, is on the other side. In the

[8] Booker T. Washington, *op. cit.*, p. 757.
[9] R. R. Wright, "The Negro in Times of Industrial Unrest," *Charities*, Oct. 7, 1905, pp. 71-72.
[10] *Ibid.*

words of President John Fitzpatrick of the Chicago Federation of Labor:

> The Negro sets himself up as a destructive interest in the community, and the leaders are trying to get his mind in such condition that he will continue to do that. Now the other races do not do that. They are susceptible of organization and education on these questions. . . .

> The leaders of the Negro race advise the Negroes not to have anything to do with the whites, to keep themselves separated, and when the white workers go on strike to wipe out a bad condition of employment and to bring about an increase of wages, that the Negro jump in there and prevent the white from accomplishing his purpose.[11]

There is truth in Mr. Fitzpatrick's statement. The dominant Negro leadership is hostile to trade unionism and favorable to the employer. In the past an important section of it has favored strike breaking as a matter of racial policy, thus drawing the vicious circle of the Negro's distrust of organized labor based on the latter's discriminatory attitude and organized labor's distrust of the Negro based upon his willingness to scab. The moralist, eager to assess blame, might easily lay responsibility for the situation at the door of white unions. He might cite in support of his judgment a long list of instances of trade-union double dealing and bad faith with the black workman. Yet his judgment would be only half true. The basis for present distrust between white labor and black goes back to the days of slavery when white freeman and Negro slave competed against each other, the one having the advantage of freedom, whiteness, and a little political power in the towns, the other having the advantage of the support of the socially, economically, and politically dominant slaveholding class. Distrust which has roots so deep is hard to overcome.

The anti-union Negro leader maintains that the white employer is willing to give the black man a chance but is held in check by the attitude of his employees. The excuse, "I have no

[11] Testimony before the Chicago Commission on Race Relations, Aug. 16, 1920, MS. pp. 30-31.

objection to hiring colored labor but my employees would quit if I did," has been heard so often by Negro job seekers that they have come to believe it and to assume that if only the opposition of white labor were removed the Negro could readily find employment. And now that the necessities of the war-time labor shortage have broken down the barriers and given the Negro a place in most of the country's leading industries, the conciliation of the employer is considered all the more imperative if the black man is to remain secure in his place and to win industrial advancement. Professor Kelly Miller of Howard University declared:

There is every indication that it is the intention of the great industries to foster and favor the Negro workman to the fullest extent of his merit and efficiency. For the Negro wantonly to flout their generous advances by joining the restless ranks which threaten industrial ruin would be fatuous suicide.

At present the capitalist class possess the culture and conscience which hold even the malignity of race passion in restraint. There is nothing in the white working class to which the Negro can appeal. They are the ones who lynch and burn and torture him. He must look to the upper element for law and order.

But the laborers outnumber the capitalists ten to one and under democracy they must in the long run gain the essential aims for which they strive. . . . How will it fare with the Negro in that day, if he now aligns himself with capital and refuses to help win the common battle?

Sufficient unto the day is the industrial wisdom thereof! The Negro would rather think of the ills he has than fly to those he knows not of. He has a quick instinct for expediency. Now he must exercise the courage of decision. Whatever good or evil the future may hold in store for him, today's wisdom heedless of logical consistency demands that he stand shoulder to shoulder with the captains of industry.[12]

Shortly before the publication of these views of Professor Kelly Miller, a prominent Negro churchman declared:

[12] Kelly Miller, "The Negro as a Workingman," *American Mercury*, Nov., 1925, p. 313. A more recent statement by Professor Miller on this subject appears in a letter to the editor of the *New York Herald Tribune*, July 13, 1930.

I believe that the interest of my people lies with the wealth of the nation and with the class of white people who control it. Labor and capital cannot adjust themselves by rival organizations; they must work together.[13]

The doctrine of race separatism and its labor corollary, "beware the white man's union," is found in its extreme form in the "back to Africa" movement of Marcus Garvey. Though this was largely a Negro counterpart of the Zionist movement in that it was interested in establishing a Negro state in Africa, its effect on Negro thought and policy in relation to organized labor was not unlike the preachings of Kelly Miller and Bishop Carey. Garvey's purpose was to arouse Negro race consciousness and nationalist feeling. According to him, equality with the white race in a white man's country was an "impossible dream" which would "never materialize" and which only served to distract the Negro "from the real solution and objective of securing nationalism." [14] He advised the Negro to beware of the labor movement in all its forms from "the American Federation of white workers or laborers" to the "present brand of Communism or Workers' partizanship as taught in America." [15] His advice to the black worker was to side with the employer until such time as he could achieve economic independence and become his own employer Expanding his doctrine he declared: [16]

It seems strange and a paradox, but the only convenient friend the Negro worker or laborer has in America at the present time is the white capitalist. The capitalist being selfish — seeking only the largest profit out of labor — is willing and glad to use Negro labor wherever possible on a scale reasonably below the standard union wage . . . but if the Negro unionizes himself to the level of the white worker, the choice and preference of employment is given to the white worker.

White unionism is now trying to rope in the Negro and make him a standard wage worker, then, when it becomes generally known that

---

[13] Bishop Carey, in the Chicago *Whip*, March 29, 1924.

[14] Amy Jacques-Garvey, *Philosophy and Opinions of Marcus Garvey* (1926), Vol. II, pp. 70-71.

[15] *Ibid.*, p. 69.   [16] *Ibid.*, pp. 69-70.

he demands the same wage as the white worker, an appeal or approach will be made to the white capitalist or employer, to alienate his sympathy or consideration for the Negro, causing him . . . to discriminate in favor of the white worker as a race duty and obligation.

The danger of Communism to the Negro in countries where he forms a minority of the population, is seen in the selfish and vicious attempts of that party or group to use the Negro's vote and physical numbers in helping to smash and overthrow by revolution, a system that is injurious to them as the white underdogs, the success of which would put their majority group or race still in power not only as Communists but as white men. . . . Fundamentally what racial difference is there between a white Communist, Republican or Democrat? On appeal to race interest the Communist is as ready as either to show his racial superiority. . . .

If the Negro takes my advice he will organize by himself and always keep his scale of wage a little lower than the whites until he is able to become, through proper leadership, his own employer; by doing so he will keep the good will of the white employer and live a little longer under the present scheme of things.

Though Garveyism has had a tremendous hold among Negroes in all parts of the country, its principal influence was among the new migrants in northern cities immediately after the World War. These simple people, fresh from the fields and unaccustomed to their strange new environment, turned to this emotionally satisfying movement offering them an escape from their ills through new freedom in a land of their own. The more sophisticated industrial workers were less impressed. Sometimes they attended Garvey's meetings and cheered his speeches, but they failed to follow his industrial advice. This was particularly true of the miners and longshoremen whose unions had large colored memberships and long traditions of equal treatment to all races.

There is little wonder in view of the expressions of race-conscious leaders,[17] that white labor should have gained the impression that the Negro group, in its efforts to overcome its

[17] Compare these attitudes with those of the clan leaders of immigrants. See David J. Saposs, "The Mind of the Immigrant Community" in *Public Opinion and the Steel Strike* (1921), pp. 224-242.

disadvantages, had allied itself with capital against the interests of white labor. Race leaders have not let the issue stand with mere expressions of opinion. Negro ministers and Y. M. C. A. secretaries, politicians, and social workers, have not only fought labor unions, black and white alike, by refusing to allow them to meet in their halls and churches, but have actually recruited strike breakers in times of industrial conflict. And these anti-union activities have been directed not against white unionists alone but against colored labor as well. The attempt to organize the Pullman porters has been fought by Negro editors, ministers, and politicians with the same vigor as attempts to organize the colored workers in the stockyards or coal mines.[18] Here there was no question of the duplicity of white labor. The Pullman porters were a Negro union organized and led by Negroes. Yet the Negro leaders cautioned their people not to fight their friend, the Pullman Company. The Chicago *Whip*, urging the porters to continue to rely upon the company union, advised "the black people at large to align themselves as far as possible with the wealthier classes in America." [19]

A certain amount of corruption inevitably followed in the trail of this pro-employer policy. Sometimes leaders preaching the doctrine were paid to do so by interests seeking to prevent the Negro's unionization. And sometimes leaders threw their influence on the employer side and found that rewards followed almost automatically without solicitation.

During the steel strike, according to a report to the A. F. of L., a colored minister at Gary urged the men to return to the mills and received a donation of $2,000 from one of the steel companies.[20] In Alabama, an itinerant preacher with an office in Birmingham fought the United Mine Workers with great energy. He declared that he made his living by doing "welfare work" and that the "industrial institutions" around

---

[18] See below, pp. 435-39.

[19] Chicago *Whip*, May 15, 1926.

[20] Testimony before the Chicago Commission on Race Relations, Aug. 16, 1920, MS p. 24.

Birmingham contributed between \$3,700 and \$4,000 for his work so that he did not "have to worry for support." He edited a paper, now defunct, known as the *Southern Industrial Fraternal Review*, organ of a paper organization called the Southern Afro-American Industrial Brotherhood. He declared that he was "bitterly opposed" to unions because they discriminated against the black man while the employer gave him a chance. He therefore preached the gospel of "work and individual betterment," or "you do the job better than the next man." [21]

Although there is strong circumstantial evidence of outright or semi-corruption on the part of Negro papers and Negro leaders, most of them want no more than the recognition of the right of black men to equal opportunity for work. Many leaders have used their power and influence to wring concessions from white labor even though the concessions they got were small, while the policies they blocked were of major importance. In 1925, four Negro legislators in Illinois almost defeated the enactment of the State Federation of Labor's injunction limitation bill. The Federation leaders were shocked and angered at having the Negroes assert their power and focus attention upon their grievances at so inconvenient a time. But it was of course this very time which made the opposition so effective. The Federation had to meet Negro criticism in order to win needed Negro votes. A meeting of twenty-six Negro trade-union officers and members was called at the Federation offices where a memorial was prepared asking the recalcitrant legislators to change their votes on the ground that opposition to legislation desired by organized labor was no way to remedy race prejudice in the labor movement. A committee of colored labor men carried this plea to the state capitol.[22] A deal was finally arranged under which the Negro legislators voted for the anti-injunction bill in return for a

[21] Information through interview, April, 1929. See also below, pp. 463-64.

[22] Eugene Staley, *History of the Illinois State Federation of Labor* (1930), pp. 464-65.

promise on the part of the unions to organize Negro electricians and give them an equal chance to get work.[23]

When the Shipstead anti-injunction bill was in the hands of the Judiciary Committee of the United States Senate, two Negro leaders appeared before the committee to oppose it. One of these was Charles W. Chestnutt a well-to-do Cleveland lawyer, the other was Harry E. Davis, the leading Negro Republican politician of Ohio. They based their opposition on the ground that the unions discriminated against the Negro and kept him from working and often struck to prevent his employment. If the powers of the courts to curtail the activities of the unions were limited, the colored worker would be denied essential protection.[24] "It must be apparent to this committee," said Davis, "that if a colored worker is denied the protection which union membership gives him, even where he is willing to become a member, there is only one place where he can have his employment rights protected if they are assailed and that is in our courts. For all practical purposes the proposed bill would take away this right from the group of independent workers for whom I am speaking and it would mean their subjection to a state of economic serfdom." [25]

The great increase in the Negro population of the northern cities after 1916 was accompanied by the rise and growth of social-service agencies. Chief among these was the National Urban League. This organization received its financial support from both Negroes and whites, but chiefly the latter. It was composed of a national body and autonomous local units, both directed by boards composed of white and black persons, but the actual administration was in the hands of Negroes. The League, originally known as the National League

[23] Interview with Warren B. Douglas, Negro Republican representative from Chicago in the State Legislature, Oct., 1928.

[24] Hearings before subcommittee of the Committee on the Judiciary, U. S. Senate, 70th Congress, 1st Session on S. 1482, 1928, pp. 603-14.

[25] From Harry E. Davis' brief filed with the Senate Committee on the Judiciary. See "Spokesman for Negroes Condemns Anti-Injunction Bill," *Law and Labor*, Feb., 1929, p. 24.

on Urban Conditions among Negroes, was founded in 1910, but it was not until the pressure of the colored population in the cities became acute that the organization became a factor of real importance in Negro life. The character of the League differed from city to city, but everywhere the outstanding characteristic of its policy was opportunism. The purpose of its industrial departments, like that of the Negro leadership in general, was to get jobs for colored workers. It tried to break down the barriers against the employment of Negroes by visiting plants and talking to employers, by running "Negro-in-industry weeks" calling the attention of employers to the desirable qualities of black workers and acquainting them with the favorable experiences of other employers. Many local Urban Leagues ran employment bureaus which became clearing houses for the placing of colored labor, and sent Negro welfare workers into the plants to help the adjustment of the black workers.[26] Many of the largest industrial concerns came to regard the local League as a useful agency for procuring labor and as a conservative stabilizing force in the colored community, and contributed substantially to its support. In Detroit, where more than half of the Negroes employed in the city were placed through the League's employment office, employers considered the activity of the industrial department so important that the Employers' Association financed its work and paid the salary of the industrial secretary.[27] During a strike in the metal trades in 1921 the Detroit Urban League freely furnished Negro labor to plants affected. On one occasion the industrial secretary personally brought over 150 colored strike breakers to the Timkin Company's works, marching them past the pickets who were afraid to attack so large a group. The secretary himself, after having delivered his men, left the plant, unnoticed, by a side exit.[28]

[26] See below p. 258.

[27] J. T. Clark, "The Urban League and Its Relation to Industry." National Association of Corporation Schools. 8th Annual Convention, New York, 1920, p. 669.

[28] Interview at Louisville, Ky., Oct. 25, 1928.

The Newark, New Jersey, Urban League acted in much the same way during a strike in the Sayre-Fisher brickmaking plant at Sayreville, New Jersey, in the late spring of 1923. The League helped to recruit a force of Negro strike breakers and allowed the company the temporary use of its secretary to keep tab on the efficiency of this labor.[29]

Charges of strike breaking have been made against local Urban Leagues in several cities. It was charged by strikers during a fig and date packers' strike in Chicago during the winter of 1926-1927, that the Urban League sent girls to shops on strike without informing them that a labor controversy was in progress. However, Foster, the local executive secretary, at a meeting at the Chicago City Club, called to make plans for a "Negro-in-industry week," denied that the League had ever knowingly engaged in furnishing strike breakers.[30] Yet the Chicago League showed exceedingly little interest in the question of unionization. The program at the meeting in question was silent on the matter of seeking union coöperation. None of the executive officers of the League had any knowledge of trade unionism. The secretary had previously declared that he had all of the layman's prejudices against organized labor and that he had never read a book on the labor movement.[31]

The Chicago League's coldness toward organized labor was not confined to the white labor movement, where the question of discrimination against the Negro might have justified its attitude. It was as unfriendly to the Negro Pullman porters' movement as it was to the plumbers' union. Unfortunately for the Chicago League, the porters' drive for the moral support of the colored community reached a high point in the midst of the League's 1926 drive for funds. Mr. Eugene K. Jones, executive secretary of the National League, publicly endorsed the porters' organization. Immediately the Chicago

[29] One of the authors, not knowing of the strike, took work at the plan' at the time of these events.

[30] Meeting held early in the winter of 1927.

[31] Interview in Chicago, December, 1926.

League, which had always received a contribution from the Pullman Company, got a letter asking it whether Mr. Jones was speaking for the whole Urban League or merely expressing his personal viewpoint. For a while the Chicago officers were in a quandary, but finally they explained to the Pullman Company that the National Urban League handled national questions and had no control over the policies of the locals. The Pullman Company made its contribution.

Unfriendliness to union labor did not extend to the whole Urban League organization. During the war and the years immediately following, when the demand for labor was keen, the New York Urban League acted as a clearing house for the placing of colored workers in the entire metropolitan area. It was careful never to send workers into a city in response to an employer's request without first asking the local central labor body whether there was a strike going on in the town or whether the presence of additional workers would be likely to depress labor standards. Before the adoption of this policy the New York League had supplied labor indiscriminately wherever it was requested. Its activity resulted in the breaking of several strikes in Connecticut cities. The local labor leaders protested to the League's board of directors, and the liberal members of that body forced the change in policy to which the League has since adhered.

The National League has believed that expediency dictated a conciliatory policy toward organized labor. It has felt that the Negro could get work more readily if he and the labor unions were on friendly terms with each other, and it set about to overcome the mutual suspicions of the parties. In 1918 a statement was presented to the American Federation of Labor by a group of Negro leaders, headed by Eugene K. Jones of the National Urban League, urging more serious effort at organizing the Negro.[32] The Federation acknowledged this request and a similar one made two years later, in 1920, by the passage of good resolutions.[33] In 1919 the Na-

[32] American Federation of Labor, *Proceedings*, 1918, pp. 198-99.
[33] *Ibid.*, p. 205; 1920, pp. 276-77, 311. See also Chapter V, pp. 107-11.

·tional League at its convention at Detroit passed resolutions favoring the unionization of Negro workers and ever since the national body has tried to maintain friendly relations with the American Federation of Labor. When it established its Industrial Relations Department in 1925, the League offered to pay half the expenses of a Negro national organizer with offices in the American Federation of Labor Building. The offer was not accepted. While the League thus has a very real grievance against the Federation for the latter's persistent coldness towards its advances, it should not be overlooked that the League's attitude was based entirely on grounds of expediency. It showed no evidence of conversion to the idea of working-class unity. It was still a middle-class social-service body interested in getting jobs for Negroes and in breaking down trade-union barriers in order to accomplish this end more effectively.

Answering Professor Kelly Miller's advice, quoted above, counselling the Negro to align himself with the captains of industry, the National Urban League declared through its organ, *Opportunity*:

The competitive struggles of the past have as their basis the unwarranted and mischievous belief that the two branches of American labor are striving after different and irreconcilable ends. It is not enough that there should be coöperation between Negro leaders and cultured whites. Harmonious relations depend not upon the manipulations of racial diplomats, but upon the interchange of friendly feeling, confidence and respect between all groups of both races. Professor Miller would stop precisely where the work of the future begins. To take this advice seriously is to abandon the very essence of all inter-racial effort.[34]

Yet, the "manipulations of racial diplomats" was the very policy which the Urban League had pursued. Its attempts to reconcile the white and black workers have never reached down to the rank and file, but have been confined to dealings with high officials of the trade-union movement.

While several local leagues have adopted resolutions urging

[34] *Opportunity*, Jan., 1926, p. 5.

the unionization of the Negro, only two have really gone out of their way to aid such a program. These were the New York and Brooklyn Leagues during the drive to unionize the ladies' dress industry in the winter of 1929-1930. The union making the drive, the International Ladies' Garment Workers' Union, is one of the most radical in the American Federation of Labor, and has always made special efforts to obliterate the color line. It has been almost unique in its intelligent handling of the colored workers, mostly women, who came into its industry.[35]

Many middle-class Negroes whose interest in organized labor extends beyond the Urban League's desire to get jobs and equal treatment for black workers have realized that the traditional attitude of the "race" leadership to the labor movement as well as the attitude of white labor toward the Negro are harmful to the best interests of all workers. No better expression of these views of the Negro liberals can be found anywhere than in the following open letter addressed "to the American Federation of Labor and other groups of organized labor" by the National Association for the Advancement of Colored People:

For many years the American Negro has been demanding admittance to the ranks of union labor.

For many years your organizations have made public profession of your interest in Negro labor, of your desire to have it unionized, and of your hatred of the black "scab."

Notwithstanding this apparent surface agreement, Negro labor in the main is outside the ranks of organized labor, and the reason is, first, that white union labor does not want black labor, and secondly, black labor has ceased to beg admission to union ranks because of its increasing value and efficiency outside the unions.

We face a crisis in inter-racial labor conditions; the continued and determined race prejudice of white labor, together with the limitation of immigration, is giving black labor tremendous advantage. The Negro is entering the ranks of semi-skilled and skilled labor and he is entering mainly and necessarily as a "scab." He broke the great steel strike. He

---

[35] See Chapter XVI.

will soon be in a position to break any strike when he can gain economic advantage for himself.

On the other hand, intelligent Negroes know full well that a blow at organized labor is a blow at all labor, that black labor today profits by the blood and sweat of labor leaders in the past who have fought oppression and monopoly by organization. If there is built up in America a great black bloc of non-union laborers who have a right to hate the unions, all laborers, black and white, eventually must suffer.

Is it not time then that black and white labor get together? Is it not time for white unions to stop bluffing and for black laborers to stop cutting off their noses to spite their faces?

The association then went on to propose the creation of an interracial labor commission to find the facts regarding the Negro's position in the labor unions and "to organize systematic propaganda against racial discrimination on the basis of these facts." [36] Aside from revealing the attitude of certain Negro liberals towards the labor movement, the effect of this letter was nil.

The influence of the attitude of race leaders toward the Negro's position in the labor movement will in all likelihood diminish as time goes on. Since 1916 the Negro's relation to industry has changed from that of a labor reserve to be drawn on in emergencies to a permanent part of the labor force. The Negro has attained a firm footing in most of the leading industries. It is no longer so necessary for him to scab in order to get employment. The chances are that the longer he stays in industry and the more closely he associates with other workers, the less influence his outside leaders will have on his industrial attitudes. In those organizations in which he has already made a real place for himself such as the longshoremen's union, the miners' union, or the radical movement, he has begun to develop a new leadership of his own grown out of the movements themselves and having nothing to do with the traditional leadership of the race. In the long run the Negro's

[36] The letter was sent by the 1924 Convention of the National Association for the Advancement of Colored People.

relations to organized labor will be determined not by editorials in the Negro press, the manifestoes of social-service agencies, or even the sermons of Negro ministers, but by the policies of the labor unions themselves.

PART III

THE NEGRO AS AN INDUSTRIAL RESERVE

Chapter VIII

TAPPING THE NEGRO INDUSTRIAL RESERVE

UNTIL the World War, industry outside of the South was manned almost entirely by white workers. A steady flow of immigrants from abroad had furnished employers with a constant supply of cheap labor to meet the needs of industrial expansion. Negro labor, engaged chiefly in agriculture and personal service, was largely disregarded as a source of industrial man power except in such emergencies as acute labor shortages or strikes. Even in the South where the Negro slave had competed successfully with the white man in almost every branch of industry, the tradition of the separation of the races operated after emancipation to check the full and free use of Negro labor in industry. The industrial backwardness of the section made the more extensive use of black labor unnecessary and left the traditional relation between the races undisturbed.

Northern employers drew upon the reserve of Negro farmers and servants to help them break their strikes as long ago as the middle fifties,[1] but it was not until the eighties, when Negro farmers began to find it too difficult to eke a living out of the soil, that the black man went to the cities in large numbers and offered serious competition to white labor. These migrants first settled in the cities of the South. Their further movement northward was determined by opportunity for employment. This opportunity came as a sudden windfall at the opening of the World War.

In 1915-1916, when large numbers of recent immigrants returned to their former homes in response to the call to arms, huge waves of southern Negro labor began pouring into north-

[1] See below, Chapter IX, p. 197.

ern industries. Still more of this labor drifted northward under the impetus of the war-time industrial expansion created by the entrance of this country into the conflict. When the war ended foreign immigration was restricted, and the northward trek of Negro labor continued on into 1924.

This mass movement, which reached its height during the war and early post-war years, was but a greatly accelerated phase of the general drift of the Negro population from the country to the cities which had been going on for half a century in increasing volume. The following figures, showing the percentages of Negroes living in rural and urban areas at each census since 1890, indicate the pace of the drift:

Year	Rural	Urban
1890	80.6	19.4
1900	77.3	22.7
1910	72.6	27.4
1920	66.0	34.0

There is nothing peculiar to the Negro population in this march from the farm to the town. The American people as a whole, as well as the people of every other industrial nation, have been moving in the same direction. In recent years the movement among the Negroes has been especially large and rapid. In 1910, 23.1 per cent of the total number of persons engaged in agricultural pursuits were Negroes. By 1920 the figure had fallen to 19.9 per cent. During this decade the number of Negroes employed in agriculture dropped from 2,893,375 to 2,178,888, a decline of 24.7 per cent. At the same time the Negro urban population rose from 2,684,797 to 3,559,473, an increase of 874,676 or 32.6 per cent. While southern and northern cities all shared in the results of the migration, the growth in the number of Negroes in the North has, because of its greater social and economic importance, justly commanded more attention.

During the period from 1870 to 1910 the number of southern born Negroes in the North increased at an average of about 67,000 in each ten-year period. Between 1910 and 1920 the net increase was 321,890, more than the aggregate number for the preceding forty years and about five times the average for the preceding ten years.[2]

The migration responsible for this increase began about 1910 and rose to great heights between 1916 and 1919. This wave was followed by a movement of equal, if not greater, proportions, beginning late in 1921 and ending in 1924. An estimate of the United States Department of Labor based on data gathered before this second movement had run its course placed its extent at 478,700.[3] There are no census figures to indicate the net increase in the Negro population of the North and West resulting from these two waves of migration, but an estimate of one million would probably not be far out of the way.

Nearly all the Negroes who left the South found their way to the industrial centers of the North and Middle West. The following table shows the increase in the Negro population of the most important industrial cities of the two sections:

TABLE V

INCREASE IN NEGRO POPULATION IN TEN LEADING
INDUSTRIAL CENTERS, 1910-20

City	1910	1920	Per Cent Increase
New York	91,709	152,467	66.3
Chicago	44,103	109,458	148.2
Philadelphia	84,459	134,229	58.9
Detroit	5,741	40,838	611.3
Cleveland	8,448	34,451	307.8
St. Louis	43,690	69,850	58.9
Pittsburgh	25,623	37,725	47.2
Cincinnati	19,639	30,079	53.2
Indianapolis	21,816	34,678	59.0
Kansas City	23,566	30,719	30.4

[2] Joseph A. Hill, "Recent Northward Migration of the Negro," *Monthly Labor Review*, March, 1924, p. 478.

[3] United States Department of Labor, Office of the Secretary, Oct. 24, 1923.

There are no reliable figures to show the increases in these cities since 1920. There is no doubt that they have been considerable, in some cases greater than the increase for the preceding decade. A school census taken in Detroit in 1925, after the second migration had ended, placed the Negro population at 81,831, or double the 1920 figure.

The great bulk of these Negroes have found their way into industry. The census records 886,810 Negroes employed in manufacturing and mechanical industries in 1920 as against 631,280 in 1910, an increase of 40 per cent. At the same time the number of Negroes in industries concerned with transportation increased 22 per cent, and the number employed in the extraction of minerals increased 20 per cent, while the number in the Negro's traditional occupation, domestic and personal service, declined 5.5 per cent. It must not be forgotten, however, that despite the 24.7 per cent decline in the number of Negroes engaged in agriculture and the 5.5 per cent decline in the number in personal and domestic service, these two occupations at the last census still engaged the great bulk of the gainfully employed Negroes — 3,301,150 out of 4,824,151, or 68.75 per cent of the total. Manufacturing, mining, and transportation claimed a total of 1,272,460.

Most of the Negroes who came North went into lower paid work requiring little or no skill or experience. The bulk of them became unskilled or semi-skilled operatives in the steel mills, automobile plants, foundries, and packing houses. Many went to work at road building and other construction jobs. Others, and this includes many women, went into the commercial laundries, food industries, and the less skilled branches of the needle trades. In some cities certain of the specialized sewing trades, for example, the making of lamp shades in Chicago, have come to depend very heavily upon the labor of Negro women. Between 1910 and 1920 the number of Negro women in manufacturing and mechanical industries increased from 67,937 to 104,983, while the number engaged in domestic and personal service declined from 853,387 to 793,631.

The increase in the number of Negroes in the packing houses has been one of the largest. In Chicago, the largest single meat center, the laborers in the packing houses in 1910 numbered 8,426. Of these, 34 were Negroes. The semi-skilled workers numbered 2,414. Of these, 33 were Negroes. In 1920 the laborers numbered 7,032 and the semi-skilled workers 6,931. Of the former number, 1,397 were Negroes; of the latter 1,558. At the beginning of 1919, two Chicago packing houses, employing an average of about 20,000 persons, employed about 4,000 Negroes. In the larger house, which employed some 14,000, Negroes constituted 20 per cent of the total. In the smaller firm they constituted about 16.6 per cent.[4] In 1928, 30 per cent of the employees of the larger company were Negroes.

In the steel industry in 1910, 6.35 per cent of the unskilled workers were Negroes, as against 17 per cent in 1920. The United States Immigration Commission in 1907 estimated that Negroes constituted 4.7 per cent of the total number of steel workers. This colored personnel accounted for 39.1 per cent of all the steel workers in the South; 0.5 per cent of those in the Middle West, which included the Ohio, Indiana, and Illinois districts, and 1.1 per cent of those in the East, which included Pennsylvania and New York.[5] Complete figures indicating the present proportion of Negroes in the steel industry are unavailable, but there are fragments which throw some light on the situation. In 1919, at the United States Steel Corporation's Homestead plant, the largest in the Pittsburgh district, 11.8 per cent of the employees were Negroes.[6] The personnel officer of the Carnegie Steel Company, the United States Steel subsidiary which owns the Homestead works, declared in the summer of 1928 that the number of Negroes on

[4] George E. Haynes, *The Negro at Work during the World War and during Reconstruction* (United States Department of Labor, Division of Negro Economics, 1921), pp. 52-56.

[5] Report of the Immigration Commission (1907), Vol. VIII, p. 34.

[6] Investigation of the Strike in Steel Industries. Hearings before the United States Senate Committee on Education and Labor (1919), p. 480.

the company's pay rolls had fluctuated between 10 and 12 per cent since the close of the war. A survey by the Pittsburgh Urban League in 1923, covering twenty-three mills in the district, reported the employment of 16,000 Negroes, or 21 per cent of the total force.[7] A check up of the most important steel companies in the Chicago district in the winter of 1926 – 1927 showed 4,164 Negroes, or 10 per cent of a total force of 41,081.[8] These were distributed as follows in the companies or individual plants covered:

Plant Number	Total Force	Negroes
1	1,867	348
2	735	176
3	25,000	2,829
4	8,479	611
5	5,000	200
Total	41,081	4,164

The United States Steel unit in the district, the Illinois Steel Company, employed 11 per cent Negroes, who constituted 2.57 per cent of the skilled workers, 10.6 per cent of the semi-skilled, and 21 per cent of the unskilled. In all the other plants the overwhelming proportion of the Negroes was unskilled.

The automobile plants in Detroit began to hire Negroes in 1916. Ten years later three large automobile plants were employing 11,000. The Ford works at River Rouge employed 6,000 of these, or 11 per cent of its total force of 55,000. The Ford Highland Park plant had no record of the number of its Negro employees, but estimates placed the number at about 4,000.[9] The Dodge Brothers works employed 915 Negroes, distributed in nineteen different departments. The Hupp plant, according to figures published in 1929, em-

[7] John T. Clark, "Negro in Steel," *Opportunity*, March, 1926, p. 87.
[8] These figures were obtained directly from the plants.
[9] Robert W. Dunn, *Labor and Automobiles* (1929), p. 68.

ployed 12 per cent Negro labor; the Studebaker, 10; McCord Radiator, 10; Cadillac, 5; Murray Body, 4; Chevrolet, 3.5; Dodge, 3.5; Packard, 3; Timkin-Detroit Axle, 2.5; Chrysler, 1.5; Hudson, 1.2; Lincoln, 1.0; Paige, 1.0; while many other plants employed less than 1.0 per cent.[10]

Although a large number of these Negroes were employed at semi-skilled labor, the overwhelming majority of them were unskilled. Only a handful were doing really skilled work. The Ford Highland Park plant had only two skilled Negroes out of an estimated 4,000.[11] At the Dodge plant 75 per cent of the Negroes were unskilled,[12] while similar or greater proportions held for the Packard and Hudson plants. It was stated in 1926 that 65 per cent of all the Negroes employed in the city of Detroit were engaged in unskilled work. The remaining 35 per cent included all those engaged in work above the grade of rough manual labor.[13]

This is generally true throughout all industry. In the building trades Negroes constitute but a small percentage of the skilled mechanics. In 1920 they were 3.8 per cent of the carpenters, 8 per cent of the masons, 2.9 per cent of the painters, 5 per cent of the paper hangers, 15.2 per cent of the plasterers, 1.7 per cent of the plumbers, whereas their proportion of the laborers was 21.6 per cent. In the chemical industries in 1920, 23.4 per cent of the unskilled workers were Negroes, while the semi-skilled were only 4.6 per cent Negro. In the cigar and tobacco factories 66.8 per cent of the laborers and only 12.9 per cent of the semi-skilled workers were Negroes.

The jobs into which the Negroes went were usually those which native Americans or Americanized foreign-born white labor did not want. This largely accounts for the almost spectacular increase in the proportion of Negroes in the iron and

[10] Dunn, *op. cit.*, p. 68.

[11] File of the study of the Negro in Detroit, made in 1926 by the Detroit Bureau of Government Research. Published in 1927.

[12] *Ibid.*

[13] *Ibid.*

steel foundries where the work is dirty, hot, and unpleasant. The foundries and metal works in the Chicago district and in the Middle West generally began to employ Negro labor between 1916 and 1921 when they could no longer get an adequate supply of foreign workers, although some had been experimenting with Negro labor before that time. A number of large mid-western works which had employed practically no Negroes until the war period or after employed the following numbers and percentages in 1927:

Plant Number	Number of Negroes	Per Cent of Total Force
1	541	38
2	388	42
3	731	17.4
4	166	30.6
5	88	37.5
6	15	10
7	300	30
8	30	15
9	129	27
10	20	10
11	26	35
12	20	10
13	15	10
14	36	8
15	285	28.5
16	15	30
17	242	32.5

Although the great majority of these Negroes were unskilled, the number of skilled workers in actual foundry operations showed a marked increase. In 1910, out of a total of 112,122 iron molders in the country, 2,156, or 1.9 per cent were Negroes. Ten years later there were 6,310 Negroes in a total of 114,031, or 5.5 per cent. The following table shows the distribution of Negro molders in four important foundry centers in 1910 and 1920:

TABLE VI

DISTRIBUTION OF NEGRO MOLDERS IN FOUR IMPORTANT FOUNDRY CENTERS, 1910-1920

City	1910		1920	
	Total	*Negroes*	*Total*	*Negroes*
Chicago	6,356	31	5,796	536
Cleveland	3,531	6	3,945	430
Pittsburgh	1,798	25	1,015	59
Birmingham	393	78	594	329

The increase in the number of Negroes in skilled foundry jobs did not stop in 1920. Nearly every plant in the above list employed Negroes in skilled places, although when they first began to use them they employed them only for common labor and unskilled work. In 1924 twelve representative foundries in the Cleveland industrial district employed from 10 to 60 per cent colored labor. Their average was 33 per cent. In all but one of these plants Negroes advanced from common labor to semi-skilled work and skilled work.[14]

Negro leaders eager to find jobs for members of their race cite figures from time to time of substantial percentages of Negroes doing skilled work. They contend that if the Negro can rise to skilled places, he has qualities which make him a good workman, and that the feeling of employers that he is capable only of the roughest labor and is by nature unsteady and unreliable even in such capacities is unfounded. Figures frequently cited show that more than one-fifth of the Negroes in the United States shipyards during the war, and over 27 per cent after the war, were engaged in skilled work.[15] Another much cited survey, made in 1923 by the Department of Labor at Washington, showed that in 273 firms employing 60,421 Negroes, 14,951, nearly 25 per cent of the total, were classified as skilled. It also showed that of 18,050 new colored

---

[14] United States Bureau of Labor Statistics, *Handbook of Labor Statistics 1924-1926*, Bulletin No. 439, p. 401.

[15] George E. Haynes, *op. cit.*, p. 58.

workers who entered industry between September 1, 1922, and August 31, 1923, 4,157 were classified as skilled. For the country as a whole it estimated that in the same period the number of Negroes in skilled occupations increased 38.5 per cent and those in unskilled work 44.1 per cent.[16]

While deductions based on sampling of this character are always open to question, it is possible that once Negroes are accepted as a permanent factor in industry some will rise in the industrial scale to take the places of older employees who drop out. Besides, mechanization is constantly changing the meaning of "skill," so that union opposition or craft tradition which has stood in the way of the Negro's entrance into certain recognized "skilled trades" will count less and less. In the old trades the union may actually oust him from places he has long filled. The "big four" brotherhoods may drive him out of occupations on the railroads which he has held for years. He may lose his predominance in the standard crafts in the South. The machinists or carpenters may keep him out of their trades in the North. Due largely to such craft opposition, in spite of the Negro's progress in the foundry and metal industries, there is hardly a metal works in the North that does not have an all-white machine shop. The same is true in the packing houses, where the great mechanical departments are practically all white, but where at the same time Negroes hold some of the most highly skilled and best paying jobs in the butchering departments. Yet it seems that for a long time to come the Negro's place in industry will in the main be at the bottom of the scale.

The Negro's position in the standard crafts has not changed appreciably in a generation, as the following table of percentages of Negro workers in eight leading trades indicates. The figures are based upon the census:

[16] United States Department of Labor, Office of the Secretary, Releases, July 7, and 19, 1923.

TABLE VII

PERCENTAGE OF NEGROES IN EIGHT LEADING CRAFTS IN THE
UNITED STATES, 1890-1920

Craft	1890	1900	1910	1920
Carpenters	3.6	3.4	3.8	3.8
Masons	6.0	8.7	7.3	8.0
Painters	2.0	2.0	2.6	2.9
Plasterers	10.0	10.5	14.2	15.2
Plumbers	1.1	1.2	2.4	1.7
Blacksmiths	5.0	4.4	4.7	4.3
Machinists	0.4	0.4	0.6	1.1
Printers [a]	0.5	0.9	0.9	1.1

Most of the Negro craftsmen of the country live in thirteen southern states: Maryland, Virginia, North Carolina, South Carolina, Georgia, Florida, Mississippi, Alabama, Louisiana, Texas, Arkansas, Tennessee, and Kentucky. The following table shows the total number of Negroes employed in the above-listed crafts and the number who lived in these southern states in 1920:

TABLE VIII

NUMBER OF NEGROES IN EIGHT CRAFTS IN UNITED STATES AND
IN THE SOUTHERN STATES, 1920

Craft	Number in United States	Number in South
Carpenters	34,243	28,171
Masons	10,609	8,102
Painters	9,332	7,210
Plasterers	7,097	3,518
Plumbers	3,516	2,444
Blacksmiths	8,521	7,058
Machinists	10,286	4,584
Printers	1,540	401

At the close of the Civil War 100,000 out of a total of 120,000 artisans in the southern states were Negroes.[17] But

[a] This classification changes from census to census. The figure is therefore no more than a rough approximation. See Chapter II, p. 21.

[17] Charles H. Wesley, *Negro Labor in the United States*, p. 142.

between 1865 and 1890 the proportion of Negro artisans in the South declined sharply as a result of the pressure of white competition and trade-union exclusion after emancipation.[18] Since 1890, however, the proportion of Negroes in the crafts has remained fairly constant, as the following table shows:

TABLE IX
PERCENTAGE OF NEGROES IN EIGHT CRAFTS IN THE SOUTH, 1890-1920

Craft	1890	1900	1910	1920
Carpenters	16.1	15.1	14.7	13.1
Masons	28.2	36.4	34.8	35.6
Painters	10.9	10.7	12.8	14.0
Plasterers	33.2	34.9	38.4	40.6
Plumbers	—	8.0	8.6	7.9
Blacksmith	20.3	16.6	15.0	14.4
Machinists	2.5	2.3	3.5	4.7
Printers	2.7	3.4	2.1	2.2

In the five leading industrial centers of the North in which the Negro population showed a heavy increase at the 1920 census, the number of Negroes in these crafts increased far more than for the country as a whole. The following table shows the change between 1910 and 1920 for four of the eight crafts listed above:

TABLE X
INCREASE IN NUMBER OF NEGROES IN FOUR CRAFTS IN FIVE NORTHERN CITIES, 1910-1920

City	Carpenters		Masons		Machinists		Plumbers	
	1910	1920	1910	1920	1910	1920	1910	1920
Chicago	92	275	67	126	95	431	39	105
New York	148	737	77	149	78	370	24	90
Philadelphia	177	688	148	116	111	455	24	102
Detroit	30	406	7	185	32	712	4	39
Cleveland	51	220	49	107	37	264	5	23
Total	498	2,326	348	683	353	2,232	96	359

[18] Carl Kelsey, "The Evolution of Negro Labor," *Annals of the American*

Despite these marked increases the Negro is still an insignificant minority in these trades. The following table shows the total number of persons and the number of Negroes employed in the four crafts in 1920:

TABLE XI

TOTAL NUMBER OF PERSONS AND NUMBER OF NEGROES IN FOUR CRAFTS IN FIVE NORTHERN CITIES, 1920

City	CARPENTERS		MASONS		MACHINISTS		PLUMBERS	
	Total	Negroes	Total	Negroes	Total	Negroes	Total	Negroes
Chicago	23,404	275	5,303	126	36,211	431	7,781	105
New York	42,478	737	9,985	149	39,723	370	19,354	90
Philadelphia	18,934	688	3,818	116	28,591	455	9,746	102
Detroit	14,152	406	2,700	185	31,885	712	4,327	39
Cleveland	9,510	220	2,351	107	20,666	264	2,741	23

It will be seen from the foregoing tables that the proportion of Negro machinists has increased markedly since 1910, even though foundries and metal works employ few, if any, of them. During this same period the number of white machinists more than doubled. These increases are due to the growth of mechanization generally and to the automobile in particular.

Race prejudice naturally put difficulties in the way of the Negroes' entrance into industry. White employers sometimes refused to hire them and white employees sometimes refused to work with them. This was particularly true of smaller plants, although some large works like the Wisconsin Steel Company in Chicago, a subsidiary of the International Harvester Company, boast of their all-white character. The reason for this company's refusal to use Negroes when the other plants of the Harvester Company in the Chicago district employ over 2,000 of them is simply that the superintendent does not like them. Often an employer is doubtful of the Negro's ability to do his work or is fearful that his white employees may object to the black worker's presence. There have been

---

Academy of Political and Social Science, Vol. XXI, Jan., 1903, p. 70. See also Chapters I and II, pp. 15, 32-33, above.

instances of white workers objecting so strongly to the use of
blacks that they have left their jobs. Between 1880 and 1900
there were thirty strikes reported against the employment of
Negro workers, eight in the decade 1880-1890 and twenty-
two in the decade 1890-1900.[19] There are no available figures
for subsequent years though it is well known that strikes
against the Negro have occurred. The East St. Louis riots in
1917 and the Chicago riots two years later, though springing
from complicated circumstances, were not without their labor
angles.[20]

The intensity of this race feeling was caused largely by
heavy importations of Negro labor. Not all of the Negroes
who poured into the northern cities between 1916 and 1924
came of their own initiative and found their way into industry
by themselves. Thousands were brought up by the labor
agents of large employers. An officer of the Illinois Central
Railroad told how Negro labor was used to carry out its huge
construction program after the war. "We took Negro labor
out of the South," he said, "until it hurt." Referring to the
importation of Negroes into East St. Louis, Illinois, during
the war, Mr. Victor Olander, secretary of the Illinois State
Federation of Labor, explained that the process began in a
"persistent effort to secure workers for a definite situation,"
and "later developed into a general propaganda in East St.
Louis to bring them (Negroes) there and dump them there,
and to let them run wild in the city without any place to sleep
or live after they were through with them. At the time of the
riot, every shed and shack in that town was filled." [21] This
was substantiated by the report of a congressional committee.
"Responsibility for this influx of 10,000 or more Negroes
into East St. Louis," it declared, "rests on the railroads and

[19] United States Bureau of Labor: *Sixteenth Annual Report of the Commissioner of Labor* (1901), pp. 413-65. See also Eric W. Hardy, *The Relation
of the Negro to Trade Unionism* (Master's Essay, University of Chicago, 1911).

[20] See above, Chapter V, p. 112.

[21] Testimony before the Chicago Commission on Race Relations, Aug. 16,
1920, pp. 8-9.

the manufacturing establishments. . . . It is a lamentable fact that the employers of labor paid too little heed to the comfort or welfare of their men. They saw them crowded into wretched cabins, without water or any of the conveniences of life. . . ." [22]

The very fact that Negro labor was cheap and would accept such conditions as the committee described overcame the employer's preconceptions as to its inefficiency. When employers short of labor turned to the Negro and found that he had no innate characteristics which made him a poor workman, they continued to draw upon the black industrial reserve. When the labor shortage ended, those Negroes who had proved their use were retained in service in substantial numbers. In the summer of 1928 several officials of the Carnegie Steel Company declared that they could well get along without the Negro, but that they did not choose to do so. Instead, they kept him in their plants in a ratio of about 10 per cent of the total number of employees. The Negro is now recognized as a permanent factor in industry and large employers use him as one of the racial and national elements which help to break the homogeneity of their labor force. This, incidentally, fits into the program of big concerns for maintaining what they call "a cosmopolitan force," which frees the employer from dependence upon any one group for his labor supply and also thwarts unity of purpose and labor organization. Or, as the personnel manager of a very large company near Chicago put it: "It makes fraternizing among the employees difficult."

The chief obstacle to the continued, not to speak of increased, employment of Negro labor after the employer's initial doubts and fears had been overcome by sheer necessity were difficulties in adjusting the newcomer to his strange industrial environment. The Negro migrant, who was for the most part a southern farm hand, unaccustomed to the discipline of

[22] Report of the Special Committee Authorized by Congress to Investigate the East St. Louis Riots, July 15, 1918, pp. 2-3.

industry, had his difficulties in adjusting himself to his new situation. Even those Negroes who came from southern cities and had had experience in the factories and mills had to make adjustments to the greater exactions and faster pace of northern industry. Employers complained that the Negro was unsteady; that he would lay off after pay day and spend his wages; that he would only stay on a job long enough to get some ready money and would then lay off until the money was spent, after which he would return to work and repeat the performance. Complaints over wage garnishments were frequent, but not more so than in the case of foreign immigrants. Both lacked resources and it is hardly strange that they ran into debt.

All these criticisms diminished as time went on and the Negro workers became accustomed to the discipline of northern industry. Testimony is general among the employers questioned that it is harder in the first instance to get an efficient force of Negroes than of white workers.[23] The process of assembling such a force commonly requires a high turnover. In Pittsburgh during the war it frequently required a turnover of 300 per cent to keep the steel mills manned with colored workers. But when the Negro group is once assembled, it is about as steady as the white group. Thus the International Harvester Company, which employed 2,093 Negroes in the Chicago district in 1926, had a turnover of 4.6 per cent per month for the Negroes in one of its plants as against 4.8 per cent for the whites, and 5.5 per cent in the other plant as against 4.6 per cent for the whites. The same company, reporting on daily absenteeism among the two races in its two Chicago plants and the foundry in another plant, declared that the average in one plant and in the foundry was about the same, while in the other plant it was much higher among Negroes.

The Chicago By-Products Coke Corporation, according to its labor manager, employed over a thousand Negroes from 1922 through 1925, of whom about 250 were efficient workers.

[23] See reference to experience of the Tennessee Coal & Iron Company below, pp. 246-47.

In February, 1926, the company employed 101 Negroes in a total force of 646. Since 1923 Negro turnover has been no higher than white.

A large foundry in Alliance, Ohio, in the northeastern part of the state, which had been employing Negro labor since 1915, reported a turnover of Negro labor for the six months from February through July, 1926, of 2 per cent. Thirty per cent of the plant's 731 colored employees had been at the works for five years or more. A metal works in Indianapolis reported its Negro labor turnover at 1.4 per cent for a typical month.

A study of Negro labor in Cleveland showed that lay-off among Negro workers was no worse than among European immigrants. Many employers who brought Negro labor North to meet the war-time shortage, the survey found, were, in their eagerness to fill the gaps, far less careful than they would have been in picking local labor. To quote: "Too often the employer has turned to the southern Negro in the hope that he could be pulled out of a tight labor difficulty in this fashion. The result is that the employer puts the newcomer on what might be termed turnover work — work not fitted to the man's training and upon which there would be a constant change of employees under any circumstances." [24]

Yet, seventy-five typical plants in the Cleveland area, employing 32.33 per cent Negroes, showed an average turnover among these employees of 36.67 per cent, making the Negro but slightly more responsible for the shifting of jobs than other classes of workers. It should be remembered that turnover among common laborers and unskilled workers is nearly always higher than in other departments and that it is in these lower branches that the Negro is usually employed.

The following table shows the percentage of Negro employees and the turnover due to colored workers in fifteen typical Cleveland plants: [25]

[24] John B. Abell, "Negro in Industry," *Trade Winds*, March, 1924, p. 18.
[25] United States Bureau of Labor Statistics, *Handbook of Labor Statistics 1924-1926*, p. 401.

TABLE XII

PER CENT OF NEGROES AND PER CENT OF TURNOVER DUE TO
NEGROES IN FIFTEEN TYPICAL PLANTS IN CLEVELAND, 1924

Nature of Plant	Per Cent of Negroes	Per Cent of Total Turnover Due to Negro Workers
Metal Working	50	35
Chemical	15	15
Railroad Labor	40	80
Foundry	50	20
Chemical	25	35
Steel Mill	10	60
Machinery	10	75
Foundry	35	55
Paints	15	20
Castings	25	30
Foundry	25	15
Foundry	30	20
Machinery, Castings	35	10
Foundry	50	20
Foundry	55	60

According to a report of the American Management Association:[26]

It would naturally be expected that Negroes show a high percentage of turnover owing to external and internal conditions. Workmen, otherwise contented, have often to leave because of lack of housing, and, as is generally known, the new worker has the highest percentage turnover. In spite of this the Chicago report indicates no very great difference except where the foreman was actually unfavorable. Mr. D. T. Farmhan found, in 1918, unskilled Negroes had fifty per cent higher turnover than whites, but the percentage was reduced by careful selection. Mr. Eugene Benge records over a period of five months in 1921 a turnover of fourteen and twenty-one per cent for white and colored workers respectively. It is, hence, fairly safe to say that, given intelligent employment methods, the disparity would not be great.

The Chicago report referred to above was that of the

[26] *The Negro in Industry* (Survey Report No. 5, American Management Association, 1923), p. 25.

Commission on Race Relations appointed after the 1919 riots. It declared that of 52 employers expressing an opinion, 24 considered labor turnover of whites and blacks about equal, while 20 considered turnover greater among Negroes.[27]

Many managements have traced high turnover and general unadaptability of Negro workers to hostile or unsympathetic foremen. In several instances supervisory officials have been transferred or discharged for showing race prejudice. Large employers, once they have brought the Negro into their works and made him a permanent element in their labor force, are careful to guard against outbreaks of race hostility. The Pullman Company was obliged to displace the superintendent of its Calumet shops because of his opposition to the company's plan to bring in Negro labor at the time of the railway shopmen's strike. At the South Works of the Illinois Steel Company in Chicago several department heads during the 1921 depression singled out Negroes for lay-off. When the superintendent of labor discovered this, he immediately put a stop to it. In the blast-furnace division, in which the most serious manifestations of prejudice occurred, the assistant superintendent was removed after fourteen or fifteen years of service while the foreman under him was reduced to a common laborer.

Unquestionably, discrimination against Negroes in lay-offs occurs frequently. Yet it occurs with nothing like the frequency that is generally supposed. Employers want a supply of loyal labor upon which they can depend. They use Negro labor now because they need it. When slack times appear and it becomes necessary to cut down forces, employers will hardly be likely to antagonize an important portion of the labor supply upon which they will again have to depend when good times return. Moreover, it is frequently cheaper to keep a class of employees on the pay roll than to release them and later be compelled to hire and train a new force. Yet the epi-

[27] Chicago Commission on Race Relations, *The Negro in Chicago* (1922), p. 377.

gram "the Negro is last hired and first fired" has been repeated so often that it is generally taken on faith. Lay-offs,
however, take place as a rule on the basis of seniority and
station. The common laborers and unskilled workers go off
first and the semi-skilled and skilled workers and supervisors
are moved down in the scale. If the Negroes suffer heavily, it
is usually due to their junior position rather than to race
prejudice. A survey by the Pittsburgh Urban League showed
that during the 1924 depression Negroes were in many instances actually kept on the payroll in larger proportions than
whites. The A. M. Byers Company retained its entire Negro
force, although its output was reduced 60 per cent, by letting
out white workers. In the Clark Mills of the Carnegie Steel
Company 42 per cent of the total force were Negroes during
the peak of production in 1923, as against 56 per cent during
the 1924 slump.[28]

Even in the South where, in accordance with tradition,
white men and black men do different kinds of work, many instances might be cited in which the theory of white and black
jobs breaks down. In the men's clothing factories in New
Orleans whites and blacks do the same work and are paid at
the same rate. When the United States Steel Corporation
came into Birmingham in 1907 it found that, except for miners
and a few handy men about the mines or plants, such as pipe
fitters' helpers, engine tappers, or helpers about the blast furnaces, or blacksmiths' helpers, the Negro in Birmingham industry was used largely for common labor. To-day the company employs Negroes as skilled workers and supervisors. In
the mines they now hold jobs as motorman, blacksmith, mason,
machine runner, lineman, rockman, machinist, pipe man, etc.,
which were formerly considered white men's jobs. Mining as
a whole in Alabama is slowly becoming a Negro occupation.
The white man is also leaving other occupations, such as longshore work at many ports and foundry labor, and the Negro
is taking his place. Between 1910 and 1920 the proportion of
Negro iron molders in Alabama rose from 10 to 24 per cent

[28] John T. Clark, "Negro in Steel," *Opportunity*, March, 1926, p. 87.

of the total. At the same time the white worker is making inroads on jobs formerly held almost entirely by Negroes.

White encroachment on the Negro's practical monopoly of the skilled crafts in the South has been proceeding gradually since the Civil War. At present the railroad brotherhoods are actively engaged in pushing the Negro out of train and yard service. In border cities like Louisville, Kentucky, white folks from the hills are undercutting Negro wages and pushing the blacks out of places in the building trades that they have held for years. Such tendencies are taking place not only in skilled trades but also in such occupations as barbering or personal service in which the Negro has had an almost complete monopoly, yet this displacement has not reduced the number of Negroes in these trades. The growing demand of the Negro group for personal service which the whites refuse to meet has absorbed them.

Though details may change, the fundamental traditional distinction between white men's and black men's jobs remains. In general Negroes and whites in southern plants are engaged in different types of work. Positions of authority, of course, go to the white man. The less attractive and lower paid jobs go to the black man. Instances are common in which Negroes receive lower pay than white men for the same work. Sometimes the differential is applied openly, as it was on the railroads prior to federal control and as it still is in many manufacturing plants. Sometimes it is applied by calling Negroes' jobs by different names. According to the superintendent of a plough factory in Kentucky:

> Negroes do work white men won't do, such as common labor, heavy, hot and dirty work, pouring crucibles, work in the grinding room, and so on. Negroes are employed because they are cheaper. Negro common labor starts at thirty cents an hour and soon gets thirty-five cents, whereas white labor starts at forty-five to fifty cents. On piece work whites make sixty to sixty-five cents an hour. The Negro does a different grade of work and makes about ten cents an hour less.[29]

---

[29] Interview with superintendent of a plough factory in Evansville, Kentucky, April 28, 1929.

It would be hard to find a better summary of the Negro's position in southern industry. That position has its roots in the southern caste system which relegates the Negro to a place of permanent inferiority. The two races must not mix or compete. But if economic pressure does throw them into competition, white southern society seeks to minimize the situation by ranking the white man's job above the Negro's. This, of course, is seldom a conscious operation. The system, the result of long established social habit, works automatically.

As the system operates, the black man digs a ditch. Then the white man steps in and lays the pipes and the black man covers the ditch. The black man cleans the tank and then the white boilermaker comes on and makes the repairs. A white man and a black man work together on a mold. In Chicago, where this happens frequently, both men are called molders and receive a molder's rate. In the South the white man is a molder and the black man a molder's helper. The white man gets about 79 cents an hour and the black man about 40 cents.

The following table of the average wage rates in the foundry industry in the Birmingham district further illustrates the point. The figures, which are as of May 1, 1926, are for a nine-hour day, but in many, if not most cases, wages are paid on an eight-hour basis with time and one half for the ninth hour:

TABLE XIII

AVERAGE RATES FOR WHITE AND NEGRO WORKERS IN THE FOUNDRY INDUSTRY, BIRMINGHAM, ALABAMA, 1926

White			Colored	
Craft	Rate	Calculated Day Rate[a]	Craft	Rate
Machinists	$0.77 per hour	$6.16	Molder's Helpers	$3.60 per day
Molders	0.79	6.32	Clippers	3.60
Pattern			Crane Operators	4.75-5.25
Makers	0.81	6.48	Cupola Tenders	3.85
Blacksmiths	0.81	6.48	Rammers	4.00
Electricians	0.79	6.32	Pit Foremen	4.50
Carpenters	0.75	6.00		
Core Makers	0.79	6.32		5.00
Core Foremen	5.50-6.00 per day		Core Foremen	

[a] On basis of eight-hour day.

It will be noted that white core foremen received from $5.50 to $6.00 a day, whereas colored core foremen received $5.00 a day. There are, of course, Negro molders, machinists, carpenters and blacksmiths, but they are not supposed to work in the same foundries as white craftsmen. If they actually do, in violation of social custom, they are usually classified as helpers.

In the Baton Rouge refinery of the Standard Oil Company of Louisana, which had 1,757 colored employees (one third of its force) in April, 1927, when the following data were obtained, the only job at which both white and black men worked was bricklaying. The rate was $1.25 an hour and the two groups, according to the company, were equally efficient. While black and white men were employed as common labor, the Negroes alone were classified as laborers. The white men were called helpers. The starting rate of pay for the Negro laborers was 31 cents an hour. The rate after a year was 37 cents and after eighteen months 38 cents. The white helpers began at 47 cents an hour and received the maximum of 55 cents after a year. Other Negro jobs were lead burners at 41 cents an hour; kitchen helpers, mostly women, $2 a day and meals; porters, 38 cents an hour; process laborers, 42 cents; pressmen in the parafin works, 51 cents at the start and 61 cents after a year; and grease makers, at 60 cents an hour, whereas a white man, according to the superintendent, would receive about 75 cents for such work.

While all of these jobs were manned exclusively by colored workers, the following jobs were held exclusively by white men: boilermakers' apprentices, 62 cents an hour; boilermakers, 94 cents; welders, 94 cents; pipe fitters, 85 cents; timekeepers' helpers, 47 cents; timekeepers, 80 cents; railroad switchmen and firemen, 77 cents; locomotive engineers, 88 cents. These were the full rates. The initial rates were lower. Welders' rates, for example, began at 61 cents and went up to 94 cents.

Other instances of the disparity in wage rates of white

and colored labor are found in the official figures of the Department of Labor and Industry of the Commonwealth of Virginia. The following table shows the daily rates of pay for white and colored employees in the Virginia building trades: [30]

TABLE XIV

Daily Rates of Pay for White and Colored Employees in Virginia Building Trades, 1928

Occupation	White	Colored
Apprentices	$ 3.37	$2.45
Bricklayers	10.57	8.11
Carpenters	6.02	5.09
Cement Workers	6.99	4.53
Engineers	7.50	6.00
Helpers	3.62	3.29
Hod Carriers	4.70	4.18
Laborers	3.49	3.07
Lathers	4.03	4.66
Painters, etc.	5.73	4.00
Plasterers	9.22	8.11
Plumbers and Gas Fitters	8.24	4.30
Sheet Metal Workers	7.07	6.00

There were no Negro electricians, iron workers, slaters and tile setters, steam fitters, or stone masons. Aside from the lathers, where the rate for Negroes was higher than that for whites, the table shows a substantially higher rate for every class of white worker.

A similar situation prevails in Virginia's manufacturing and other industries. The following table shows the average hourly rate for white and colored wage earners, exclusive of office help, in a number of the state's leading industries.[31]

[30] Report of the Department of Labor and Industry of the State of Virginia, 1928, p. 9.

[31] Figures compiled from Report of the Department of Labor and Industry of the State of Virginia, 1928, pp. 11-69.

TABLE XV

AVERAGE HOURLY RATE, VIRGINIA INDUSTRIES, 1928

Industry	Males		Females	
	White	Colored	White	Colored
Abattoir, Meat Packing	.50	.35	.34	.25
Automobiles, Accessories and Repairs	.42	.32	.37	.25
Bakery Products	.50	.34	.30	.22
Boots and Shoes	.42	.22	.25	.20
Brick and Tile	.42	.31	—	—
Candy, Chewing Gum, etc.	.45	.26	.28	.17
Cannery Products	.36	.23	.23	.22
Cotton Mill Products	.32	.27	.24	.17
Crabs, Oysters, Clams	.43	.31	.25	.25
Creamery and Dairy Products	.39	.33	.24	.23
Fertilizer and Guano	.46	.31	—	.22
Fish Oil and Fish Guano	.43	.40	—	—
Flour and Grist Mills	.32	.26	.38	—
Furniture, etc.	.40	.32	.29	.26
Garments	.59	.34	.28	.16
Knitting Mills	.44	.28	.22	.14
Lime, Cement, Limestone	.35	.30	.35	.36
Laundries	.47	.33	.20	.18
Paper and Pulp Mill Products	.42	.33	.28	.27
Paper Boxes, Bags, Twine	.44	.28	.25	.25
Peanut Cleaning and Coffee Roasting	.51	.27	.24	.14
Public Utilities	.37	.28	.32	.25
Railroad Activities	.60	.46	—	.39
Sash, Doors, Blinds, etc.	.46	.28	.22	—
Saw Mill Products	.30	.23	—	—
Shipbuilding	.72	.46	—	—
Silk Mill Products	.40	.30	.27	.22
Stoves	.62	.28	—	—
Tannery Products	.35	.34	—	—
Tobacco and Its Products	.44	.27	.26	.15
Trunks, Bags, etc.	.34	.29	.28	—
Wood Products	.35	.25	.22	.13
Woolen Mill Products	.36	.39	.24	—

Some of the lesser industries have been omitted from this table, but in all of them, as in all but two cases listed above, the average rate of pay for Negroes was lower than that for whites. The two cases in the above table where the colored rate exceeded the white were females in the lime, cement, and limestone industry and males in the woolen mills. In the former case two Negro women were listed, in the latter, one Negro man.

In the North the Negro, like every new immigrant group, has for the most part gone into unskilled and low paid branches of industry.[32] His earnings are less than those of white men because he generally does different work. Discrimination on the part of employers and foremen, which keeps him on jobs yielding a lower return and which frequently denies him advancement to which he is entitled, of course occurs, but such discrimination is practiced against individuals and races in plants where Negroes have never been employed. There is in the North, as a rule, no discrimination as to wage rates. With few exceptions when a Negro does the same work as a white man he receives the same rate of pay. But where Negroes constitute a large proportion of the personnel of a plant, the general wage scale is frequently lower than where he is but a small minority. A well-known employer in Cleveland who has won high praise from Negro leaders for opening up skilled and technical jobs to colored workers, has made it a practice to employ a high percentage of Negroes. The wages he pays are notoriously low. During a community chest drive a few years ago he remarked that it was right that contributions should be deducted from the wages of his workers because there were more applications for charity from the employees of his plant than from any other factory in the city.

It has not been possible to get very accurate comparative data on the wages of Negro and white workers in northern plants, but the following figures give some indication of the situation. A medium-sized steel foundry in Chicago, employ-

[32] See above, pp. 152-58.

ing 35 Negroes in a total force of 135, reported in 1927 the average weekly wage of its white workers as $37 and of its colored workers as $29. Of the 35 Negroes, but 2 were skilled men, a molder and a ladleman, receiving 75 and 70 cents an hour respectively. Eleven were semi-skilled chippers and grinders, getting 55 cents an hour. The remaining 22 were unskilled laborers at 50 cents an hour. Table XVI shows the average weekly wage in another Chicago foundry, employing 31 Negroes out of a total force of 211.

TABLE XVI

AVERAGE WEEKLY EARNINGS IN A CHICAGO FOUNDRY, 1925-1926

		Skilled Labor		General Labor	
		1925	1926	1925	1926
January	White	33.81	40.57	26.36	38.58
	Colored	33.81	41.33	25.92	42.67
February	White	34.87	39.75	27.64	39.28
	Colored	35.30	40.19	28.00	39.23
March	White	40.31	39.75	43.70	35.28
	Colored	40.25	39.46	40.03	29.61
April	White	37.50	40.71	41.19	26.19
	Colored	37.12	40.07	38.80	34.53
May	White	39.75	41.55	31.30	38.65
	Colored	39.99	40.08	32.79	38.20
June	White	47.03	39.80	27.50	42.75
	Colored	42.21	42.99	29.29	49.64
July	White	47.24	39.43	26.50	40.36
	Colored	42.63	40.50	27.63	22.43
August	White	39.75	39.79	33.36	35.78
	Colored	39.82	40.13	33.38	36.11
September	White	39.00	39.75	33.36	35.78
	Colored	33.82	40.63	33.38	36.11
October	White	39.75	39.50	34.44	43.86
	Colored	40.74	42.01	31.80	43.48
November	White	39.34	40.88	28.50	44.54
	Colored	40.26	43.32	28.50	38.84
December	White	39.00	40.51	29.16	34.17
	Colored	40.85	34.25	35.60	37.66

Although these figures show no differences in earnings attributable to race, certain northern communities where the influence of southern tradition is stronger than in Chicago do have different wage rates for white and Negro labor. Discussing the effects of this practice, John P. Frey, a high official of the International Molders' Union, declared in 1925:

Now, from my personal knowledge, taking the city of Cincinnati to begin with, and the cities of Dayton and Springfield and others . . . the Negro molder receives from 20 per cent to 45 per cent less wages for the same output as the white molders in this state. If you would go with me and talk with the Negro molders who are employed in a foundry in Cincinnati . . . they would tell you that they thought the organization might be a good thing for them, but if they became members of the trade union movement they would immediately lose their jobs.[33]

Variations in wage scales to fit minute classifications of jobs on the basis of complexity and skill often make discrimination against individuals or groups easy. White men are usually assigned to the more exacting and higher paid operations because of a widespread and deep-seated feeling on the part of employers that the Negroes — who once dominated the skilled trades in the South — have certain innate racial characteristics which make them incapable of doing skilled work. The table below of the average hourly wage rates in the Pittsburgh district in 1925 shows a lower scale for colored workers.[34] This is brought about by assigning to the Negro the cruder operations and is no evidence of the kind of wage discrimination practiced in the South. "Where the wage scale is higher, the preference is given to the white worker," according to a study of the position of the Negro worker in Pittsburgh, "but where the same job is concerned, the wages are same." [35]

[33] *Toward Interracial Coöperation* (Proceedings of First Interracial Conference held under auspices of Commission on Church and Race Relations of the Federal Council of Churches and the Commission on Interracial Coöperation, Cincinnati, Ohio, March 25-27, 1925), p. 119.

[34] Ira De A. Reid, *The Negro in the Major Industries and Building Trades of Pittsburgh* (Master's Essay, University of Pittsburgh, 1925), p. 17.

[35] *Ibid.*

TABLE XVII

RATES OF PAY FOR NEGRO AND WHITE WORKERS IN THE METAL
INDUSTRIES, PITTSBURGH, 1925

Occupation	Negro	White
Boilermakers	.70-.90	.70-.90
Chippers	.50 and bonus	.45-.65 and bonus
Core Makers	.60	.60-.90
Grinders	.55	.40-.60
Machinists	.60	.70-.90
Machinists' Helpers	.60	.60
Millwrights	.60-.90	.60-.90
Molders	.60	.75
Polishers	.55	.65
Rolling Mill Hands	.60	.75
Mill Laborers	.40-.50	.40-.50

Instances of the tendency to employ Negroes at the lower
end of the industrial scale could be drawn from almost every
class of employment. It is as pronounced in the laundries and
needle trades of New York as in the metal works of Pennsylvania and the Middle West. The majority of New York's
laundry workers are women and a large majority of these are
colored. Plants rarely employ white and black women at the
same time, but use one race or the other. White and black
workers get the same pay, about 12 or 18 dollars a week.
Median earnings, including the wages of foreladies, were
$14.88 in 1927.[36] The better jobs for men, such as drivers,
markers, and assorters, who make from $30 to $40 a week,
go to whites. The same is true of washers, who are skilled
workers making from $50 to $60 a week. On the other hand,
assistant washers, wringers, and pullers, who make from $20
to $25 a week, are colored.

As in the laundries, most of the colored employees in the
needle trades are women and the overwhelming majority of

[36] State of New York, Department of Labor: *Hours and Earnings of Women
Employed in Power Laundries in New York State* (Special Bulletin No. 153,
Aug. 1927), Pt. IV, especially pp. 26-31.

them are unskilled. Colored needle trades workers are employed principally in the women's dress industry. Men's clothing outside of the South employs practically none. In the
women's industry the Negro is becoming an increasingly important factor. There are probably 2,000 Negroes, mostly
women, employed in the women's dress industry in New York
City alone.[37]

Prior to the dress strike in the winter of 1930, all but a
few hundred of these Negro women worked in non-union shops
at much lower wages and for considerably longer hours than
prevailed in the organized shops. Though by no means alone
in their willingness to work under conditions below the union
standard, they were nevertheless a factor in depressing the
labor market. A group need not be large in order to play such
a part and Negroes have played it frequently even when their
numbers have been few as compared with totals employed in
particular industries or occupations. As an instance, the Negroes outside the South are a small factor in the building
trades, yet they have been able to depress the market here
and there, in Chicago, Pittsburgh, Cleveland, and elsewhere,
to an extent sufficient to cause bitter complaint from the white
unions which commonly bar them from membership. Many
Negroes who came North had been craftsmen in the South,
but found employment in the mills or factories more profitable
than following their trades. But when the demand for mill
and factory labor declined, these colored workers drifted back
into their trades, and their numbers, though small, were sufficient to create an oversupply of certain types of building labor
and to depress established standards, even though no attempt
was made to undercut prevailing rates.[38]

Many employers declare that the industrial labor market
is constantly affected by a temporary shifting of Negroes from

[37] Estimate of Mr. Julius Hochman, general manager, Joint Board, Dress
and Waistmakers' Union, New York. See also Chapter XVI, p. 342.
[38] Interview with officials of the Building Trades' Council, the Elevator
Constructors', Cement Finishers' and Plumbers' Unions, Pittsburgh, July, 1928.

both agriculture and personal service to industry. The shifting in the case of agriculture is of a seasonal character. Colored workers go into the northern factories in the spring and go back home in the fall. It is impossible to determine the volume of such shifting at the present time. Negro labor, dropped during the fall and winter slack, frequently remains in town and becomes a burden upon public relief agencies, returning to industry in the spring when normal production is resumed. But employers who observed the Negro when he first entered industry still believe that this seasonable interchange between farm and factory labor persists. The mills in the Pittsburgh and Chicago districts report that appreciable shifting of this character still occurs. Farther south the seasonal shift becomes more extensive. In factories of southern Ohio, or in works like the Sparrow's Point plant of the Bethlehem Steel Corporation in Maryland, it is said to be a factor of great importance. Undoubtedly such movements were prevalent during and directly after the migrations, but now that the Negro is permanently settled in the North the autumn trip "back home" is becoming a thing of the past. But whether the seasonal lay-off sends the Negro temporarily to the farms or to the city streets, the depressing effect upon the labor market is identical.

The relations of personal service to industry are affected by changes in style which throw colored workers out of jobs and compel them to seek new lines of work. A few years ago the storekeepers on a fashionable shopping street in New York decided to put on a "white front." Colored doormen and elevator men were dismissed and white men put in their places. The same thing happened a few years ago in Chicago, when certain hotels changed from colored waiters to white. Changes of this kind are constantly occurring and, though they do not affect large numbers at a time, the general practice of following styles in the color of servants has its effect upon the market. Conversely, the style of employing colored servants turned two generations of Negroes away from industry and

kept them untrained for industrial life while white men pre-
ëmpted all the jobs.

The most distinctive characteristic of the Negro's position
in the world of labor is his relegation to occupations in which
he does not compete with white workers — in short, the perpetuation of the tradition of black men's and white men's jobs.
This tradition is not confined to the South, but extends
throughout the country. Pullman porters and dining car waiters are almost invariably black, while railroad conductors,
locomotive engineers, subway guards, motormen, sales persons
in stores, clerks and white-collar employees of every sort are
almost without exception white. Certain of the skilled crafts
which Negroes have followed in the South for years are practically barred to the Negro in the North by union regulations
or craft tradition where there is no union.

A complicated and inconsistent set of rationalizations has
grown up to justify the system. The Negro cannot be a locomotive engineer because he is unfit to be entrusted with lives
or property to such an extent. Yet as a slave he ran locomotives
in the South and even carried Confederate troops to the front
to fight for his enslavement. The Negro cannot be a mechanic
because he is naturally incapable of doing skilled work although he followed skilled trades when they required a much
higher degree of artisanship and skill than they do in this
mechanical age. The Negro cannot be a clerk or white collar
worker because these are positions of social dignity which
members of an inferior race should not hold. Yet a number of
cities and the federal government employ Negroes in all
sorts of clerical and administrative posts.

Between 1917 and 1929 the number of Negroes in the
public service of the city of New York increased from 247 to
2,275. While this latter figure included 894 laborers and a
great many messengers and office boys, it also included police,
attendance officers, engineers, clerks, and school teachers.
Many Negro teachers in New York and other northern cities
teach white children. Between 1910 and 1928 the number of

Negroes employed in the federal civil service increased from 22,540 to 51,882, making the United States government by far the largest employer of colored labor in the land. The colored workers on the government's pay roll include in addition to thousands of clerks all sorts of professional, technical, and administrative employees. This growing recognition in the public service is due to the colored citizen's increased political power, a by-product of the northward migration which may in time become a factor of first rate social importance.

All of this shows that the obstacles to Negro employment break down and that the rationalizations which support them go by the board when circumstances make such employment necessary or expedient. Where it is still possible to take advantage of the Negro and pay him less than a white man for the same work or to use him as a tool to keep down labor standards, the practice is followed. But where circumstances make this impossible or inexpedient the Negro receives the same treatment as the white man. Whether the Negro will hold the position in industry which he has won since 1916, whether he will become the victim of new inventions and new methods of production, whether he will withstand or give way under competition of white farmers who move to the towns, or of Mexican, South American, or other immigrants who come into this country, the future alone can tell. All that can be said at present is that the Negro has become an integral part of the labor force in nearly all of the country's basic industries.

CHAPTER IX

THE NEGRO LONGSHOREMAN

THE longshoremen constitute one of the largest industrial groups in the Negro community of nearly every shipping center. In the South the Negro has been in longshore work since the days of slavery. In the North he began to come into the work during the Civil War. In the past twenty years he has been a factor of great importance in the industry in every port from New York to Galveston, as well as in several ports of the Great Lakes.

Work on the water front is hard and has elements of hazard. It is casual and oversupplied. In the sense in which the word "skill" is usually employed it is unskilled, although it does require a degree of special competence which raises it above the level of what is known as common labor. It is a trade which contains most of the elements which make labor unionism difficult. Yet in most of the larger ports, and particularly among the men concerned with deep sea shipping, labor organization is fairly strong and active.

About 30 per cent of the country's longshoremen are Negroes, or, according to the federal census of 1920, 27,337 out of a total of 85,928 persons classified as longshoremen or stevedores. More than 5,000 of these colored workers were employed at the port of New York. In some southern ports like Charleston or Savannah practically the entire force is colored. At the larger southern ports, such as Baltimore, the harbors of the Hampton Roads district, New Orleans, and Galveston, the forces are mixed.

It was among the longshoremen that the first successful Negro labor organizations were formed. In 1867 their union at Charleston, the Longshoremen's Protective Union Association, was referred to in the press as "the most powerful organization of the colored laboring class in South Carolina." [1] Eight years later, in 1875, the union had over eight hundred members and was able to gather five hundred for its parade, which the papers described as "exceedingly creditable, the members being well dressed and a good looking body of men." [2] But this union was no mere dress-parade unit. Even at this time, a decade after the end of the Civil War, it had a long record of vigorously conducted strikes. [3]

During these years similar activity was also going on among the Negro longshoremen of other ports. In 1871 a union was formed in Baltimore which, within a month after its establishment, succeeded in having wages increased from 20 to 25 cents an hour. [4] A year later, in 1872, the longshoremen of New Orleans formed the Longshoremen's Protective Union Benevolent Association, which is still alive and functioning and has the distinction of being the oldest Negro labor union in the country. Up to 1923 it was also one of the strongest.

The importance of the Negro's place in their industry has made it impossible for the longshoremen to ignore him in their organizations. He probably plays a more important rôle in their movement than he does in any other labor union. The International Longshoremen's Association has three Negro vice-presidents and regularly seats several score of Negro delegates at its national convention. Race prejudice and interracial competition have by no means been abolished, but the white and black workers have effected a working arrangement which harmonizes their differences sufficiently to enable them to work together in a single organization.

In New Orleans, where the working arrangement between the two groups has operated with much success, there is an

[1] Charleston *Daily News*, Jan. 5, 7, 9, 1867, also Feb. 25, 1868.
[2] Charleston *News and Courier*, Jan. 26, 1875.
[3] *Ibid.*
[4] Charles H. Wesley, *Negro Labor in the United States*, pp. 184-85.

old tradition of labor solidarity cutting across race lines. Whites and blacks, as elsewhere in the South, have separate unions, but coöperation has been close and effective. As noted in an earlier chapter, one of the most inclusive sympathetic strikes in this country occurred in that city during the eighties, when practically every organized craft quit work because the employers, refusing to deal with "niggers," would not sign an agreement with the colored draymen's union.[5]

Commenting on the success of interracial coöperation in the southern port, the German economist Sartorius von Waltershausen said in 1886, "In New Orleans the unions were able, despite the occasional outbreak of racial antipathy, to harmonize the opposing factors, and have undertaken, through the recognition of black labor, a problem in civilization whose solution they will probably not live to see." [6]

The black and white workers, the latter being mainly Irish, were organized in separate locals. Work was divided between the two races on an equal basis and joint committees of the white and black locals handled matters of common concern. A uniform wage scale was maintained.[7]

During and immediately following the Reconstruction, the greater part of the business of the southern ports was the export of cotton. Each class of labor engaged in the handling of the goods was organized in a separate union. In New Orleans there were eight such groups: the longshoremen who unloaded the cotton on the wharf and put it on the ship; the draymen or teamsters who transported it; the yardmen who unloaded the cotton in the yards and brought it to the warehouse and the cotton press; the cotton classers who classified the cotton according to its quality; the scalehands who put the cotton on the scales and took it off after weighing; the weighers and reweighers who did the actual weighing; the pressmen

---

[5] Report of the United States Industrial Commission (1900), Vol. VII, p. 647.

[6] August Sartorius, Freiherr von Waltershausen, *Die nordamerikanischen Gewerkschaften unter dem Einfluss der fortschreitenden Productionstechnik* (1886), p. 94.

[7] Report of the United States Industrial Commission (1900), Vol. VII, p. 647.

who operated the cotton press; and, finally, the screwmen who stored the cotton in the hold of the ship.[8]

Before the invention of the present high-power cotton press the work of the screwmen required extraordinary dexterity, skill, and strength. For the export of cotton to be profitable, as many bales as possible had to be packed into the hold of the vessel. In the eighties and nineties the bales, even after they had been through the press, were soft and bulky, while the capacity of even the largest vessels was small compared to ships of today. The screwmen screwed the bales down with hand screws to reduce their volume and increase the size of the cargo. In addition to cotton the screwmen stowed tobacco, which also had to be packed carefully in the smallest possible space. The difficulty of their work and the strength and skill which it required made the screwmen the best paid workers in the port. During the eighties they received six to seven dollars for a ten-hour day.[9]

Dock labor in New Orleans as well as in other southern ports had been largely black since the Civil War, but the screwmen, the aristocracy of the port, were an entirely white group and no Negro could stow cotton in New Orleans until the nineties. Yet screwmen who were too lazy to do their own work frequently called on Negro longshoremen to help them heave the screws, and in this way a number of Negroes became initiated into the mysteries of the craft. In the early nineties the white screwmen's union struck and one of the shipping companies mustered a group of Negroes who had learned the trade to do their work. One man who knew the job was put in charge of four green men. In this way the strike was broken and the Negro screwman won his foothold in the port. At the next strike the Negro was in a position to demand half the work in consideration for supporting the strike by refusing to take the white men's places. Out of this situation there grew the black screwmen's union in 1903, and from that date on-

8 Von Waltershausen, *op. cit.*, pp. 142-43.
9 *Ibid.*, p. 144.

ward the black and white screwmen's organizations shared their work on a fifty-fifty basis.

The equal division of work between the white and black unions was the formula which maintained peace between the two races and enabled them to preserve a united front for more than half a century. The formula now operates in every southern port where white and black longshoremen are organized. Like all working principles it by no means operates with full and equal justice. Since the great majority of the longshoremen in the South are colored, there are a great many more black applicants for a job than white. Accordingly, with the work equally divided among the two unions, the white men get much steadier employment than the black and much better than the even break which the agreement aims to preserve. It is common when a ship ties up at the pier for every white man to get work and for a hundred or more Negroes to be turned away. The percentage of Negro dock labor in the South has increased steadily since the beginning of the century. Less than twenty years ago in New Orleans the two races were about evenly divided. At the outbreak of the longshoremen's strike in 1923 New Orleans had 4,400 Negro and 1,400 white longshoremen.[10] Today the proportion of Negroes on the docks is even greater.

The strike of 1923, which seriously interferred with the business of the New Orleans waterfront for many weeks, marked a turning point for unionism. It ended in a disastrous defeat for organized labor, breaking the hold which it had on the port for half a century and nearly ending the career of both the white and colored longshoremen's unions. Prior to the walkout, the Negro longshoremen's union had 1,956 members. The strike brought this number down to 300. Although subsequent gains have brought the membership back to about 1,500, the loss of the strike so thoroughly changed conditions on the waterfront that the union has become comparatively

---

[10] Figures from Mr. A. J. Neeson, superintendent, Cotton Docks, New Orleans, La.

unimportant. Its treasury, which had contained more than fifty thousand dollars, is empty. Its territory, which had included all shipping lines calling at foreign ports, is now confined to the vessels of the United States Shipping Board, or between 25 and 30 per cent of the shipping of the port. The losses of the white union were equally severe. The strike was even more disastrous to the coastwise longshoremen whose organizations were completely destroyed. The colored coastwise union before the strike had about 700 members and twenty thousand dollars in the treasury.

The strike of 1923 was the culmination of a long series of labor disturbances. Leadership in these conflicts was almost without exception in the hands of the white men. This was well illustrated in 1916 when the workers were becoming restive under the pressure of the rising cost of living. One of the points of contention which brought the conflict to a head and resulted in a walkout was a dispute as to how many flour sacks should go on a truck. The Negroes said not a word while the white men were becoming more and more agitated over the question of excessive loads. But when the strike was called under the leadership of the white men, the Negroes all walked out.

Between 1916 and 1923 there were four strikes in New Orleans, all of which resulted either in compromise contracts or defeats for the union. The weakening of the union's position during these years was due to an excess supply of labor. It was the custom when there was insufficient union labor at the pier for the employers to hire such other labor as was standing around. This extra or "rabbit" labor, as it was called, was usually colored, though minorities of whites were also at hand. It was to these "rabbits" that the companies turned for a nucleus of trained labor when their regular men were on strike and it was through "rabbits" that organized labor's hold on the port was broken.

But even before the strike of 1923 broke unionism's hold on the business of the port, organized labor had begun to suffer serious set-backs on the New Orleans docks. Two years before the strike the United Fruit Company broke with the organization and began to hire non-union labor. The next year the Southern Pacific Lines followed suit. This non-union labor was almost entirely colored. The Negro union, seeing that this trained labor together with the "rabbits" would be used against it, opposed the white men's effort to force a strike. It could see no use in striking for higher wages when two of the largest shippers were already getting all the labor they wanted under non-union conditions. But the agitation for higher pay continued. I. W. W. organizers, seeing a fruitful opportunity, became active about the docks and further increased the unrest.

The real force behind the strike agitation was the white screwmen's union. In the old days when a ship carried about 7,000 bales of cotton, it paid to stay in port from ten days to two weeks to get such a cargo screwed in, for the screws increased the capacity of the ship by 15 per cent. But when the modern vessel with capacity for 20,000 bales came along, screws were used less frequently. To screw an entire cargo of this size after the manner of the cargoes of former days would have taken from twenty-five to thirty days and have meant a net loss of from two to three voyages a year. So the general use of screws no longer paid. Cotton was stowed by hand and the screwmen were obliged to use their instruments only upon comparatively rare occasions. The invention of the high-density cotton press shortly before the World War made the use of screws altogether unnecessary. This machine reduced the "standard bale" of cotton from 29 cubic feet to 17 cubic feet.

But despite the fact that the modern ship and the modern cotton press made his work unneccessary, the screwman stayed on and his union continued to claim the sole right to stow cotton or tobacco. No longshoreman, whether a union man or not, could put a single bale of cotton or a single hogshead of tobacco into the hold of a ship. That was the screwman's exclusive right.

The continuance of this arrangement, after all reason for its existence had ceased, was a constant source of irritation and expense to the shipping companies. Frequently, when longshoremen were at work on one kind of cargo and it became necessary to stow cotton or tobacco, the longshoremen would have to be called off and a new group of workers put in their places. Or, if it became necessary to put a load of staves or other small cargo between the tobacco or in broken places between the cotton bales which the screwmen were stowing, longshoremen would have to be called in to do the work. There were always plenty of longshoremen at hand, but screwmen were often scarce. It was expensive to keep them at hand on the pier to step in when needed, for, once hired, they had to be paid even if they were not working. Consequently the foremen or stevedores only assembled gangs when they needed them, and not infrequently inability to muster a gang of screwmen resulted in long delays in the final dispatch of the vessel. In addition, the screwmen, under their 1921 contract with the companies, were paid piece rates which varied according to the position of the stowage.[11] There were twenty different rates and there were always contests concerning them.

When the Southern Pacific Lines broke with the union, the screwmen began to see the writing on the wall. Their jobs and their privileges were threatened, for they well knew that companies hiring non-union labor would not continue to observe the meaningless distinction between screwmen and longshoremen. In a final effort to save their jobs they began their strike agitation in the summer of 1923, believing that the winning of the strike would give them a new lease of life. The group primarily responsible for this agitation were the so-called "double headers," screwmen who held membership in

11 Agreement between United States Shipping Board and Screwmen's Benevolent Association, Local 412 and Local 237, International Longshoremen's Association, 1921, pp. 2-3.

the longshoremen's union so that they might have work during the seasons when no cotton or tobacco was stowed. This "double heading" was a common practice among members of both races, but it was the white group which was the active agitating force. A large measure of the confidence of this group during the strike agitation lay in its close relations with the political machine which controlled the New Orleans city government and also exercised great influence in state affairs. Von Waltershausen commented upon the dockmen's political power as long ago as 1886, ascribing it principally to the fact that the majority of the white workers were Irish, "who, as is well known, have a particular aptitude for demonstrations, agitations and conspiracies and, because of their common racial, national and religious sentiments, stand or fall together as a man." [12] Irish domination of the active faction was undiminished in 1923.

The demands of the union were for increased pay and shorter hours. They asked eighty cents per hour and time and one half after eight hours instead of the existing arrangement of sixty cents per hour and time and one half after nine hours. When the ship owners refused these demands, a joint union meeting was called. A white official in sympathy with the screwmen was in the chair. The Negro union opposed a strike as dangerous and inopportune. A vote was taken and most of the Negroes as well as many whites voted not to strike. Many present at the meeting declared that the motion was lost. But the chair ruled otherwise. [13] A strike was proclaimed and the white and black unionists all walked out.

Strike breakers were used freely; the "rabbits," Southern Pacific and United Fruit Company labor, forming the nucleus around which green workers were organized. A very large portion, if not an actual majority, of these strike breakers were

[12] Von Waltershausen, *op. cit.*, pp. 146-47.

[13] Interviews with the president, ex-treasurer and other officials and members of the Colored Longshoremen's Union, March, 1927; also with the white president and secretary of the New Orleans Trades and Labor Council.

white. Many of the Negro strike breakers were the sons or relatives of the strikers.[14] Though the strike seriously interfered with the business of the port for a number of weeks, its failure was apparent from the very beginning. The I. W. W., which had been most successful in organizing both white and black lumber workers in southern Louisiana, was unable to attract longshoremen despite its activity along the docks and its appeal to solidarity. The Negro workers who were promised full equality and equal treatment were as cool as the whites. The old A. F. of L. organization, in spite of its shortcomings, had been too effective to give the radical organization a foundation upon which to build.

Yet the Negro dock worker at New Orleans had a real grievance against the white worker, for in spite of the seeming equality guaranteed him in the agreements under which he worked, the white man insisted on pinning a badge of inferiority upon him. A tradition handed down from old sailing-ship days, when the white man refused to work alongside of the Negro, forbids the latter to work wherever he wants on the ship. As the price of accepting the Negro as a co-worker, the white man declared that the black man would have to work where he did not want to. He created different positions on the vessel for the two races, taking the side of the ship next to the wharf for himself and assigning the side away from the wharf to the Negro. Although this form of Jim Crowism worked no actual hardship, it was an indication of the absence of real labor solidarity. Far more important is the fact that the foremen who hired labor and who were themselves members of the white union and were supposed to divide the work equally between the two races seldom gave the Negro his due. A white man who served the Leland Line for many years as timekeeper declared that in not a single year of his service did the Negro gangs check out equally with the white gangs. The difference, and this official declared that this was applicable to other lines as well as his own, amounted to from two to three

[14] Interview with Dr. Evans, former timekeeper of the Leland Lines.

days' labor and frequently more during the year.[15] The easy jobs invariably went to the white men. It was common, too, in order to speed up the work, to play one group against another, to tell the white men on the starboard side of the ship that the blacks were doing all the work and to tell the black men on the port side that the whites were doing all the work. Each side was suspicious enough of the other to be ready to accept such taunts at their face value.

Despite all this, the I. W. W. plea for real labor solidarity fell flat. However, five years earlier, in 1916, a similar plea to dock workers in Baltimore met with hearty response. Negro labor had always been employed in this port. It will be remembered that it was here among the longshoremen that one of the first successful Negro trade unions was formed.[16] But it was not until 1900 that the Negro came to be a factor of first rate importance. That year the German workers, the largest group in the port, led a strike against Sunday work. One of the firms involved imported a body of Negroes from its docks at Norfolk, and used them to check the walkout. From then on the number of Negro longshoremen increased. Many of the stevedores preferred them to white workers because "you can tell them what to do and they'll do it." [17]

In 1912 the International Longshoremen's Association began to organize Baltimore. The Negro was organized as a matter of course. A number of unions were formed, but the Negroes were concentrated in two mixed locals known as Numbers 826 and 829. Before very long a disagreement between the white and black members of the latter body, which contained most of the Negroes, led to a split. The black members withdrew and asked the International for a separate charter. This was opposed by the white members who claimed that the Negroes were not entitled to a charter which read like their own, but only to a charter as "dock men." If the International

[15] Interview with Dr. Evans, former timekeeper of the Leland Lines.

[16] See above, p. 183.

[17] This opinion was expressed by those who handled Negro labor at every southern port.

had accepted this contention, it would have made it practically impossible for the Negro to get work, since there is very little "dock work" to do. The white men lost their case and the Negroes received a regular charter, authorizing them to handle all freight on ships and docks. The new local thus chartered has but one white member.

There are two places in Baltimore where the union's efforts to organize have failed completely. These are the coastwise companies and the piers of the Baltimore and Ohio and the Pennsylvania Railroads. Together, these unorganized docks employ about 1,000 men. Negroes first came to work on the Baltimore and Ohio and the Pennsylvania piers in 1916 when they were brought in to break a strike. Prior to that time no black man could get work at these docks. The Negroes who work there today feel that the white unions were responsible for this discrimination and therefore cannot be approached on the question of union affiliation.

For years prior to the 1916 strike, the all-white railroad piers were a source of deep dissatisfaction to the black workers and served to keep many Negroes lukewarm toward the International Longshoremen's Association. So when the Marine Transport Workers of the I. W. W. entered Baltimore in 1916 with their plea of labor solidarity, they quickly won a sympathetic response and within a year had 1,400 Negroes paying dues to their organization. But the war and the government's opposition soon put an end to the I. W. W's activities. It was no match for the International Longshoremen's Association, which had active government support. I. W. W. strength ebbed as quickly as it had risen, and today the International Longshoremen's Association is in complete control of the organized forces in the port. It has five locals; two mixed, one colored, and two white. In April, 1929, it had a membership of about 2,200, of whom 1,116 were Negroes.[18]

The Negro longshoremen of Baltimore strongly resent the discrimination practiced against their race by the white unions.

[18] Interview with J. F. Barry, secretary of Local 858, I. L. A.

The colored longshoremen's local showed its feeling by refusing to affiliate with the Baltimore Central Trades and Labor Council, where colored delegates were segregated at meetings. Though this particular controversy was patched up, the
Negro union leaders still make strong mental reservations in
their support of the A. F. of L. The secretary of the Baltimore Negro longshoremen declared that he found it distaste-
ful to support the union label when Negroes could not get into
scores of organizations. Once, he said, he actually found it
necessary to defy organized labor in order to employ Negro
bricklayers and carpenters to remodel the longshoremen's offices.[19]

The local labor movement's attitude toward the Negro
has strengthened the hostility of the local Negro leadership
to all union labor. The fact that Negroes play a prominent
and important part in the longshoremen's organization has in
no way lessened this feeling. Yet the movement in Baltimore
has not had to contend with the same type of open hostility as
that which met Negro longshoremen in the Hampton Roads
district. There, attempts of the longshoremen to bring the
shipyard workers into their organization were blocked by the
Negro Y. M. C. A. secretary, who admitted that both his
salary and the chief support of his "Y" came from the Newport News shipyard. This secretary serves as the yard's labor
agent. Through his influence over the hiring and firing of
Negro employees he wields tremendous power over the entire
colored labor force. And he exercises this power despite the
fact that the company has appointed a Negro and white committee to handle the men's grievances. He has fought the
union with every means in his power. He denied it the right
to meet in his "Y." He attacked the white unionists' motives,
opposing the organization of whites and blacks in the same
union because, he said, the white unionist never wants the
black man unless he is in trouble.[20]

[19] *Ibid.*
[20] Interview with Secretary Williams of the Newport News Negro Y. M.
C. A., April, 1929.

A few years later, in 1921, the Negro coal trimmers at Hampton organized as a local of the International Longshoremen's Association, struck for higher wages. Their efforts were opposed by all of the most influential local Negro leaders and particularly by the Negro preacher. In this atmosphere the shipping board found no difficulty in importing strike breakers, both black and white. In spite of this the union won out in the end, for after about four weeks, the effort to break the strike was abandoned and the old men were restored to their places at the rates they had demanded.

As this indicates, the colored longshoremen in the Hampton Roads district, which includes Newport News, Norfolk and Hampton, have organized successfully in spite of the most serious opposition. Unions organized under the wing of the old Knights of Labor flourished at Newport News as far back as the nineties. In 1910 the Negro longshoremen of Norfolk formed the Transportation Workers' Association of Virginia. For five years or more this group functioned as a local fraternal society, paying little attention to economic problems. It was never able to achieve recognition or to enter into contracts with the employers. Finally, during the World War, it ceased to function as an independent body and became part of the International Longshoremen's Association. The absorption came about as a result of the decision of the United States Shipping Board, giving the Association complete jurisdiction in the port.

In 1914 the coal trimmers, a craft under the longshoremen's jurisdiction, formed a union and demanded relief from such intolerable working conditions as twelve-hour days without sufficient time off for food for several days at a stretch, and pay at the rate of twenty-five cents per hour. The union had hardly begun to function when its president, George Millner, who later became third vice-president of the International Longshoremen's Association, was discharged for his activities. When his reinstatement was refused, the coal trimmers struck and stayed out until he was restored to his position. Within a short time the coal trimmers received several increases in pay and finally obtained a written contract from their employers.

The Coal Trimmers' Union was chartered by the A. F. of L. as a federal labor union. It was absorbed by the International Longshoremen's Association after the Shipping Board's war-time ruling. At this time the general longshoremen's union in the International Longshoremen's Association at Newport News had no Negro members. The Negroes, instead of attempting to get into the regular body, formed an independent local of their own which came into the International in 1917 along with the Transportation Workers' Association and other independents in the district. As a result of the government's support, the International Longshoremen's Association was able, during the war, to organize the entire Hampton Roads waterfront of between eight and nine thousand men. Fully six thousand of these were Negroes. After the war union strength declined rapidly. Between three and four thousand Negroes employed on coastwise ships dropped out of the organization. They were followed before long by the dumpers on the railroad piers. Today, of about six thousand men employed in the district, 2,200 are organized. Of approximately 4,000 unorganized workers, about 500 are white and 3,500 black. Of the organized workers about 200 are white and about 2,000 colored.

The colored worker thus dominates union affairs in the district. Of the nine locals seven are black and two white. There are no mixed locals due, first, to the strength of the southern tradition of racial separation and, second, to the preference of the Negroes themselves for their own organizations. They feel that they can control these themselves through officials of their own race without the necessity of sharing power with the whites.[21] The Negroes now have twenty-one of the twenty-seven representatives on the Hampton Roads Longshoremen's

[21] Interview with George Millner, 3d vice president of the International Longshoremen's Association. See also Chapter IV, pp. 72-73.

District Council, while the whites have only six. Representation is on the basis of three from each union. The president of the Council is a Negro. The members of the arbitration committee, which handles all matters affecting the longshoremen, white and black, are all Negroes.

Yet it would be a grave mistake to assume that race distinctions have been swept away. Separation between the white and black locals in the various activities, and the distinctions between the black and white man's place at work are almost as hard and fast as in any southern community. Working gangs are mixed only on the very rarest occasions, while the custom of maintaining separate places on the ship for white and black men, the former usually working on the top deck and the latter below, is almost universally observed. There are Negroes employed in supervisory capacities, such as timekeepers, paymasters, and foremen. Checkers and weighers, however, are always white.

Institutionalized racial distinctions of this kind are not found in the northern ports, though restrictions and barriers which deny the Negro equal treatment are prevalent. The Negro came into longshore work in the North before the Civil War. He was brought in for the most part as a strike breaker or as an instrument to divide and weaken white workers. His use for such purposes was so extensive that his presence came generally to be resented, even when his employment was altogether innocent of anti-organization designs. This resentment was frequently so bitter as to result in riot and bloodshed. Such a riot broke out in New York in 1855 when Negroes were used to break a water front strike.[22] The situation was repeated in Buffalo in the summer of 1863 when the boss stevedores tried to fill the places of former white workers with Negroes and provoked a serious fight in which twelve black men were badly beaten, while one was killed in the fighting and two were drowned.[23] The predominant longshore group

[22] Charles H. Wesley, *Negro Labor in the United States*, pp. 79-80.
[23] *Fincher's Trades' Review*, July 11, 1863.

of the day was the Irish, who were then seldom employed at anything but the cheapest common labor and, accordingly, resented competition in new and better kinds of work in which they were just gaining a foothold.[24] Riots almost as serious as that in Buffalo were reported in Chicago, Detroit, Cleveland, Albany, New York, Brooklyn, and Boston when Negro strike breakers, brought in to take the places of Irish strikers, were greeted by floods of bricks, stones, and broken bottles. During the spring of 1863 rioting between the two races along the New York water front was frequent, and injury and death often resulted.[25]

In June of that year, shortly before the trouble in Buffalo, three thousand Irish longshoremen in New York lost a strike for higher wages largely because of the introduction of black labor under police protection. A month later these defeated Irish longshoremen led the draft riots in an attempt to resist forced military service in behalf of Negroes whom they feared and hated as their industrial rivals.[26]

Despite indications and the fears of the Irish, the Negro failed to gain a prominent place in longshore work at this time. In fact, his rôle along the water front in New York and the North generally became less and less important, while the Irish held their own. They continued to dominate the trade down to 1887 when the shipping companies in New York turned to Italians to break the "big strike," led by the Knights of Labor.[27] Several lines also used Negro strike breakers on this occasion, but let most of them go when their old men returned.[28] Six years later, in an extensive strike in Brooklyn, Italians and Negroes brought from the South were again used as strike breakers,[29] but it was the former, who had been be-

[24] See Chapter I, pp. 12-13.

[25] E. D. Fite, *Social and Industrial Conditions in the North during the Civil War* (1910), pp. 189-90.

[26] *Ibid.*, p. 190. See also De A. S. Alexander, *Political History of the State of New York* (1906), Vol. III, p. 68.

[27] Charles B. Barnes, *The Longshoremen* (1915), p. 8.

[28] *Ibid.*, pp. 8-9.

coming an increasingly important factor in the industry for the past six years, who really broke the strike.[30] Fights and brawls between the Irish strikers and Italian scabs took place all along the water front. At times the situation became so serious as to require the calling of police reserves. Soon the strike took on an interracial aspect and became a fight against the Italians. Every Italian who came near the water front, even though he had nothing whatever to do with the strike, was in danger of attack. The fruit vendors and peanut men who used to ply their trades along the docks dared not show themselves. In one instance, according to the newspapers, an Irishman who was mistaken for an Italian "because he wore a sloven hat" was chased for blocks and pounded before he could explain.[31] Apparently, it is not the Negroes alone who have suffered as a group because some of its members have taken the places of men on strike.

Negroes first got a permanent footing on the New York docks in 1895 when the Ward Line used them to break a local strike. For some years after the strike this company used Negroes exclusively.[32] Today, with about half its force colored, this company still uses Negro labor more extensively than any other line in the port. Strikes in 1899 and 1907 further strengthened the Negro's position on the New York water front, while the labor shortage incident to the World War finally made him a factor of major importance.

The Negro's presence in the port is now accepted by the white man. He has a right to be there; he has a right to work; he has a right to belong to the union. Yet he is by no means regarded as an equal. "We are in the union today," said a Negro union official, "because the white man had to take us in for his own protection. Outside the organization the Negro could scab on the white man. Inside he can't. In return for

[29] Mary White Ovington, "The Negro in the Trade Unions of New York," *Annals of the American Academy*, Vol. 27, May, 1906, p. 555.

[30] *New York Tribune*, August 24, 1893.

[31] *Ibid.*, August 25, 1893.

[32] Barnes, *op. cit.*, p. 9.

this we get a share of work, the protection of the union contract and organization support." [33]

There are many piers in New York which refuse to employ Negroes. Most piers which do employ Negroes work four or five Negro gangs along with eighteen or twenty white gangs. The Ward Line, as already mentioned, is an outstanding exception, employing approximately half white and half black labor. During the war the Negroes who had previously enjoyed an even larger share of the work on this line objected to the company's policy and a race riot was barely averted.[34] Some companies have tried to use black labor as a club against their white workers. The stevedore of the French Line once planned to use Negro longshoremen to break the control of the white group on his pier, but his men, by going over his head and protesting directly to the company, forced him to abandon his plan. Since then the white group on the French Line has been more strongly entrenched than ever. Stevedores, like many employers, frequently become accustomed to employing labor belonging to particular racial groups. Thus the Kerr Line in New York employs only Italians. Other lines prefer Irish or Hungarians or Slovaks, and will take workers from these groups if they are available. Frequently, when Negroes unable to get work on certain piers lay the fact to race prejudice they are really suffering from such prejudice no more than groups of white workers who do not happen to belong to the nationality to which the stevedore has become accustomed.

Another factor making it difficult for Negroes to work at certain docks is the system of hiring labor. This is done largely through a class of job brokers called gang handlers. In most instances the gangs gathered become permanent organizations held together by bonds of personal loyalty between group and leader. Each is dependent upon the other. No outsider, black or white, can get into a gang without com-

[33] Interview with an official of the Negro Local at Brooklyn, N. Y.

[34] Franklin Frazier, *Negro Longshoremen* (1921). (MS in library of the Russell Sage Foundation.)

mon consent. Any gang leader who obtained jobs for men outside of his group would be considered guilty of an unpardonable breech of loyalty which, under the strong-arm methods
of the longshoremen, might well be punished by death. There
are Negro gang handlers as well as white, and a Negro outside
of a particular gang is just as much an outsider as a white man.

Yet there have been instances of race prejudice on the part
of both employers and employees, operating very crudely and
openly. Negroes complain bitterly that the best jobs generally
go to the white men. If there is unpleasant work to do, such
as handling ore or dirty goods, the Negro is likely to get the
job. If there are two jobs open, one to last a week and another
two days, the white man would get the long job. Negro union
leaders claim that the white longshoreman gets much steadier
employment than his colored brother and consequently makes
much more money. This seems altogether likely, although
there are no statistics available to substantiate the Negroes'
claims.[35]

A flagrant instance of race prejudice occurred a few years
ago when white members of the longshoremen's unions in
Brooklyn formed an unofficial committee which went from
pier to pier asking the stevedores to give preference to white
labor. Officially the union frowned on this. The longshoremen's organization prides itself on the position of official
equality which the Negro enjoys in its ranks and resents having the spectre of race prejudice drawn from its closet. When
the president of a colored local in New York reported discrimination against Negroes in the district to the international
convention of 1919 at Galveston, Texas, the white union officials on their return to New York refused to have anything to
do with him.[36] Ten years after this incident the Negro longshoremen of New York were complaining of discrimination as
bitterly as ever. Their militant tactics having failed, they now
turned to conciliation. In February, 1929, the Negro local

[35] Interviews with Negro and white longshoremen at the port of New York.
[36] Frazier, *op. cit.*

gave a dinner in honor of the international officers. They set
forth their complaints at length and appealed to the white
man's sense of justice. But the position of the Negro at the
port remained unchanged.

Negroes in the New York district are free to belong to
any local they choose, and they commonly join a union near
their home or near the pier where they most frequently work.
There is, however, a Negro local, Number 968, situated in
Brooklyn, with Negro officers and a Negro membership which
fluctuates between six and eight hundred. The local also has a
white membership of from eighty to a hundred and twenty-
five. This leaves two thousand or more union Negroes in the
port who are scattered through the various locals under the
control of the whites.

Race and nationality play a very large part in the organization arrangements of the New York longshoremen. There
are so-called Irish locals, Italian locals, Hungarian locals, in
fact locals of almost every national or racial group that plays
an important rôle in the longshore work of the port. Yet all
of these groups in turn contain many other racial minorities.
They are, like the Negro union in Brooklyn, purely social in
their origin. There are no "Jim Crow" locals in the port.
During the war there were two other Negro locals which have
since disappeared, and there has recently been an attempt to
form a new colored union in Port Newark, where many Negroes are employed. The leaders of the Negro longshoremen
in New York, like the leaders at Hampton Roads, prefer to
have the members of their race join their own locals because
it gives them direct representation and power and influence
in both district and international councils which they would
not have if they remained minorities scattered in various white
unions.[37] There was a Negro union in New York, Branch 6,
when the dock workers were organized in the Longshoremen's
Union Protective Association, the L. U. P. A., before the
International Longshoremen's Association began to function

[37] See above, Chapter IV, pp. 72-73.

in the port. The Italians were the first racial group in the new International Association to have separate unions,[38] and the tendency continued as the members of new national groups came into the trade and joined the union movement.

Sometimes racial and national issues which have nothing to do with industrial relations have been raised among the workers of the port. In the fall of 1920 a group of Irish longshoremen backed up a demand for the release of Mayor Terence McSweeny of Cork by refusing to work on British vessels. Two hundred and fifty Negroes employed on the docks affected joined in the strike.[39] Now this might well be interpreted as a demonstration of conscious labor solidarity, and to some of the Negroes who joined the strike it undoubtedly was just that. The large majority, however, struck because there was a general walkout on their docks. The International Longshoremen's Association opposed this strike as a violation of the union contract, but the union's authority was remote, so far as the colored strikers were concerned, when compared to sympathy with and loyalty to the group with which they constantly worked.

There has been a tendency among the Negro dock workers in New York, which they share with other minority groups, to follow the leadership dominant in the locality in which they work. Dual and secession movements were common occurrences in the port in the years immediately following the end of the World War. In 1919 a man named Vacarelli, who was defeated for the vice-presidency of the International Association, withdrew from the latter and organized the Waterfront Workers' Union. The new body's chief strength was among the Italian locals, a number of which seceded from the I. L. A. Negroes in the locality, in general, went along with the secessionists. Two years later, in 1921, the International Association was forced to accept a severe reduction of wages and a lengthening of hours. A forty-four-hour week became a forty-

[38] Barnes, *op. cit.*, pp. 124-25.
[39] *Messenger*, Oct., 1920, p. 102.

eight-hour week, and the wage scale was reduced from a range of 80 cents to $1.20 an hour to a range of 65 cents to $1.00 an hour. A strong minority led by a man named Butler who had been president of the Longshoremen's Union Protective Association (the L. U. P. A.) before its absorption by the International Longshoremen's Association, fought the concession. Butler had opposed T. V. O'Connor for president of the International in 1917 and was defeated. In 1921 he capitalized the discontent growing out of the wage reduction and joined hands with Vacarelli and other discontented leaders and formed the United Cargo Workers. Again most of the Negroes in the section affected joined the movement, but — as in the earlier Vacarelli movement — the great body of colored workers, like the majority of white workers, remained loyal to the International Longshoremen's Association.

During these secession movements, during the war, and for many years before the war, the I. W. W. was active in New York. Though it gained some strength among the Italian workers in Brooklyn and among various groups in Hoboken, it was unable, despite its attacks on race discrimination and its plea for industrial brotherhood, to attract any appreciable following among the colored workers. This was due partly to the Negro's lack of interest in the I. W. W.'s revolutionary theories, and partly to the fact that the mass of workers in the sections where the Negroes were employed also failed to respond to the movement.

Yet in Philadelphia, where the majority of the dock workers are Negroes, the I. W. W. controlled the port for more than seven years. It rose to power during a strike in May, 1913, and maintained its position throughout the war despite the efforts of the International Longshoremen's Association with government backing to win away its following. In 1920 a series of ill advised strikes forced by the Communists who were trying to gain control of the I. W. W. finally ended the latter's career in Philadelphia. In this manner the International Longshoremen's Association finally gained the control of the port which it had been unable to wrest from its rival when the latter was strong and united. The relations of the Philadelphia longshoremen to the I. W. W. will be treated below in Chapter XV. It is sufficient to say here that the tradition of labor solidarity and racial equality which it established at the port has been carried on unchanged by the International Longshoremen's Association.

CHAPTER X

THE NEGRO IN THE COAL MINES

THE early history of the Negro coal miner is an integral part of the expansion of the bituminous coal industry in the southern fields of West Virginia, Virginia, Kentucky, Tennessee, and Alabama. While it is true that Negroes were employed sporadically in Illinois and Indiana and in the northern Appalachian region, Pennsylvania and Ohio, in the early eighties and nineties during labor difficulties, few of them have found permanent employment in these sections until very recently. Even today the greatest number of Negro miners is found in the rich southern Appalachian fields, Alabama and West Virginia.

When the United States Coal Commission made its report in 1923, there were 147,456 anthracite and 525,152 bituminous miners in the country. Of this total of 672,608 coal miners, 42,489 were Negroes. In other words, in 1923, a little over 6.3 per cent of the total number of coal miners in the United States were Negroes, few of whom were engaged in the mining of anthracite. In fact only 46 Negroes were employed in the whole anthracite industry. (See Table XVIII.)

TABLE XVIII [a]

MINE WORKERS IN ANTHRACITE AND BITUMINOUS FIELDS
CLASSIFIED BY RACE AND NATIONALITY

Race and Nationality	Anthracite Mines	Bituminous Mines	Total
U. S. White	69,645	310,719	380,364
U. S. Colored	46	42,443	42,489
Foreign Born	77,765	171,990	249,755
Total	147,456	525,152	672,608

[a] Adapted from the Report of the United States Coal Commission (1923), Pt. 3, pp. 1419-22.

The negligible number of Negroes in the anthracite region is due to the economic features and geographic location of the industry. The anthracite coal area is compact and covers a small territory which is much more urbanized than the bituminous coal area.[1] In the adjacent urban communities are industries that compete with the anthracite coal mines for a labor supply, and in periods of slackened production of anthracite coal some of the redundant labor finds employment in near-by establishments. Consequently there is not as much shifting in the anthracite mining population as in bituminous, nor as frequent occasion to recruit labor from distant localities. Other reasons for the small number of Negroes engaged in the anthracite industry are the earlier development of anthracite as compared with bituminous fields and the greater difficulty in mining anthracite coal, which necessitates greater skill and a longer apprenticeship. When anthracite mining was first developed in the United States the skilled workers were the experienced British miners, while the native white Americans, and, later, the non-English-speaking whites comprised the unskilled. As the industry expanded and immigration of British workers to the United States fell off sharply, both the native American and the non-English-speaking whites broke into the ranks of the skilled. But neither the cessation of British immigration nor the moving of the native American and non-English-speaking whites into the ranks of the skilled has necessitated the acceleration of the amount of Negro labor used in anthracite coal mining, since, until the passage of the Immigration Act of 1924, additional increments of labor could always be obtained from southern Europe. Moreover, the anthracite industry is not an expanding one like bituminous coal mining, where instability in production and a relatively slight degree of technological and managerial improvements make continual additions to the labor force necessary. In fact, the increased mechanization of bituminous coal mining resulting in the lowering of older skill requirements; the rapid expan-

[1] See the Report of the United States Coal Commission, Pt. 3, p. 1414.

sion of bituminous coal mining since the nineties of the past century; the negligible rôle that immigrant labor seems destined to play in future American industrial development; the proximity of the richest deposits of bituminous coal to the centers of Negro population; and the ease with which Negro labor, because of limited industrial opportunity and low economic standards, can be used in labor difficulties are the combination of causes back of the increase of Negroes in the bituminous industry.

In the bituminous mining areas, 42,443, or 8.1 per cent of all labor employed, are Negroes. Until about ten years ago, the Negro miners were concentrated in Alabama and West Virginia, and especially in the southern mines of West Virginia. In 1920, 43 per cent of all Negroes employed in bituminous mining were found in West Virginia, and 16.1 per cent in Alabama, while only 5.3 per cent were employed in Pennsylvania, 2.1 per cent in Ohio, 4.3 in Illinois, and 27.6 per cent scattered throughout the rest of the bituminous states.[2] In West Virginia the Negro constituted almost 20 per cent of all miners in the state in 1923. In Alabama 52.7

TABLE XIX[a]

BITUMINOUS MINE WORKERS BY STATES, CLASSIFIED BY RACE AND NATIONALITY, NUMBER AND PER CENT

State	Native Born White		Foreign Born White		Negro		Total All Nationalities	
	No.	Per Cent	No.	Per Cent	No.	Per Cent	No.	Per Cent
Penn............	68,843	43.2	88,387	55.4	2,288	1.4	159,512	100.00
West Va.........	55,491	·60.1	18,490	20.0	18,376	19.9	92,357	100.00
Illinois............	47,836	59.3	30,857	38.3	1,927	2.4	80,614	100.00
Ohio.............	32,322	67.6	14,606	30.5	902	1.9	47,830	100.00
Indiana...........	19,947	81.1	4,252	17.3	384	1.6	24,583	100.00
Alabama.........	5,667	43.7	469	3.6	6,843	52.7	12,979	100.00
Other States.....	80,613	75.2	14,941	13.9	11,723	10.9	102,277	100.00
U. S..............	310,719	59.2	171,990	32.7	42,443	8.1	525,152	100.00

[a] Adapted from the Report of the United States Coal Commission (1923), Pt. 3, pp. 1419-22.

[2] The other bituminous states are Colorado, Iowa, Kansas, Kentucky, Maryland, Michigan, Missouri, Oklahoma, Tennessee, Virginia, and Wyoming.

per cent were Negroes. But in none of the other leading bituminous states was the number of Negro miners more than 2.5 per cent of the total.

The development of the northern Appalachian region was in the hands of British immigrants. But as newer fields developed, occasioning the migration of these older stocks, and as the native white Americans moved up into the ranks of the skilled, southern and eastern European labor was employed. The increased employment of immigrants from southern and eastern Europe in the mines of Pennsylvania became especially noticeable in the eighties (see Table XX, below) when the movement of English, Scotch, Welsh, and Irish from Pennsylvania to the Middle West and to the Southwestern fields of Kansas and Oklahoma began.[3] This movement occurred during the disturbances in Ohio and Pennsylvania, where the Miners' National Association had reached the apex of its development. This organization in 1875 had 347 lodges, with

TABLE XX [a]
RACIAL DISPLACEMENT IN THE COAL INDUSTRY

Year	Nationality of Workers	Pennsylvania	Ohio	Indiana	Illinois	West Virginia
1870	All Workers [b]	41,997	12,501	1,109	6,954	1,525
	South Europe	121	50	2	43	4
1880	All Workers [b]	103,917	16,331	4,469	16,301	4,497
	Other Countries (Non-English Speaking)	2,037	356	100	604	25
1890	All Workers (Anthracite)	124,203	—	—	—	—
	Slav & Italian (Anthracite)	31,202	—	—	—	—
	All Workers (Bituminous)	53,712	19,591	6,532	24,323	9,952
	Slav & Italian (Bituminous)	26,806	2,509	87	6,095	151
1901	All Workers (Anthracite)	141,780	—	—	—	—
	Slav & Italian (Anthracite)	67,118	—	—	—	—
	All Workers (Bituminous)	111,229	25,963	10,593	46,005	23,914
	Slav, Italian & Rumanian (Bituminous)	86,855	8,243	378	14,249	1,792

[a] Arthur E. Suffern, *Conciliation and Arbitration in the Coal Industry of America*, p. 36.   [b] Bituminous and Anthracite.

[3] Report of United States Commission on Immigration, Vol. 6, Pt. 1, p. 22.

a total membership of 35,355. In Pennsylvania there were 20,840 members; in Illinois, 5,122, and in Ohio, 4,734.[4] The frequent labor disturbances arising in the eighties and nineties over the miners' attempts to organize were met by the operators with imported Negro labor.

On March 17, 1880, miners from Ohio and Pennsylvania held a conference at Pittsburgh and demanded payment by weight, fortnightly payment of wages, the eight-hour day, and the abolition of the company store. The operators were given until August 1 to grant the demands. But the operators refused and the miners were forced to carry out their threat of striking.[5] The Hocking Valley miners of Ohio abandoned the struggle, but the Tuscarawas Valley miners held out for nine months, when they were finally forced to capitulate before the tide of southern Negro labor imported by the operators under military protection.[6] At about the same time a strike at one of the mines in the Pittsburgh district was combated with 50 Negroes imported from Virginia. After 1882 the policy of bringing southern Negro labor into the Pittsburgh district was continually resorted to by the operators during labor shortages, especially as a means of combating unionism and strikes.[7]

After the formation of the United Mine Workers in 1890, the work of organizing took on a more serious aspect. Between 1890 and 1896 the Southwest field was organized, but the request for recognition of the union met the stern opposition of four large companies termed the "Big Four," which operated mines in Arkansas, Oklahoma, and Kansas. Immediately upon the calling of the strike, the "Big Four" companies, following the policy of importing southern Negro labor which they had inaugurated in earlier labor disputes in Oklahoma and Arkansas, sounded a call for Negro labor for their

[4] Arthur E. Suffern, *op. cit.*, pp. 50-51.
[5] *Ibid.*, p. 20.
[6] *Ibid.*
[7] Report of the United States Industrial Commission (1901), Vol. 12, p. cxlix.

Kansas mines. Handbills were circulated in Birmingham, Alabama, which read:

Wanted! Colored coal-miners for Weir City, Kan., district, the paradise for colored people. Ninety-seven cents per ton September 1 to March 1; 87½ cents per ton March 1 to September 1, for screened coal over seven-eighths inch opening. Special train will leave Birmingham the 13th. Transportation advanced. Get ready and go to the land of promise.

Colored Coal Miners Wanted for Weir City district, Kansas. Coal 3 feet 10 inches high. Since issue of first circular, price paid for mining has been advanced to one dollar per ton in winter and ninety cents in summer, for lump coal screened over seven-eighths inch screen. Pay-day, twice a month, in cash. Transportation will not exceed ten dollars, which will be advanced. Special train leaves Birmingham Tuesday night, June 13. Leave your name at Kansas City railway office, 1714 Morris Avenue.

The first importation induced by the circulars numbered about 175 Negroes. They were brought in by the Western Coal and Mining Company over the Missouri Pacific Railroad. The striking white miners met the Negroes when they were being unloaded at a stockade at Fleming Camp. They explained the situation, with the result that 125 of the new workers refused to go into the stockade. The Negroes had had no previous knowledge of the strike. Some were willing to join the strikers when the union gave assurance of support, but most of the first importation received transportation back to their homes.[8] Further interference with these importations was restrained when the coal companies obtained a federal injunction against the union. After this the importation of Negroes continued.[9] Out of this struggle at least one Negro character, Milton Reed, emerged to play an important part in organizing the Negroes who had been imported by the West-

[8] *Coal Miners' Strike in Crawford and Cherokee Counties*, Fourteenth Annual Report of the Kansas Bureau of Labor and Industrial Statistics (1898), pp. 338-39.

[9] Suffern, *op. cit.*, pp. 50-51. Also, see George McNeill, *The Labor Movement* (1887), p. 260.

ern Coal Company and the Central Coal and Coke Company
to break the strike.[10]

When the 1897 general strike occurred, the Illinois operators threatened to use Chinese labor. This was opposed by
the governor of the state. As an alternative the operators
erected stockades about the mines and Negroes were brought
in from Alabama. Governor Tanner also refused to sanction
this, taking the view that many of the Negroes were probably
criminals who had learned their trade under the convict-labor
system in the South. The governor ordered out the militia
with instructions to prohibit the disembarkation of the Negroes.[11] Shortly afterwards the importation of southern Negroes again occurred at Virden and Pana, Illinois. The appearance of Negroes at Virden precipitated a clash between
the striking miners and the armed guards, resulting in the
death of nine miners and ten guards. The colored miners escaped to the mines. At Pana a riot between the white and
Negro miners was fomented when an armed group of the
recently imported Negroes attempted to prohibit the exodus
of a part of their number who, under the influence of the
miners' union, attempted to leave the scene.[12]

In Western Pennsylvania the H. C. Frick Coal and Coke
Company imported southern Negro coal miners as early as
1892. Three years later the same company, because of labor
disputes, employed more Negroes.[13] The introduction of Negroes into the coke fields by the Frick Company was a further
extension of the practice of using Negro labor in times of
stress which was inaugurated somewhat earlier by coal operators in the Pittsburgh Coal district. Yet almost three decades
passed before Negro labor, aside from sporadic importations,

[10] "In Praise of Milton Reed, Negro Organizer," *United Mine Workers'
Journal*, July 25, 1901, p. 1.

[11] Suffern, *op. cit.*, pp. 47-48.

[12] Report of the United States Industrial Commission, Vol. 12, pp. 38-39
and 51-52.

[13] Gerald Allen, *The Negro Coal Miner in Western Pennsylvania* (Master's
Essay, University of Pittsburgh, 1927).

played any considerable rôle in mining Pennsylvania coal. As late as 1920 there were hardly more than 3,000 Negro miners in Pennsylvania.[14] The inconsequential increase in this state was largely confined to the Connellsville coke section until the labor disputes which followed closely upon the World War, and again in 1922, 1925, and 1927.

The number of Negro miners in the Far West, and likewise in Ohio, Illinois, Indiana, and the Southwest has never been large. According to the testimony of two witnesses before the United States Industrial Commission, the Colorado Fuel and Iron Company, operating coal mines in Colorado and a number of iron mines and coke ovens in other western states, imported about 2,000 Negroes under contract from the southern states between 1890 and 1896.[15] When the testimony of the secretary of the corporation was taken, he stated that at that time, out of their 7,500 employees, 500 were colored miners and laborers in the steel plants.[16] But these importations did not continue. At one time it was rumored that 3,000 Negroes were being imported into the anthracite region of Pennsylvania where they had never been employed.[17] Later it was also reported that the importation of Negro miners was threatening trouble in Winnipeg, Canada.[18] For some reason the rumored importations never materialized.

In the initial development of the bituminous areas in the southern states, Negroes and native whites were principally used. But after the nineties, when the industry expanded more rapidly in Alabama, West Virginia, Kentucky, Tennessee, and Virginia, foreign white labor was used to supplement that of the native white and the Negro. Some idea of the rapidity of

[14] See Table XIX.

[15] Testimony of Harry E. Lee, commissioner of mines, Colorado, and James T. Smith, deputy commissioner of labor before the United States Industrial Commission, Report, 1901, Vol. 12, pp. 222 and 248.

[16] Testimony of D. C. Beaman, secretary and attorney of Colorado Fuel and Iron Company before the United States Industrial Commission, Report, 1901, Vol. 12, p. 281.

[17] *Crisis*, December, 1911, p. 55.

[18] *Ibid.*, January, 1912, p. 96.

the expansion of the bituminous industry in these states from
1890 to 1908 is gained from the statistics of production of the
period. In 1908 the annual production of bituminous coal in
West Virginia was six times greater than it was in 1890. During the same period the yearly output was trebled in Alabama.
In Kentucky, Virginia, and Tennessee combined, it was increased
fivefold.[19] This remarkable expansion increased the demand
for labor, and when the supply of native white and Negro
labor proved inadequate, or too indolent to meet productive
requirements, foreign labor was imported. Tables XXI and
XXII indicate the extent to which the development of the
southern bituminous fields rested upon the Negro and native
white labor. Although the presence of immigrants from Great
Britain and Germany was noticeable in West Virginia and
Alabama before 1890, the great bulk of labor continued to be
supplied by Negroes and native whites. But by 1900 the expansion in West Virginia necessitated an increase of immigrant
miners not only from Great Britain and Germany, but from
the eastern and southern European countries as well. A similar increase in miners of European birth was characteristic of
the Alabama mines after 1900. In this same period the Virginia fields, which had from the outset employed almost exclusively native whites and imported southern Negroes, began
displacing these with Austro-Hungarians, Italians, and Poles.[20]
These tendencies became more striking in the period from
1900 to 1907 when a further expansion took place in the
southern fields, causing the employment of more immigrants
from southern and eastern Europe. Sometimes this foreign
labor was used to supplement the native white and Negro, as
in West Virginia and Alabama, while at other times it displaced some of the native white and Negro labor, as in Virginia. Tennessee and Kentucky alone of the southern coal
states continued to rely almost exclusively upon Negro and
native white labor.[21]

[19] Report of the United States Commission on Immigration, Vol. 6, pp. 21-22.
[20] Ibid., Vol. 6, pp. 23-24.   [21] Ibid., Vol. 7, pp. 136-37.

TABLE XXI [a]

DISTRIBUTION OF MINERS BY RACE AND NATIVITY IN SOUTHERN
COAL STATES, 1890 AND 1900

State and Year	Native White Native Parents	Native White Foreign Parents	Foreign White	Colored Native and Foreign
Alabama				
1890	2,487	300	1,492	3,687
1900	5,984	606	1,573	9,735
Kentucky				
1890	3,165	369	581	976
1900	6,135	487	471	2,206
Tennessee				
1890	3,439	181	500	769
1900	7,223	265	310	3,092
Virginia				
1890	1,811	38	375	1,700
1900	4,150	89	479	2,651
West Virginia				
1890	5,523	791	1,375	2,016
1900	12,028	1,181	2,968	4,620

[a] Adapted from the Report of the United States Commission on Immigration, Vol. 7, p. 136.

TABLE XXII [a]

NEGRO COAL MINE OPERATIVES, 1920 AND 1910, AND NEGRO MINE
AND QUARRY OPERATIVES, 1900 AND 1890

State	Miners	Quarrymen	Miners and Quarrymen	Coal Mine Operatives	
	1890 [b]		1900	1910	1920
Alabama	3,687	369	9,735	11,189	14,097
Illinois	566	—	1,368	1,512	2,194
Indiana	172	13	399	376	614
Kentucky	976	—	2,206	3,888	7,407
Ohio	578	42	780	1,004	1,389
Pennsylvania	849	206	1,616	1,773	2,930
Tennessee	769	482	3,092	1,609	913
Virginia	1,700	527	2,651	1,719	2,450
West Virginia	2,016	—	4,620	11,237	17,799

[a] Compiled Jan. 31, 1929, by Leon E. Truesdell, chief statistician for population, Bureau of Census, United States Department of Commerce.

[b] Persons of Negro descent, Chinese, Japanese, and civilized Indians; but almost exclusively Negro.

West Virginia, which has some of the richest deposits of bituminous coal in the world, has been of importance as a coal-producing state since its formation in 1863. But the industry's most striking growth began about 1893. In 1863 the state produced 444,648 short tons of coal, while in 1893 it produced 10,708,578 short tons. This increase has continued down to the present and the state has competed in markets long considered the natural outlet for the coal mined in the central competitive field.[22] In 1907 the state produced 48,091,583 short tons,[33] and in 1926, 144,603,574.[24]

The state of West Virginia is divided into four territories, each possessing varying characteristics as to output, quality of coal, developmental age, and labor supply. The southern part of the state contains two important districts, viz., the New River-Kanawha and Pocahontas. The former includes Nicholas, Putnam, and Raleigh Counties. The counties that make up the Pocahontas district are McDowell, Mercer, Mingo, and Logan. The Elk Garden and Fairmont districts constitute the northern sector. The former is made up of Tucker, Mineral, and Grant Counties, and the adjoining Fairmont district contains the counties of Barbour, Harrison, Marion, Monongolia, Preston, and Taylor.

The development of coal mining in West Virginia first began in the southern territory, in Fayette and Kanawha Counties of the New River district, and in McDowell County of the Pocahontas district. This development began in an important way, almost simultaneously with the construction of the Chesapeake and Ohio Railway. And in 1876 Negroes were brought into the New River-Kanawha district from Virginia. By 1886 there were probably more than 1,000 Negroes in the coal fields of Fayette County.[25] The Pocahontas field

---

[22] The central competitive field embraces western Pennsylvania, Illinois, Indiana, Ohio, and northern West Virginia.

[23] Report of the United States Commission on Immigration, Vol. 7, pp. 144-45.

[24] West Virginia Department of Mines, Annual Report (1926), p. 106.

[25] Files of the West Virginia Bureau of Negro Welfare and Statistics, Courtesy of T. E. Hill, director of the bureau.

was not developed until the construction of the Norfolk and Western Railway in 1882. The first mines were operated at Pocahontas, Virginia, and just over the line on the West Virginia side. When the mines opened, Negroes from the agricultural sections of Virginia and North Carolina entered the field. Very soon the operators began sending out agents to induce more Negroes to come.[26] Shortly after the Pocahontas district opened, the Mill Creek Coal and Coke Company opened a mine at Coopers, in Mercer County. From the beginning of its development until 1895 Negroes constituted more than 90 per cent of all employees at the mine.[27]

From the earliest period of bituminous coal development in West Virginia until more recent times, when an unprecedented expansion has been witnessed, Negro labor has been steadily employed. In the Pocahontas district, where 19,438 miners were employed in 1908, 6,738 or 34.7 per cent were Negroes. In McDowell County of this district, there were 11,487 miners employed in 1908. Almost 5,000 or 43.1 per cent of these were Negroes. Although the mines in the New River-Kanawha district never employed as many as the Pocahontas field, Negro miners constituted 21 per cent of the total number of miners in the district in 1908.[28] Table XXIII shows the number of Negro miners as well as native white and foreign born in both the northern and southern districts in 1923, 1925, and 1926.

In the northern part of the state, in the Fairmont and Elk Garden districts, the Negro miners have increased in numbers only since about 1917. When the mines in these districts were first opened, native whites from the immediate vicinity supplied the labor. As production expanded, the operators attempted to introduce Negroes. In 1892 two carloads of Negroes were brought in from North Carolina, South Carolina, and Virginia. These did not prove satisfactory. Italian

26 Report of the United States Commission on Immigration, Vol. 7, p. 156.
27 Hill, *op. cit.*
28 Report of United States Commission on Immigration, Vol. 7, pp. 156-59.

TABLE XXIII [a]

DISTRIBUTION OF MINERS BY RACE AND NATIONALITY IN SOUTHERN
AND NORTHERN WEST VIGRINIA 1923, 1925 AND 1926

	1923		1925		1926	
	Number	*Per Cent*	*Number*	*Per Cent*	*Number*	*Per Cent*
SOUTHERN TERRITORY:						
Pocahontas District						
American (Native) White..	21,101	54.9	22,230	55.1	23,680	55.7
Other Nationalities...............	8,123	21.2	6,832	16.9	6,885	16.2
Negro...	9,162	23.9	11,276	28.0	11,982	28.1
All Miners.............................	38,386	100.0	40,338	100.0	42,547	100.0
New River-Kanawha District						
American (Native) White..	21,527	64.9	19,243	63.7	21,319	66.0
Other Nationalities...............	3,813	11.5	3,113	10.3	3,332	10.3
Negro...	7,835	23.6	7,844	26.0	7,648	23.7
All Miners.............................	33,175	100.0	30,200	100.0	32,299	100.0
NORTHERN TERRITORY:						
Fairmont District						
American (Native) White..	16,702	55.1	14,829	61.9	17,148	60.9
Other Nationalities...............	11,425	37.7	6,536	27.3	7,637	27.1
Negro...	2,192	7.2	2,590	10.8	3,356	11.9
All Miners.............................	30,319	100.0	23,955	100.0	28,141	100.0
Elk Garden District						
American (Native) White..	1,450	68.5	1,102	71.8	1,184	71.7
Other Nationalities...............	619	29.3	388	25.3	437	26.5
Negro...	46	2.2	45	2.9	30	1.8
All Miners.............................	2,115	100.0	1,535	100.0	1,651	100.0

[a] Compiled from West Virginia Department of Mines Annual Reports.

labor was next tried. During 1893 and 1894 many Italians
were secured from New York. Later about 200 Slavs and
Poles were brought in from New York through labor agencies.[29] Thus in 1910 Negro miners were only 3.4 per cent of
the operatives in the Elk Garden and Fairmont districts, while
the American white and the Italian workers were 52.5 per
cent and 18.6 per cent, respectively. Although the numbers of
Negro miners in these two districts are still numerically small
in proportion to the total mining population, they have gradually increased since the World War. In 1923 Negro miners

[29] Report of the United States Immigration Commission, Vol. 7, pp. 145-47.

were 9 per cent and in 1926, 12 per cent of the total number of miners employed in these sections of the state. This is an increase of about 51 per cent in three years. In these years the native whites have not increased as rapidly as the Negro. They have, however, maintained their numbers rather consistently. On the other hand, the number of foreign miners has shown a decided falling off, as is shown in Table XXIII. The first appreciable increase in Negro miners in northern West Virginia came in 1918, when several hundred left the mines in the southern counties of the state to obtain work in the northern counties where some of the operators had entered into wage agreements with the United Mine Workers. Many were brought in from Alabama.[30] And with the occurrence of the 1919 strike in Alabama, others who thought it unsafe to remain in the Alabama mines, because of a long history of trade-union activity including the disastrous 1908 strike of which the Negro unionists were the backbone, now migrated to the Fairmount and Panhandle sections of West Virginia, and to the neighboring mines of Ohio.[31] But the greatest increase of Negro miners in the northern part of the state came with the 1925 strike. A large proportion were natives of Alabama, Mississippi, South Carolina, and Virginia, who entered the northern end of the state by way of western Pennsylvania where, following the restriction of immigration and the labor disputes in the coal mining and steel industries, they had been employed in large numbers. Others that came in the 1925 strike were floaters who, like birds of prey, flock to the scene of any labor disturbance in the hope of earning easy money without expenditure of legitimate effort.[32]

The racial antipathies which had already existed in north-

[30] Files of the West Virginia Bureau of Negro Welfare and Statistics. Courtesy of Hill.

[31] Interview with Joseph Smith, president, Local of United Mine Workers, Stewartville, Ohio.

[32] Abram L. Harris, "The Strike of 1925 in Northern West Virginia," *Annual Report of the West Virginia Bureau of Negro Welfare and Statistics,* 1925-1926, pp. 29, 30, 36.

ern West Virginia as the result of the introduction of a medley
of nationalities were intensified with the importation and increased employment of Negro miners. These animosities,
which had largely originated in Europe, when combined with
the problem of American white-Negro relations made the
union vulnerable to any disposition of the operators to play
one race against the other. Many of the operators, proceeding
upon the theory of *divide et impera*, inaugurated the practice
of mixing the different races.[33] These conditions have given
to the history of the miners' unions in this section a large degree of uncertainty, forcing the union to go over old territory
and organize the newcomers as they displaced the older organized miners.[34] The confusion of nationalities in the northern
tier of counties was far worse than in the southern part
of the state. But the United Mine Workers' attempts to
organize the southern counties have not only failed to bring
about permanence in organization; they have encountered the
bitter opposition of the southern coal operators, often ending
in bloodshed and violence, after which the union was driven
out. The failure of the union to gain permanence in the southern districts can not, of course, be attributed to mere employer
opposition. Nor should it be explained wholly on the basis of
race prejudice between white and black miners, despite the
great importance of this factor. Aside from the industrial and
geological features which give southern West Virginia a competitive advantage over the older unionized central competitive field, one of the chief causes of the ineffectiveness and instability of the miners' union here has been the ease with which
the operators have been able to import redundant Negro labor
from the neighboring states of Virginia, Tennessee, and Kentucky, and from Alabama and other southern states. The existence of such a store of labor in the southern communities has

[33] *Report of the United States Commission on Immigration,* Vol. 7, p. 147.
Also *Labor Relations in Fairmount, West Virginia,* United States Dept. of
Labor, Bulletin No. 361, July, 1924, p. 4.
[34] John L. Lewis, *The Miners' Fight for American Standards* (1925),
pp. 85-86.

given to the operators in West Virginia, and in practically every other mining section of the country, an industrial reserve army which may be used either to defeat the purposes of unionism or to meet an increased demand for labor caused by the expansion of the industry.

It is not easy to generalize about the extent to which employers prefer labor from one race rather than that from some other. If the present examination of labor in the coal industry offers an analogy for other industries, it seems that employers will use that proximate and available supply of labor the productive efficiency [35] of which they estimate to be highest for the industry. As has already been pointed out, the early development of the coal fields in the northern and middle western states fell to the lot of the English-speaking immigrants and the native white Americans. Strikes and the early attempts of these classes to form unions, coupled with the increased demand for coal paralleling the country's industrial expansion in other lines, stimulated the importation and increased employment of Italians, Hungarians, Poles, Slavs, and Magyars. In the early period Negroes, when used, were employed as strike breakers. The failure of northern coal operators to employ Negro labor continuously in the developmental period of the industry, and their hesitancy to import it more frequently and in larger quantity during labor disorders was due to their preference for eastern and southern European immigrants.[36] The latter could easily be procured from the eastern seaboard cities if sufficient numbers failed to come into the mining areas voluntarily. It was also due, perhaps, to the operators' reluctance to recruit labor from a race that was then, to a greater degree than it is now, assumed to be shiftless and inefficient. Sometimes even when there is slight doubt about the Negro work-

[35] Productive efficiency is used here in the sense of general satisfaction to the employer and not in the purely technical or economic sense of effectiveness in material output.

[36] It is doubtful that the foreign immigrants' standard of living was lower than that of the southern agricultural Negro, or that the former was really more efficient as a worker. The employer's preference was determined by race.

er's efficiency, other considerations enter to render him unsatisfactory. That these other considerations do condition the employers' willingness to hire Negroes was amply demonstrated in the hearings conducted by the Senate Committee that investigated the 1927 coal strike. The following is the verbatim testimony of Mr. F. D. Welsh, superintendent of the Clearfield Bituminous Coal Corporation, before the Committee:

SENATOR WHEELER: While the clerk is getting the pay rolls, let me ask you this: As Superintendent of the mine do you find that you can get as efficient help at the present time as you could under organized labor?

MR. WELSH: We have done so. As a matter of fact, our labor has been improving, and it is almost entirely from right here in Pennsylvania, and they are experienced and practical miners.

SENATOR WHEELER: Are they colored or white?

MR. WELSH: They are entirely white. We have never employed colored men. We have drawn the line at Mexicans and Spaniards and people of that class.

SENATOR WHEELER: You do not feel that the Mexicans and colored are as efficient miners as white men?

MR. WELSH: Colored men are very efficient miners in many cases, but it makes a very undesirable element in the community. We take great pride in our schools, and take great pride in our churches, notwithstanding what has been said about this injunction, and we contribute to them. We contributed $22,000 to a school building in addition to our contribution by way of taxes. We do not want to bring in colored men and undesirable people and decrease the standing of the community, and particularly the schools.

SENATOR WHEELER: And you feel that the bringing in of colored labor in any community has a demoralizing effect?

MR. WELSH: I do.

SENATOR WHEELER: Upon the community as a whole?

MR. WELSH: I do, and I would not do it.

SENATOR WHEELER: Is it not a fact that it lowers the standard of morality of the people as a whole to bring in a large number of colored people?

MR. WELSH: I have not had any actual experience and have never employed them, but from what I have observed in other places I think that is the result.

SENATOR WAGNER: Their way of living, their accommodations, the way they sleep and live generally make a great deal of difference in the matter of the morality of the people.

MR. WELSH: You are entirely right.[37]

But strong as traditional racial attitudes involving the American Negro may be, they seem quite flexible when employers are faced with labor shortage or strikes and so-called union agitation. Impelling necessity seems to transform reluctance to employ Negroes into complete satisfaction with their labor in an emergency. To use the language of a Colorado coal operator who never employed Negro labor until the strikes of the nineties: "... They are in general quite satisfactory, fully as much so as correspondingly unskilled white labor. They are less given to strikes and not so subject to agitation and are fully equal to white labor in endurance and steadiness of work. The present turbulence among the white laborers will have a tendency to increase the number of colored ones wherever it exists." [38] This statement we shall find to be very much like those recently made by some of the operators concerning the Negro labor employed by them in the 1927 coal strike.[39] And it should be borne in mind that not only was Negro labor used along with native white labor in the early development of coal mining in West Virginia, Tennessee, and Kentucky, but that it played an historic rôle in the strikes that occurred in these states in the late nineties and the early 1900's. When the Hopkins County, Kentucky, strike occurred in 1900, various companies transported Negroes from the southern states to man the mines.[40] Similarly the 1902 strike in the New River-

[37] Hearings before the Committee on Interstate Commerce, United States Senate, 70th Congress, 1st Session (S. Res. 105), 1928, Pt. 2, p. 294.

[38] Beaman before the United States Industrial Commission, *op. cit.*, p. 281.

[39] On the efficiency of the Negro miner during 1927 strike, see testimony of Horace Baker, Pittsburgh Terminal Coal Company, Hearing sub-committee, United States Senate, *op. cit.*, p. 2769.

[40] United Mine Workers of America, *Minutes of the Thirteenth Annual Convention* (1902), pp. 38-39.

Kanawha Field, West Virginia, which synchronized with the great anthracite strike, led to the importation of Negroes from Virginia, North Carolina, and South Carolina.[41] The storm of protest that the importation of Negro strikers into Tennessee, West Virginia, and Kentucky provoked in these years is indicative of the extent of its effect upon the labor movement in these states. One of the protests [42] was directed to "Our Colored Fellow-Men." It read:

Those colored workmen who, in case of a strike or any other labor trouble, take the places of white workmen, make a mistake. It is foul play. They ought to be ashamed of themselves. They are guilty of a dirty trick. They are mean, dishonorable and perfidious. They do a wrong to all labor. They raise prejudice against their own race. They bring themselves into contempt. . . . We say these things because of the efforts that have recently been made to use colored men as "strike breakers." Within a year, numbers of them have been railroaded from the South to the North as labor mercenaries, and several capitalists threaten to hire thousands of them in case the white wage workers make trouble. In two or three Western states, attempts have been made to use them against the coal miners, and in other places, to turn them to account in the skilled industries, as in the steel works at Chicago, Pittsburgh and elsewhere. Large numbers of colored men in the Southern States are now learning all the trades, not only in workshops, but in training schools, and plenty of them would like to get jobs in the North. . . . They are ready to cut under their white competitors, ready to take small wages, to work as many hours as they can, to live in a scrubby manner, and to promise that they will never, never go on a strike against their masters. . . . With a horde of these darkies, and another horde of Chinese, in the Northern states, there would be a great time for the boss of the billion dollar trust, which holds steel works, coal pits, railroads, iron mines, real estate, and lots of ships, as well as the fat Schwab. . . . Let the colored men be warned in time. It would be bad for them, bad for the community, bad for all labor, and particularly bad, in the long run, for the capitalists, the trusts, and the billion dollar gangs. Be sure of that. This is a country where all

[41] Report of United States Commission on Immigration, Vol. 7, p. 151.
[42] *United Mine Workers' Journal*, October 3, 1901, p. 5. Also, *Ibid.*, Aug. 25, 1892, p. 3; Sept. 29, 1892, p. 8; and May 2, 1901.

human rights have not yet been destroyed. . . . We give notice, there-fore, to our colored fellow-men, whose welfare can never be promoted by injuring other people, don't try to cut under white workers. Don't let anybody use you as strike breakers. Don't live as mere tools.

The employment of the Negro industrial reserve was strikingly revealed by the 1925 strike in northern West Virginia, and the recent but more general strike of 1927. The following table compiled from interviews [43] with mine superintendents and union officials shows the number of Negroes employed at 24 mines before and during the strike of 1925 in northern West Virginia. At the time the investigation was made, 24 mines formerly operating upon a union basis in Harrison, Marion, and Monongolia Counties were employing almost a thousand Negro miners, while prior to the strike these mines had not employed over five hundred. If our investigation of the strike had included the mines at Lowesville and Everettsville, it is probable that the total would have been found to be around 1,500 for twenty-six mines. If the total number of Negroes employed by the mines investigated is any indication of the number employed by operators elsewhere in the district, the 1925 strike gave rise to a tremendous increase in the employment of Negroes in the northern counties. This conclusion is substantiated by the Bureau of Mines Reports for 1923, 1925, and 1926. In 1923 there were not more than 2,600 Negro miners in the whole Fairmont district, but three years later there were 3,356. (See Table XXIV.)

The oustanding features of the facts presented in the following table are that the number of Negroes employed during the strike was over twice as great as it had been previously, and that Negro labor was 32 per cent, excluding two uninvestigated mines, of all labor employed during the strike, while it was less than 7 per cent in the normal times that preceded it. Many of these new Negro miners had migrated North in 1920, and some of them, because of industrial depression in bordering industrial sections, drifted into West Virginia. And even if

[43] See Abram L. Harris, *op. cit.*

TABLE XXIV

Comparative Estimates of Negro Labor Employed before and during Strike of 1925 in Northern West Virginia

Name of Company	Name of Mine	County	Total Number, All Miners		Total Number, Negroes		Status of Mine Prior to Strike
			Prior to Strike	During Strike	Prior to Strike	During Strike	
Fairmont Cleveland Coal. New Eng. Fuel and Transportation Co.	Parkers Run / Federal No. 1 (Grant Town)	Marion	400	125	Did not employ Negroes	30	Union
Consolidated Coal Co.	Consolidation No. 97	Marion	600	500	50 / Not on Strike	225	Union
Bethlehem Mines Corp.	Dakota No. 42	Marion	150	150	25	25	Union
Consolidated Coal Co.	Ida May	Marion	300	200	200	95	Union
Jamison Coal and Coke Company	Jamison No. 8	Marion	450	Closed temp.	20	Closed temp.	Union
	Jamison No. 9	Marion	400	125	10	30	
Bethlehem Mines Corp.	Bethlehem No. 41[a]	Marion	350	200	9[b]	50	Union
Fairmount-Chicago Coal.	Chesapeake	Marion	475	150	30	75	Union
Hutchison Coal Co.	Erie No. 2	Harrison	150	47	30	6	Union
Dawson Coal Co.	Dawson	Harrison	85	40	7	3	Union
Elkhorn Coal Corp.	Elkhorn No. 52	Harrison	250	140	12	50	Union
Despard Fuel Co.	Despard	Harrison	150	116	3	2	Union
Howard-Guthrey	Snake Hill	Harrison		60		30	Union
Clarke Coal & Coke Co.	Pitcairn	Harrison	115	80	22	20	Union
Clarke Coal Co.	Eagle	Harrison	100	84		12	Union
Hitchman Coal Co.	Hitchman	Marshall	250	250		22	Union
Sheeling Steel Co.	Beachbottom	Brooke	150	No Negroes[c]	No Negroes[c]	No Negroes[c]	Non-Union
West Va. Pittsburgh Coal	Locust Grove	Brooke	300	75	5	125	Non-Union
Brady Warner Coal Corp.	Osage Nos. 1 and 2	Monongolia	200	175		100	—
Chaplin Collieries Co.	Virginia-Louisa	Monongolia	160	No Negroes[c]		No Negroes[c]	—
Connellsville By-Prod. Co.	By-Pro. No. 1	Monongolia	450	No Negroes[c]	No Negroes[c]	No Negroes[c]	—
Sopher Mitchell Coal Co.	Berry / Jere	Monongolia	400	140	20	12	Union
Total			5,885	2,657	443	912	

[a] Information supplied by union officials.

[b] Sometimes about 20.

[c] Mine did not employ Negroes.

these Negroes had been experienced union miners, many of them would have been unable to secure employment at some of these mines in normal times. Where the non-employment of Negroes occurred, prior to the strike, it seemed attributable in some instances to the desire of management to keep out recent immigrant workers and Negroes, and in other instances to the refusal of white workers, especially of native Americans, to work with Negroes.[44] But it was difficult to ascertain which of these two attitudes determined the non-employment, or to discover the degree to which employers, under the influence of current racial attitudes, assumed that the employment of Negroes with whites would produce conflict and thus disturb production. Whenever the fact of the non-employment of Negroes was placed before the operators, it was in most instances attributed by them to the white workers' hostility to the Negro. And whenever it was presented to the striking white workers, it was attributed to the operators' refusal to hire Negroes. For example, white union miners pointed out that the Paisley interests had consistently refused to hire Negro miners before the strike of 1925, but that when the strike occurred, this company had filled its mines with Negro workers, informing them that they had not previously been employed because of the white workers' hostility to them. The local union officials contended that prior to the strike the union had adopted resolutions requesting the employment of Negro union miners, but that their committees could never gain an audience with the mine officials. Similar experiences were cited by Mr. Van Bittner, chief representative of the United Mine Workers in West Virginia, who said that Negro union miners had actually been sent to jobs, but were given poor equipment or broken machines to work with, causing the Negroes to become discouraged and to quit.[45] All of the responsibility for the Negro's inability to obtain employment

[44] See *Labor Relations in Fairmount, West Virginia*, United States Department of Labor, Bulletin No. 361, July, 1924.

[45] See Abram L. Harris, *op. cit.*

during normal times can not, however, be saddled upon the
operators, for white miners, union and non-union, in northern
West Virginia, Pennsylvania, and Ohio have often refused to
work with Negroes, and in some places have struck or
threatened to strike if they were employed. Some of the mines
visited during the 1925 strike were called "white workers'
mines." Wherever the responsibility for the non-employment
of Negroes chiefly rests, it seems safe to conclude that their
employment did not occur in normal times at those places
where race prejudice existed, whether on the side of management or on that of the employees, or both — assuming, of
course, the availability of labor from other racial groups.

These complicated cross-currents were again exhibited in
the 1927 strike in Pennsylvania and Ohio. The two largest companies in the Pennsylvania bituminous area are the Pittsburgh
Coal Company and the Pittsburgh Terminal Coal Company.
The normal labor force of the former is about 11,000.[46] That
of the latter is about 3,000. Prior to the strike Negro miners
employed by the Pittsburgh Coal Company were about 7 per
cent of the company's total labor force.[47] At the mines of the
Terminal Company, Negro miners constituted about 2 per
cent of the total before the 1927-1928 strike.[48] The statistics on employment of Negroes for the three last months in
1927 and the first two in 1928 are as follows for the Pittsburgh Coal Company:[49]

Month	White	Negro	Total	Per Cent Colored
October, 1927	4,754	3,443	8,197	42.0
November, 1927	5,135	3,468	8,603	40.3
December, 1927	5,301	3,534	8,835	40.0
January, 1928	5,500	3,516	9,016	38.9
February, 1928	5,666	3,458	9,124	37.9

[46] J. D. A. Morrow, Testimony before the Senate Committee on Conditions
in Coal Fields, 1928, op. cit., Pt. 9, p. 2643.

[47] Interview with C. A. McDowell, manager of safety and personnel,
Pittsburgh Coal Company, July 9, 1928.

[48] Gerald Allen, op. cit.   [49] Interview with C. A. McDowell.

The figures which were given for the Pittsburgh Terminal Company [50] at the hearings of the Senate committee investigating conditions in the coal fields in 1928 were:

Mine Number	White	Negro	Total	Per Cent Colored
2	150	0	150	0
3	430	195	625	31
4	213	367	580	63
8	620	180	800	22
9	200	220	420	52
10	70	0	70	
Total	1,683	962	2,645	42[51]

While Negro miners employed by the Pittsburgh Coal Company never averaged more than 350, or 7 per cent of its labor force, prior to the 1927 strike, they made up 3,600, or about 36 per cent of all miners employed at the height of the strike. And while the number employed in normal times never exceeded 100 in all the mines of the Pittsburgh Terminal Company, it almost reached 1,000 or over 40 per cent of the mine force, during the strike. The percentage of Negro miners employed at different mines of the same company varied. At the Shannon Mine No. 3 of the Pittsburgh Coal Company, where it was reported that mine officials had formerly refused to hire Negro labor, even when sent by the local union, Negroes constituted almost half the workers.[52] The same situation obtained at the Hornig and Coverdale mines of the Pittsburgh Terminal Company.[53]

The facility with which labor can be recruited in a crisis such as the strike of 1927 depends very largely on the state of employment in other industries. At the time of the 1927

[50] Horace Baker of the Pittsburgh Terminal Company, before the Senate Committee, *op. cit.* Pt. 9, p. 2781.

[51] This appeared in the original as 36 per cent.

[52] Interview with J. D. Higgins, Local 2363, United Mine Workers of America, July 7, 1928.

[53] Interview with President Carroll, Local 5085, United Mine Workers of America, July 9, 1928.

strike, employment in many other industries was far below
normal. Especially was this true in the steel mills in the Pittsburgh district and in the neighboring coal fields of northern
West Virginia and in the more remote southern counties. From
these sources as well as from a large class of floating migrants
— recently from the southern states — the supply of Negro
labor was recruited for the emergency. Whenever the responsibility for importing this labor was placed upon the coal companies it was always disclaimed by them. Such a disclaimer
was made when one of the leading operators in the Pittsburgh
district was interviewed. According to him, his company imported no labor. The supply was plentiful and advantage was
taken of it. Furthermore, he said that his company "will use
any kind of labor it can get unless use of a particular group
makes trouble" for the company. But the mine superintendent's weekly statement on the number of men hired shows
clearly upon whom the responsibility rests. A copy of the superintendent's report form follows:

WEEKLY REPORT OF MEN HIRED

....Mine   Week Ending......................

	White	Black	Total
Friend at mine			
Budd Davis Agency			
Lovan Service Company			
Pgh. Coal Co. — Employment			
United Employment — Cleveland			
Other Agency (Name)			
Came in self			
Circular letter			
Newspaper advertisement in			
*Brought in by			

*Does not include Company driver.

_____

Superintendent

The fact that each of one company's 173 newly employed Negroes considered some occupation other than mining as his regular occupation seems to indicate that the strike was being used quite generally as a means of temporary relief from unemployment in other lines. Twenty-six of these employees gave common labor as their regular occupation; five were stationery firemen; three were concrete workers; twenty-three were steel workers; two were glass workers; five were coke workers; eight were bricklayers; seven were auto-repairmen; six were cement finishers; six were plasterers; four were riveters; three were grinders and chippers; three were janitors; ten were locomotive firemen (evidently from the South); three were truckmen; four were crane operators; three were tailors; and twenty-six had no specific occupation. From where did they come? The last place of residence of 25 per cent of them was Pittsburgh. West Virginia was the last place of residence of another 25 per cent. But 18 per cent came from other parts of Pennsylvania; 8 per cent came from Michigan; 7 per cent, from Alabama; and 6 per cent came from Ohio.[54] The effects of the Negro migrations from the South were also in evidence. Alabama was the birthplace of 25 per cent of these new employees; South Carolina, 10 per cent; Pennsylvania, 9 per cent; Virginia, 9 per cent; North Carolina, 9 per cent; West Virginia, 6 per cent; Tennessee, 5 per cent; Kentucky, 4 per cent; and Mississippi, 17 per cent.[55] As has been stated the two reports from which these figures were taken covered only about 20 per cent of the total number of Negro miners employed by this company. In the absence of reliable information one is left to conjecture the extent to which these factors of migration and unemployment, as revealed by the reports, are typical of the whole Negro mining community.

[54] *The Causes of Labor Turnover among Newly Employed Negro Miners of the Pittsburgh Coal and Pittsburgh Terminal Companies.* (Two investigations by Alonzo C. Thayer, secretary, Urban League of Pittsburgh, Feb., 1928.)
[55] *Ibid.*

The local union officers, in releases to the press [56] and in interviews, maintained that over 60,000 men, half of whom were Negroes, had been brought into the large mines in western Pennsylvania in a period of fourteen months. Similar statements were made concerning the mines of eastern Ohio, or what is known as Sub-District 5, of District 6, United Mine Workers of America. District 6 covers Brooke, Ohio, Hancock, and Marshall Counties in West Virginia, and Jefferson, Belmont, and Harrison Counties in Ohio. In the whole district there were about 20,000 miners, 3,000 of whom were Negroes. There were about 450 Negroes in Sub-District 5, all members of the unions, as few mines in Eastern Ohio are non-union. But it is alleged that two mines alone imported 20,000 Negroes from the beginning of the strike to September, 1928. Many of them were inexperienced at mining, and, upon finding it harder work than they anticipated, floated from mine to mine. Others, having had no previous knowledge of the strike, were easily persuaded by union pickets to leave the scene, the union agreeing to pay the railroad fare of those who were penniless.[57] Although too much reliance should not be placed upon estimates given in a time of great bitterness by union members and officials aiming to show the extent to which the operators employed imported Negro labor as a means of combating the strike, it does seem to one who witnessed the great trucks loaded with fresh recruits of Negro labor enroute to the mines that the importations must have been tremendous. Perhaps nothing would tell the story more convincingly than statistics on labor turnover. But these facts were not obtainable even when requests for them were made of officials of the companies against whom the largest importations were charged. Fortunately, however, one is not forced because of the unavailability of employment statistics to draw wholly upon one's imagination to visualize the results that followed upon this sudden introduction of large masses of new people

[56] *Pittsburgh Press*, March 24, 1927, quoted by Allen, *op. cit.*

[57] Interviews with John Chinque, president, and with Negro members of Sub-district 5, U. M. W. of A., Bellaire, Ohio.

into the striking mining communities, in which the feeling current among the strikers was that the newcomers were willing instruments in the employers' subjection of the miners to a modern serfdom. And the antagonism which is always characteristic of strikers and strike breakers was intensified because the American race problem was injected. As a Negro union miner said during the strike, "You hear . . . honest-to-goodness white miners say: 'I do not mind the white scab, but I be damned if I will stand for a Negro scab.'" [58]

The results of the importation of Negroes were written large with violence, bloodshed, loss of life, and the destruction of property in western Pennsylvania from about September, 1927, to February, 1928. The outstanding instances of conflict were at Bruceton, Broughton, and Hornig, Pennsylvania. At Broughton a group of the newly employed Negroes of the Pittsburgh Terminal Company fired into the schoolhouse while it was in session. The striking unionists charged the company's coal and iron police with bribing the colored miners to do the shooting. But the testimony submitted by Mr. Horace Baker in behalf of the company disclaimed the company's responsibility for the incident and discounted the newspaper reports and miner's testimony on the seriousness of the shooting. He attributed the whole affair to the Negro miner's determination to fight back after being subjected to terrible abuse by the white strikers and their friends.[59] It is undoubtedly true that the white striking miners, working upon the assumption of class war, did perpetrate abuses of varying degrees of severity upon Negro strike breakers, and it should be pointed out, upon the whites as well. These acts some of the strikers freely admitted when interviewed by the author. But that these acts of vengeance visited upon the Negro strike breakers were ever so outrageous as to warrant a reprisal that jeopardized the lives of innocent school children could hardly be established before an impartial tribunal.

[58] A. W. Johnson, secretary, Local 2950, U. M. W. of America, Wellsburg, W. Va. Quoted from the *Messenger*, May-June, 1928, p. 99.
[59] Horace Baker, Testimony before Senate Committee, *op. cit.*, p. 2781.

The following list of murders of Negroes taken from affidavits based upon the certified records from the coroner's office
in Allegheny County, Pennsylvania, presents the picture of the
bloody drama occasioned by the strike. It is by no means a
comprehensive statement.

TABLE XXV [a]

NEGRO MURDERS COMMITTED IN AND ABOUT THE CAMPS OF THE
TWO COAL COMPANIES DURING THE 1927 STRIKE

Name	Company Worked For	Cause of Death	Place of Death
Arrie May Wilson	Pittsburgh Coal Co.	Shock and hemorrhage following gun shot and wound of chest	Blythesdale, Elizabeth Township, Pa.
John P. Black	Pittsburgh Coal Co.	Shock and hemorrhage following gun shot wound of neck	Pittsburgh, Pa.
Otis Simon		Shock and internal hemorrhage following gun shot wound of left side of chest	En route McKeesport Hospital, Mc-Keesport, Pa.
Laura Holyfield		Shock and hemorrhage following a compound fracture of skull due to blows on head with ax	Bethel Township, Pa.
James Lawrence	Pittsburgh Coal Co.	Shock and hemorrhage following gun shot wound of chest	Moon Run, Robinson Township, Pa.
Frank Snapp	Pittsburgh Terminal Coal Co.	Shock and hemorrhage following gun shot wound of chest and neck	Bruceton, Pa.
Robert Holsley	Pittsburgh Coal Co.	Shock and hemorrhage following gun shot wound of chest	Cliff Mines, North Fayette Township, Pa.
Floyd Sidney	Pittsburgh Coal Co.	Shock and hemorrhage following stab wound of heart	North Fayette Township, Pa.

[a] Certified records of the Coroner's office. Hearings before Senate Committee, *op. cit.*, Pt. 5, pp. 1041, 1046, 1048, 1049, 1051, 1059, 1060, 1061.

The clashes between white strikers and Negro strike breakers, frequent and often resulting in serious injury on either one side or the other, do not account for all the bloodshed and loss of life that took place. Some of it resulted from drunken brawls and gambling dissensions arising among the strike breakers themselves. Another source was the frequent clashes between the strike breakers and the coal and iron police inside the mining camps where the power of the coal companies is supreme. The camps are the companies' privately owned and controlled communities into which not even a magistrate may enter without the company's permission. These little self-contained communities remind one of a manorial estate with the exception that the latter existed under feudal agrarianism while the former is a feature of contemporary industrialism. In them are the company's general store and the company-owned homes in which its workmen live, as well as its mines and mining property.

The bringing of five or six thousand people into these small inaccessible mining communities gives rise to two problems which in themselves are sources of discord and violence. One is the problem of housing the new employees, and the other is that of protecting them and the company's property and intangible property rights from interference by striking employees. The first problem the coal companies met by building barracks when their existing houses proved inadequate. The other problem was met by the employment of so-called coal and iron police, deputized by the state but paid by the coal companies. The Pittsburgh Coal Company alone spent $800,000 for coal and iron police during the strike.[60] The power of the coal and iron police does not extend beyond the company's property. They are usually recruited from the roughest elements in neighboring communities, and have a reputation among both strikers and strike breakers for their brutality and their zeal in the exercise of petty authority. Whenever one of the new employees desired to leave the camp

---

[60] Morrow, testimony before the Senate Committee, *op. cit.*, Pt. 9, p. 2644.

he would have to obtain a pass from the police. An applicant for a pass must tell the captain of the coal and iron police where he is going and when he expects to return. Admittance to the camps is gained only by presentation of the pass. It was alleged by one of the officials of the United Mine Workers that the coal and iron police follow every strike breaker who leaves the company in order to find out where he is going and the nature of his business. Very often, according to the testimony, quitting workmen have been stopped by the coal and iron police, severely clubbed or otherwise beaten. Afterwards, the victims would be carried before a magistrate who was friendly to the employer and heavily fined or jailed for disorderly conduct.[61] Fear of the coal and iron police was clearly exhibited by Negro miners with whom the author talked during July and August when the strike was subsiding. These miners claimed that the company police made "wild west raids" on their homes, while such raids were never made upon the whites. They said that the slightest provocation from a Negro miner would cause the police to give him a severe beating and then jail him on the charge of resistance and disorderly conduct.

The conditions that surrounded the lives of the newly recruited miners in one of the camps were portrayed in the report of the Senate sub-committee.[62]

These barracks were partitioned into rooms something like 24 feet long and about 12 feet wide, in which there were eight bunks — four double bunks on each side of the room with a narrow passage through the center. There was a small window in each end of the room for ventilation. Generally, these barracks were occupied by colored miners; they were poorly ventilated, filthy, unsanitary, and some of them, your committee learned were infected with vermin and hardly fit to house beasts, much less human beings who are employed in the mines all day where the sun's rays never penetrate, and where at best the air they breathe is never very pure. . . . A number of miners were interviewed

---

[61] Phillip Murray, vice president of the United Mine Workers, before Senate Committee, *op. cit.*, Pt. 2, p. 17.

[62] Hearings before Senate Sub-Committee, *op. cit.*, Pt. 2, p. 346.

in this mine by your committee, but found few of them were satisfied with their conditions, and some of them expressed great discontent.

The committee further pointed out that little effort was being made by the authorities to curb immorality and vice. "No effort was made to invoke law and order or to maintain police protection except through the coal and iron police, and they were found to be the outstanding ones who showed little regard for law and order or for the improvement of morality." [63] The Committee found that the operators themselves generally paid little if any attention to the morals of the community and made no efforts to improve them. This description of the civic and moral atmosphere of the company barracks and camps was denied by the spokesmen for the companies. One of them pointed out that the barracks were not permanent quarters and housed single men only. He said that the men who went to the barracks were largely of that class that move about a good bit, and that men with families remain in the barracks only until houses could be provided.[64] Yet Negro miners in voicing their complaints to one interviewer protested against dirty beds, soiled linen, ill-kept barracks, and men who did not bathe after leaving the coal pit.[65]

When one of the authors, in company with an official of one of the coal companies, made an inspection of some of the houses occupied by Negroes, he found them with leaky roofs, broken plastering, and surrounded by foul-smelling pools of stagnant water, and old privies without doors or otherwise exposed. The houses of the Negro miners were segregated from those of the whites, and this official advised that white and black workers got along much better when segregated. The Negro houses were usually the less desirable. At one of the mines visited the Negro houses were alongside the road, giving rise to numerous complaints of exposure to the attacks of union strikers and sympathizers. At another mine new

[63] *Ibid.*, p. 359.
[64] Horace Baker, *op. cit.*, Pt. 3, p. 2762.
[65] Alonzo Thayer, *op. cit.*

houses were under construction for the white miners. No such houses were being built for the Negroes. The Negro miners were assured, however, that they would be moved off the road into the houses vacated by the whites as soon as the new houses were completed. Segregation, according to statements from Negro miners, was carried to the point of providing separate sections of the bath house, different food, and separate dining rooms for the two races. Because of their acceptance of these conditions and their faith that the company would soon remove all sources of irritation, the new Negro employees of the company in question were highly praised by one of the officials. He said that the Negro had accepted conditions during the strike that no other group of people would have accepted. The Negro's other admirable traits which their use as strike breakers revealed were that "he will do what you tell him; is more easily satisfied than the white worker; does not act in concert; and is submissive." [66] Any discussion of these traits from the standpoint of their being inherent racial characteristics transcends the limited purposes of the present study. But it should be said that one would hardly expect a group of people composed largely of peasants — recent migrants from the southern states — and unmarried men who drift from mine to mine, and from one industrial occupation to another, to be deeply concerned about united action in the protection of what other men might be willing to die for as "human rights." The indifference manifested by the newly recruited Negro miners in the matter of demanding reforms in employee-employer relations may be attributed to "a submissiveness of race," or to any other apparently more appropriate disposition, but that some of them, even though inarticulate, were conscious of their grounds for complaint was evidenced in their large labor turnover.

The great instability of the new Negro miners of two companies caused a local Negro welfare organization to ask permission to ascertain the causes for it. The investigations re-

[66] Interview with C. A. McDowell of the Pittsburgh Coal Company.

vealed numerous grievances and the absence of machinery for ascertaining and adjusting them. Here follow some of the characteristic complaints brought out in the interviews, held in February and March, 1928, with more than 200 Negro miners in the employ of the Pittsburgh Terminal Coal Company and the Pittsburgh Coal Company.[67]

1. There is no hope on the job. — [Leaving.]

2. We must live in special houses; under union conditions we live anywhere in the patch.

3. Superintendent refused to put Negroes at work at Library. Can't use any more Negroes.

4. A man loses much time and money because somewhere ahead of him a man has failed to put over his job. . . . Some days a man goes into the mine and stays from half a day to a day mining without being able to cut. It is no fault of his, but he gets no pay for it.

5. Men come to the mines purely for love of money, not mining like me. I have worked for twenty years in the mines. . . . Green men know nothing about the run of veins. . . . They think they can loaf and get credit for a lot of work, but they can't. They get disgusted and leave. . . . But they have men they pay to instruct these new men, but they don't teach them right. They put them in a room and tell them what they pay, but they don't tell them how it is figured. That's the cause of these money-mad boys quitting so soon.

6. We are having a hard time out here. On Saturday, Jan. 21, we nearly froze — no heat in the bunk house. I went to the sergeant and superintendent about it, but neither of them could do anything. I found the men drunk.

7. I was refused powder to shoot with. I had $39.00 worth of time in the office but still I could not get powder. The pit boss told them to let me have some powder, so I paid $1.20 that I owed so that I could get powder.

8. On January they stopped my lamp — they claimed I had dirty coal. Then I went to the pit boss and explained to him that I could not stay there and pay board for two weeks of $21.00. He said that was up to me. I then asked for my time. He said that was up to me. Then I went to the superintendent who said it was up to the pit boss. I went to the main office. . . . The whole bunch don't care for the Negro.

[67] Alonzo Thayer, *op. cit.*

The manager is drunk all of the time. On June 23, the bookkeeper, police, baggage man and the fireman of the bunk houses were all drunk. I don't see why we poor fellows should suffer because all of them say that we don't want to work when the conditions in the mine are so that you can't make anything.

9. There is lots of slate in the mine. Sometimes I spend a day cleaning slate — with no pay. No materials to repair trucks. Must go from place to place looking for material. Assistant foreman does not know where material can be found. Men are reprimanded for broken rails and faulty tracks but can find no material.

10. Men sometimes crib cars so that they can get a load and a half on one car, but when weight is credited by weigh-master it is same as uncribbed.

11. Cars ought to be brought to the face of the coal. Instead they are left at the mouth of the room. This forces a man to pick and throw his coal and then make another handling necessary, requiring considerable extra time, with no pay offered. When I first came all dead work was paid for — now when you talk to the foreman about it he says the company does not allow him to pay for it.

12. Placed as snapper about three weeks ago. Taken off yesterday. First motorman had motor-boss transfer me because he refused to work with me when I complained about the unfair distribution of cars to white and colored men.

13. Have been here one month. Could not get more than 5 cars for two men. . . . Water in mines. . . . Negroes must do double on same job. Can't get bosses to listen to needs. Want men to work for nothing. New rule of picking coal at bottom before shooting, requires several hours work without pay. Work added constantly which is dead work with no pay.

14. . . . A man . . . can't get 20 cents out of the office if he was sick and wanted to go to the doctor in Pittsburgh. He would have to go and get four dollars worth of script and sell it for $2.00 to the coal and iron sergeant. If you should quit and have a hundred dollars worth of script you could only get 50 on the dollar. Then they say — "We like you colored boys."

15. Two or three cars is best we can get a day. Can scarcely make board. Cars and mine supplies lacking. Two men sent in where hours are spent cleaning up a room, then they were removed to some other place to work.

16. Men must clean rock falls and load slate without pay.

17. Negroes used as utility men — snappers on motors but are refused regular jobs as motormen. We are jim crowed, that's all. According to custom in mines, snapper or brakesman is promoted to motorman. Exception is made in cases of Negroes.

18. I've worked for the Tennessee Coal and Iron Company for years and I've led the union cause. I'm convinced that they are offering us a splendid opportunity here, but there is a great chance for improvement in the selection and the handling of the men. We are living under advanced conditions and the loyalty of my people can be used to great advantage.

In addition to the wide variety of grievances shown in the above random samples, Negro miners complained of high prices at company stores from which they said they were compelled to purchase, payment in script and inability to cash it unless at discount by company police, car shortage resulting in lowered wages, excessive dead work without pay, and the inability to obtain accessory mining supplies such as spikes, rails, and beams. In the effort to relieve the situation one company appointed a young colored man to the position of assistant in its personnel department. The appointee had been formerly engaged in recreational work for a local settlement house. As welfare worker among the company's Negro employees, his functions were conducting gardening contests, picnics, band concerts and baseball games. Whenever these activities involved financial outlays, the company defrayed the costs. In one instance baseball equipment alone cost the company $5,000. These feeble attempts at inaugurating a welfare program controlled and directed by the company in order to keep its employees satisfied and to prevent them from contemplating what the striking unionists had perceived as the miners' real welfare are the company's tacit admission of the union's efficacy. A further substantiation of it was one official's admitted desire to see established some type of organization through which the operators and the miners might adjudicate their differences. This official made it clear, however, that the company union was the type of organization he wanted established in the coal industry. But after all, welfare programs and talk of company unions may merely be scarecrows which the operators plan to demolish after the verdict of the strike is rendered decisively in their favor. What will happen afterward is hard to forecast, but some of the present tendencies observed warrant speculation.

First of all, the United Mine Workers' Union, although badly discredited and shattered from internal dissension, still possesses life. Whether it possesses sufficient internal cohesion to bring about complete revival depends upon the amount of defection from its ranks caused by the dual union which challenged it for supremacy during the strike of 1927. The second tendency is the return to work of the strikers and the gradual weeding out of much of the Negro labor brought in during the strike. Is this labor to be displaced?

During the months of July and August, when the strike was quieting, the opinion that the Negro miner would be gradually let out of the industry was quite generally expressed by the Negroes themselves. The following are some of their statements:

1. Some of the operators would not use Negro before strike. The "Red Necks" are returning and they are being given the places that Negroes had. The Negroes are gradually leaving. Negroes irresponsible. Soon as they make some money they lay off and get drunk.

2. I've been working at Bluefield, West Virginia, but I thought I could make more money in Pennsylvania. All the company wants to do is break strike. After this it won't give damn about Negro.

3. "Red Necks" returning. Negroes are discharged on trumped-up charges to give places to returning strikers.

4. Every miner lays off. But when the Negro lays off he is discharged and his place given to a "Red Neck."

The return to work of "red necks," meaning strikers, was interpreted by many of the Negro miners as signifying that their usefulness to the coal companies was rapidly waning. And, as in the 1925 strike in northern West Virginia, white union miners contended that the Negro strike breakers, having served the operators' purpose, were being gradually let out of the mines. The prevalence of such an opinion is due to the Negro workers' industrial experience prior to 1915, when in most instances he was employed only in emergencies, the passing of which meant his displacement. Today American industry can not tap the foreign sources of a labor supply as it formerly did. The traditional displacement of Negro labor following its employment in times of stress is somewhat counteracted by the restriction of foreign immigration to the United States. From the number of Negroes employed in northern West Virginia at present, it does not seem that the 1922 and 1925 strikes were followed by any sweeping displacement of the Negro labor introduced in the strike periods. As a matter of fact it seems that it was then that Negro labor got its first secure foothold in the coal mines of the northern counties. We have noted that there were almost twice as many Negro miners in the northern fields of West Virginia in 1926 as there were in 1923. It was unthinkable, however, that all the Negro labor that entered northern West Virginia in 1925 would remain when the strike was over. Unsatisfactory or undesirable Negro as well as white labor was eliminated. The same process is in all likelihood taking place [68] in western Pennsylvania. At four mines of one of the leading companies in western Pennsylvania there were about 900 Negroes and 800 whites employed at the height of the strike in January, 1928. Eight months later, September, 1928, when the disturbance had considerably subsided, there were about 1,500 whites and only about 750 Negro miners at the same four mines.

[68] This was written in September, 1928, before the strike had officially ended. Since then Mr. Ira Reid of the department of research, National Urban League, reports in a survey of Negro Pittsburgh that the Pittsburgh Coal Company was employing 2,500 Negro miners in all of its mines on September 15, 1929. Negro miners were 25 per cent of the total number of miners. While the number reported for September, 1929, is eight times higher than it was at any time before the strike, it was more than 30 per cent less than the total number employed at the height of the strike.

Despite an apparent weeding out of the Negro, or a voluntary shifting of them to other pursuits, the number is still twice as great as it was at all of this company's mines before the 1927 strike. It would be rash to venture an opinion as to how many of the 750 will ultimately remain in the industry. But it can be tentatively assumed upon the basis of results that followed the 1922 and 1925 coal strikes and strikes in other industries that a large number of those introduced into the coal mines of western Pennsylvania will remain. Even so, the Negro industrial reserve army, which the southern sections of the country and unstable industrial conditions in other parts can furnish, will not have been robbed of its potentialities for a transitory yeoman's service in the future. But the coal industry's absorption of even a small contingent of the reserve army places the portion absorbed in a new relation to itself and to the unabsorbed, and in relation to the older white industrial workers. Probably this new class of workers in undergoing industrial orientation will align itself with the white workers to revive the now discredited and shattered miners' union. It may, on the other hand, become the entrenched bulwark against unionism. In the event that the former development occurs, the Negro miner becomes the agency through which the future introduction of other Negroes into coal mining might be controlled by the union more easily than heretofore. If the latter should take place, the labor movement in the coal industry faces a circumstance similar to that in the steel, automobile, and packing industries. That the former rather than the latter series of events will come to pass is a warrantable conclusion in view of the life still remaining in the miners' union and its demonstrated capacity for surviving catastrophes.

To conclude from the foregoing discussion that the relation of all Negro labor to unionism in the coal-mining industry has consisted solely of strike breaking and the lowering of living standards among the older white workers would be erroneous. In the early days Negro labor was used intermittently, i. e., during strikes. Only a very small proportion of this imported southern labor was usually retained after a disorder. Thus in scattered sections of the West and the North some of these older Negro union miners are to be found today. But Negro labor secured a foothold in the northern fields during and after the World War. A small percentage of this became organized. In the southern fields Negro labor was used from the beginning, and some Negro miners in Alabama and West Virginia have been affiliated with the union since the days of the Knights of Labor. Thus while it is true that Negro labor secured its foothold in the northern fields by strike breaking, the same is not true of the southern field. But the proximity of the southern fields to the reserves of Negro agricultural labor made it possible to introduce new and low-standard Negroes into the mines, as occasion warranted, lowering the effectiveness of unionism among southern Negroes and whites. This story of unionism and its relation to the Negro miner is told in Chapter XVII.

Chapter XI

THE NEGRO AND THE UNIONIZATION OF STEEL

The steel industry has always relied upon a steady supply of cheap labor. In the North until the World War the principal source of this supply was the foreign immigrant. In the South it was the Negro. In 1907 the Immigration Commission reported that Negroes made up 39.1 per cent of all the steel workers in the South, as against 1.5 per cent in the East and 0.5 per cent in the Middle West.[1] Most of the southern Negro workers were concentrated in the great centers of the industry in Alabama and Maryland, but many were also employed at the smaller mills and furnaces scattered through Virginia, Tennessee, Kentucky, and other states.

The largest operator in the far South, the Tennessee Coal and Iron Company, became part of the United States Steel Corporation in 1907. Prior to this about 4,000 Negroes, 25 to 30 per cent of the total force, were employed in the company's manufacturing plants. An additional 5,000 were employed in its mines. Nearly all of the Negroes employed in the plants were common laborers and turnover among them was exceedingly high. They were, in the words of one of the company officials, "shiftless, thriftless, sloppy, and dirty. They were inefficient labor." But they were nevertheless indispensable to the company's operations. After an attempt to use foreign workers was abandoned because the supply was too difficult to obtain, it became apparent that the Negro would have to play the part that the immigrant played in the North. Yet if the company's plants were to operate with an efficiency comparable to the mills of the North, the quality of Negro

[1] Report of the United States Commission on Immigration, 1907, Vol. 8, p. 34.

labor would have to be raised. This the Tennessee Company set out to do in a systematic and thoroughgoing fashion. It exercised great care in the selection of its help. It inaugurated a comprehensive welfare and educational program. It made pay days fortnightly instead of monthly to provide the worker with a steadier flow of cash and discourage requests for advances. It abolished the privilege of discounting advances at the company commissaries. Housing standards were raised and rents made slightly higher in an effort to attract a higher type of colored worker. Schools, recreational facilities, social work among mothers and children, hospitals and clinics were provided in an attempt to improve the Negro's standard of living and raise the quality of his work.

The facilities provided for the employees and the welfare work done among them were of excellent quality. There are few companies in the country which could match its completeness and its efficiency. The standards of health, education, and efficiency of white and black workers alike were raised considerably. Care in the selection of employees contributed equally with welfare work to the improved quality of the colored force. Of one hundred Negro applicants for jobs, twenty, according to the president of the company, would as a rule meet the necessary standards, whereas eighty of every hundred white applicants would do so. As a result, labor turnover in 1928 for the company's mills and mines was reduced to 25 per cent and this, as is usually the case, was chiefly in the cheaper positions.

All this gave the company a working force with which trade unionism could make little headway. Even in the mines, where labor was far more mobile than in the mills and where there was a long tradition of militant labor activity, the union was not successful. In the manufacturing plants, organization effort was hopeless from the start.

The first attempt to organize the steel industry in Alabama came during the war in 1918 when the machinists, blacksmiths, electricians, sheet metal workers, molders and other unions of the metal trades launched a campaign to organize all the metal-working shops and steel mills of the Birmingham district. At the time not only the large plants but most of the independent shops were engaged directly or indirectly on government contracts. The workers demanded a basic eight-hour day and other advantages set forth in the various pronouncements of federal agencies dealing with labor standards. The steel mills, which were operating on a ten to twelve hour basis, ignored the workers' demands and a general metal-trades strike resulted.

The metal trades unions were all white, but they knew that their efforts were bound to fail unless the Negroes in the less skilled branches of the industry were included in their movement. To this end the International Union of Mine, Mill, and Smelter Workers entered the field and attempted to organize the miscellaneous employees, white and black, in the ore mines, blast furnaces, and steel mills who were not included in the various metal trades. About 70 per cent of the ore miners in the district were colored, while the proportion of Negroes in the steel plants was between 40 and 45 per cent. The proportion in the blast furnaces alone was larger. The Negro was thus a factor of major importance to the whole strike movement.

The companies, aware of this situation, fought the strike by playing up the race issue. The Negroes at first were willing enough to come into the movement, but threats and intimidations soon frightened them away. During the course of the organizing campaign a white general organizer of the Mine, Mill, and Smelter Workers and a local Negro organizer were kidnapped in North Birmingham while trying to hold a meeting. They were carried several miles into the woods where both, but particularly the Negro, were badly beaten and then left to themselves. Efforts on the part of the local labor leaders to get indictments for kidnapping against the gang leaders, one of whom was a city policeman, were unsuccessful. Another Negro organizer's house was dynamited.

Eight-hour agreements were obtained in a number of independent shops in the district but no headway was made with the steel plants and the strike was finally called off. The effort showed the utter futility of attacking the steel industry at any one spot alone. The breadth of its operations is so great that it can, by transferring work or men from one place to another, easily defeat any local movement before it really gets started.

As a result of the loss of the metal-trades strike, Birmingham played little part in the great nation-wide steel strike of the next year. It would have been too much to expect wholehearted coöperation on the part of the southern workers so soon after their recent defeat. The Negroes took no part at all in the second walkout. They had been so thoroughly intimidated during the first strike that they refused to have anything whatever to do with the second.

In the smaller steel mills and blast furnaces scattered through various parts of the South there had long been labor organization. The principal groups were the Sons of Vulcan, dominated by the puddlers, the Associated Brotherhood of Iron and Steel Heaters, and the Iron and Steel Roll Hands' Union. None of these, however, had any Negro members. In fact, the Sons of Vulcan, the most important group, barred Negroes by constitutional provision. The shortsightedness of this policy of Negro exclusion was demonstrated as early as 1875 when Negro puddlers from Richmond, Virginia were brought to Pittsburgh to take the place of white strikers.[2] These were, as far as is known, the first Negroes to enter the steel industry in the North.

When the Amalgamated Association of Iron and Steel Workers was formed the next year, 1876, through a combination of existing unions, its constitution declared it to be an organization "embracing every iron and steel worker in the country." But this did not alter the prejudices of the white rank and file and make it easier for Negroes to get into the new group than it had been for them to get into the old asso-

[2] *Wage-earning Pittsburgh* (The Pittsburgh Survey, 1914), p. 106.

ciations. In fact the new union at its first annual convention in 1877 refused definitely to declare Negroes eligible for membership.[3]

The effect of the policy of Negro exclusion, quite the opposite of what was intended, was to hasten the Negro's entrance into the northern mills. Almost every labor disturbance between 1878 and the middle eighties saw Negroes used as strike breakers. The Black Diamond Mill at Pittsburgh, the Moorhead Mill at Sharpsburg, and the Clark Mills at Pittsburgh, one after another used colored workers to take the places of white strikers.[4] The climax of the practice came when strikers at the Elba Works near Pittsburgh attempted to resist the introduction of Negroes and precipitated a serious riot. In the course of an investigation which followed, the district attorney in open court denounced the employers for "importing classes of labor which resulted in disturbance of the peace."[5] In every instance the Negroes brought in were men trained in the mills of the South.

These hard lessons soon taught the union that the Negro steel worker could no longer be ignored. In 1881 Negroes were declared eligible to membership in the Association.[6] Following this action, colored men were taken into the organization at Richmond, Virginia, the principal source of supply of Negro strike breakers for the Pittsburgh district, and shortly afterwards the Negroes in the Pittsburgh plants were organized. Wherever possible, separate Negro lodges were established. This practice was not confined to the South, but extended to the union's entire jurisdiction. In 1887 a separate colored local, the Garfield Lodge, was established in Pittsburgh.[7] The colored workers were duly cynical about the

[3] Jesse E. Robinson, *The Amalgamated Association of Iron, Steel and Tin Workers* (1920), p. 46.

[4] Helen A. Tucker, "Negroes in Pittsburgh," *Charities and The Commons*, January 3, 1909, p. 602.

[5] From President M. T. Tighe of Amalgamated Association of Iron, Steel and Tin Workers, Pittsburgh, July 5, 1928.

[6] Robinson, *op. cit.*, p. 46.

[7] *Ibid.*, p. 47.

whole performance, declaring that the white unionists had acted merely to insure themselves against further Negro strike breaking.[8]

The Amalgamated Association grew steadily from the middle eighties down to 1891. Though it never succeeded in organizing the entire industry, it had contracts with most of the leading companies.[9] In 1892 the "big strike" against the Carnegie Steel Company took place and the tide began to turn. After the strike, Carnegie Steel broke with the union and a number of other large producers followed within the next few years. During this strike a number of Negroes in the Clark Mills quit work while a number of others found employment as strike breakers in the Homestead Works and other plants. Many of the latter were local residents. Some Negro strike breakers, as on previous occasions, were imported from the South, but contrary to prevailing impression, their numbers were not large and they formed but an insignificant proportion of the total number of strike breakers used.[10]

In spite of its decline following the 1892 strike, the Amalgamated Association continued to be a factor in the steel industry down to 1901, when it called a strike against the United States Steel Corporation. Among the men who answered this call were a number of Negroes, members of the Lafayette Lodge of the Association, who were employed in the Butler Street plant of the Carnegie Company. Three of these Negro strikers, together with a white officer of their local, went down the river to get work at a union plant not affected by the strike. The superintendent promised them work if the white men would work with them. But the white men, their union brethren, refused. The pleas of the union official accompanying the Negroes were unavailing. The colored men, incensed, returned to their mill and told the other colored strikers that they were being used as the white man's pawns

[8] *Wage-earning Pittsburgh*, p. 108.

[9] John A. Fitch, "Unionism in the Iron and Steel Industry," *Political Science Quarterly*, March, 1909, p. 71.

[10] Helen A. Tucker, *op. cit.*, p. 603.

and would never get a square deal from the white man's union. Thereupon all of the colored strikers returned to work. As soon as the international president heard what had happened down the river, he ordered the charter of the offending local revoked unless the white men consented to work with Negro members of their union. But in spite of the stand of the international organization, the faith of the colored men in the association was completely shattered and they remained at work.[11]

There is little question but that the Negro workers' attitude was justified. They were not admitted to the organization in the first place until "past experience . . . taught the craft that they were indispensable."[12] The union was not interested in extending its advantage to all employees of the industry, but merely desired to prevent a certain class of workers whom its members would not receive on equal terms from breaking its strikes and undercutting its scale.

In the South the refusal of white men to work with Negroes was frequent. The question was repeatedly brought to the attention of the national convention of the union, but without results.[13] Sometimes employers, knowing the union's attitude towards the Negro, offered to make concessions to its prejudices. A mill superintendent in Birmingham, eager to have a strike in his plant called off, proposed to the union "to put all of the 'niggers' on one side of the mill and the white men on the other side if they would go back to work."[14] But the union wanted more. The mill in question employed a large force of colored workers, particularly in the less skilled branches, at very low pay. The union delegation asked the superintendent if he would "discharge all the niggers" if they called

<hr>

[11] From President M. T. Tighe of the Amalgamated Association, July 5, 1928.

[12] Amalgamated Association of Iron and Steel Workers, *Proceedings*, 1881, p. 708. See also Robinson, *op. cit.*, p. 47.

[13] Amalgamated Association of Iron and Steel Workers, *Proceedings*, 1900, p. 5874; 1905, p. 7255.

[14] *Ibid.*, 1908, p. 8333.

off the strike. When the latter said he had no authority to do this without consent from the head office at Pittsburgh, the delegation informed him "that under the circumstances it could do nothing towards throwing the mill open." [15] Headquarters rejected the union's demand, declaring that they would "operate their Birmingham mills to suit themselves and without the aid of the Amalgamated Association." [16] While these efforts to eliminate the Negroes at Birmingham were in progress, the very delegation which was carrying on the negotiations stopped at another of the company's southern mills at Knoxville, and, in the words of the head of the delegation, "explained the situation to the colored men in that mill and got them to promise to keep away from Birmingham by telling them that if the company succeeded in forcing a reduction at Birmingham, it meant another reduction in Knoxville." [17]

Even when steps to take positive action to bring Negroes into the union were proposed, the colored man's interests were but an incidental consideration. Thus, when a resolution to organize the Negroes was introduced at the 1908 convention of the Amalgamated Association, the delegates were asked for their support so that the union might "use him [the colored man] to maintain fair wages and conditions instead of allowing the manufacturer to use him to lower conditions of the working man." [18] The union's great mistake in the past, according to the sponsor of the resolution, was that when it lost a strike through the use of colored men, it left the mill entirely to them, "thus enabling them to teach others the iron and steel business." [19]

"For example," said the delegate, "I will take Moorhead's mill at Sharpsburg where they operate thirty puddling furnaces, three teams with colored men, and we were told by the men themselves that each furnace produces a new puddler

15 *Ibid.*, p. 8338.
16 *Ibid.*
17 *Ibid.*, p. 8334.
18 *Ibid.*, p. 8340.
19 *Ibid.*

each year. This goes to show that if they were members of the
A. A., they would be scattered about and could be prevented
from learning any more." [20]

Responsibility for the Negro's undercutting was placed
squarely at the door of the union. The speaker went on to say:

> I have talked during this year a great deal to colored puddlers and
> finishers, and every one that I have talked to blames the A.A. for their
> actions. They claim that the A.A. refuses to take them in and give
> them the privilege of working in any union mill where they might
> secure a job, and manufacturers, knowing this to be a fact, compel him
> to work for what the manufacturer wishes to give. If the colored man
> complains and makes a stand for the scale price, the manufacturer tells
> him that if he has to pay the scale prices he will employ white men and
> sign the scale with the result that he is between the devil and the deep
> sea. [21]

The situation today, more than twenty years after these
remarks were made, is practically unchanged, except for the
fact that the union's influence is completely eliminated from all
the great companies and its jurisdiction confined to but a small
and highly specialized segment of the industry, namely, skilled
workers in small plants manufacturing iron requiring skilled
processing. Although there are a number of Negroes in such
plants which the union could organize, it hesitates to do so
because it feels that it could not guarantee them equal treatment. "If colored men should strike after unionization," the
international president declared, "the union would not be able
to guarantee them work in the white plants because of the attitude of the whites." [22] The anti-Negro tradition in the ranks
of the organization is as strong as ever. Much of the
work in the plants under the union's jurisdiction is done by
groups or teams and the white men are reluctant to work with
colored men as "buddies," though there is no objection to
working with them in the same plant on other jobs and in other
divisions.

[20] *Ibid.*
[21] *Ibid.*
[22] Interview with President M. T. Tighe at Pittsburgh, July 5, 1928.

Obstacles of this character have appeared again and again in other occupations and have been overcome under the pressure of circumstances. The Amalgamated Association, however, feels that its position is exceedingly precarious and hesitates to do anything which might in any way threaten what it now has. It wants no dissension in its ranks and, above all, it wants to continue friendly relations with the employers who now recognize it. Union officials report that, time after time when attempts have been made to organize Negro workers, employers say, "we'll deal with organized labor if we are driven to it, but if we must deal with organized labor we'll have white organized labor." [23]

The Amalgamated Association is one of those many organizations characteristic of the American labor movement today so overawed by the size and power of the employers in its field that it has given up all effort at really organizing its industry and is content to withdraw its activities to a narrow segment of the field, just large enough to keep the union going but without the will, the power, or resources to expand.

When the National Committee for Organizing Iron and Steel Workers was set up in 1919, the Amalgamated Association took its place in its councils as one of the twenty-four unions with jurisdiction over workers in the iron and steel industry. Throughout the strike and the organizing campaign which preceded it the National Committee was seriously handicapped by constant bickering and contention among the two dozen crafts. This was one of the major causes of the defeat of the steel workers' movement. "Perhaps the strike would have been won in spite of the odds against the workers," said an article in *Advance*, the organ of the Amalgamated Clothing Workers, "if there had been complete harmony among the twenty-four internationals represented on the Committee. As it was, there were twenty-four separate bodies loosely held together." [24]

[23] *Ibid.*
[24] *Advance*, May 6, 1920, p. 4.

To this dissension the Amalgamated Association of Iron and Steel Workers contributed a major share.[25] Its financial contribution to the National Committee was exceedingly meager, only $11,881.81, despite the fact that the association had jurisdiction over 50 per cent of the workers in the mills including all the strategic steel-making trades, and actually had about 150,000 members at the height of the campaign.[26] The association, although that it demanded the lion's share of control in the organizing campaign, was interested primarily in the skilled worker and particularly in its continued control over skilled employees in the mills where it had contracts. Unskilled laborers were a secondary consideration even though it organized a great many of them. In several plants where the association had contracts covering the skilled men, the laborers struck in response to the general call. When the skilled men went out in support of the laborers, the Amalgamated officials forced both back to work to get the mills into operation. This was done in the name of the sanctity of contracts. Yet when the steel strike was but two months old, the Association, forgetting its understanding with the National Committee and the other organizations, attempted to obtain separate agreements with both the Bethlehem and the United States Steel Corporations.[27]

Most of the Negroes in the mills were unskilled workers. This fact in addition to the Amalgamated's traditional attitude towards the race made it a rather ineffective agency for bringing the colored worker into line for the strike. But in spite of all drawbacks, it was more liberal than a number of other important organizations represented on the National Committee, such as the machinists and electrical workers which barred Negroes entirely, or the blacksmiths which admitted them only to auxiliary lodges subordinate to the white

[25] William Z. Foster, *The Great Steel Strike* (1920), pp. 249-54.

[26] Hearings before United States Senate Committee on Education and Labor; *Investigation of Strike in Steel Industries* (1919), p. 353. See also Foster, *op. cit.*, p. 250.

[27] Foster, *op. cit.*, pp. 69-72, 173-75, 249-51.

locals. In Cleveland the Amalgamated opened its doors to Negroes after the machinists had refused to admit them. At Youngstown one lone Negro machinist who struck to the very end was never admitted to the machinists' union.[28] From the very start the National Committee was thus handicapped in its efforts to organize the whole iron and steel industry by the fact that certain of its constituent organizations were lukewarm or hostile to the idea of organizing the increasingly important group of colored workers.

The Negro became an important factor in steel during the war-time labor shortage. "If it hadn't been for the Negro at that time," said a former official of the Carnegie Steel Company in Pittsburgh, "we could hardly have carried on our operations." When the migration failed to bring colored labor to the mills in sufficient numbers, the companies sent their agents to the South and brought thousands of black workers back with them. "The nigger saved the day for us," declared a company official who had personally supervised the importation of thousands of colored men into the Pittsburgh district. In some places, as previously pointed out, it required a turnover as high as 300 per cent to keep the plants manned with this colored labor.[29]

But by the time the National Committee for Organizing Iron and Steel Workers began its work, the Negro migrations had subsided and the importations had ceased. The colored worker was no longer regarded as a mere makeshift. He had become a recognized element of the labor force. In the area from Chicago east to Buffalo, where the strike was really fought, the Negro, according to William Z. Foster, secretary of the National Committee, constituted anywhere from 1 to 20 per cent of the workers in the mills.[30] In the Chicago dis-

[28] Commission of Inquiry, Interchurch World Movement, *Report on the Steel Strike of 1919* (1920), p. 177.

[29] Information in this paragraph obtained through interviews with men who had been officers, welfare workers, and agents of the company during the war period.

[30] Foster, *op. cit.*, p. 206.

trict, the maximum was about 10 or 12 per cent. In Pittsburgh the proportion was higher, reaching 15 to 20 per cent in some larger plants, and 35 to 40 per cent in some of the smaller ones.

From the start the National Committee failed to realize that this group, new to industry and ignorant of the aims of the labor movement, needed special attention. Many of these Negroes, fresh from southern fields, judged their conditions in the mills by standards different from those of the white workers. They felt that their pay was good. They accepted other working conditions without question, knowing little as to whether they were good or bad.

At this time the Pittsburgh Urban League occupied a position of great strategic importance in the local industrial community. On its initiative eighteen Negro welfare workers were placed in eleven plants employing the overwhelming majority of the Negroes in the industry. These welfare workers maintained close contacts with the employees and had ready access to the managements. When the organization of the mills began, John T. Clark, the executive secretary of the Urban League, and other Negro leaders suggested to William Z. Foster that the strike committee use Negro organizers. Foster was willing but his associates were cold. A number of conferences held with Clark and other Negro leaders got nowhere. The impression became current among influential Negroes that the labor leaders were merely making a gesture at organizing the Negro, and that many of them looked forward to eliminating him from the mills after the strike was won.[31] Foster, however, was in earnest in his desire to organize everyone and consented to address a mass meeting of colored steel workers which Clark arranged in a large church. But Clark, wanting it known that the Urban League had not thrown its influence behind the union movement but was merely giving its spokesmen a chance to reach the colored workers, insisted that A. L.

[31] Clark declared that he got this impression from his talks with Foster. Interview with John T. Clark at St. Louis, April 27, 1929.

Manly of the Philadelphia Urban League (the Armstrong Association) also tell the meeting of his experiences with organized labor and the Negro, which of course were by no means all favorable to organized labor. The meeting was packed to overflowing and many company spies were scattered through the hall.

After the mass meeting, the Urban League, feeling that it had done its part, washed its hands of the union movement and assumed an attitude of complete neutrality. Clark directed his welfare workers at one of the weekly meetings he held with them to tell the men in the mills to use their own judgment about joining the strike. The effect of all this was detrimental to the union cause. Foster charged the League and its agents with hostility to the unions, while Clark rejoined that his attitude was the inevitable result of the organizers' failure to give adequate recognition to the race.

Only a handful of Negroes in the Pittsburgh region answered the strike call. "A dozen," said Foster, "would cover those from among the large number employed in the mills in Pittsburgh proper who walked out with the 25,000 whites on September 22." [32] But this could hardly have been due to the Urban League's attitude, for colored workers in other districts were equally apathetic. "In the entire steel industry," Foster declared, "the Negroes, beyond compare, gave the movement less coöperation than any other element, skilled or unskilled, foreign or native." [33] In the plants around Pittsburgh, the response was as poor as in the city itself. At the Homestead Works of the United States Steel Corporation there were 1,737 Negroes among the plant's 14,687 employees. Of these Negroes only eight joined the unions and but one struck, while 75 per cent of the white unskilled workers joined the unions and 90 per cent struck. In Duquesne of 344 Negroes employed not one struck. In Clairton six out of 300 joined the union and struck for two weeks. In the Braddock

[32] Foster, *op. cit.*, p. 207.
[33] *Ibid.*

plants not one of the several hundred Negroes employed struck.

At the South Works of the Illinois Steel Company at least 85 per cent of the colored workers walked out on the first day of the strike. But they were merely following the lead of the mass.[34] They had little conception of the meaning of unionism or the causes of the strike, and at the first opportunity they went back to work.[35] This was due partly to the strike leaders' failure to realize that organizing the Negro was a special problem requiring special attention. Most of the Negroes who worked in the Chicago mills lived in the black belt far away from the steel plants. They did not attend union meetings voluntarily after they returned home and the union made no special efforts to reach them.

The attitude of the National Committee was that, since the Negro was a comparatively small factor in the industry in most places and since the unions were obliged to deal with so many thousands of workers drawn from a dozen or perhaps a score of nations, it was impossible to concentrate on any particular race. The committee therefore "made a general appeal, pretty much in English. . . ." [36]

But in some places where the Negro was a factor of great importance, as in Pueblo, Colorado, where he numbered about 2,000 out of 6,000 employees, the unions made vigorous efforts to win him. Yet the result was as unsatisfactory as in the other districts. "We put on a campaign," said Foster, "which should have gotten 99 per cent of the men into our unions, but we could not get more than 2 per cent of the colored men in the organization." [37] The only place where the Negro workers really supported the strike was Cleveland. There the Amalgamated Association was particularly active and the colored

[34] See reference to similar action among the longshoremen p. 203, below
[35] From well-informed employees who ask that their names be withheld.
[36] William Z. Foster's testimony before the Chicago Commission on Race Relations, August 16, 1920, MS p. 77.
[37] *Ibid.*, p. 78.

men working in the mills before the walkout joined the union one hundred per cent strong.

The Negroes who remained in the plants were in many instances assigned to the work of men who were striking. In addition, thousands of new Negro strike breakers entered the mills. According to the famous Interchurch Report, "the successful use of strike breakers" was one of the main causes of the failure of the unions. And according to the same source, these strike breakers were "principally Negroes." [38] The report continued:

Negro workers were imported and were shifted from plant to plant; in Gary, the Negroes were marched ostentatiously through the streets; in Youngstown and near Pittsburgh, they were smuggled in at night. "Niggers did it," was a not uncommon remark among company officers. Besides the comparatively small bands of avowed strike breakers, shifted from plant to plant, it is evident that great numbers of Negroes who flowed into Chicago and Pittsburgh plants were conscious of strike breaking. For this attitude, the steel strikers rightly blamed American organized labor. . . . Through many experiences Negroes came to believe that the only way they could get into a unionized industry was through strikebreaking. . . . [39]

The National Committee reported to President Gompers of the American Federation of Labor that something like 30,000 Negro strike breakers were used. [40] Foster put the number between 30,000 and 40,000. [41] Eight thousand, Mr. Gompers was told, were used in Chicago. Most of these were residents of the city or persons who had come to the city voluntarily in the hope of finding work in the mills. The companies did no importing. Their agents were able to recruit all the labor they wanted on State Street. In fact the supply of colored labor in Chicago actually exceeded the demand and some 500 who were unable to get work there moved on to Cleveland where they

[38] Commission of Inquiry, Interchurch World Movement, *Report on the Steel Strike of 1919*, p. 177.

[39] *Ibid.*, pp. 177-78.

[40] Letter to President Gompers, March 30, 1920.

[41] Foster, *op. cit.*, p. 207.

took the places not only of white men but also of black men on strike. The Cleveland mills could get no local Negroes to act as strike breakers.[42]

In the Pittsburgh district importations were heavy.[43] They were reinforced by many who came from mills which were largely shut down. In many places serious clashes occurred between the pickets and the Negro strike breakers. In Pittsburgh and the neighboring towns of Braddock and Monesson the presence of the black men was resented not only by the strikers but by the white strike breakers as well. Bloody fights resulting in injuries and deaths took place in the plants themselves, despite the constant efforts of the state constabulary and the sheriff deputies to prevent them.[44] Both the authorities and the companies did their best to suppress this fact. "We couldn't get any information from public sources," declared John Fitzpatrick, chairman of the National Committee to Organize Iron and Steel Workers. "We went to the City Hall. We went to the Health Department. We went to the coroner's office . . . to get information, and there was no information from anybody. The only information that we could get was from the undertaker, and the undertaker gave us this information: 'No man or woman has died in this community in the last week. If you want to know anything further, go out to the graveyard and see the number of new graves made there, and you will get an indication of what has happened in the steel mills between the white and colored workers.' "[45]

The strike did little to change the Negro's position in the steel industry. He had already won his place before the strike began, and the part he played in the struggle neither increased his numbers nor gave him advancement in the mills. Nearly all the Negro strike breakers who came into the plants from

[42] Report of the National Committee to President Gompers, March 30, 1920.

[43] Ibid.

[44] Testimony of John Fitzpatrick before the Chicago Commission on Race Relations, op. cit., p. 28.

[45] Ibid.

outside lost their places when the walkout ended, while those already employed who had remained at work and had been advanced to the better jobs of the men who struck went back to their old places when the old employees returned.

Any future attempt to organize the steel industry will have to face in earnest the problem of organizing the black worker. This is true not only of the North but to an even greater extent of the South, where the industry rests upon Negro labor receiving a decidedly lower rate than the northern worker. Steel companies are tending more and more to do business on a national scale. In this new competition the northern mills will be at a disadvantage if they are required to pay more for their labor than their competitors. Thus far the balance has been equalized by the fact that southern plants are for the most part behind the rest of the country in productivity.[46] And for this fact Negro labor is again responsible, for it is so cheap and plentiful that many companies have been able to operate profitably with machinery which the North would consider antiquated. But when the southern operators replace their old furnaces and machinery with modern equipment, the balance will swing in favor of the South. A situation may well develop not unlike that in bituminous coal, where the West Virginia and Alabama mines, manned to a large extent by Negroes, have been able to undersell the Pennsylvania fields.[47] When the United Mine Workers failed to organize West Virginia and Alabama, it began its own destruction. In the same way any movement to organize steel which does not take the southern Negro steel worker into account will be foredoomed to failure.

[46] United States Bureau of Labor Statistics, *Productivity of Labor in Merchant Blast Furnaces*, Bulletin No. 474, 1929, p. 12.

[47] See Chapters X and XVII.

CHAPTER XII

THE NEGRO IN THE STOCKYARDS

THE Negro's real entrance into the packing industry was in the rôle of a strike breaker. True, Negroes had been employed in the industry ever since 1880, when the first member of the race joined one of Armour's killing gangs in Chicago;[1] but it was not until 1894, when the butcher workmen, affiliated with the Knights of Labor, struck in sympathy with Debs's American Railway Union, that Negroes came into the industry in significant numbers. When the strike broke out, the whole number of Negroes employed in the yards was about five hundred.[2]

Shortly after the strike began the *Chicago Tribune* noted that "an offer was received by one of the larger packing firms to supply several hundred Negroes to fill the places of the strikers."[3] Some of these Negroes had worked in slaughter houses and abattoirs in the southern and border states. Most of them, however, had had little or no experience in the meat industry. Skill in the old sense of the word was coming to mean less and less in the packing industry even as long ago as 1894. Specialization was making the employment of cheaper labor possible.[4] Poles, Lithuanians, and Bohemians made up the bulk of this cheap unskilled labor and the supply seemed so plentiful that the companies, according to the same item in the *Tribune*, refused the offer to use Negro strike breakers on

[1] United States Bureau of Labor, *Influence of Trade Unions on Immigrants*, Bulletin No. 56. Jan., 1905, p. 2.

[2] *Ibid.*

[3] *Chicago Tribune*, July 13, 1894.

[4] Edna Louise Clarke, *History of the Labor Controversy in the Slaughtering and Meat Packing Industry in Chicago*. (Unpublished Master's Essay, University of Chicago, 1922), Copy No. 4, p. 48.

the ground that "it was not necessary or advisable policy to antagonize the whites."

But the opportunity to get labor to help break the strike was evidently too tempting to forego for very long. Within a week Negro workers were in the yards. Their presence immediately made trouble, and before long "indignation" and "displeasure" resulted in numerous attacks on colored persons.[5] Even supervisory employees who did not join the strikers objected to the black strike breakers. One foreman resigned his place when he was told to work with Negroes. Anti-Negro demonstrations were frequent and the papers told how:

Swinging from the cross tree of a telegraph pole at the corner of Root and Halsted Streets, near the entrance to the yards, the effigy of a Negro roustabout was suspended. A black face of hideous expression had been fixed upon the head of straw and a placard pinned upon the breast of the figure bore the skull and cross bones with the words "nigger-scab" above and below in bold letters.[6]

Few of the Negroes who came into the yards during the trouble of 1894 stayed on after the strike was settled, and their number grew but little during the ten years of industrial peace which followed. The colored working force in 1904, ten years after the sympathetic strike, was probably less than 5 per cent of the entire force in the yards.[7] Nearly all of these were unskilled laborers, receiving a wage of 18 cents an hour.[8]

In May, 1904, the Amalgamated Meat Cutters and Butcher Workmen of North America formulated a scale of wages and working conditions which, among other things, called for a minimum wage rate for unskilled workers of twenty cents an hour. The packers replied by offering the union a uniform scale for the unskilled of 16.5 cents an hour, claiming that the supply of labor was plentiful and that they

[5] Chicago *Record-Herald*, July 19, 1894.

[6] *Ibid.*

[7] Eric W. Hardy, *The Relation of the Negro to Trade Unionism.* (Master's Essay, University of Chicago, 1911), pp. 35-36.

[8] John R. Commons, "Labor Conditions in Slaughtering and Meat Packing." *Trade Unionism and Labor Problems* (1905), pp. 223-28.

could get all the workers they wanted at that rate.[9] The union, seeing that the employers were in earnest, dropped its demand for an increase and turned its energies to preventing a general reduction. A number of plants in which agreements with local unions expired actually put the 16.5 cent rate into effect. The union asked that "negotiations be immediately opened upon an 18.5 cents minimum for all common labor."[10] The controversy ended in a strike involving 23,000 workers in Chicago alone and over 40,000 throughout the entire country.

Michael Donnelly, the president of the union, realized at once that, despite the strength of his organization, he faced a serious task. "We must," he said, "get everybody into the organization, including the women and Negroes."[11]

The packers turned immediately to the well-supplied labor market of which they had boasted and directed their main efforts towards securing strike breakers. They brought salesmen and employees from their branch houses to take over the skilled positions, and for the rougher work they imported large numbers from outside. Most of these were foreigners, many fresh from abroad, and Negroes from the South. The wages of these unskilled strike breakers were unusually high, ranging from $2.25 to $2.50 a day, together with free board and lodging.

Frequently the workers brought in to break the strike knew nothing of where they were going or what they were doing. Immigrants with the "passed" tags of the New York customs authorities still on their luggage were brought to Chicago in special trains, unloaded at obscure points about the yards, and smuggled into the various departments in groups of ten or twelve.[12] Sometimes, when they found out what they were doing, workers refused to continue at their jobs. A colored strike breaker told of how a whole train load of Negroes brought up

[9] Clarke, *op. cit.*, p. 75.

[10] Amalgamated Meat Cutters and Butcher Workmen of North America, *Proceedings*, 1906, p. 7.

[11] Interview with Miss Mary McDowell of the University of Chicago Settlement.

[12] *New York Tribune*, Aug. 5, 1904.

from the South refused to go to work when they learned they were to take the jobs of men on strike.

Most of the Negroes, however, and many of the immigrants, had no idea as to what a strike or a union was. The Negroes, being easiest to obtain, were the largest strike-breaking element. They were brought to work in such numbers that it was thought for a time that the packing industry was going to become overwhelmingly black. Estimates place the number of Negroes employed in the plants as high as 10,000.[13]

To prevent violence strike breakers were housed in the yards. Sanitary and moral conditions were so bad that Ogden Armour himself is reported to have said after a visit to his plant, "My God, I can't stand that."[14] A business men's association in the vicinity of the yards adopted resolutions condemning as "a menace to the city of Chicago" the employment as strike breakers of "Greeks and Negroes brought from the vilest slums of the leading American cities" as well as "the most ignorant immigrants . . . direct from Ellis Island." The resolution ran, "To any reasonable man it is plan that such people cannot permanently be retained by the trust and hence must be poured out upon the city at the beginning of the winter season. They are a menace as future paupers."[15]

After the stream of Negroes had continued to pour into the yards for nearly six weeks, strike leaders and other union officials addressed an appeal to Booker T. Washington to use his influence to prevent Negroes from working in the plants until the strike was settled, and to address a mass meeting of colored citizens in Chicago on the subject: "Should Negroes Become Strike Breakers?" Mr. Washington declined the invitation because of a previous engagement, and there is no record of his having made the appeal the labor leaders requested.[16]

[13] Hardy, *op. cit.*, pp. 35-36.
[14] Interview with Mary McDowell.
[15] Resolved by the Ashland Avenue Business Men's Association, quoted by Clarke, *op. cit.*, p. 88.
[16] *New York Tribune*, Aug. 25 and 27, 1904.

Evidently the great majority of the Negroes who were brought into the stockyards in 1904 lost their places when the more experienced men who had walked out returned to work. Six years after the strike the census of 1910 showed that there were but 67 Negroes in a total of 10,840 semi-skilled and un-skilled workers in the Chicago industry. For the next six years the situation remained essentially unchanged until the shutting off of immigration from Europe and the rise of the war indus-tries began to restrict the supply of white labor. This, to-gether with the Negro migrations to the cities, soon began to increase the proportion of Negroes in the yards, until in Jan-uary, 1918, it reached 20 per cent.[17] Some of the colored men who were old hands in the plants were promoted to more skilled jobs, while many migrants from the South and such centers as Cincinnati and St. Louis, with experience as butchers and skilled workmen, came to Chicago and other northern cities and obtained skilled jobs. In Cincinnati a school was established by an important local packing concern, where Negro butchers were trained. Before long a similar school was opened at the Negro Y. M. C. A. in Chicago under the auspices of the leading packers. Labor was scarce and the com-panies needed trained men.

In the spring of 1916 the Amalgamated Meat Cutters and Butcher Workmen again began to organize the packing-house workers. With labor becoming scarce and prices going up, the time seemed particularly opportune for an organization drive. The packers tried to block the progress of organization by in-creasing wages. During the middle of 1916 the pay of un-skilled workers was increased to 20 cents an hour. This was the first change in the scale since 1904. Later in the year a second increase was granted which was followed by several more in 1917, until the wage rate for unskilled workers had

[17] Data presented by Mr. O'Hearn of Armour and Co. to Judge Alschuler in the First Arbitration Proceedings before the United States Administrator for Adjusting Labor Differences Arising in Certain Packing House Industries, Jan., 1918.

risen to 27.5 cents an hour. Similar increases were granted to piece workers, mechanics, and skilled butcher workmen.

These increases did not arrest the progress of organization. By the summer of 1917 the movement had gathered such strength that the packers became seriously alarmed. The Swift management sent out instructions directing its executives to dispense with the services of active union members "as soon as practicable." The local representatives were urged to handle matters so as not to force a strike and were cautioned to find reasons "other than being members of labor unions" for discharging undesirables.[18]

At the same time the various plants were asked to increase their percentage of colored labor. In answer to this suggestion the manager of the Denver works wrote that they had recently started an employment bureau at the plant to handle such matters. "We shall start at once," he said, "to increase the percentage of colored help on the plant with the intention of getting it to fifteen per cent or higher as soon as we possibly can." [19] The packers were banking on the traditional difficulty of organizing Negro workers as well as upon the fact that many of the organizations having jurisdiction over crafts represented in the yards did not accept Negro members.[20] Before long the number of Negroes in the Chicago yards alone reached 12,000, and it soon became clear to those interested in organizing the industry that no movement which did not include the Negro could be successful. A conference of all local unions with jurisdiction over packing-house workers was called, and a special federal body known as the Stock Yards Labor Council was set up.[21] John Fitzpatrick, president of the Chicago Federation of Labor, William Z. Foster, and John Johnstone were placed in charge of the work of organ-

[18] Clarke, *op. cit.*, p. 102.

[19] *Ibid.*

[20] *Ibid.*, p. 105.

[21] William Z. Foster, "How Life Has Been Brought into the Stock Yards," *Life and Labor*, April, 1918, p. 63.

ization. "We approved the situation," explained Fitzpatrick, "of bringing all the workers in the stockyards into the organizations already established. We didn't want any Jim Crow situation out there."[22]

Yet a few organizations, like the carmen and machinists, had "white" clauses in their constitutions, or rituals. Fitzpatrick took up with the American Federation of Labor the question of overcoming these obstacles to the inclusion of colored workers and it was decided that the Negro must be organized. The Federation promised to grant special federal labor union charters to such groups of Negro craftsmen as were barred from the regular internationals. The Meat Cutters and Butcher Workmen, the key craft in the yards, while remaining outside of the Stockyards Labor Council, followed its traditional policy of organizing all eligible members without regard to race or color.

After devoting two months to making their plans and perfecting the structure of their machine, the Stockyards Council set to work with a corps of organizers in September, 1917. Two of these organizers were Negro coal miners whose services were contributed by the miners of Illinois. When the Illinois district of the United Mine Workers met in convention in the spring of 1918, Fitzpatrick and Foster, in the name of the "stockyards union," sent them a telegram thanking them for the coöperation of these organizers, Bell and Robinson, "whose efforts made it possible to organize the Negroes in the industry."[23]

Membership grew rapidly when the organization began to function. Within two months the union claimed 40,000 members in Chicago and 30,000 in the other meat centers of the country.[24] In Chicago Negroes joined the Meat Cutters and Butcher Workmen's Union in large numbers. Although they received equal treatment with the whites in the yards, there

---

[22] Testimony before the Chicago Commission on Race Relations, August 16, 1920, p. 33.

[23] *Ibid.* p. 65.

[24] First Arbitration Proceedings, 1918, pp. 105 and 38.

were many complaints that Negro union butchers were unable to use their cards in organized shops outside the yards, whereas white men could use their cards anywhere.[25] The proportion of northern Negroes who joined the various unions was high, one leader estimating it at 90 per cent.[26] But on the whole, the organizers were disappointed in the response of the colored workers. At the height of the organization drive but 4,000 to 5,000 Negroes, or only about one third of those employed in the Chicago yards, joined the unions.[27] The organization spokesmen drew up a list of demands and attempted to see the heads of the several companies, but the packers refused to meet them. A strike vote followed on Thanksgiving eve, 1917, in all of the great packing centers of the Middle West. Ninety-eight per cent of the employees favored a strike, but the war and government intervention brought about the arbitration of the dispute. One of the workers' demands which the packers accepted without submission to arbitration provided: "There shall be no discrimination towards any employee or prospective employee because of creed, color or nationality." [28]

The era of compulsory arbitration lasted until September 15, 1921. Throughout this period union activity went on unabated, for the strength of the workers under arbitration, as under the strike, depended upon organization. Every crisis in the arbitration proceedings led to increased union activity and to anti-union tactics on the part of the packers. And every such crisis was accompanied by attempts to arouse distrust between black workers and white.

One of the principal agencies for keeping this division alive was an organization known as the American Negro Protective League. The League was founded by J. T. Scott,

[25] Interview with Mr. George Arthur, secretary of the Negro Y. M. C. A., Chicago, Feb., 1927.

[26] Clark, *op. cit.*, p. 106.

[27] Foster's testimony before the Chicago Commission on Race Relations, Aug. 16, 1920, p. 75.

[28] Number 11. See First Arbitration Proceedings, pp. 58-61.

a Negro editor of Carroll, Illinois. Scott was an ambitious politician and founded the League chiefly to further his own political ends. In 1916 he ran for President of the United States, doubtless largely to advertise himself. He is said to have received 2,521 votes.[29] Naturally, the declared purpose of the League was to protect the Negro in his rights and extend his privileges. The organization seems to have fallen into decay after the campaign of 1916, but was shortly revived in Chicago by a Negro leader named R. E. Parker.

President Fitzpatrick of the Chicago Federation of Labor charged that Parker was an agent of the packers designated to keep the colored workers out of the labor movement.[36] Parker admitted that he was responsible, when the unions first began their organization drive in 1916, for distributing some 20,000 posters and handbills in the neighborhood of the yards reading:[31]

BEWARE THE STOCKYARDS UNION.

All Colored Working Men in the Stockyards —
Do Not Join Any White Man's Union
Save Your Jobs
Come tonight to 35th and Forest Avenue, corner
restaurant, hear the Protective League Speakers.
R. L. JACKSON, Chairman.   R. E. PARKER, President.

Parker claimed that the packers had nothing to do with the financing of this propaganda. "I paid for them myself," he said. "I did it for my race and for my personal interest in my race."[32]

An investigation of Parker's activities, undertaken by the authorities of the State of Illinois, indicates that whatever may have been the connection of the packers with Parker's

[29] Investigation of R. E. Parker, president of the Negro Protective League, Oct. 1, 1917. Submitted to the Commission on Race Relations, Aug. 16, 1920.

[30] Statement to Chicago Commission on Race Relations, *op. cit.*, pp. 59-61.

[31] *Ibid.*

[32] *Ibid.*

20,000 handbills and posters, the employers' relations with Parker were close. The report read in part:[33]

> Parker stated that Swift and Co. and Armour and Co. were expecting a strike at any moment and are prepared to fill the strikers' places with Negroes sent from the South. . . .
>
> He (Parker) said that he went South last winter for Swift's, Armour and Co. and the Steel Trust and imported more Negroes than any man in Chicago . . . and now any time a Negro wanted work, he can give him or her a note, and they will be given work in the stockyards, but if they join a union, they can't.

Parker claimed that he was against the Negro joining the white man's union "because the white man is never satisfied and will strike when he is most needed." He also declared that he was against strikes and that if the white man struck the Negro should take his place.[34]

The packers also, according to the Chicago Federation of Labor, "subsidized Negro preachers and Negro politicians and sent them out among the colored men and women to induce them not to join the unions." A Negro Y. M. C. A. secretary and two aldermen were charged with serving on the packers' staff and participating actively in their campaign. One of these aldermen was accused of going to the attorney for the unions while he was preparing his case for presentation to the arbitrator and urging him not to ask for a preferential union shop.[35]

This opposition of the Negro leadership was largely responsible for the Negro's comparatively poor response to the union appeal. — "It seemed to make no difference what move we made," said William Z. Foster, "there was always an argument against it." Later he wrote:

> . . . the propaganda was sent forth that the only reason the whites were willing to take the blacks into their locals was because the latter, being in a minority, could exert no control; that the whites would not

---

[33] *Ibid.*
[34] *Ibid.*
[35] *New Majority*, Aug. 9, 1919.

dare to give them a local of their own. This was met by the establishment of a Negro local of miscellaneous workers in a convenient neighborhood. Then the Jim Crow cry was raised that the whites wanted
the blacks to herd by themselves. This the organizers answered by
insisting that a free transfer system be kept up between the white and
black locals. . . .

But even this did not satisfy; the anti-union propaganda went on
undiminished and with tremendous effect.[36]

The unions attempted to meet this hostile Negro campaign
by giving particular care to the demands and grievances of the
Negroes who joined the unions. These workers constituted
but a tenth of all the organized stockyard employees. Yet,
Foster stated, "40 per cent of the total amount of grievances
that were presented by all the workers in the stockyards came
from these colored workers and the standing instructions were
to look after them very carefully." [37] A second method of
overcoming Negro hostility was counter propaganda by the
unions showing the part the Negro was playing in the stockyard workers' movement. One such bulletin, issued by Federal
Labor Union No. 15805, composed of colored stockyard
workers, was addressed to "Fellow Colored Workers" and
read in part:

A conference was held on Sunday, November 11th in Omaha,
Nebraska, representing the workers in all the packing houses outside of
Chicago, for the purpose of drawing up a working agreement suitable
to all the workers involved.

It is significant of the times that fifteen delegates present at that
conference, were of our race and helped very materially in shaping that
agreement . . .

So you see, Brothers, that the slogan amongst the Stockyard workers
is *"Each for all and all for each,"* irrespective of race, creed, color,
nationality or sex. So come and hear what we are demanding from the
packers, in conjunction with our white Brothers who are thoroughly
organized and going down the line with us.

---

[36] William Z. Foster, *The Great Steel Strike*, p. 211. See also Foster's
testimony before the Commission on Race Relations, Aug. 16, 1920, pp. 73-77.

[37] Testimony before the Chicago Commission on Race Relations, Aug. 16,
1920, p. 75.

The labor unions charged that the packers, in spite of their denials,[38] imported large numbers of Negroes from the South into Chicago and other centers in order to weaken the unions and depress the standard of working conditions.[39]

During the middle of 1919 the unions presented demands for further wage increases to Judge Alschuler, the arbitrator. While preparing their case they redoubled their organizing activities, particularly their efforts to get Negro members. Street meetings were held every day at the time the workers were leaving the yards. The police tried persistently to break up these meetings until the unions succeeded in having the captain in command of the stockyards district transferred to another precinct.

In connection with their organizing campaign the unions planned a great mass meeting and demonstration to take place on Sunday, July 6, 1919. Black and white workers were to parade together throughout the stockyards district and then gather in a park or playground to listen to speeches. On the day before the demonstration the packers asked the police to revoke the parade permit, or at least to require the whites and Negroes to march separately. This, they doubtless felt, would emphasize race distinctions and make the task of unionization more difficult. On the morning of the day set for the demonstration the chief of police summoned the union leaders to his office and told them that a trade-union parade through the stockyards district would precipitate a race riot.[40] The packers, it seems, had informed the police that the Negroes were arming to assault the whites.[41] Efforts were made to induce the unions to call the parade off. The police were ready to revoke the permit, but a compromise was effected under which whites and blacks marched separately, but joined together at the playground for a joint demonstration. According to the report in a labor paper:

[38] Testimony before Chicago Commission on Race Relations, May 13, 1920.
[39] *New Majority*, Aug. 9, 1919.
[40] *Ibbid.*, July 12, 1919.
[41] *Ibid.*, Aug. 9, 1919.

As the procession [of the white workers] moved along the streets of the colored district, the air echoed with cheers of thousands of colored workers who lined the sidewalks, windows and doorways, and hundreds joined the throng and marched to the Bentner playground to hear the speakers.[42]

The marchers carried placards and banners addressed to the colored workers. One read:

The bosses think that because we are of different color and different nationalities we should fight each other. We're going to fool them and fight for a common cause — a square deal for all.

The organ of the Chicago Federation of Labor, the *New Majority*, described the parade under the headline:

YARDS EMPLOYE PARADE INSPIRES COLORED WORKERS WITH UNION IDEALS

Not long after this demonstration the race riots occurred. They grew out of a misunderstanding at the bathing beaches and in their immediate outbreak had nothing to do with the labor situation.[43] The packers, however, according to Fitzpatrick, at once tried to make them seem a labor affair and tried to use the situation to increase friction between the races.[44]

For several days, as a result of the rioting, the colored people were kept in their own districts. This prevented thousands of stockyard employees from getting to work. The labor unions were planning to go into the colored and white districts to hold a series of meetings aiming to dispel distrust and restore harmony between the races. Describing the plan President Fitzpatrick of the Chicago Federation of Labor declared:

We are going to explain to them that there won't be any fight between Negro and white workers. Their interests are in common, for

---

[42] *Ibid.*, July 12, 1919.

[43] See *The Negro in Chicago*, Chapter I.

[44] Testimony before the Chicago Commission on Race Relations, Aug. 16, 1920, p. 49.

they are working together that, when they are in the stockyards, they are on common ground, trying to earn their daily bread and they must stand together.[45]

While in the midst of formulating these plans the union officials learned of a conference in Armour's office between representatives of the company and the city and state authorities at which arrangements were made to escort Negro workers to the yards under a police and military guard.

Whether the plan was merely short sighted or whether, as the union leaders charged, it was maliciously designed "for the purpose of creating a riot actually in the stockyard district,"[46] it was certainly dangerous. The officers of the stockyards' organization hastened to the conference at Armour's and demanded admission. When they entered the meeting room, after first having been denied admission, they were quoted as having told the men around the table: [47]

We have worked day and night to keep this situation in hand. Not your police, not your soldiers have stopped this rioting, but the union men and women of the stockyards district.

The longer it has gone on, the harder it has been to hold. Five days of race riots have got some of our white workers alarmed and even inflamed, until we do not know how much longer we can control them.

But this we know. Union men will not work with machine guns pointed at them. They will not work under the spur of bayonets. If you do the thing you are planning here, we will not be responsible for the blood that will be shed. You will be responsible.

These men will be on the killing floor of the packing plants. They will have cleavers and knives. They know how to use them. The machine guns will not be able to stop what will happen unless they mow down the workers, white and black. You must be insane to attempt such a thing.

The union officials tried to get the police to postpone their plans, but the chief claimed that he had orders from the mayor

45 *Ibid.*, p. 52.
46 *Ibid.*, p. 50.
47 *New Majority*, Aug. 9, 1919.

and was going to put them through.[48] Neither the governor
nor the mayor could be reached in spite of persistent efforts to
locate them all through the night. The plan was to go into
effect the next morning. As a last resort Fitzpatrick and his
lieutenants called a meeting of colored and white leaders of
the stockyard workers. He addressed them in front of the
Congress Hotel from the running board of an automobile,
saying:

> Now it is your duty to go into the black district and notify every
> man you come in contact with not to go to the stockyards to-day. This
> is a job perpetrated by "Big Business." They are going to start a riot
> and make a labor war out of this situation and we want to avoid that.
> Now go to these districts and tell these workers not to be fooled by this.[49]

As a result of these efforts, several thousand Negroes and
perhaps 20,000 white workers were induced not to go to work
that morning. Some 600 lost their jobs for not reporting, but
no race riot took place.

There is, of course, no way of telling whether or not the
union's tactics actually prevented another interracial outbreak,
but the situation was certainly tense and the scene was set for
almost anything to happen. Not only were the scars of the
terrible July race riots still fresh, but the situation in the stockyards district was further aggravated after the rioting had
stopped by the burning of the homes of several hundred
workers, chiefly Poles and Lithuanians who had comparatively
little anti-Negro prejudice. No one knew who did the firing,
but the whites suspected the Negroes, the Negroes suspected
the whites, and organized labor suspected the packers.[50] Besides, the yards and surrounding districts were flooded with
posters of the type already noted, telling the Negro to beware
of the white man's union. That the situation did not become
more serious is as surprising as it was fortunate.

[48] Fitzpatrick's testimony before the Commission on Race Relations, Aug. 16,
1920, p. 53.
[49] *Ibid.*, p. 55.
[50] *Ibid.*, and also *New Majority*, Aug. 9, 1919.

Interracial strain became relieved after the passing of the crisis of 1919, and it was not until early in 1921 that the Negro again came to play a dramatic rôle in the stockyards situation. Suddenly, in February of that year, the packers notified the federal government that, inasmuch as the war was actually over, they considered the Alschuler agreement at an end. On March 6, 1921, two days after Harding's inauguration, they announced a wage cut of 8 cents an hour for common labor and 12.5 cents for piece workers. Proposals to lengthen hours were made at the same time. The reductions were to go into effect a week later, on March 14th. The unions made a hasty appeal to the President and succeeded in extending the Alschuler agreement for another six months.[51]

The week between March 6th and March 14th was a crowded one, and it looked for a time as though a strike might be precipitated if the proposed cuts became effective. In the midst of this crisis R. E. Parker, of the American Negro Protective League, again came into prominence. Speaking as the head of a new organization, the American Unity Labor Union and Colored Welfare Club, Parker announced through the daily papers:

We do not believe that striking at this time will help the cause of labor, as there are thousands of men out of employment. We will refuse to coöperate with the Amalgamated Meat Cutters and Butcher Workers' Union in any way and will not strike.[52]

At the same time Parker sent the following open letter to the several packing companies:[53]

Writing you this open letter from the American Unity Welfare Labor Union of six thousand of colored laborers, most of whom belong to the American Unity Welfare Labor Union and are experienced workers in all departments of packing houses.

We, the colored laborers of the packing plants, accept 20 per cent

[51] Clarke, op. cit., p. 132; also Benjamin Stolberg, "The Stock-Yard Strike," Nation, Jan. 25, 1922, p. 92.
[52] Chicago Tribune, March 13, 1921.
[53] Dated March 9, 1921.

reduction of wages on skilled labor and 10 per cent reduction on un-skilled labor, as you have agreed to give.

We are willing to sign an agreement on these terms for one year and work colored laborers of our organization in every department of the packing plants.

We further agree to work eight hours for a day's labor with time and a half for overtime and double time for Sundays and holidays, unless a day off is given with pay for Sundays and holidays.

We have no affiliation with the American Federation of Labor or the Amalgamated Meat Cutters' Union and we refuse to strike on the day that they have set to strike. We believe we are better off by not being in the white union as they have always been unfair to colored laborers; that is the reason we organized the American Unity Welfare Labor Union five years ago.

The Chicago Federation of Labor denied Parker's right to speak for 6,000 Negroes. The entire number of Negroes in the yards at the time did not number that many and most of them belonged to the regular unions. "The American Unity Labor Union," the Federation declared, "is not a bona fide organization. It is a strike-breaking agency. Parker tried to hold a meeting of his 'union' last Sunday to offset the Chicago mass meeting of the stockyards workers. Less than a hundred were present. Thousands of Negro workers joined the white workers in the union demonstration." [54]

The threatened strike of March, 1921, which was post-poned by the extension of the Alschuler agreement, finally took place in December of the same year. The proposed wage reductions which the arbitrator had refused to approve were finally put into effect with the approval of the representatives of employee-representation machinery which had been estab-lished by all the large packers. [55]

Though greatly weakened by internal dissensions and pre-vailing unemployment, a substantial proportion of the workers answered the strike call. The employers, as on similar occa-sions, employed strike breakers. Morris and Company is said

[54] *New Majority*, March 19, 1921.
[55] See Stolberg, *op. cit.*, also Clarke, *op. cit.*, pp. 148-49.

to have opened an employment office in the heart of the Chicago Negro district and strike leaders claim that colored workers were also brought up from the South to Chicago, St. Paul, Omaha, Kansas City, and to every other center in which the great packers operated. The payrolls of one of the great companies in Chicago showed that during January, 1922, the proportion of Negro employees rose from 25 to 33 per cent of the total.[56] Another company, perhaps the largest operator in the yards, increased its Negro force from a little over one sixth of the total in 1921 to more than a third of the total in 1922.

This injection of the race issue intensified and embittered the industrial struggle. One Negro was murdered,[57] and two thousand police were sent to the scene of the strike, turning "Packingtown" into an armed camp. The old story of recriminations and clashes between strikers and "scabs," between the police and the workers, between white men and black was repeated. The strike lasted for nearly two months. It ended on January 31, 1922 in the complete defeat of the workers. The unions were driven from the yards and have never since been able to regain a footing.

The use of the Negro as a strike breaker seems to have led the white unionists to forget that the Negro also played his part in the conflict as a striker. "Our union workmen," said the *Chicago Defender*, the largest Negro paper in the country, "obeyed the dictum of their superior union officials and did exactly what their white brothers did — struck. The packers scoured for non-union help and in the dragnet many of our group were found." [58]

Yet neither the *Defender* nor any other prominent Negro paper or Negro leader in Chicago suggested that there was anything odious about strike breaking, about taking the job of a man who was struggling for better conditions. Instead,

[56] Clarke, *op. cit.*, p. 149.
[57] Stolberg, *op. cit.*, p. 92.
[58] *Chicago Defender*, Dec. 17, 1921.

the *Defender* set out to give a rational and logical explanation of why the Negro does break strikes. It said:

> The prospect of a job in these times of near-starvation looks good to any idle worker, black or white. Self-preservation is the first law of nature; add to this the knowledge that such opportunities only come to the black worker on occasions like this and it can be readily seen why he fills the union worker's place. It is an ill wind that blows no one good, and while there is much to be said in favor of unionism, the powers that be must be made to realize that no strike can be effective in this country unless the black worker is part and parcel of it.[59]

Although many Negroes who worked as strike breakers in 1922 won permanent positions in the yards, the black worker won his place in packing, as in steel, as a result of the war-time labor shortage rather than as a result of strike breaking. It may be well to recall that, while the Negro broke the strike of 1904, there were but 67 Negroes among 10,840 semi-skilled and unskilled workers in the Chicago yards six years later, in 1910.

One of the two largest operators in the country reported in 1929 that it had 2,638 Negroes on the payrolls of its larger plants and that these constituted 19 per cent of all its employees in these plants. In 1925 these same plants employed 2,949 Negroes or 22.5 per cent of the total force. They were distributed as follows in the three general categories of skill:

Year	Per Cent Unskilled	Per Cent Semi-Skilled	Per Cent Skilled
1925	33.6	40.9	25.5
1929	28.2	46.7	25.1

They constituted the following percentages of the total number of employees in each of the three categories:

Year	Per Cent Unskilled	Per Cent Semi-Skilled	Per Cent Skilled
1925	30.7	29.4	13.0
1929	22.7	26.9	11.0

[59] *Ibid.*

This is a representative company and its figures are a cross section of the industry as a whole. If figures for Chicago alone were available they would probably show an even larger percentage of Negro employees. Another company, also one of the "big four," employed over 2,200 Negroes in Chicago alone in 1928. These constituted 30 per cent of its total force. While most of the Negroes in the industry do the harder, less pleasant, and lower paid work, many of those in the skilled class hold some of the best paying and most highly skilled jobs in the yards. A few firms employ Negroes in supervisory posts. While these colored foremen as a rule supervise the work of colored gangs, one occasionally finds a Negro foreman in charge of a gang which includes both white and black workers. There is no question that the Negro now has a secure and important place in the packing industry.

With every vestige of trade unionism stamped out of the yards, the packers turned to company unionism and employee representation. All such representation plans include Negroes in prominent places. In 1927 two Negroes served as representatives on the Armour assembly, while the Swift plan had a Negro secretary.

With the Negro occupying the place he does in the packing industry, it would be difficult for the race leaders to condone strike breaking in the event of another industrial struggle. It could not bring the Negroes industrial opportunities which they have not already gained. It could only help to undermine their established standards.

Chapter XIII

THE NEGRO ON THE RAILROADS

THE four transportation brotherhoods, the engineers, the conductors, the firemen, and the trainmen dominate the railway labor world. Two of these organizations, the Brotherhood of Locomotive Engineers and the Order of Railway Conductors, have almost from their inception barred Negroes from membership. In view of the fact that the occupations which they represent involve the exercise of authority and responsibility, these two brotherhoods have been able to keep the jobs of conductor and engineer exclusively in the hands of white men. The trainmen and firemen, however, though also barring Negroes from their brotherhoods, have not been able to bar them from their crafts.

The employment of Negroes in these crafts has been confined almost entirely to the South. It was usual before the world war for southern railroads to employ Negro firemen on from 50 to 60 per cent of their runs, while some roads employed 85 to 90 per cent colored firemen, or practically the entire firing force exclusive of apprentice engineers. In 1920, according to calculations based upon the census, Negroes constituted 27.4 per cent of the firemen, 27.1 per cent of the brakemen and 12.3 per cent of the switchmen in the southern states of Alabama, Arkansas, Florida, Georgia, Kentucky, Louisiana, Mississippi, North Carolina, South Carolina, Tennessee, Texas, Virginia, and West Virginia.

The four transportation brotherhoods are not alone in drawing the color line. Several of the shop crafts as well as the telegraphers, the clerks, and the maintenance-of-way employees follow their example, and either bar Negroes altogether or refuse to admit them on a basis of full equality with whites. Even an insurgent industrial union, like the American Federation of Railroad Workers, has a white clause in its constitution, while a weak craft body like the Switchmen's Union of North America has tried to outdo its rival, the Brotherhood of Railway Trainmen, in its hostility to the Negro.

Yet the Negro is represented in almost every branch of railroading. Figures issued by the United States Department of Labor in 1924 [1] showed 136,065 Negroes in the industry distributed as follows in the various occupations:

Baggage Men and Freight Agents	111
Boiler Washers	2,377
Brakemen	4,485
Conductors	33
Engineers	111
Firemen	6,478
Foremen and Overseers	1,195
Inspectors	202
Laborers	95,713
Porters, Train and Pullman	20,224
Superintendents	2
Switchmen and Flagmen	2,874
Telegraphers	97
Telegraph and Telephone Linesmen	202
Miscellaneous	1,961

These employees were scattered through every state of the Union, though the great majority of them were employed in the southern or border states. Georgia led the list with 10,865, while the other states, employing more than a thousand, followed in the order named: Louisiana 9,141, Virginia 9,010, Alabama 8,844, Texas 8,391, Tennessee 8,100, Mississippi 7,744, North Carolina 5,321, Florida 5,091, Illinois 4,554, Arkansas 4,184, Kentucky 3,916, South Carolina 3,858, Missouri 3,706, Pennsylvania 3,560, Ohio 3,219, Maryland

[1] United State Bureau of Labor Statistics, *Monthly Labor Review*, Nov., 1924, p. 161.

2,221, West Virginia 2,052, Oklahoma 1,807, Indiana 1,167, New York 1,127.

The Negro's position in the railway service is an anomalous one. He is unorganized in the midst of a highly organized industry. He is ineligible to promotion in the transportation departments, despite the fact that American railroading in these branches is built upon the theory of promotion by seniority. Until recently he received lower pay than the white men even when he did the same work. All of this has had a profound effect not only upon the white railway man in the South but upon railway service in the South as well. Southern railway managements, hostile to trade unionism, frankly used the Negro to weaken the organizations which barred him from membership. They also used him to depress the current wage standard. Engineers were obliged to be cautious for fear that the roads might some day decide to employ colored engineers. White firemen and trainmen who faced direct Negro competition were obliged to accept lower wages and less favorable employment contracts in "Negro territory" than firemen and trainmen in other parts of the country.

The Negro's presence has also profoundly affected the efficiency of the all-white conductor and engineer services. In the North these posts are commonly filled by the promotion of trainmen and firemen. In the South, where custom has made this impossible for Negro trainmen and firemen, the roads have been obliged to hire conductors and engineers from outside. Not a few of those hired have been men who had lost their places on northern roads because their efficiency was below par, while another large group has been made up of so-called "boomers" who come to one place for the cotton rush and then go to the next for the wheat rush. Though the public has suffered in quality of service the companies have seemed satisfied. They were able to weaken trade unionism on their lines and to keep wages down. They could ignore the more efficient performance of the northern roads since they were obliged to compete only among themselves.

Satisfaction, however, did not extend to the white employees, who seldom missed an opportunity to protest against the competition of unorganized and cheap black labor.

"Every time the firemen ask for an increase in wages or for overtime due them," complained a white fireman on a southern run, "they are told by the superintendent, 'Why I can get a Negro in your place for one dollar, while I am paying you $1.50 per day.' " [2]

"Since 1885," ran an article in the *Locomotive Firemen's Magazine*, "The Brotherhood of Locomotive Firemen has been victorious. The fireman of today knows nothing of what the fireman suffered before, through organization, they had thrown off the yoke of slavery. But why does not the Brotherhood accomplish similar results in the South? The answer is: 'The Negro.' " [3]

Two methods of coping with the situation presented themselves. The first, as some northern members suggested, was to take the Negro into the brotherhood and "teach him and educate him" and fight discriminatory working conditions on a united front.[4] The second was to force the roads to eliminate the Negro from train and engine service. The condition of the southern labor market made the second alternative impossible while the first course was rendered equally unrealizable by the attitude of the white brotherhoods.

The southern locals insisted that despite their economic aim they were social organizations.[5] The fraternal aspect of labor unionism, particularly of the four railway brotherhoods, is of great importance. In the United States where fraternal orders play so important a rôle in social life the labor union is sometimes almost as important as a lodge as an instrument of economic protection. During periods when there is no outstanding economic issue to interest the group the fraternal aspect increases in importance and does much to hold the mem-

[2] *Locomotive Firemen's Magazine*, Aug., 1899, p. 203.
[3] *Ibid.*, May, 1899, p. 541.
[4] *Ibid.*, Aug., 1902, p. 286.
[5] See above, Chapter IV, p. 167.

bership intact. It is not strange, therefore, that the southern locals should persist in regarding themselves as social organizations and insist that to admit the Negro to their ranks would be to admit him to social equality. "Social equality is something that will never be tolerated in the South," wrote a railroad man from Virginia. "When the Negro presents himself to become a member of a southern labor organization, on the day of the balloting, black marbles will be at a premium." [6]

An angry member from Louisiana wanted to know what the Negro had done to merit recognition by the firemen. "The Negro can organize on his own responsibility if he likes," he wrote, "but he can never affiliate with southern organizations of any kind. The firemen of the South have a great work to do without crossing the color line." [7]

Other members showed deeper personal race prejudice. "As for the Brotherhood of Locomotive Firemen taking in the Negro, I hope and pray that I may never live to see the grand old B. of L. F. so disgraced as to take into its protecting folds this class of God's creation." [8]

"A 'burr-bear' to become a member of our grand organization," said another member. "Just think of that! No, never! I would like to know how we would go about organizing Negro firemen." [9]

At the same time a similar controversy over the race question was going on in the ranks of the trainmen's brotherhood. In 1899 the issue was brought to the floor of the national convention through a resolution calling upon the four brotherhoods to "give their support toward clearing our lines of this class of workmen." The resolution was adopted after an attempt to table it, moved by H. R. Fuller, was overwhelmingly defeated. [10] Since then no brotherhood official has dared to espouse the Negro trainman's cause. At the same time oppo-

[6] *Locomotive Firemen's Magazine*, Sept., 1902, p. 427.

[7] *Ibid.*, p. 426.

[8] *Ibid.*, p. 432.

[9] *Ibid.*, April, 1901, p. 440.

[10] Brotherhood of Railway Trainmen, *Proceedings*, 1899, p. 59.

sition to the Negro has become better and better organization politics. The railroad labor movement has thus been obliged to adjust itself to the social prejudices of the South. Any attempt on the part of the northern majorities to force the southern locals to accept the Negro as an equal, assuming such desire on their part, would disrupt trade unionism south of the Mason-Dixon line.

The issues between the white and black railwaymen were dramatically brought to public attention in 1909 when the management of the Georgia Railroad removed ten white assistant hostlers, members of the Brotherhood of Locomotive Firemen, who were getting $1.75 a day, and filled their places with Negroes at $1.25 a day. At the same time Negro firemen were given equal seniority rights with white employees with the result that in several cases, where length of service warranted it, Negroes had better runs than white men.[11] The Brotherhood of Locomotive Firemen protested in vain. Finally it called a strike and succeeded in crippling a large part of the Georgia Railroad's service.

Since 1904 or 1905, when the Georgia Railroad first began to hire Negroes in large numbers, the effects of their lower wages were felt by the white workers. Prior to the employment of Negroes on a large scale firemen received 50 per cent of the engineers' wages. In 1907 the pay of engineers was raised but the firemen got no increase. Subsequently the engineers' scale was again raised by 6 and 10 per cent, while the firemen were positively refused an advance. As a result their wages fell to less than 47 per cent of the engineers' scale, while other roads in the territory were paying their firemen from 53 to 60 per cent of what they paid their engineers. At the same time the Negro firemen who were held responsible for their white brothers' low estate were getting $1.75 for runs for which white men received $2.77, and $2.62 for runs for which white men received $3.62.[12]

[11] *Outlook*, June 5, 1909, p. 310. Also *Locomotive Firemen's Magazine*, Aug., 1909, p. 267.

[12] *Locomotive Firemen's Magazine*, Aug., 1909, p. 261.

The strike brought the whole question of the colored fire-man's status into the foreground. The union, instead of mere-ly demanding the correction of its immediate grievances, asked that Negro firemen be eliminated altogether from the road. In its efforts to make a case it called witnesses before the arbitration board who testified that Negroes were incompetent and inefficient workers. Most of these witnesses were en-gineers and they were nearly unanimous in declaring that the Negro fireman was not as a general rule to be trusted; that he was constantly liable to fall asleep if he was not watched, that on cold days he went to sleep before the furnace, while on hot days he crawled into the shade and took a nap; that he was inefficient and unintelligent about his work, firing "to make smoke and not for steam." Witnesses also stated that most Negro firemen could not read or write or understand orders and train signals. They also declared that the company recognized the Negro's inferiority by not requiring as high standards for admission into the service as it did for white men; also by accepting a lower standard of performance when they were once employed.[13]

The railroad, on the other hand, declared that the Negro had brain and brawn enough to be a competent fireman.[14] It admitted frankly that it employed Negroes because they were cheaper. "If we can get what we want cheap," said the com-pany's spokesman, "is it a crime to take it? We give the Negro less because his scale of living is lower. We give the white man more because we do not wish to bring his scale down to the level of a Negro." [15]

Instead of recommending the elimination of the Negro as the strikers demanded, the arbitration board decided that Negroes employed as firemen, hostlers, and hostlers' helpers should be paid the same rate of wages as white men working in the same capacities. "If this course is followed by the com-

[13] *Ibid.*, pp. 255-56.
[14] *Ibid.*, p. 257.
[15] *Ibid.*, pp. 257-58.

pany," said the Brotherhood of Locomotive Firemen, "and the incentive for employing Negroes thus removed, the strike will not have been in vain."

The principal effect of the strike was not any particular tangible gain to the brotherhood but rather the crystallization of sentiment for the elimination of the black man from the railroad transportation service. "Brothers, I say," read a communication in the Locomotive Firemen's Magazine six months after the Georgia strike, "the Negro firemen must go, and now is the time, as we have the 'mired wheel' started." [16]

Two years later, in March, 1911, the employment of Negro firemen on the Cincinnati, New Orleans and Texas Pacific Railroad, generally known as the "Queen and Crescent" line, precipitated a strike of unusual violence and bloodiness in which ten firemen were killed and many more were injured. The issue which precipitated this strike was not unlike that which led to the walkout on the Georgia Railroad two years before. The firemen's brotherhood objected to the company's policy of granting equal seniority rights to white and black men. They claimed that the latter, being ineligible for promotion to the post of engineer, were acquiring most of the preferred runs on the road and permanently blocking them to white men, requiring the latter to remain upon heavy freight runs and locals. This, the brotherhood claimed, was in direct violation of its agreement with the railroad that "firemen will have preferred work, runs or promotion according to age in service, experience, merit and ability being equal." [17] The word "firemen" in this proviso, the brotherhood claimed, meant white men eligible to promotion. Negroes were to occupy a fixed status at the bottom of the industrial scale in places which the white man did not want. [18]

Two weeks and two days after the strike broke out a settlement was reached which provided that Negro firemen were

[16] *Ibid.*, Jan., 1910, p. 127.
[17] *Ibid.*, April, 1911, p. 519.
[18] *Ibid.*; also *Crisis*, May, 1911, p. 15.

not to be employed on the company's line north of Oakdale and Chattanooga, Tennessee, and that the percentage of Negro firemen thereafter employed was not to exceed the percentage in service on January 1, 1911, "provided a sufficient number of competent white men" could be secured. The agreement also stipulated that Negro firemen should not be assigned to more than one-half of the passenger runs or to more than one-half of the preferred freight runs, provided always that such assignment be made only on the basis of seniority and fitness. Hardly was this settlement reached when the white firemen on the Southern Railroad of Georgia threatened a walkout for reasons almost identical with those which caused the Queen and Crescent strike. The strike was averted by the railroad agreeing to employ no Negro firemen north of a given point on its line. The agreement also fixed the differential in pay for the same work between white and black firemen and hostlers at 30 per cent.[19]

During these conflicts the newspapers in the towns through which the roads passed usually supported the white firemen. The local labor unions also supported the brotherhood and passed resolutions expressing sympathy with its stand.[20] One newspaper, the *Daily Sun* of Jackson, Tennessee, was quoted with approval by the *Firemen's Magazine* [21] as saying:

> The question of doing away with the Negro firemen has been mooted for several years and like Banquo's ghost, it will not down. Therefore it is hoped that the various roads will begin now to prepare for accepting the inevitable, for Americans have determined that neither the Negro, the Chinaman or the Japanese will "run" either this country or its railroads. If the "cause" of the strike had been removed, much bloodshed and suffering would have been avoided.

The agreements on the Queen and Crescent and the Southern of Georgia roads marked the beginning of a definite attempt by the white brotherhoods to stop the extension of Ne-

---

[19] *Ibid.*, Sept., 1913, p. 224.
[20] *Locomotive Firemen's Magazine*, May, 1911, p. 656.
[21] *Ibid.*, p. 657.

gro employment in engine service. Ultimately Negroes were to be eliminated from the fireman's craft, but in the meantime the brotherhood planned to direct its efforts to the more practical program of confining Negro employment to certain districts and of limiting the proportion of Negroes to the percentage in the service on a given date.

The policy thus inaugurated by the firemen, following a bitter strike, had been put in force by the Brotherhood of Railway Trainmen a year before, when that organization wrote the following clause into an agreement signed with southern roads at Washington:

No larger percentage of Negro trainmen or yardmen will be employed on any division or in any yard than was employed on January 1, 1910. If on any roads this percentage is now larger than on January 1, 1910, this agreement does not contemplate the discharge of any Negroes to be replaced by whites; but as vacancies are filled or new men employed, whites are to be taken on until the percentage of January first is again reached.

Negroes are not to be employed as baggagemen, flagmen or yard foremen, but in any case in which they are so now employed, they are not to be discharged to make places for whites, but when the positions they occupy become vacant, whites shall be employed in their places.

Where no differences in the rates of pay between white and colored employees exists, the restrictions as to percentage of Negroes to be employed does not apply.[22]

This agreement, by explicitly barring the future entrance of Negroes into specific occupations, went further than that subsequently signed by the firemen of the Queen and Crescent and the Southern Railroad of Georgia.

Not the least interesting portion of the trainmen's agreement was the section waiving the restrictive percentages where no difference existed in the rates of pay between white and colored employees. The roads, after all, used Negro labor because it was cheaper than white. If Negro labor should

[22] Agreement between the Brotherhood of Railway Trainmen and the Southern Railroad Association, Jan., 1910.

cease to be cheap, then the incentive to employ it would disappear and the white unions' problem would be automatically
solved. It will be remembered that a year earlier the arbitration board in the Georgia Railroad strike recommended that
white and colored employees receive the same rate of pay
for the same work.[23] The provision in the agreement forced upon the Southern Railroad of Georgia in 1911 fixing the differential between white and colored labor at approximately 30
per cent was also a move in the same direction. It was not,
as a prominent Negro journal implied, an attempt to force a
discriminatory wage rate upon Negro employees[24] but, on
the contrary, an effort to control the differential between white
and black labor so as to prevent the latter from becoming too
attractive to employers.

As long ago as 1901 the *Locomotive Firemen's Magazine*[25] printed a plea from a southern member urging "those
brothers who are forced to come in contact with a Negro on
an engine to try to make him understand that if he does a
white man's work he is entitled to the treatment and pay of a
white man and that if he makes the attempt the company and
the engineers will be compelled to respect them."

Important as were these various contracts and declarations
of policy, they effected no fundamental change in the Negro's
position on the railroads. Such changes had to wait until the
United States government took control of the roads during
the World War.

The war, as has been constantly pointed out, opened up
new industrial opportunities for Negroes in both North and
South, and it was not long before the high wages of the shipyards and other war industries began to draw Negroes from
the railroads in large numbers. It looked for a time as though
the aim of the white brotherhoods to force the Negro out of
railway employment was suddenly to be realized. The propor-

---

[23] See above, pp. 290-91.
[24] *Crisis*, Sept., 1913, p. 224.
[25] *Locomotive Firemen's Magazine*, Jan., 1901, p. 112.

tion of Negro workers began to fall rapidly. Several lines became so exasperated at the Negro's newly developed unsteadiness as seriously to consider his elimination from their service. Finally on May 25, 1918, on the plea of Robert L. Mays, head of a Negro union, the Railway Men's International Benevolent and Industrial Association, Director General McAdoo issued his general order number 27 providing that from June 1, 1918 on "colored men employed as firemen, trainmen, and switchmen shall be paid the same rates as are paid white men in the same capacities." Secretary McAdoo, a southerner, in his report to the President, referred to his order as "an act of simple justice." [26] The act stayed the Negro's drift away from the railroads and put an end to the talk among railway executives of eliminating him because of his unsteadiness. With railroad jobs made attractive, the Negro was glad to have them. The predictions of the brotherhoods that if the pay of the two races were equalized the Negro would disappear from the transportation services went unrealized. Labor was scarce and the roads were glad to have steady and experienced employees no matter what their color.

But the desire of the trainmen's and firemen's brotherhoods to eliminate the Negro from their occupations continued undiminished, and when hostilities ended in Europe and war industries began to shut down, the white railwaymen's hostility to the Negro increased. In January, 1919, with the roads still under federal control, a committee of white employees on the Illinois Central and its subsidiary, the Yazoo and Mississippi Valley, served notice on their employers that all white switchmen would leave the service in a body unless all yard engines were manned entirely by white men. Ever since the great strike of 1894 the Illinois Central and Yazoo Railroads had employed Negroes on train and engine service. Switching crews which consisted of three or four men were almost invariably mixed, crews of four consisting of a white foreman, one white and two colored helpers, while crews of

[26] Report of the Director General of Railroads, 1918, p. 15.

three consisted of a white foreman and a white and a black helper. At one of the company's properties, the Nonconnah Yards, where a method called "hump" switching was used, shifts consisted of two white foremen, seven white "liners," and eighteen colored "car riders."

Prior to 1918, 60 per cent of the roads' switching force at Memphis had been colored. But during the war the proportion of colored switchmen declined, leaving a majority of jobs in the hands of white men. With colored men getting the same pay as white, their jobs became desirable. White foremen began to find incessant fault with the black men's work. Negroes were penalized and discharged on the slightest pretext, and as their places became vacant white men were appointed to fill them.

The colored employees protested to the local railway officials through an organization of their own, the Colored Association of Railway Employees. The latter attempted to adjust the situation by replacing eighteen white men in the terminal by colored men who had just been laid off in one of the company's yards where the force had been cut.

The white switchmen, instead of proceeding in accordance with the terms of the brotherhood's contract with the roads and filing a protest with the local brotherhood lodge, sent a committee to the railroad officials announcing, as mentioned above, that they would quit in a body at a given hour that same day unless all colored switchmen were discharged and their places filled with white men. The white workers objected to working with Negroes because the latter were "inefficient, disorderly and boisterous," and because they objected to the Negro's receiving the same pay as white men.[27] The company rejected the committee's demand and insisted that the matter be handled in the regular manner through the brotherhood. The committee, however, insisted that the matter was not an organization matter but a question which the employees themselves expected to settle.

[27] Statement of Facts from the Grievance Committee of the Colored Association of Railway Employees, Memphis, Tenn., Jan. 17, 1919.

The committee made good its threat. At the hour set all the white switchmen at the Memphis end of the Yazoo and Mississippi Valley Railroad walked out. The strike quickly spread to the Illinois Central where certain employees refused to take out passenger and freight trains. On the following morning the strikers were joined by employees of the Frisco System and on the next day by the white switchmen of the Union Railway of Memphis and the Southern Railroad. Estimates placed the number of strikers at from four to six hundred.[28]

President Lee of the Brotherhood of Railway Trainmen demanded that the men return to work at once and file their grievances in the usual manner. But E. P. Tucker, leader of the switchmen, insisted that the men were not on strike. "This is not a movement of organized labor," he declared, "though all are union men. . . . We have been working under conditions no man would tolerate in being forced to work with incompetent and unreliable Negro employees. Now the crisis has come and we refuse to longer risk the sacrifice of life and limb." [29]

Tucker further declared that sentiment was so strongly behind his movement that not only was it likely that the switchmen on the roads not yet affected would quit, but also that a general walkout of firemen, engineers and conductors in the district would probably take place if his men's demands were not met.[30] His statement proved an idle boast. Twenty-four hours after it was made the collapse of the strike was complete. Not only did the other crafts fail to respond to the switchmen's call, but the conductor's and firemen's brotherhoods joined with the trainmen in inducing the strikers to return to work. The Brotherhood of Railway Trainmen fought the movement for the sake of organization discipline, not because it disapproved the switchmen's grievances. The brotherhood charged that its rival, the Switchmen's Union of North America, an

[28] *Ibid.*, also *Railroad Trainman*, March, 1919, p. 200.
[29] Memphis *Press*, Jan. 14, 1919.
[30] Memphis *News-Scimiter*, Jan. 14, 1919.

A. F. of L. union, aided the strikers and had agents on the scene thoughout the trouble.[31]

The strike failed but the white switchmen remained as determined as ever to force the Negro out of their craft. Open efforts gave way to secret activity and terrorization. These tactics reached their height on the Illinois Central system where special agents reported a plot to kill Negro trainmen who refused to give up their jobs. A price of $300 was said to have been placed on the head of every Negro trainman. Negro employees, firemen as well as trainmen, received letters signed "Zulus" ordering them to leave the service and threatening them with death if they refused.[32] One colored fireman was shot in the face with a shotgun as his train was nearing a station. In several instances trains were stopped by white men armed with clubs and guns. Negro brakemen were beaten up for holding "white men's jobs" and were threatened with death if they were caught running in the territory again. Black trainmen were ambushed and beaten on their way to or from work. One brakeman was kidnapped at Lambert, Mississippi, under the eyes of the train crew, while he was making an inspection accompanied by the white flagman. His story runs:

We arrived at Lambert, Mississippi, at 9:15 P.M. While the engine was being supplied with water, the flagman, Mr. Shields, and I were looking the train over, beginning at the caboose and proceeding toward the engine. When I reached a point of about 40 car lengths, I was suddenly stopped by three white men, who had passed the flagman, Mr. Shields, and did not interfere with him, but halted me demanding that I throw up my hands at the point of pistols.

They snatched my lantern and threw it away, and had me to march across the field about a mile. They asked me didn't I know that they didn't want any Negroes braking on the head end of those trains. One of them wanted to beat me up, but the other two insisted he not do it, "because he is a good old Negro, I know him," is what one of them said. They warned me not to come through there. After being closely questioned and threatened with violence, they finally turned me loose.

---

[31] *Railroad Trainman*, March, 1919, p. 200.
[32] New York *World*, Aug. 1, 1921.

By this time my train was gone, and train No. 51 going south had arrived at Lambert. They commanded me to leave Lambert on this train, so I ran and caught train No. 51 and explained to the train crew what had happened. Mr. Gary, the conductor, took a statement of same and said he would give it to the operator at Swan Lake, Miss.[33]

Several Negro trainmen, less fortunate than the man who told this story, were killed by the terrorist "Zulus" in the course of their campaign. Such violence was confined largely to lines in the far South, particularly Mississippi. Though the method succeeded in driving a great many colored men from the roads, it affected the mass of Negro railwaymen far less than the deliberate and persistent peaceful attack on their position by the train service brotherhoods.

This attack, which had resulted in the trainmen's agreement of 1910 limiting the percentage and territory of colored employees [34] and in similar agreements affecting the firemen on certain southern lines,[35] was resumed in 1919 while the railroads were still under federal control. Following the "outlaw" strike among the switchmen at Memphis, the trainmen's brotherhood forced the Railroad Administration, under threat of tying up the southern lines, to enter in agreements revising working rules. These new regulations, which became effective in September, 1919, looked eminently fair and just. A casual reading would hardly indicate that they were deliberately aimed at the Negro, a fact which both the brotherhood [36] and the Railroad Administration [37] made no effort to conceal. In fact the regional director of railroads for the territory affected admitted in an interview with a delegation of Negroes who had come to protest against the new rules that he had complied with the demands of the white trainmen rather

[33] Statement of Bob Grant, colored brakeman, 65 McLemore Ave., Memphis, Tenn. Incident occurred Feb. 15, 1921.

[34] See above, p. 293.

[35] See above, p. 293.

[36] *Railroad Trainman*, Nov., 1919, p. 798.

[37] Letter from Walter White of the N. A. A. C. P. to Walker D. Hines, Director General of Railroads, Dec. 19, 1919.

than endure a strike because "it was better to inconvenience a few men than tie up the entire South for an indefinite length of time." [38]

The rules in question provided:

1. All men entering the services on and after September 1, 1919 to fill positions of brakemen, flagmen, baggagemen, and switchmen will be subjected to and required to pass uniform examinations and comply with regulations as to standard watches and to know how to read and write.

2. Discipline will be applied uniformly, commensurate with the facts of the case, without distinction as to color.

3. When train or yard forces are reduced, the men involved will be displaced in order of their seniority, regardless of color. When a vacancy occurs, or new runs are created, the senior man will have preference in choice of run or vacancy, either as flagman, baggageman, brakeman or switchman; except that Negroes are not to be used as conductors, flagmen, baggagemen or yard conductors.

4. Negroes are not to be used as flagmen except that those now in that service may be retained therein with their seniority rights. White men are not to be used as porters, no porter to have any trainman's rights except where he may have established same by three months continuously in freight service.

In addition to the above, it was also agreed that trainmen on the extra board would be permitted to select runs or positions in accordance with their seniority.

The purpose of these new rules, according to brotherhood officials, was to put an end to "discrimination against white trainmen" by raising the requirements for admission and the standards of performance in the service for colored trainmen to the level required of white trainmen.[39] But while abolishing this disadvantage to white employees the rules, through the operation of apparently just seniority provisions, put Negroes out of places they had long held. In fact President Lee of the Brotherhood of Railway Trainmen called attention to this,

[38] Letter from W. S. Lovett to Walter White, Jan. 17, 1920.
[39] *Railroad Trainman*, Nov., 1919, p. 804.

saying, "under this agreement a large number of white trainmen either on the extra list or out of service, who had been
denied work as brakemen (head end) were permitted to select
positions as brakemen in order of their seniority." [40] Custom,
in most places where mixed crews were employed, had given
the Negro the post of brakemen at the head end of the train,
while the post of flagman at the rear end was reserved for
white men. In some states the rule barring Negroes from the
rear end of the train was actually written into the law.

Now the new agreement, while giving the white man the
privilege of exercising his rights on the head end, barred the
Negro from the rear end. The result was that on line after
line, after the new rule became effective, the senior white men
gave up their positions as flagmen and claimed their rights at
the head end, while the younger white men took the job at the
rear end which the Negro was not permitted to fill. The principle of seniority on which railroading was supposed to be
founded became to a large extent seniority for white men only.

The following list illustrates the situation. The list is made
up of flagmen and brakemen on a district of the Illinois Central for ten freight train crews of two men each.

Name	Color	When Employed
J. H. Moppins	White	Jan. 1, 1901
C. J. Walton	Colored	July 15, 1901
G. G. Hubbard	White	Jan. 10, 1902
S. M. Richardson	Colored	June 16, 1902
W. B. Brown	White	Feb. 21, 1903
John Poole	Colored	Aug. 25, 1903
H. J. Kincaid	White	March 5, 1904
M. H. Green	Colored	Sept. 12, 1904
S. P. Gibson	White	April 14, 1905
F. D. Best	Colored	Oct. 11, 1905
George Williams	Colored	May 2, 1910
Will Dickerson	Colored	June 3, 1912

[40] Circular of Instructions, No. E-3 Grand Lodge, Brotherhood of Railway
Trainmen, Oct., 1919.

Name	*Color*	*When Employed*
P. C. Bradley	Colored	Nov. 6, 1914
Robert Wood	Colored	Dec. 29, 1916
Paul Woodard	Colored	July 9, 1918
R. H. Bostic	White	Jan. 7, 1922
H. C. Huff	White	June 8, 1922
P. J. Rowlett	White	Feb. 13, 1922
J. R. Sherley	White	Sept. 14, 1923
S. E. Patterson	White	Jan. 17, 1924

Ten of the above names are white and ten colored. The five senior white men have been in service just a few months longer than the five senior black men, but the five junior black men have been in service many years longer than the five junior white men. Yet if business fell off so as to require a reduction of staff so that but five crews were needed to do the work previously done by ten, the five senior white men on the rear end would be permitted to displace the senior Negroes on the head end, while the five junior white men would be permitted to take the places vacated by them at the rear end, eliminating all the Negroes from actual service. To take specific names on the list, Moppins (colored) who had been in service since 1901 would be out of work while Patterson (white) who had been in service since 1924 would have a good job.

The new rules, it will be noted, provide that white men are not to be used as train porters and that no porter is to have trainman's rights unless he has established the same by serving three months continuously in the freight service. When this rule was announced there were over 7,000 train porters, practically all Negroes, in the railway service. These employees are not to be confused with Pullman porters, though their duties are similar to those of Pullman porters on parlor cars. A large proportion of the train porters, in addition to performing their regular porter duties, serving the passengers on the chair cars and coaches, helping them with their baggage, keeping their cars clean and properly heated and ventilated, perform the duties of head-end trainmen. A number of roads find it profitable to substitute porters for head-end trainmen but pay the former a porter's instead of a trainman's wage. Even on lines where porters are not permitted by the rules to perform tasks which regularly belong to the trainmen, they nevertheless frequently do trainmen's work under the orders of the conductor.

Under the Railroad Administration rules intended to abolish inequalities in pay, porters who did trainmen's work were classified as trainmen or "porter-brakemen" and received trainmen's pay. This in many instances meant an increase in wages from $50 or $55 a month to a minimum of $120 plus overtime and plus such extra money as the porter made on tips and from the sale of pillows to passengers at twenty-five cents apiece.

Over night the job of porter changed from that of a low paid menial doing a trainman's work as well as his own, to a place of sufficient income and dignity to arouse the interest of the white trainmen. "Porter," if the title and pay of "brakeman" were attached to it, ceased to be a "black man's job." Railway rules recognized the fact by providing that "in reductions of force where white trainmen displace porter-brakemen, they will perform the duties of porter in addition to those of brakeman. . . . Any brakeman who fails to comply with the above may be displaced by a colored porter-brakeman." [41]

The elevation of the porter-brakeman was not an unmixed blessing to the Negro, for along with equal pay there went, on many roads, equality on a general train and yard service seniority list.[42] The old practice of keeping the Negro porter in a separate category was abandoned, and all train and yardmen regardless of color were placed on a general list. This seemed manifestly fair. Now that the Negro received a standard wage for his labor it appeared only just that he take his chances along with the rest. To do less would be to ask for special privileges. Yet the new regulations raised a storm of protest among the Negro employees, who complained that

[41] Missouri Pacific Rules, Nov., 1920.
[42] Ibid., Oct. 1, 1920.

their operation under the interpretation of the white Brotherhood of Railway Trainmen was threatening the Negro's right
to remain in railway service.

The rules made the white man eligible to the post of porter-brakeman without at the same time lifting any of the bars
against the Negro's entrance into places exclusively open to
white men. The brotherhood, the most important factor in
the interpretation of the rules, not only barred the Negro
from membership but was doing its best to force him out of
the service. The rules obliged the Negro, now that his job had
become attractive to the white man, to take all the white man's
risks without sharing his advantages and without having the
organized protection he enjoyed.

Another regulation, innocent enough on the surface, which
has worked hardship on the Negro trainman is that providing that "porters shall have no rights as trainmen except where
such rights may have been established by three months continuously in freight service." Under the standard contracts of
the Brotherhood of Railway Trainmen, which bars Negroes,
the latter can have no standing as trainmen in passenger service because they cannot begin work as freight service trainmen. Besides, many roads now having colored freight trainmen have not hired Negroes since the war. Hence, on such
roads no colored man could transfer to passenger service as a
trainman under the terms of the contracts. This seemingly
innocent regulation together with the apparently fair seniority
rule has thus turned out to be an economic "grandfather
clause" designed to force the Negro out of train service as
quickly as possible under the forms of due process of law.

The white trainman's hostility to the Negro train porter,
having its roots in the latter's willingness to do a trainman's
work for half the standard wage, is no recent manifestation.
It actually antedates the formation of the present Brotherhood
of Railway Trainmen. As long ago as 1881 the present union's
predecessor, the old Brotherhood of Railroad Brakemen,
made agreements providing that the front man on passenger
trains was to be a regular brakeman. But the union was too

weak to compel the observance of its contracts so the agreement was generally ignored, the porter continuing to do the
brakeman's work. Former President Lee of the trainmen's
brotherhood dates the determination of the white trainmen to
do away with Negro competition from this time. "The Negro
porter today," he told a colored labor leader, "is not the victim of the white trainmen's greed but of the railroads' av-
arice." [43]

Even today the brotherhood's attitude is partly due to
the common practice of requiring the train porter to perform
regularly designated trainman's duties under the conductor's
orders, a practice which was made a regular rule of the service
by the federal regional director of the southeastern district
under the United States Railroad Administration. The colored
railwaymen's organizations fought the rule at the time as a
discrimination against the Negro worker, for it required him
to perform trainmen's work for porter's pay. But the rule
stood and the practice has continued with a resulting increase
in the number of colored train porters and a decrease in the
number of colored trainmen.

One of the consequences of the practice of using the low
paid porter for the high paid trainman's work has been a revival of the full-crew movement. This movement, fostered
largely by the Brotherhood of Railroad Trainmen and supported by the other railway unions, aims at legislation to regulate the size of train crews and the standards of railway employment. The bill most commonly introduced provides that a
crew shall consist of five persons; an engineer, a fireman, a
conductor, a brakeman and a flagman. The legislation is urged
in the interest of safety, but it is well known that other motives,
such as providing jobs and reducing the work of individual
train-service employees, have not been absent from the minds
of its sponsors. [44]

[43] Statement by Lee to R. B. Lemus, head of the Brotherhood of Dining
Car Employees.

[44] Interviews with union officials. See also Bureau of Railway Economics,
Arguments for and against Train-Crew Legislation, 1915, especially pp. 23-24.

Full-crew legislation has not been aimed primarily at the Negro. In fact the movement began in the North, where there were no Negroes in train service. The first bill was introduced in Massachusetts in 1902. Between 1910 and 1913 a new wave of agitation resulted in the passage of several new full-crew laws as well as in the enforcement of measures which had been dead letters for a decade. It was then that the Negro began to suffer. Train porters doing brakemen's work were not "brakemen" in the eyes of the law or under the definitions of the brotherhood's contracts with the railroads. On several lines Negro porters who had been doing brakemen's work for many years, and regarding whose competence no question was raised, were forced out of the service because they were not "brakemen." [45]

The opposition of the railroads stemmed the tide of the full-crew movement for many years. Its recent vigorous revival, like the earlier movement, is not aimed primarily at the Negro. It is rather an attempt to counteract the effects of improved mechanical devices which have been making it possible for the railroads, without appreciably increasing the number of their employees, to lengthen their freight trains and handle an increased volume of traffic. The present bills, which have been introduced in many states, seek to limit the length of trains and fix the minimum number of the crew. Negro organizations have offered to support these measures if they are so framed as not to discriminate against colored employees, or, specifically, if the words "brakemen or porter" are substituted for "brakeman." The white brotherhood, however, interested in the elimination of the Negro, has refused this concession.

Like the trainman the Negro fireman also seems to be headed out of the service. New contracts between the roads and the Brotherhood of Locomotive Firemen and Enginemen negotiated during the last few years have prevented the Negroes from regaining the old place which they held on the southern roads before war industries attracted so many of

[45] *Crisis*, Oct., 1911, p. 254.

them to more remunerative jobs.[46] The Southern Railroad, where the firing force was 80 per cent black before the war, now employs but 10 per cent colored firemen on its central division. On the Atlantic Coast Line the percentage has been reduced from 90 to 80. On the Seaboard Air Line the ratio has fallen from 90 to 50 per cent and the brotherhood has recently been seeking a contract to reduce it to 40 per cent. On the Shreveport division of the Illinois Central, where white firemen worked on a fifty-fifty basis, the brotherhood has also been seeking a contract confining the blacks to 40 per cent of the jobs.

Several lines which have always employed colored men on train and engine service have recently signed contracts with the brotherhoods going beyond the customary provisions restricting the percentage and territory of colored workers and providing instead that Negroes be replaced by white men as rapidly as vacancies occur. While most of these agreements have been on smaller lines, the action of the great St. Louis and San Francisco system in issuing regulations in the fall of 1928 pointing to the eventual elimination of all Negroes from shop, train, and yard service indicates the headway which the white organizations have made in their anti-Negro campaign. In 1926 President Robertson of the Brotherhood of Locomotive Firemen told his convention that he hoped to be able to tell the next meeting that not a single Negro remained on the left side of an engine cab.[47] That, of course, was a political speech which the membership doubtless discounted. However, there is no better index of the hopes of a constituency than the exaggerations of its politicians.

The decision of the St. Louis and San Francisco Railroad to replace Negroes with white men when vacancies occurred doomed the black man not only in train and yard service, which are under brotherhood jurisdiction, but also in shop

[46] See above, pp. 294-95.
[47] Speech at the convention of the Brotherhood of Locomotive Firemen and Enginemen, Detroit, 1926.

service over which the brotherhoods have no control. The Negro has never occupied a position in the railroad shops comparable in importance to his position in the transportation departments. As in the latter service, his rôle has been confined chiefly to the South, and his part has been that of helper and laborer. It has long been usual on many southern lines to find a very substantial part of the helper force in the shops colored. A number of shops have made it a practice to employ only colored helpers. In the northern shops the Negro has been used only as a common laborer.

Prior to the shopmen's strike of 1922 the number of Negroes in the skilled shop crafts, North or South, had been negligible. The one exception to this rule was the Illinois Central System where Negroes had been brought into the shops in large numbers in 1911 to break a strike which affected the entire system from Chicago to New Orleans. This strike lasted officially for about three years. The shops were filled with Negroes who were put to work under white foremen and instructors and taught specialized operations. White strike breakers were also used for finer operations for which the employers thought the Negroes incompetent. A substantial proportion of the colored men who came into the Illinois Central shops at that time are still employed there.

When the shopmen's strike began in 1922 Negro helpers who were organized went out and stayed out as long as the white mechanics. There was not a sufficient supply of skilled colored labor available for the Negro to be used effectively as a strike breaker. While an effort like that of the Illinois Central, eleven years before, might succeed on a single road, it was impossible to try it with any hope of success in a nation-wide strike. The roads wanted strike breakers who had some experience and skill and naturally turned chiefly to white men. Yet as a result of the strike Negro mechanics in small numbers did find permanent places in the New York Central shops at Cleveland, in the Erie shops at Buffalo and Cleveland, and in the Illinois Central shops at Memphis.

Negro labor was used along with white labor wherever it

was available, but it was only in the Pullman Company's shops that it was a factor of major importance. These shops had been unionized during the period of federal control. When the general shopmen's strike was called late in the summer of 1922, the Pullman shops were affected along with those of all the other carriers. The company immediately took advantage of its close relations with the Negro world. For years it had been its custom to put some five to six hundred additional porters into service during the summer season to handle the increased rush of business. When the shopmen struck the company got in touch with its former summer porters and offered them and, through them, other Negroes an opportunity to work in its shops. Thousands responded and were put to work as fast as they reported at the various plants. They started at the mechanic's-helper rate of 47 cents an hour.

The group of colored strike breakers was a particularly good one and an unusually high percentage remained in the shops after the strike was settled. The helper rate was subsequently raised to 52 cents an hour. The management made employment of Negroes a permanent policy. Regular promotions are now made from laborer to helper, to helper-apprentice, to mechanic. Helper-apprentices are promoted by 2 cent raises in the hourly rate until they reach the maximum of 65 cents. The mechanics' rate is 70 cents an hour, though some get 72 and 75 cents. Today, about 60 per cent of Pullman shop workers are colored. They are engaged on practically every skilled operation. None, however, occupy supervisory positions. Even in the battery house at the Calumet works in Chicago, where all of the workers from laborers to electricians are Negroes, the supervisors are white. But in spite of the fact that it finds this labor perfectly satisfactory, the executives of the company stated that they would continue to use Negro labor only as long as it was unorganized. If they were compelled to deal with union labor again, the president of the company declared that white labor would be restored.[48]

[48] Interview with President Carry, Vice-President and General Manager Hungerford, and the assistant to the president, James Keely, Chicago, Feb., 1927.

Aside from the Pullman Company and the few other places mentioned, the Negro has no place in the shop crafts. The practice of discriminating against him through contracts negotiated by the white unions without the presence of his representatives is followed here in the same manner as in the transportation services. All the regular shop craft unions either bar the Negro or discriminate against him in some fashion. Of the sixteen "standard" unions in the Railway Employees' Department of the American Federation of Labor, only five jurisdictions have Negro members, and in all of these Negroes are put in auxiliary or subordinate locals.[49] These jurisdictions are maintenance-of-way, firemen and oilers, railway carmen (wash cleaners), blacksmiths, railway clerks (freight handlers).

In 1924 six unions known as the Six Federated Shop Crafts made an agreement with the International Brotherhood of Firemen and Oilers to organize the Negro shop-craft helpers.[50] The organizations concerned were the machinists, the sheet-metal workers, the boilermakers, the electrical workers, the blacksmiths, and the railway carmen. Under this agreement colored helper locals were chartered by the firemen and oilers which undertook to organize the Negro helpers, collect their dues, and handle their benefits. Representation before the railroads under this agreement is in the hands of local shop committees and the system federations, the latter receiving a per capita contribution from the firemen and oilers for each colored man organized.

This arrangement helps to protect the shop crafts from the use of helpers as strike breakers in time of trouble. It brings the Negro to the support of the white organizations in return for certain benefits and protection, while at the same time consigning him to a position of permanent inferiority. On some roads the very unions which entered into this arrangement with the firemen and oilers had contracts providing that

[49] See Chapter IV, pp. 57-58.
[50] Railway Employees Dept., A. F. of L. File 8-112, April 10, 1924.

"none but white English-speaking helpers shall be employed when available." [51]

With the scales thus weighted against them what were the Negro railwaymen to do to protect their interests in their dealings with their employers and in their relations with their white fellow workers? Organization seemed the first requisite, and ever since the early years of the century there have been attempts among colored railwaymen to organize in defense of their interests. In fact every wave of attack upon the Negro's position on the railroads was accompanied by the formation of protective organizations.

The first organization of Negro railwaymen, the Colored Locomotive Firemen's Association, was formed in Georgia in 1902 or 1903. This step was taken during a period of hot discussion of the Negro question in the firemen's brotherhood,[52] but since the discussion resulted in no overt attempt against the colored worker, the association functioned only as a benefit society.[53]

When the full-crew agitation reached its high point around 1913, an organization was formed "to guard against attacks upon colored railway employees, such as the full-crew bills which have been recently introduced into the legislatures of several states." [54] Two years later, in May, 1915, another group known as the Railwaymen's International Benevolent and Industrial Association was formed in Chicago to bring every class of railway worker into a single union. The group, according to its leader, Robert L. Mays, grew up in protest "against unfair and bad working conditions of the employee and against unfair practice of the American Federation of Labor and the railway brotherhoods." [55] For nearly three

[51] Agreement between the Missouri Pacific Railroad and the Boilermakers, Sheet Metal Workers, Machinists, Carmen, Blacksmiths, Electrical Workers, Painters, their Helpers and Apprentices. Effective Dec. 21, 1918, pp. 14, 21, 30, 38, 42.

[52] See above, pp. 287-88.

[53] *Locomotive Firemen's Magazine*, March, 1904, p. 416.

[54] *Crisis*, June, 1913, p. 63.

[55] Chicago Commission on Race Relations, *The Negro in Chicago*, p. 409.

years the association hardly functioned. At the beginning of 1918 it had fewer than one hundred members. But when the government took control of the roads during the war and by its policies encouraged organization in all branches of the service, the group came into its own. During 1918 and during the first two or three years following the return of the roads to private ownership, the number of Negro unions grew rapidly. One investigator in 1923 reported fifteen such groups,[56] and there may actually have been twice that number. These organizations included those in services of which the Negroes have near monopolies, such as dining car employees and sleeping car porters, as well as those in services in which Negroes compete with white workers. The Railwaymen's International Benevolent and Industrial Association, the largest and most active of all the groups, had 187 branches in thirty states and claimed a membership of 35,000. It actually had about 15,-000 members at the height of its career in 1920.

In the beginning the organization made its way by the sheer boldness of its leaders. In February, 1918, when President Wilson asked representatives of the various railway unions to appear before a commission on wages and working conditions, headed by Secretary Lane, the Railway Men's International, with almost no membership except its officers, sent a delegation to Washington to present the Negro worker's case against existing discrimination in pay and treatment. The association claimed that Mr. McAdoo's order equalizing the pay of white and black workers was the result of its efforts. On a number of subsequent occasions during and after federal control, the association appeared before various labor adjustment boards and the United States Railway Labor Board in behalf of colored railwaymen. Its efforts resulted in several victories, particularly for the Pullman porters and dining car employees both of whom received substantial increases in pay.

[56] Annette M. Dieckmann, *The Effect of Common Interests on Race Relations in Certain Northern Cities* (Master's essay, Columbia University, 1923), p. 88.

During 1921 attempts were made to unite the various groups of colored railwaymen to counteract the brotherhoods in their efforts to force the Negroes out of the industry. Notwithstanding the seriousness of the threats, not only did no strong federation of colored unions result, but the Railway Men's International Association, torn by internal dissension, declined rapidly and soon disappeared.

There are in the field today four well-established groups of colored railway workers, outside of the Pullman and dining car services, which have no problem of interracial competition. These are the Association of Train Porters, Brakemen and Switchmen with about 1,700 members; the Protective Order of Railway Trainmen, with about 1,000 members; the Association of Colored Railway Trainmen with about 3,000 members; and the Interstate Order of Colored Locomotive Firemen, Engine Helpers, Yard and Train Service Employees and Railway Mechanics. The last is a revival of the Railway Men's International Association without dining car employees or Pullman porters. The others are organizations of long standing.

These organizations have protested against discrimination. They have argued the Negro workers' cause before the Railway Labor Board and other tribunals. They have won some few concessions but they have been powerless to prevent the white unions from steadily forcing the Negro out of all the better railroad jobs. They have no political influence and are thus powerless to affect legislation. They cannot strike to prevent the signing of discriminatory contracts, to defend their members, or to enforce their programs. Such action would once and for all drive them off the roads and give the brotherhoods their jobs. In the days of the old Railway Labor Board they could at least present their grievances to a body which would give them a hearing. But the very decision of the board which gave minority organizations a right to function made it possible for the majority to negotiate the contracts determining conditions of employment.[57] Under the present railway-

[57] Decisions of the United States Railway Labor Board (1921), Vol. II, p. 96.

labor law the hands of minority groups are tied.[58] The Negro
unions must consequently function by conciliating the management and appealing to public opinion. Whatever they get is by
grace of the railroad's generosity, or, perhaps, its sense of justice. Their position is thus hardly different from that of a company union; in fact, a number of company unions have been
able to get as much for their colored members as these independent Negro organizations.

Many Negro employees in the hope of holding their jobs
have declared themselves willing to accept lower wages than
their white competitors. On the Gulf Coast Lines, a group of
subsidiaries of the Missouri Pacific, the Negro firemen have
actually signed wage agreements fixing their wages at figures
below the standard rates. Where the standard rates per hundred miles on passenger engines, according to class, are $4.91,
$4.99, and $5.07, the rate for Negro firemen on the same class
of engines is $4.50. Where the standard rates on the next
heavier engines are $5.23 and $5.31, the rates for Negroes
are $4.66 and $4.75. On through freight, white and Negro
wages compare as follows: $5.40 and $4.80; $5.48 and $4.80;
$5.64 and $4.88; $5.80 and $5.05; $5.96 and $5.22. On local
freight the figures are $5.80 and $5.22; $5.88 and $5.22;
$6.04 and $5.30; $6.20 and $5.47; $6.30 and $5.64. On
switch engines white firemen receive $5.63 and $5.75, while
Negroes receive $4.71.[59]

Thus the brotherhoods' determination to force the Negro
off the railroads has led to the revival of the pre-war system of
wage differentials to which the unions had always objected as
a threat to their standards. But the return to a lower wage
scale for Negro railway men has not become widespread. Nor
has it been generally accepted by the Negro railway organizations as a method for saving the Negro's job. These groups

[58] See Chapter XX, pp. 451-60.

[59] Basic rates of pay for the southeastern railroads as fixed by the arbitration award of May 1, 1927. Rates for the colored firemen of the Gulf Coast
Lines as fixed by the agreement between the colored firemen and the management, effective September 1, 1929.

seem to be at a loss as to what to do. Their program shows that they are well aware of the weakness of their position. They know that they are doomed but they hope that there may still be a chance to save themselves by acquainting the public with the injustice of their fate. Their present plan is to appeal to the press, to prominent citizens, to leading politicians, and, above all, to the stockholders of the roads whose executives are signing contracts that force them out of the service. They still rely upon the rich white man's sense of justice as their best protection. But unless all signs fail, their appeals will be in vain. With technological changes threatening the jobs of white men as well as black, it is only natural that the white workers, who are effectively organized, will continue their efforts to protect their interests by eliminating their black competitors.

PART IV

INDUSTRIAL UNIONISM AND LABOR
SOLIDARITY

Chapter XIV

RADICAL AND INDUSTRIAL UNIONISM

When industry was less specialized and mechanized the craftsman's skill gave him a quasi-monopoly over his job. In this phase of industrial development the trade union represented a fairly strong alignment of the skilled workers against the employer. As business expanded and industry became more integrated, new techniques and complex processes took precedence over simple industry. Specialization and machinery made progressive encroachments on the skilled worker's craftsmanship by simplifying the productive process through minute division of labor, and thereby enabling the employers to supplant the skilled worker with the cheaper and the less skilled. The effects of this industrial change were visible in the nineties but did not come to the fore until the nineteen hundreds.

In the realm of trade unionism one manifestation of this industrial change took the form of an increasing number of jurisdictional disputes.[1] Specialization and machinery caused the importance of many traditional unions of highly skilled workers to decline and at the same time gave rise to new occupations. Jurisdiction over some one of these new occupations was often claimed by two or more unions. This precipitated disputes and frequently led to the expulsion of one of the disputants from the Federation. Another manifestation of the effects of industrial change upon the labor movement was the demand of radicals and progressives for the transformation of traditional trade-union philosophy and structure. The radicals

[1] See Report of the President, American Federation of Labor, *Proceedings*, 1902 Convention, "Jurisdictional Disputes Threaten Progress of the Labor Movement," p. 16. Also, Louis Levine, "Federated Labor and Compromise," *New Republic*, Dec. 5, 1914, p. 19; and David J. Saposs, *Readings in Trade Unionism*, pp. 123-43.

were divided into two schools, namely, the opportunist radicals [2] and the revolutionary radicals.

The opportunist radicals, like the progressives, were as a rule content to remain in the American Federation of Labor and agitate for a break with "pure and simple" craft unionism. They were usually socialists. Their stronghold was in such unions as the United Mine Workers, the International Ladies' Garment Workers, the International Cloth, Hat and Cap Makers, the Brewery Workers, the Bakery and Confectionery Workers, and the International Association of Machinists. The mission of the opportunist radical was threefold. He was to capture his trade union for political socialism by pursuing the policy of "boring from within"; to educate the members of the conservative unions to industrial unionism; and to bring the Federation to a definite sponsoring of "amalgamation." The first function of the opportunist radical was more important to official socialism than either the second or third. The Socialist party wished to become the political expression of the proletariat but did not wish to interfere with trade-union policy and method of organization. This official position of the party did not prevent individual socialists from advocating industrial unionism and "amalgamation" at the convention of the American Federation of Labor. The opportunist radicals were not dual unionists. They wanted the transformation of trade unionism to take place through education and voluntary acceptance by the unions, yet they desired that the Federation advocate the change.

Unlike the opportunist radicals, the militant and revolutionary radicals were impatient of "evolution" and "boring from within." They believed that a labor movement whose power rests upon skill, job monopoly, and wage consciousness is by nature indifferent to the unorganized and less skilled workers. A labor movement organized on these principles was "class collaborationist" rather than "class conscious," was

[2] For an able discussion of opportunist radicals, see David J. Saposs, *Left Wing Unionism* (1926), pp. 33-48.

separated by craft jealousy rather than united in class solidarity. Such a labor movement, it was predicted, would eventually find itself in a precarious position before the advance of machine technique which whittled away the importance of skilled craftsmanship and facilitated the introduction of heretofore unskilled workers into the higher ranks of industry.

Voluntary overhauling of trade-union structure did not satisfy the revolutionary and militant radicals' demands. While it was acceptable to the "opportunist" radicals as a step in the direction of their ideal, it did not necessarily envisage the transformation of trade-union ideology which the revolutionary radicals insisted should be in terms of the class struggle. The revolutionary and militant radicals realized this and proceeded to form independent or dual unions of a more or less industrial structure.

The atmosphere which radical dual unions like the Amalgamated Clothing Workers and the more revolutionary I. W. W. wished to create in the labor movement was more conducive to the organization of the masses of Negroes than the traditional and laissez-faire policy of the American Federation of Labor. Since the radical dual union was more often than not founded upon the old unions' neglect of the under dog [3] and upon the ideal of working-class solidarity, it is

[3] Mr. David J. Saposs declared: "The economic factors that were responsible for neglect of the immigrant workers centre around the time-worn struggle between the newcomer and those on the ground floor, a struggle which embodies the suspicion and hostility of those who have found a strategic entrenchment which they guard against all comers. This conflict has manifested itself in the attitude of many unions towards women, Negro and other workers less favourably situated, but who might threaten the privileged position. The immigrant worker was likewise regarded as an intruder who by injecting himself into the arena controlled by the union would cut in on the established standards. . . . An equally stimulating economic factor in the formation of dual unions by recent immigrants is the ignoring or subordinating of the interests of the unskilled and semi-skilled by the skilled. In many of the industries employing large numbers of immigrant workers the existing or A. F. of L. unions constitutionally assume jurisdiction over all the workers. In actual practice they have been largely motivated by the craft or skilled worker spirit. *Left Wing Unionism*, pp. 102-3.

less inclined than the conservative craft union to proscribe a member because of race. The kind of organization that the radical unionists advocated was one in which the interests of an industrial group like the Negroes could best be satisfied.

That the problem of the Negro workers is, in the main, that of the unorganized, unskilled, and largely neglected workers, calling for some type of industrial unionism, was pointed out in the chapters on the exclusion of Negroes by the craft unions and the policy of the American Federation of Labor. It has been noted that hardly more than 4.3 per cent of the Negroes employed in the manufacturing industries are trade-union members. In those industries where unionism is weakest, having capitulated to the offensive of welfare capitalism, or where craft unionism makes little headway because of integration and specialization and the inertia of conservative trade-union leaders, the greatest numbers of Negro industrial wage-earners are found, and chiefly in the heavy and less skilled branches of the industry. In iron and steel there were 106,000 unskilled and 24,000 semi-skilled Negroes in 1920. At the same time there were 28,000 unskilled and 16,000 semi-skilled in the food industries, mainly packing; 18,000 unskilled, and 8,000 semi-skilled in textiles; 107,000 unskilled in lumber and furniture; 20,000 semi-skilled and 21,000 unskilled in tobacco; and in the automobile industry there were from 20,000 to 30,000.

Negro labor has become an important factor in all the foregoing industries, except textiles and tobacco, only since 1912, although it had been employed to break strikes in the steel and the packing and slaughtering industries in the eighties and nineties. In tobacco, where the employment of the Negro was traditional in both skilled and unskilled capacities,[4] he had been organized by the Tobacco Workers' International Union. Just prior to and after the World War over 3,500 Negroes were members of the union. But the union's inability to com-

[4] Very few Negroes are employed in the skilled branches of tobacco manufacture now.

bat the open-shop movement of the trust has caused its entire membership white and black, to dwindle to 4,000. In an interview with the secretary of the union, the authors were informed that there had been about 3,000 Negroes in the local at Winston-Salem, North Carolina. He said that the Negroes were backward and ignorant of the purposes of trade unions, and that as soon as wage increases were obtained they dropped out of the union. The picture which the secretary drew of the white tobacco workers was equally distressing, but, judging from the extent of organization among tobacco workers in Louisville, Kentucky, where the union makes its headquarters and where it makes childish attempts to organize the large companies like Liggett and Myers, it seems that the officials themselves have accepted defeat with complacency and with the hope that by the dissemination of the "unfair list" the sole remaining union shop can be kept from going non-union.[5]

The assumption underlying the attitude of the officials of the tobacco workers' union has been given official endorsement by President Green himself.[6] The theory is: first, that the so-called under-privileged workers, the less skilled and backward workers, are difficult to organize; and, second, that these workers must themselves manifest a desire for unionism before their organization can be successfully undertaken. This attitude, which is largely responsible for the retardation of an understanding of trade unionism among the Negro workers, separated by race feeling and custom from the main currents of economic and political affairs, was the very one against which radicals and progressives inside and outside of the Federation protested. This same point of view delayed aggressive trade unionism in the southern textile industry, where the bulk of the Negro textile workers are employed. Now that the United Textile Workers' Union is attempting to organize the

[5] Resolution No. 55, presented to the 1929 Toronto convention of the American Federation of Labor, *Proceedings*, p. 146.

[6] See William Green's letter to E. A. Carter, editor of *Opportunity*, Dec., 1929, pp. 381-82.

southern industry, it remains to be seen what it will do with the 25,000 or more unskilled Negro textile workers, very few of whom were brought into the textile controversy. Judging from the action of the Federation's November conference on the organization of the South, especially the textile industry, no attempt will be made to organize the Negro for some time to come. Mr. A. Philip Randolph of the Sleeping Car Porters' Union was present at the conference and stated that the Negro in the South was ripe for organization, but he did not press the matter. An Alabama delegate insisted that some Negroes could be organized immediately. But the conference steered clear of the question, and the report of the committee did not even refer to it.[7] Only the communists have as yet dared to advocate racial equality and a united front of white and black textile workers. The communists' appeal for white and black solidarity in the struggle in the textile industry was dramatic, but it was premature since so few Negroes were involved, and their statements on this question were used against them with telling effect by the prosecution in the trial of their organizers in 1929. Nevertheless their anticipation of a probable employment of Negroes by the employers to defeat the unionization of the white textile workers, and, therefore, the necessity of early organization of the Negro textitle worker, however unskilled, is vindicated by the history of unionism in such basic industries as steel, packing, automobile, and rubber.

The position which Negro labor occupies today in these industries was won through the favorable conjuncture of mechanization — which facilitated the employment of the less skilled — industrial expansion, the cessation of immigration, strikes, and the open-shop movement. The story is fully told in the chapters on the "Negro as an Industrial Reserve." But it might be well to recall here the tactics of the leaders of in-

[7] See *Labor's News*, Nov. 23, 1929, p. 6. A conference of American Federation of Labor leaders on organizing the South was held in Washington, Nov. 14, 1929.

dustrial unionism in the coal fields, which, while not wholly successful, were in striking contrast with those of the conservative craft unions.

In Chapter X it was shown that Negro labor, in addition to its normal employment in the early development of the southern coal fields, was used in the same period to break strikes in the central competitive field and in Colorado and Kansas. The leaders of the United Mine Workers' Union realized that their ability to hold the northern states was dependent upon unionization of blacks and whites in the South. In attempting to execute its ideal the union was not handicapped by craft structure. It was industrial and its jurisdiction embraced the whole industry. It never experienced such craft jealousies and jurisdictional disputes as arose when attempts were made in 1917 and 1919 to organize the steel and packing industries, the failure of which is responsible for the present absence of organization among the white and black workers in those industries. Had other American Federation of Labor unions been able to follow the strategy of the United Mine Workers, it is not illogical to assume, judging from the success of the I. W. W. among the Negro and white lumber workers in Louisiana,[8] that at least the seeds of working-class solidarity would have been sown among the masses of Negroes and whites before the northern hegira.

The contention here is not that all industrial unions admit Negroes equally with white members, for the Railway Carmen, an American Federation of Labor union, and the American Federation of Railroad Workers,[9] an independent union, do

[8] See Chapter XV, pp. 331-33.

[9] Negro railroad workers under the jurisdiction of the American Federation of Railroad Workers are organized into separate unions. "The American Federation of Railroad Workers being composed exclusively of white wage railroad workers, and believing that colored railroad workers should be organized for the same purpose and with the same aims and objects, appropriated a certain amount of its funds for the purpose of establishing an organization to be known as the Colored Railroad Workers' Union to be affiliated with the American Federation of Railroad Workers. That the Grand Lodge Officers of the latter are to be the Grand Lodge Officers of the former,

not. The contention is rather that the industrial union is better adapted than the craft union for organization in the large basic industries and for protecting the interests of the less skilled workers. A union having jurisdiction over a whole industry would imperil its own existence by neglecting any large section of workers in that industry. Because the ideology of industrial unionism is usually socialist or radical, the industrial union signifies aggressive and comprehensive working-class alignment, and is, therefore, more solicitous than the conservative trade union about the welfare of underprivileged minorities like the Negro. The attitude of such unions as the Amalgamated Clothing Workers and the now defunct Amalgamated Metal Workers, the Amalgamated Food Workers, and the Industrial Workers of the World toward Negro affiliation is in striking contrast to that of traditional unionism. These unions were independent of the American Federation of Labor. They were socialist or radical in philosophy, and more or less industrial in structure. With the exception of the I. W. W. none of them ever had jurisdiction over industries in which any appreciable number of Negroes were employed. They manifested their concern for the colored man by welcoming all workers regardless of race or by making some similar statement in official pronouncements. These unions and the socialist unions in the American Federation of Labor, the International Ladies' Garment Workers and the Brewery Workers, gave moral and financial support to the propaganda of Negro radicals because they thought it heralded the awakening of the Negro "proletariat." In contrast it will be recalled that old-line trade unions like the machinists, plumbers, and boilermakers, sought to forestall the competition of the Negro by excluding him from membership. Many of the unions which did not debar Negroes constitutionally were forced to

---

performing similar duties and acting in like capacities for the Colored Railroad Workers' Union." — Preamble, Constitution and Due Book, Colored Railroad Workers' Union, affiliated with the American Federation of Railroad Workers, p. 4.

organize them into segregated locals or leave them unorganized, as the leader of the molders did in Nashville, Tennessee, when the white molders objected to the organization of the Negro and the latter, knowing that the whites would not support them, hesitated to embrace unionism for fear of discharge. Above all, the organization of the great body of Negroes, the unskilled, had never been seriously undertaken by the American Federation of Labor, its declarations of good intentions to the contrary notwithstanding.

CHAPTER XV

THE NEGRO AND THE I. W. W.

THE first attack against "pure and simple" trade unionism was led in the nineties by the Socialist Trade and Labor Alliance and the Socialist Labor party, the forerunners of the Industrial Workers of the World. Daniel De Leon was the acknowledged leader of the assault. He was convinced, as one of his followers expressed it, "that without the organization of the workers into a class-conscious revolutionary body on the industrial field socialism would remain but an aspiration."[1] The logical implication of this statement is that the indifference of "pure and simple unionism" to politics and the class struggle was as much an underlying cause of De Leon's hostility as was its craft structure. De Leon was not interested in building industrial unions, per se; but rather in constructing a new unionism that would serve as a basis for the political activity of the Socialist Labor party. The Alliance was, therefore, a mere tail of the party. It was launched in 1895. From then until its absorption by the I. W. W. its union membership never exceeded 16,000.[2] None of the available records show that Negroes were members of the Alliance or of the party, but that does not mean that the party and the Alliance were anti-Negro, for despite the absence of records it seems that there were a few Negro members. R. T. Sims,[3] who played an important part in the National Brotherhood Workers,[4] was one.

[1] Quoted by Paul F. Brissenden, *The History of the I. W. W.* (1920), p. 48.
[2] *Ibid.*, p. 52.

[3] Mr. Sims was a member of Local 184, Brotherhood of Painters and Decorators Union, Milwaukee, Wisconsin. Upon the formation of the I. W. W., he joined as a member of the Socialist Trade and Labor Alliance. Later he was appointed national organizer for the I. W. W. Correspondence with R. T. Sims. See also Milwaukee *Free Press*, January 7, 1906.

[4] See Chapter VI, pp. 117-19.

But special appeals such as were later issued by the Socialist party to the Negro and in his behalf, were never indulged in by the Socialist Labor party. The S. L. P. followed the theory that caused Eugene V. Debs at a later date to request the Socialist party to withdraw its proclamation to the Negro. The theory was that special pronouncements in favor of any section of the proletariat would distinguish that part of the working class from other parts, and thus create divisions among the proletariat. Socialism, it was argued, knows only the class struggle. It is oblivious to race. This explanation, never actually given by the early De Leonites, is today accepted by the Socialist Labor party as substantially the correct interpretation.[5] The philosophy of solidarity and the opposition to craft unionism epitomized in the Socialist Trade and Labor Alliance, and, later, in the Industrial Workers of the World was not new to the labor movement. It was championed in the seventies and eighties by the non-class-conscious Knights of Labor which made serious efforts to enlist Negro workers. And while the fortunes of the Negro workers may not have been consciously envisaged by this socialist "industrialism" of the late nineties, any realization of the ideal would have of necessity included them. But it was not until the formation of the I. W. W. in 1905 that earnest attempts were to be made to capitalize trade-union race discrimination and to capture Negro working-class sympathy.

At the founding of the I. W. W., William D. Haywood, the moving spirit of American syndicalism, said, "the American Federation of Labor which presumes to be the labor movement of this country is not a working-class movement. It does not represent the working class. There are organizations . . . affiliated with the A. F. of L. which in their constitution and by-laws prohibit the initiation of or conferring the obligation on a colored man; that prohibit the conferring of the obligation on foreigners. What we want to establish at this

[5] Correspondence with Arnold Peterson, national secretary, Socialist Labor party.

time is a labor organization that will open wide its doors to every man that earns his livelihood either by his brain or his muscle." [6] At a later date Justus Ebert pointed out that one-fifth of the native American workers were Negroes whose exclusion was in part due to the color line in the A. F. of L. But he declared:

> The I. W. W. organizes the Mexican miner, the Spanish fireman, the Negro worker, in fact, all races, regardless of religion, color of skin, shape of skull or kinks in the hair. As long as they are wage workers, and can straighten out the capitalist kinks in their brains, the I. W. W. welcomes . . . every one of them. [7]

This spirit was manifested at the inception of the I. W. W. when its constitution was made to provide that "no working man or woman shall be excluded from membership in unions because of creed or color." [8]

The practical purpose of trade unionism never occupied the attention of the I. W. W. leaders as it has that of the leaders of the American Federation of Labor. The I. W. W. was looking forward to the establishment of a new society, a non-political federalism. The establishment of this new society meant the industrial emancipation of Negro and white workers. "The workers," said Haywood, "have no interest, have no voice in anything except the shops. . . . The political state . . . says that women are not entitled to vote . . . but they are industrial units, they are productive units. . . . The black men of the South are on the same footing. They are . . . citizens of this country, but they have no voice in its government. Millions of black men are disfranchised, who, if organized, would have a voice in saying how they should work and how the conditions of labor should be regulated." [9]

---

[6] Industrial Workers of the World, *Proceedings of the First Annual Convention*, 1905, p. 1. For an enumeration of the disabilities of craft unionism, see *Proceedings*, p. 5; also Brissenden, *op. cit.*, p. 84.

[7] Justus Ebert, *The I. W. W. in Theory and Practice* (1920), p. 94.

[8] Article 1, Section 1 of the Preamble and Constitution, Industrial Workers of the World, p. 34.

[9] *Bill Haywood's Book, an Autobiography* (1929), p. 288.

During the active part of its life the I. W. W. issued about one million membership cards. About 100,000 of these cards were issued to Negroes.[10] The important work of the I. W. W. among the Negro workers was in the southern lumber industry in Louisiana and Texas and among Negro longshoremen and dockworkers of Philadelphia, Baltimore, and Norfolk, Virginia.[11]

In 1910 the Brotherhood of Timber Workers, an independent union, was begun in the lumber camps of Louisiana, Texas, and Arkansas. During the organization's period of greatest activity it had about 35,000 members, about half of whom were Negroes. At the May, 1912, convention, the Brotherhood joined the I. W. W. as the Southern District of the Forest and Lumber Workers' Union. Bill Haywood was present at the convention. When he inquired why no colored men were present, he was told that, because the Louisiana law prohibited meetings of white and black men, the Negroes were meeting in some other place. Haywood said, "You are meeting in convention now to discuss the conditions under which you labor. This can't be done intelligently by passing resolutions here and then sending them out to another room for the black men to act upon. Why not be sensible about this and call the Negroes into this convention? If it is against the law, this is one time when the law should be broken." [12] The Negroes were asked to come and the mixed convention elected Negro and white delegates to the next I. W. W. convention.[13]

After the convention the Brotherhood of Timber Workers attempted to establish fortnightly payment of wages at the Galloway Lumber Company's mills at Grabow, Louisiana.[14] The company refused to accede to the union's demands. Likewise the Southern Lumber Operators' Association, in response

[10] These statements are made on the authority of Benjamin Fletcher, a Negro I. W. W. official.

[11] See Chapter IX, pp. 188, 191-93, 204-5.

[12] *Bill Haywood's Book: an Autobiography*, p. 241.

[13] *Ibid.*

[14] *International Socialist Review*, Aug., 1912, p. 105.

to the union demands, closed forty-six of its mills, thus affecting almost the entire industry in the state. Negroes and whites struck together. The feeling between the workers of the two races was well demonstrated in a statement issued by the strikers at Merryville, Louisiana:

It is a glorious sight to see, the miracle that has happened here in Dixie. This coming true of the impossible — this union of workers regardless of color, creed or nationality. To hear the Americans saying "You can starve us but you cannot whip us"; the Negroes crying "You can fence us in, but you cannot make us scab"; the Italians singing the *Marseillaise* and the Mexicans shouting vivas for the Brotherhood. Never did the Santa Fe Railroad, the Southern Lumber Operators' Association and the American Lumber Company expect to see such complete and defiant solidarity.[15]

During the strike the companies resorted to non-union labor and some of them tried to play one race against the other. The union attempted to organize the black and white scabs. In special appeals the Negro workers were asked not to permit themselves to be divided from their fellow white workers by the "vicious lumber trust."[16]

For a time Negroes and whites stood steadfast in joint opposition to the operators. Frequently the Negroes were intimidated by a local sheriff into organizing into a separate branch. The official policy, however, was to organize Negroes and whites in the same union.[17] And, though the union forced some of the employers to remove some of the most obnoxious causes of dissatisfaction, such as payment in scrip, company stores, and monthly payment of wages, it began to crack under the strain of blacklisting, rioting, and illegal warfare. The employers began a campaign of concessions in the form of small wage increases, preferential treatment of key employees, lower rent, and shorter hours. Latent race feeling was gradually stimulated. After three years of stubborn resistance the

[15] *Crisis*, Feb., 1913, p. 164.
[16] *Solidarity*, Sept. 28, 1912, p. 1.
[17] *Ibid.*, July 20, 1912, p. 1.

Brotherhood of Timber Workers, the I. W. W.'s greatest symbol of the solidarity of southern white and Negro labor, disintegrated.[18]

As the southern drama drew to a close, the I. W. W. became active along the Philadelphia waterfront. It rose to power there when the longshoremen, after having been out of the labor movement for fifteen years, went on strike in May, 1913. The strike began as a local movement without the support of any established organization, but it was not long before the organizers of both the Marine Transport Workers of the I. W. W. and the International Longshoremen's Association of the A. F. of L. appeared on the scene, urging affiliation with their respective unions.[19] At a mass meeting the strikers decided in favor of the I. W. W. and were chartered as Local No. 8 of the Marine Transport Workers. More than half of the union's memberships, or 2,200 out of 4,200, were Negroes. The whites were mainly Irish, Poles and Lithuanians.

For seven years the Marine Transport Workers controlled the Philadelphia longshore force, winning recognition from both deep sea and coastwise shipping interests. It maintained this control throughout the war despite the fact that the International Longshoremen's Association of the A. F. of L., with government encouragement, controlled the other harbors of the country. Throughout the war the International Longshoremen's Association tried constantly to win Philadelphia from its rival. The influence of T. V. O'Connor, member and later chairman of the United States Shipping Board and former president of the International Longshoremen's Association, was enlisted. Yet the I. W. W. not only held its own, but actually captured all stevedoring at both the Du Pont ammunition plants engaged in war work and at the United States Navy Yard itself.

Filled with confidence born of its successful career, the Philadelphia Marine Transport Workers' Union called a

18 Correspondence with Covington Hall, southern organizer for the I. W. W.
19 *Messenger*, June, 1923, p. 740.

strike in the spring of 1920 for an eight-hour day, forty-four
hour week, and increased pay. The call was answered by 5,500
dock workers; and, shortly afterwards, 3,200 sympathizing
harbor workers joined their ranks. Fully 5,000 of these
8,700 workers were Negroes. A thousand joined the movement in a single day.[20] For six weeks the Philadelphia harbor
was tied up. A hundred deep-sea vessels, unable to dock, were
anchored in the river. Business losses amounted to millions
of dollars. Throughout the strike white and black workers
stood by the organization. Efforts to use strike breakers and
to play one race against another were unsuccessful. The union
was constantly alive to the danger of the latter issue and tried
to guard against it by emphasizing its white-black character
in its strike handbills and cartoons. One such cartoon which
was widely circulated pictured a white worker and a black
worker side by side holding the ropes which tied up Philadelphia's shipping.[21] Yet in spite of everything, the strike
failed to attain its major objectives and this failure marked
the beginning of the I. W. W. union's decline.

At just about this time the communists began their efforts
to capture the I. W. W. Before long they had gained control
of the General Executive Board and in the course of the struggle for control the Philadelphia Marine Transport Workers'
local was suspended and remained unaffiliated with the I. W.
W. for about a year and a half. During this period the International Longshoremen's Association redoubled its efforts to
capture the port and this time succeeded in winning a small
following. In the spring of 1922 the old Marine Transport
Workers' local was reinstated, and in September of the same
year the communist group forced another strike for the forty-
four hour week. This move was foredoomed to failure. The
union which was unable to win its strike two years before

[20] Correspondence with Benjamin Fletcher, Negro I. W. W. organizer,
Aug. 1, 1929.

[21] Marine Transport Workers' Industrial Union, No. 8, Branch 1, *Strike
Bulletin*, Philadelphia, June 15, 1920.

when at the height of its power was in no position to carry on a new fight while still suffering from the effects of the old and while torn by factional issues and internal intrigues. In January, 1923, the anti-communist group withdrew from the Marine Transport Workers and set up an independent organization known as the Philadelphia Longshoremen's Union. Meanwhile the leaders of the old I. W. W. group had been sent to prison, along with scores of their fellows, as a result of the government's efforts to stamp out the organization. The communist efforts could make no headway and the I. L. A. fell heir to the remains of the organized waterfront.

The support which both the white and black longshoremen of Philadelphia gave to the I. W. W., had very little to do with attachment to that body's social theories. The Philadelphia Marine Transport Workers' Union was successful not because of its revolutionary idealism, but because it was a good business union, capable of winning recognition from employers and of improving working conditions. In general I. W. W. locals were looked upon as centers of revolutionary propaganda rather than as units of practical unionism. In this respect the Philadelphia Marine Transport Workers was an exception. It was one of the few I. W. W. locals which actually exercised job control. In its day-to-day relations with employers in the port it differed not one whit from a conservative union of the A. F. of L. But it did bring white men and black men into one organization in which race distinctions were obliterated in both the leadership and the rank and file. The effectiveness of the propaganda for labor solidarity was tested during the trouble of 1921-1923, when spokesmen of the Garvey movement went among the faction-torn workers preaching the doctrine of race consciousness. Despite the fact that Garveyism won a following everywhere at this time, the Negro longshoremen of Philadelphia were deaf to its pleas, for their labor movement had won them industrial equality such as colored workers nowhere else in the industry enjoyed.[22] Ac-

[22] *Messenger*, Aug., 1921, p. 234.

Chapter XVI

THE NEGRO AND THE GARMENT AND TEXTILE UNIONS

THE great majority of Negroes in the needle trades are women employed in the manufacture of women's garments. They first entered the trades in New York about 1900 through the old waist industry. The work there was highly specialized and required but a low degree of skill, and employers turned to colored girls as available cheap labor. These girls first came into the unorganized shops. An investigation made in 1906 found no Negroes in any of the New York garment unions.[1] But three years later, in 1909, when the waist workers were organized, the few Negroes whom the agents of the International Ladies' Garment Workers' Union found employed were taken into the union as a matter of course.

Negroes remained an insignificant factor in the industry down to the period of the war, when, almost suddenly, the situation changed and colored workers began to come into the trade in large numbers. The influx began in Chicago during 1917 when colored girls, who were willing to work for much lower wages than white, were brought in to break a strike. This strike was lost largely through the employment of this colored labor and when it ended some five hundred Negro girls found permanent places in the trade.

The International Ladies' Garment Workers, instead of fighting these newcomers and trying to eliminate them from the trade because they were new, because they were Negroes, and because they had been scabs, accepted them as a permanent

[1] Mary White Ovington, "The Negro in the Trade Unions of New York," *Annals of the American Academy of Political and Social Science*, May, 1906, p. 91.

part of the industry and made every effort to organize them. Those who came into the union were given full equality. Colored girls were often chosen as shop chairmen in plants employing both white and Negro help.

Colored labor was used in Chicago for two reasons, it was cheap and it was non-union. In spite of the fact that the union rate after the war for ladies' skirt and dress operators was $37.40 a week, non-union colored operatives could be employed for from $18 to $25 on the same tasks. Negroes worked as skirt and dress finishers for $15 a week, while the union rate for the same work was $26.40.[2]

Early in 1920 the manufacturers in a drive against the union opened a number of shops on the south side near the Negro districts and employed only colored help. When the union succeeded in organizing some of these all-Negro shops, Negro labor lost its attractiveness to the employer and efforts were made to replace it with white labor. In one instance the Negro workers were locked out, the employer offering to settle with the union if it would furnish him with all white help. The union refused and declared a strike. In several other instances the union found it necessary in order to carry out its policy of full racial equality to call strikes against employers who persisted in discriminating against Negro workers.

During a series of industrial troubles following the war Negro girls were invariably used as strike breakers. They were secured for the employers through a Negro minister acting as a labor agent.[3] The practice of using Negroes as strike breakers was not confined to Chicago, but was followed in New York and Philadelphia, as well as in the less important garment centers. In New York, unlike Chicago and Philadelphia, Negroes, though used extensively, were not the all-important strike-breaking element. Italians, southeastern Europeans, Latin Americans, Spaniards, and Portugese were used just as extensively. The Negro was but one of many strike-

[2] Chicago Commission on Race Relations, *The Negro in Chicago*, p. 414.
[3] *Ibid.*, p. 415.

breaking groups. He did not stand out as the chief strike breaker as he did in Chicago and Philadelphia. Frequently in New York Negro scabs were used to take the place of Negroes on strike with the union.

In Philadelphia Negro strike breakers were introduced during the women's dress strike of 1921. Shop after shop was filled with colored workers. The whites, fearing that they would be entirely displaced, became alarmed and tried to resist the introduction of Negroes by force. Bitter fighting took place between pickets and scabs. Scissors and pins were used freely by both sides, and the employers, in the hope of strengthening the determination of the strike breakers, tried to give the clashes an interracial rather than industrial color. This failed, however. The city handled the situation wisely and assigned Negro police to shops where Negroes worked.

When the strike ended the white workers, for the most part, found their way back into the shops. The Negro, however, had gained a real foothold in the industry. More than 1,000 workers, or 20 to 25 per cent of the employees, now in the Philadelphia dress shops are colored, whereas before the strike there were only about 300 Negroes employed. The industry is about 35 per cent organized and the union has about 200 Negro members.[4]

This 1921 strike, like the Chicago strike of 1917, was lost to the union through the Negro strike breaker.[5] The leaders of the Negro community overwhelmingly supported the strike breakers despite the International's scrupulously fair attitude towards the colored workers. During the entire struggle not a single influential Negro voice was raised in behalf of the union. The Armstrong Association, reputed to be one of the most progressive local Urban Leagues, remained neutral.

This attitude of the colored leaders was due largely to the fact that they were eager above all else to get the Negro

[4] Interview with Mr. Elias Reisberg, manager of the Philadelphia Dressmakers' Union.
[5] *Ibid.*

into industry. The union realized that with 20 to 25 per cent of the industry colored it had a serious problem on its hands and that its future in the city depended to no small degree on winning the influential forces in the Negro community to its side. This it set about to do with great thoroughness. Union representatives visited the Negro editors, ministers, and professional men whose word carried weight. A meeting of some of the most prominent colored citizens in the city was arranged at which the union made a plea for support. It explained that it was not only willing to accept the Negro and give him an equal chance, but that it was eager, now that he had won a permanent place in the industry, to guarantee him his position and protect him against exploitation. These pleas gradually won important Negro leaders, including ministers and editors, to the union cause. The union, both to demonstrate its good faith and further to strengthen its position, appointed the employment director of the Armstrong Association as one of its organizers.

In Baltimore, where Negro women have also been entering the women's garment industry in large numbers, the International Ladies' Garment Workers' Union has spent thousands of dollars in a futile effort to organize the newcomers.[6] The situation there has been complicated by southern traditions which hinder advancement to the more skilled branches of the trade and which separate white from colored employees in different parts of the plant. It is but natural that this situation should breed distrust towards the white workers who have the better jobs and who are insulated against contacts with and competition from the colored group.

This distrust of the white worker, which is by no means confined to Baltimore and the South, is perhaps the strongest obstacle to the unionization of the Negro. In Philadelphia some of the native American whites have refused to work alongside Negro girls. The number of Americans in the

[6] Interview with Miss Fannia Cohn, director of the Education Department of the International Ladies' Garment Workers' Union.

industry there is larger than elsewhere and this has led to barriers in the recreational and social activities of the union which have made the colored workers suspicious.[7]

The union has tried hard to overcome such distrust and gain the confidence of the Negro worker. It has not only employed Negro organizers,[8] but has made it a practice to push the Negro forward wherever possible and to encourage him to take an active part in organization affairs. The officials report, however, that most Negroes who have attained places of prominence have not taken forward parts on their own initiative but have been encouraged to do so by white leaders. The West Indians in New York are perhaps the most active of all the Negro groups. The highest union office held by a Negro, membership on the executive committee of the New York Dressmakers' Union, is held by a girl who comes from Jamaica.

Fortunately for the organization, situations such as those found in Baltimore or Philadelphia are not characteristic of the needle trades in the more important centers of the industry. The great majority of the garment workers are immigrants or the children of immigrants in whom the American color prejudice is not strong. The desire of these workers to show their good faith to the Negro has frequently resulted in the election of Negro shop chairmen even when colored workers constituted but a small minority in the factory. During its drive to organize the women's dressmaking shops in New York in the winter of 1929-1930, the International Ladies' Garment Workers made strenuous efforts to bring the Negro into the movement. A colored organizer was employed and a special campaign was launched in the Negro districts with the New York and Brooklyn Urban Leagues,[9] the Negro

[7] Consumers' League of Eastern Pennsylvania, *Colored Women as Industrial Workers in Philadelphia* (1919-1920), p. 28. Also interview with Mr. Elias Reisberg.

[8] International Ladies' Garment Workers' Union, *Proceedings*, 1925, pp. 137-38.

[9] See above, Chapter VII, p. 144.

Y. M. C. A., and the National Association for the Advancement of Colored People coöperating. Meetings to discuss plans were held in the New York Urban League office and space was turned over to the union organizer to use for an organizing headquarters.[10] As a result of this campaign the Negro membership of the union increased from about 300 to about 950, so that it now constitutes about 4 per cent of the organization.[11] Yet, due to the great increase in the membership as a whole which took place at the same time, the percentage of Negroes in the organization is now no greater than it was before the drive. The union, however, has little cause for complaint, since the Negro's strength in the organization is roughly proportionate to his strength in the New York dress industry as a whole.

Perhaps the most interesting aspect of this drive for Negro members is the light which it throws on the International's policy. It is not strange that the union should do everything in its power to organize the Negro where he plays a vitally important rôle as in Philadelphia or Chicago. It is extraordinary, however, to find an organization going out of its way to organize a group which is as unimportant strategically as the Negro is in New York. This unimportance is due not to small numbers alone. There are about 2,000 Negroes among the 40,000 workers in the New York shops. It is due primarily to the fact that the colored workers are engaged chiefly in the less skilled branches of the trade. There are practically no Negroes among the cutters or operators, the key crafts, where wages, under the union scale, are $50 and $44 a week respectively. Most of the colored girls are finishers at a weekly wage, under the union scale, of $26. There are also a substantial number of Negro examiners, drapers, and cleaners at $26, $31, and $20 respectively. There are very few colored men

[10] See *New York Times*, Nov. 26, 1929; Dec. 18, 1929.

[11] Figures from Mr. Julius Hochman, general manager of the Joint Board of the Dress and Waistmakers' Union (I. L. G. W. U.) of Greater New York, June 16, 1930.

in the industry. Most of those who are employed are pressers at $50 a week.[12]

In all likelihood, according to union officials, the Negro minorities in the various shops would have joined the organization if most of the other workers in the shops had done so. The union did not make its special drive because it was afraid that a general appeal would fail to enlist the Negro's interest, as was the case in the steel strike.[13] It made its drive because it wished to take advantage of a good opportunity to emphasize its interest in the organization of the colored worker. These tactics have not failed in their desired effect. Union officials report that the Negro is a particularly loyal member. Many have come into the movement with the zeal of converts and show an attitude of almost religious gratitude to the organization for what they believe it has done for them.

During the communist campaign between 1924 and 1928 to gain control of the International, most of the organized Negroes remained loyal to the union. At several meetings at which there was a substantial Negro attendance, representatives of the left wing charged the union with race prejudice. The Negroes themselves were first to deny these charges. "I was elected shop chairman in an all-white shop," said one girl. "The union organized every colored girl in my shop and treated them just like the white," said another. "The union made the boss stop discriminating against us," said a third. "The union called a strike to reinstate me," said a fourth.[14]

In December, 1928, the left wings of the ladies' garment workers and the furriers held conventions in New York and established a dual organization called the Needle Trades Workers' Industrial Union. Two Negroes were given places on the general executive board. In the spring of 1930 this

[12] Agreement between the Affiliated Dress Manufacturers, Inc. and the International Ladies' Garment Workers' Union; and Agreement between the Association of Dress Manufacturers and the International Ladies' Garment Workers' Union, New York, Feb., 1930.

[13] See above, Chapter XI, p. 260.

[14] Interviews with workers.

dual communist union claimed a Negro membership of 500.[15] The claim is grossly exaggerated.[16] Before the formation of the dual union, while the communists were following their policy of boring from within, very few Negroes joined the left wing. Those who did join the lefts were for the most part employed in shops in which the majority of the workers opposed the union administration. The failure of the communists to attract a Negro following in the needle trades is due largely to three causes. First, there is no race issue upon which to base an appeal. Second, the communists themselves have made no special effort to enlist Negro support, but have turned their attention to individuals or groups in strategic positions, and the Negro is not yet found in such positions either in the industry or in the union. Third, the language of communism is even stranger to the Negro than the language of orthodox trade unionism.

The International Ladies' Garment Workers have had to face all of the usual difficulties in their efforts to organize the Negro. They have had to overcome distrust of the white workers and to change the Negro's traditional loyalty to the employer into a loyalty to his fellow workers. This has been most difficult in centers like Chicago and Philadelphia, where the Negro played a prominent part as a strike breaker and where he now constitutes a large percentage of the employees. Winning his place as a strike breaker made him grateful to his employer and aroused suspicion between him and his white fellow workers. Difficulty in organizing the colored needle worker has been greater where his comparative numbers are large than where they are small. Where there are but few in a shop he mingles freely with his white fellow workers and absorbs their point of view. In New York, where this is the case, and where the white workers have little race prejudice, union organizers report that the black workers have shown no suspicion towards their white fellows and that their

[15] See Chapter XIX, p. 420.
[16] *Ibid.*

reported pro-employer attitude is absent. But where there are many Negroes in a shop the group tends to be self-sufficient and to have comparatively few contacts with the white employees. The efforts of the union leaders are regarded with distrust and the traditional Negro suspicion of organized labor remains intrenched.

But not all of the obstacles in the way of organizing the Negro have been racial in character. One of the union's greatest difficulties has been the fact that the overwhelming majority of Negroes in the needle trades are women who are new to industry and to whom the significance and language of trade unionism are foreign. The few men who have found their way into the trades are hardly less ignorant of the meaning of labor organization. In addition, as already mentioned, the great majority of colored workers are employed in the less skilled branches. This is true not only in New York but also in Philadelphia and Chicago where the colored workers are more thoroughly distributed through the shops. The union is just as eager to organize these workers as it is to organize those in more skilled operations, but the unskilled worker is less interested in unionism because his stake in the industry is smaller.

The International Ladies' Garment Workers' Union has jurisdiction not only over the ladies' dress industry but over a number of other industries as well. All of these have separate unions under the International's control. The most important of these organizations are the cloakmakers, the children's dressmakers, the raincoat makers, and the white-goods workers. Of all of these the cloakmakers are best organized but there are few Negroes in the industry. The proportion of colored workers in the other trades is larger. The head of the white-goods workers in New York estimated the proportion of Negroes in his field at 10 to 15 per cent. It is probably nearer the smaller figure. Although the industry is poorly organized, Negro membership in the union is proportionately about as extensive as white. The local having jurisdiction over the children's dressmakers also includes the makers of house dresses, bath robes, and infants' cloaks. Its membership is about 1,800 and it claims a Negro membership of about 150.

The other clothing industries outside of the International's jurisdiction have practically no Negro workers. The Amalgamated Clothing Workers of America, the dominant organization in the men's clothing trade, reports that there have never been more than two hundred Negroes in the industry in the areas in which the organization functions. The union's attitude toward the colored worker has been similar to that of the International Ladies' Garment Workers. In 1919 when the number of Negroes in the men's clothing factories reached its high mark, the Amalgamated appointed a Negro organizer and made special efforts to reach the black newcomers. The union did not limit its interest to those colored workers who were directly engaged in the making of clothing. The 1920 convention declared that "such jobs as running elevators, cleaning buildings and assisting in the packing and shipping rooms are essential to the industry" and instructed the general executive board "to encourage the organization of such workers in every city." [17]

Colored membership in the Amalgamated was largest in Chicago. There was practically none in New York, although some firms which moved to the outskirts of city to escape the union employed Negro labor because it was available and cheap. In Camden, New Jersey, in the spring of 1920, a manufacturer who had moved out of New York so that he could run a non-union shop locked out thirty colored girls who joined the Amalgamated Clothing Workers. This employer claimed that he had purposely employed colored girls because they "know nothing about the union." [18]

The men's clothing factories in the South, particularly the summer-goods houses in New Orleans, employ a large proportion of colored labor, but neither the Amalgamated Clothing

[17] Amalgamated Clothing Workers of America, *Proceedings*, 1920, p. 238.
[18] *Advance*, June 4, 1920.

Workers nor its rival, the United Garment Workers, have attempted to organize this field. The United Garment Workers, an A. F. of L. union, has no Negro members and according to its officials has made no special effort to reach them.

Other needle trades organizations, particularly the cloth hat and cap makers and the furriers, have followed the International and Amalgamated tradition in their attitude toward the black worker. Both these organizations have had practically no Negro membership since 1920 or 1921 and they never did have more than a handful. The cap and hat makers in the early post-war years were particularly eager to organize the Negroes who came into the industry and sent regular and generous contributions to the *Messenger*, the magazine of Negro socialism and radicalism.[19]

The attitude of the needle-trades unions, particularly the International and the Amalgamated, toward the organization of the Negro is due to their structure, composition, and general outlook. They are industrial unions interested in organizing all the workers of their industry regardless of their degree of skill. They are composed largely of immigrant workers who have little race prejudice. Their outlook is not limited to the narrow concept of job control which dominates most of the A. F. of L. unions. They are moved instead by a broad social philosophy which looks to the ultimate reorganization of society along socialistic lines. Race prejudice or craft snobbery would strike at their very foundations.

The textile industry is frequently associated with the needle trades in the public mind, although the two have much less in common than the making of automobiles and the making of steel. Except in some of the knit-goods industries their processes and operations are entirely different. Yet the labor movements in the two groups have much in common. The workers in both cases have been drawn largely from immigrant stocks. Both have had stormy histories marked by bitterly contested strikes. Both have been theatres of communist ac-

[19] See below, Chapters XVIII and XIX.

tivity, boring from within, and dual unionism. Both have been organized upon an industrial rather than a craft basis by organizations with broader and more progressive policies than those of most American labor unions. And both employ large proportions of women workers.

Although Negroes have been employed in textile mills since slave days, their rôle in the industry has on the whole been of slight importance. The census of 1920 showed that of 1,611,000 persons employed in the industry but 24,734 were Negroes. In the North the number of Negroes in the mills was almost negligible. In Passaic, New Jersey, during the strike of 1926-1927 but one mill, the United Piece Dye Works in the suburb of Lodi, employed colored workers. They numbered about 300 in a total force of about 3,000. About half of these 300 Negroes answered the strike call, while the rest remained at work. Those who went out worked actively for the strikers' cause. Four served as delegates to the strike committee. The strike organization, a communist group led by Albert Weisbord, in order to prove that it was without race prejudice, made one of these Negroes vice-chairman of the executive committee. The company was careful to avoid the race issue. It imported about one hundred Negro strike breakers but used them only to take the places of Negro strikers.

The employment of Negroes in the textile trades of the South dates back to the establishment of the first mills two or three decades before the outbreak of the Civil War. A few mills were run entirely by black slave labor. Many employed white and black labor side by side without friction and with efficient productive results. Describing working conditions in the cotton mills in Athens, Georgia, an English observer wrote in 1839: "There is no difficulty among them on account of color, the white girls working in the same room and at the same loom with the black girls; and boys of each color as well as men and women work together without apparent repugnance or objection." [20]

[20] J. S. Buckingham, *Slave States of America* (1842), Vol. II, p. 112, quoted in *Documentary History*, Vol. II, p. 357.

Ten years later another English visitor commenting on the rise of textile mills in the South declared, "The masters of these factories hope by excluding colored men — or, in other words, slaves — from all participation in the business, to render it a genteel employment for white operatives." [21] It is this situation rather than that described by the earlier visitor which has become the rule in the industry in the South. Though several unsatisfactory attempts were made to use Negro labor and even to operate mills under Negro management in the early nineteen hundreds,[22] the use of Negro labor does not seem to have been given serious consideration since the Civil War.[23]

"Except in rare instances," declared a recent observer, "Negroes have never been used as operatives of machines and there are almost no foreigners." [24] In a note commenting further upon the situation the same writer declared: "At present there are cases in Durham, North Carolina, and Lynchburg, Virginia, and possibly several others in which Negro labor is being used. There is, however, no general disposition towards its use. This is due partly to feeling the inability of the Negro as a machine tender, partly to social question of relationship between white and black workers, partly to a sufficient supply of cheap labor." [25]

The approximately 25,000 Negroes employed in the industry are for the most part laborers in the packing and shipping departments, assistants in the dye works, or employees in the picking rooms. The latter is the important and very unpleasant job of preparing the raw cotton for the machine. Negroes are used for this work because it is often hard to find white persons willing to do it.

When the movement to organize the textile workers of

[21] Charles Lyell, *Second Visit to the United States* (1849), Vol. II, pp. 236-37, quoted in *Documentary History*, Vol. II, p. 337.

[22] Holland Thompson, *From Cotton Field to Cotton Mill* (1906), pp. 248-68.

[23] Broadus Mitchell, *The Rise of the Cotton Mills of the South* (1921), pp. 210-21.

[24] Lois Macdonald, *Southern Mill Hills* (1928), p. 18.

[25] *Ibid.*

the South began in 1928, the problem of the Negro worker immediately presented itself. The A. F. of L. union, the United Textile Workers, wishing to avoid all unnecessary trouble in a difficult situation, did its best to avoid the race issue, and its rival, the communist National Textile Workers' Union, followed the same course when it first entered the southern field.[26] Before long, however, the communists reversed their initial position and went out of their way to appeal to the Negroes and to stress the issue of social equality. The employers and the local press immediately seized upon this injection of the race question and used it to frighten the white workers away from the union and to obscure the economic causes of the strike. The *Gastonia Gazette* wrote:

> Do you want your sisters or daughters to marry a Negro? That is what this Communist controlled Northern Union is trying to make you do. We know that no red-blooded Southern white man is going to stand for anything like that, and when these foreign agitators come down here to insult us with such a policy, our answer to them should be in the good old Southern fashion of riding them out of town on a rail.[27]

Describing the effects of the tactics of the National Textile Workers' Union one of its organizers, a colored man, declared: [28]

> . . . . some of our organizers . . . were very untactful in bringing up the question of social equality as the policy of our Union.
>
> Several speeches made by our Comrades, in which social equality was stressed, met with resentment from the white workers because the economic necessity of carrying out this policy was not sufficiently stressed. . . .
>
> The Negroes were very skeptical at first at what appeared to them as a sudden change of heart on the part of the white workers, and were very slow to respond to our call for organization.

Altogether there were not more than five or six hundred Negroes among the 25,000 mill workers in the counties center-

[26] *Labor Unity*, June 22, 1929, p. 4.
[27] Quoted in *Labor Unity*, June 22, 1929.
[28] *Ibid.*

ing around Gastonia, Charlotte, and Bessemer City, North Carolina, where the National Textile Workers' Union was active. And of these few hundred only those employed in the picking rooms, where the cotton received its first handling before the manufacturing process began, were in a sufficiently strategic position to have any effect upon the strike. The National Textile Workers' interest in the Negro, like that of the unions in the needle trades where his rôle is small, was not a matter of practical concern, but a gesture based upon a social philosophy.

CHAPTER XVII

THE NEGRO AND THE UNITED MINE WORKERS

THE rôle played by the Negro as an industrial reserve in the coal industry and his part in the development of the mines in the southern fields have been related. Attention is given here to a somewhat detailed description of the successes and failures of the United Mine Workers in organizing the Negro miner and overcoming race antipathy.

At the very beginning of unionization in the bituminous coal industry it was clear that the problem facing operators and miners alike was control over the competitive districts in the states that had a common market. It was realized that it was natural that the lowest priced coal from any part of a district having a common market would underbid the higher priced commodity from the other sections of the same district, thereby reducing the price of all coal to the level of the cheapest in that market. It was also realized that if the coal from the competitive districts having a common market was to bring the same price, control would have to be established not only over differential advantages between these districts, but also over those in the districts that had different markets, as the coal of the latter might enter the markets of the former. Control of differential advantages hinged upon the ability to equalize competitive costs which were different for each district because of a difference in natural advantages, proximity to market, freight rates, quality of coal, and the price of mine labor. Of course the union did not attempt to control all of these elements of cost. It centered its attention upon the chief one, the price of mine labor. Its purpose here was to fix a wage scale for each district so that no operator would have an advantage over the other. The union sought

collective contracts with the operators through joint conferences which fixed the tonnage rate for basing points in each district represented at the conference. A rate for each district
was to be fixed afterwards at separate district conferences. The
district rate varied with the variable costs, thickness of seam
and quality of coal in each district. It was a differential above
or below the rates agreed upon for the basing points.

By the latter part of the last century the union and the
operators had entered the described agreements in the central
competitive field — Ohio, Indiana, Illinois, and western Pennsylvania — which had a common market on the Lakes, and in
the Northwest. Here practically one-third of the workers in
the bituminous industry were employed in 1922; and the territory was almost completely unionized up to 1927. But in the
southern fields the union was never able to establish permanent
control. Yet the invasion of the Lake market by the coal from
the southern fields made their unionization imperative if control of the central competitive field was to be maintained.

The rapid displacement of union mined coal by the non-
union coal of the southern fields is described in a summary of
the Report of the United States Coal Commission. Referring
to the period between 1898 and 1914 the summary said:

Southern Ohio declined notably in relative importance among the
fields of the Appalachians competing in western markets, and, whereas
the Pittsburgh district also lost in relative standing, shipments from
northern West Virginia increased; the non-union regions of eastern
Kentucky were developed with extraordinary rapidity and an entire
new field — Logan County, West Virginia, coming into first production in 1905 — had taken rank as one of the most productive districts
of the country by 1914. Twenty years ago the coals of Hocking Valley,
Pittsburgh and eastern Ohio were regularly quoted on the Chicago
market. Today Pittsburgh has entirely disappeared from the Chicago
market and the other coals mentioned are represented only by occasional
shipments. In 1898, 86 per cent of the coal shipped up the lakes originated in the union districts of Pittsburgh and Ohio. In 1913 their
share had dropped to 67 per cent. In 1898 southern West Virginia

shipped to the lakes only 40,000 tons or less than 1 per cent of the total. In 1913, its contribution ran over 6,000,000 tons or 23 per cent of the total. Non-union eastern Kentucky first broke into the lake trade in 1909 with shipments of 7,000 tons; since then its share has increased by leaps and bounds until in 1921, the district supplied 2,600,000 tons.

Not all of these shifts in production are due to labor policy of the non-union field. In part they represent the natural rapid growth of young districts over the old where the available coal has been thoroughly staked out years ago, as for example, in southern Ohio. In large part, also, the union Appalachian coal in the Chicago market was displaced not by non-union coal, but by coal from the rapidly developing union field of southern Illinois which has grown at a prodigious rate, exceeded by few other districts of the country. And, finally, part of the apparent displacement is due to the completion of through railroad routes across the southern mountains and to the extremely favorable freight rates offered by these long-haul carriers to stimulate traffic. With due allowance for these other factors, however, it is still true that the non-union fields have been greatly encouraged by the mere fact that they could keep their labor costs below the costs of the union shippers and that they were free to operate during strikes.[1]

The labor cost of the southern territory was cheaper because of the low standard of living among both Negro and native white miners. The union sought to raise the standard among these miners so as to deprive the southern operators of a competitive advantage arising from cheap labor. In other words the union was conscious of the necessity of organizing Alabama and West Virginia if it would hold the central competitive field.

Three years after its inception the union entered Alabama. After thirty years of intermittent warfare it was driven in defeat from the state. About two years after entering Alabama it began operating in West Virginia. The West Virginia coal operators' resistance was as stubborn as that of the Alabama operators. In both West Virginia and Alabama the union's task was exceedingly difficult. The miners in these

[1] E. E. Hunt, F. G. Tryon and J. H. Willits, *What the Coal Commission Found* (1925), pp. 233-34.

districts were chiefly Negroes and native whites who were divided by race prejudice. Yet the organization of the Negro miner was particularly important because of the northern operators' reliance upon him as a strike breaker.

Prior to the formation of the United Mine Workers about 1,000 Negro miners held membership in the National Trades Assembly No. 135, Knights of Labor.[2] In 1890 the National Progressive Union and the National Trades Assembly merged into the United Mine Workers of America which, unlike many other unions, erected no barriers against Negro membership. One of its objects was "to unite in one organization, regardless of creed, color or nationality, all workmen . . . employed in and around coal mines. . . ."[3] Furthermore, the new miners' union desired to bring about greater equality in the working relations between white and black miners. This it sought to do by placing the following clause in the Constitution: "No member in good standing who holds a due or transfer card shall be debarred or hindered from obtaining work on account of race, creed or nationality."[4] Although this statement does not appear in the recently adopted constitution, the official attitude of the United Mine Workers was never an obstacle in the organization of Negro miners. For a number of years the organization employed one national and several district Negro organizers to facilitate the unionization of Negro miners. In many sections of northern West Virginia, Ohio, and western Pennsylvania, Negro miners held such local offices

[2] Interviews with J. M. Withers, a Negro who began mining coal in 1884 in Alabama, but is now employed at the Richland Coal Company's mine at Wellsburg, W. Va. Mr. Withers was in the strikes of 1904 and 1908, and was at one time a member of the Joint Convention of the Alabama Operators and the United Mine Workers. Also, interviews with J. W. Hayes, secretary-treasurer, Knights of Labor. See Knights of Labor, Convention *Proceedings*, 1886, p. 44.

[3] Article II, Constitution of International Union, United Mine Workers of America, 1924, p. 3.

[4] Article VII, Section 3, of the Constitution, United Mine Workers of America. Quoted by F. J. Warne in *History of United Mine Workers of America*, p. 35.

as president and secretary even though greatly outnumbered by the predominating foreign elements. It was not rare to find the lone Negro member of a local union holding the position of president or secretary, due to the fact that ability to write and speak English is a necessary prerequisite for the efficient conduct of these offices. Likewise, the frequent appointment of Negro miners to the mine committee is traceable to the language factor. The union wage agreement specifies that all committeemen shall be American citizens, or miners who have made application for citizenship, and who speak the English language.[5] From the viewpoint of the foreign miner the Negro possesses the qualifications for serving on the mine committee — he is a citizen and he speaks the English language. Although the holding of office by Negro miners and their appearance on the mine committee has often aroused the racial antagonism of the native white American,[6] it has undoubtedly impressed most of the United Mine Workers' estimated Negro membership of 5,000 [7] with the honesty of the organization's purpose and policy. This does not mean that white and black miners have always been found working harmoniously and on the most friendly terms; for the most frequent complaint one got from the Negro unionist in the coal fields was his inability to use his union card at some mines where the employment of a Negro had caused the white union miners to strike, or where it was believed by the operators that the employment would cause a strike. Indeed the frequent manifestations of racial antipathy against the Negro on the part of the white miners were in large measure accountable for the great defections among Negro members of the United Mine Workers during the 1927 strike. But even before 1927 many Negroes

[5] Section 23, Agreement between the Northern West Virginia Coal Operators' Association and District 17, United Mine Workers of America, February 10, 1923.

[6] *Labor Relations in Fairmont, West Virginia*, United States Department of Labor, Bulletin 361, p. 4.

[7] Charles S. Johnson, "Negro Workers and the Unions," *Survey*, April 15, 1928.

deserted the union because of the race prejudice of their white fellow unionists. They and thousands of non-union Negro miners for whom the union never seemed to offer much attraction, because of their inability or unwillingness to draw any distinction between the absence of racial discrimination in constitutional principle and the appearance of it in every day fact, have resolutely opposed the Negro miners' affiliation with the union. On the other hand, the large number of Negro miners who have retained membership in the United Mine Workers have done so because of their belief in the superiority of working conditions where the union is recognized and because of the fact that the constitutions of many districts forbid racial discrimination and penalize it when proven.

The staunch adherence of some Negro miners to union principles was exhibited in the 1927 strike in eastern Ohio where racial discrimination has been pronounced; and also in the 1925 strike in northern West Virginia. A stronger exhibition of fidelity on the part of Negro miners to the union had been evidenced in the 1908 and 1919 strikes in Alabama, where the price exacted for union affiliation was much higher than in other coal fields. The failure of the United Mine Workers to gain a permanent foothold in Alabama was not due to an industrial reserve army which the operators used to defeat the union's purpose, as had often been the case in the northern Appalachian fields, but rather to southern social prejudice.

The United Mine Workers first entered Alabama about 1893. It took the organization about seven years to obtain a substantial foothold. In 1900 many of the Alabama operators entered into contracts with the union. In 1902 about 65 per cent of the miners in Alabama were members of the organization as compared with 23 per cent in 1899. A majority of the Alabama membership was Negro. The 1900 contracts, however, were short-lived. In 1904 a strike was precipitated by the declaration of some of the large coal companies for the non-union shop. The rest of the operators continued to adhere to the agreement of 1900, but refused to renew it when it expired in 1907. Because of this, the National Executive Board of the United Mine Workers called a strike for July 6, 1908.[8] The 1908 strike lasted about two months and was called off by the union officials when they found themselves confronted with the opposition of the governor who was supported by an indignant public opinion in the mining communities affected by the strike. The tents in which the white and black strikers lived were cut down and confiscated in order to prohibit the "mobilization of Negroes in union camps." There was violence and bloodshed in which white and Negro miners partook of defeat and victory as compatriots in a common cause. Finally, the vice president of the union was visited by a committee of Alabama citizens who requested him to end the strike. They argued that no matter how meritorious the union cause, the people of Alabama would never tolerate the organization and striking of Negroes along with white men. The committee threatened to make the Springfield, Illinois, riot, which had just occurred, "look like six cents if the strike continued."[9] The demand of the citizens was reinforced by the governor's hostility. The union officials countered by offering to transport every Negro striker out of the state and to make the strike a "white man's affair." But Governor Comer said that he would not permit white men to live in camps under the jurisdiction of the United Mine Workers.[10] Faced with these obstacles, the union's only alternative was temporary abandonment of the Alabama field.

After its dismal failure of 1908, the United Mine Workers' strength in Alabama dwindled until its membership amounted to less than 5 per cent of the mine workers in the state.[11] The bitter struggles and hardships that accompanied the 1904 and 1908 strikes precipitated an exodus of white

[8] Brief of the Alabama Mining Institute before the United States Coal Commission, Aug. 31, 1923, p. 44.

[9] Twentieth Annual Conference of the United Mine Workers of America, *Proceedings* (1909), Vol. II, p. 873.

[10] *Ibid.*, p. 866.

[11] Report of the United States Coal Commission, 1923, Table 1.

miners, with the result that the Negro constituted about 75 per cent of all miners. By 1915 the union's strength had decreased to two per cent. In 1917 another attempt was made to organize Alabama. The response, while not general, resulted in increasing the union's strength to about 26 per cent. A strike was called for recognition of the union. Intervention by Secretary of Labor W. B. Wilson resulted in a contract which was unsatisfactory to the union.[12] Another agreement proposed by Dr. Garfield, United States Fuel Administrator, was acceptable to the operators and, for a time, placated the union. The award was issued October 6, 1917. It provided for an advance of 10 per cent per day to all-day labor with a 15 per cent advance on yardage, dead work, and room turning.[13] The employees' right to belong to the union was not to be abridged by the operators. But neither the check-off nor the closed union shop was granted. Tribunals were to be set up for the adjustment of the usual complaints common to mining.

The "Garfield Agreement" was to run during the continuation of the war, but not to exceed two years from April 1, 1918. The terms of the agreement, never satisfactory to the union, were acquiesced in under the spell of war patriotism. In August, 1918, the United Mine Workers appealed to the Fuel Administration for a further increase. It was denied. On November 1, 1919, over a year after the signing of the Armistice, a national coal strike was called. The United States Attorney General, at the direction of the President, had an injunction issued against the strike.[14] But neither persuasion nor threats could induce the strikers to return to work. A commission was then appointed by the President to study the problem and make an award. The Alabama operators did not appear before the commission. Letters were filed by them explaining the conditions in their mines and stating that "they

[12] Brief of the Alabama Mining Institute, p. 47.

[13] Award and Recommendation of President Wilson's Bituminous Coal Commission, 1920, p. 21.

[14] See F. B. Sayre, *Cases on Labor Law* (1922), p. 757. United States v. Frank J. Hayes, et al., United States District Court, Indiana, 1919. Unreported.

had no joint relations with the mine workers in their district."
The commission's award embodied an average increase of 14
per cent above the rate fixed by the Fuel Administration. It
recommended that the Alabama operators "arrange to meet
with representatives of the miners and put into effect the
award."[15] It seems that most of the Alabama operators were
willing to put into effect the wage scale awarded by the commission but were quite unwilling to give the union the recognition the commission had given it in the negotiations and which
was implied in its decision.[16] The union, however, insisted upon
the wage scale as awarded by the commission plus the adjustment of disputes through arbitration with the United Mine
Workers participating, and the miners' right to belong to the
union without molestation by the operators. Only a few operators signed the agreement. Local strikes were called to force
recalcitrant operators into signing. The failure of these strikes
led the national officers to order a state-wide strike for
September 7, 1920. Mr. Van A. Bittner, formerly president
of the Pittsburgh district, was sent to Alabama to take charge
of the affair.

At this time there were about 27,000 miners in Alabama.
Twelve thousand responded to the strike call. The operators
attributed so great a response to the fact that about 80 per
cent of the miners were "southern Negroes who are easily
misled, especially when given a prominent and official place
in an organization in which both races are members." [17] The
local strikes called by the district president in May had resulted in sporadic rioting and clashes between strikers and
miners who remained at work. Now the disorder spread and
took on more violent aspects. A few days after Mr. Bittner
arrived the Governor sent the Alabama National Guard to
the strike scene. Order was not restored for several months.
Men who attempted to return to work were ambuscaded; and

[15] *Ibid.*, p. 53.
[16] Brief of the Alabama Mining Institute, *op. cit.*, p. 48.
[17] *Ibid.*, p. 85.

mine guards, militia, and strikers clashed, often resulting in deaths on one side or the other. The Alabama scene was as primitive and brutal as any of the earlier coal tragedies in which white men had been the sole participants. Over 76 per cent [18] of the strikers were Negroes. They "struck and struck hard," believing that if they did not stick the union would carry out its promise of "building a fence around the state" and letting them "live in slavery the rest of their days." [19]

In the 1908 strike the union built camps to house the strikers. The state had construed this as "mobilization." In the 1920 strike a new strategy was tried. Every court order giving the operators the right to evict striking employees was contested by the union on the ground that the miners' implied leases had not expired. A favorable decision from an upper court, or a prolongation of litigation would have placed the union in a strategic position. But the law after five months' delay took its course. On January 27, 1921, the Supreme Court of Alabama decided unanimously that it was illegal for the strikers to withhold possession of the houses from the companies, and that, accordingly, the miners should be taxed with the costs. The strike began to weaken. Some of the men began returning to work while the more persistent of them held out in the hope of a settlement that would give the union at least a measure of control. About a month after the Supreme Court's decision, a compromise was effected. Mr. Van A. Bittner and the operators agreed to arbitration, each promising to abide by the decision. The union demanded: (1) recognition; (2) abolition of the sub-contract system; (3) reëmployment of strikers; (4) readjustment of the day wage rate; and (5) machinery for the adjudication of disputes. On March 19th Governor Thomas E. Kilby, the sole arbitrator, rendered a decision which doomed the union to extinction in Alabama. The award provided: (1) that recognition of the United Mine

[18] Correspondence with Mr. Van A. Bittner.
[19] Speech by Van A. Bittner, quoted in Brief of Alabama Mining Institute, *op. cit.*, p. 54.

Workers of America is not to be compelled; (2) the day wage scale and sub-contract system are to remain unchanged; (3) the existing methods of adjusting grievances are found to be fair and equitable; (4) the operators are under no obligation to reëmploy the striking miners; and (5) that freedom of contract shall be inviolate and therefore any of the above mentioned things may be done by mutual agreement of the parties.[20]

It was clear from the decision that the United Mine Workers after spending $3,000,000 to organize Alabama was to be driven from the state. The 1920 strike, like that of 1908, was opposed by Alabama public sentiment. A committee of Birmingham citizens investigated the strike. In the section of its report on the appearance of Mr. Bittner it said: "Accompanying him came a band of northern Negroes and northern whites, who went from camp to camp throughout the mining districts, Negro organizers and white organizers speaking from the same platform, arousing passions, inflaming feelings, and for the first time bringing to the Alabama miners, of whom more than 70 per cent are Negroes, the news that they were under-paid and ill-treated." [21]

In 1923 the union's strength was below 2 per cent. When the national coal strike was called in 1922, Alabama mines ran full time and shipped coal to the markets usually supplied by the central competitive field. The passing of the union and the migration to West Virginia, eastern Ohio, and western Pennsylvania of hundreds of Negro miners who were prominent in the 1920 strike left the Alabama operators unhampered in executing the long-desired freedom to deal with their employees individually. It is doubtful if the union will reappear in Alabama within a generation. Two things support this opinion. First, the shattered condition of the United Mine Workers resulting from the 1927 strike in the central competitive field. Second, the gradual inauguration of welfare

[20] Brief of Alabama Mining Institute, p. 76.
[21] *Ibid.*, p. 51.

and employee-representation plans by the leading Alabama operators.

Both the Tennessee Coal and Iron Company and the De-Bardeleben Coal Company have gone in for extensive welfare programs which contain unusual provisions for Negro miners, upon whom the operators rely for keeping Alabama non-union. At the annual meeting of the Alabama Mining Institute in 1922, Mr. Milton H. Fies, vice president of the DeBardeleben Coal Company, pointed out that:

The coal operators of Alabama . . . have proven to the nation that the right of men to work shall not be restricted in Alabama's coal mines. In his adherence to this prime essential to liberty the Alabama coal operator has the coöperation and active support of the Negro. The Negro is primarily a free agent and hence a non-union man. It is the Negro's doctrine — and it is a sound one — that every man should have the right to work where he pleases, when he pleases, for whom he pleases, and for what he pleases. You appreciate, I am sure, the measure of the Negro's contribution to non-union Alabama. . . . We should carry our "welfare work" for the Negro beyond the confines of any single mining village and apply such principles to all deserving Negroes wherever found, and thus have the Negro understand that he is to have justice and opportunity.[22]

Here was expressed determination to keep Alabama non-union through the coöperation of the Negro in the operators' counter-reformation. The racial spirit of this speech, when made known to the Negro community, would naturally cause the leaders to ally themselves with the employers. The *Southern Industrial-Fraternal Review*, a Birmingham weekly which circulates among the Negro secret societies, volunteered its support to the employers in the struggle for industrial freedom. "It is a great thing to realize," the *Review* remarked, editorially, "that at last the southern Negro miner has awakened . . . and . . . has decided a long time ago that he was through looking for the 'End of the Rainbow' through the

[22] Milton A. Fies, "Industrial Alabama and the Negro," speech before Alabama Mining Institute, Birmingham, Alabama, Oct., 1922.

ranks of the United Mine Workers, and that he was going to remain right down here in Dixie." [23] Leadership like this could be relied upon to keep the Negro workers in line. Similar support came from another quarter. Industrial paternalism and economic individualism upon which the operators' program was based were not a new philosophy to the Negro community. They were the essentials of the doctrine which Booker T. Washington, the Negro educator, had propagated untiringly in Alabama, and throughout the Negro world. Therefore it does not seem at all unnatural for the official organ of Hampton Institute, where the Washington philosophy was bred, to describe, with evident approval, the welfare capitalism existing in the Alabama coal mining industry two years after the Fies's speech:

The southern industrialist is . . . very much interested in the Negro, for he supplies much of the common labor, some of the semi-skilled labor, and more and more of the skilled labor on which southern industry depends for its operation. Now it is an axiom of business management that by and large, the more intelligent labor becomes, the more valuable it becomes; that the workman who lives in a better home is more con-

[23] "Alabama Un-Unionized Coal Fields" in the *Southern Industrial-Fraternal Review*, Birmingham, Alabama, Sept. 5, 1925. The editor of this paper is one Rev. P. Colfax Rameau, Ph.D., who, it is generally believed, receives financial support from the coal operators and other Alabama industrialists. It is interesting to note Rameau's attitude on the Muscle Shoals problem in which it is doubtful if any of his readers, or the Negro public generally, was interested. Praising the Alabama Power Company, which was at that time under investigation by the Federal Trade Commission, and the Tennessee Coal, Iron and Railroad Company, Rameau says in part, "Time and space would fail us to tell you more about these two industrial giants and what they have done to put Alabama on the industrial map, and in real economic welfare service in making better general working and living conditions for their employees and too, without any unionism to dominate and dictate what shall be done, and today we are pleading with the great Anglo-Saxon church of this Southland to rise in the power of its great Christian manhood and save at least the Alabama Power Company from the hands of a belated political mob, and send out a Christian crusade that will set ten thousand pulpits ringing with a new message of God and humanity that will be the means of saving Muscle Shoals for unborn posterity." The issue that carried this statement also carried a large advertisement of stock in the Alabama Power Company. See the *Review*, July-August, 1928. See also Chapter VII, pp. 137-38.

tented and therefore a better workman, that home ownership, habits of thrift, ideals of honest and fair dealing are big factors in making more permanent and profitable relations between employer and employee. . . . The effect therefore that industrial welfare work, now so generally carried on by large corporations, is having and will continue to have on the great masses of Negroes, North and South, promises to be a big factor in Negro progress. . . . Negroes in industry are constantly being trained on consistent constructive labor. To a large extent their intelligence is developed to a higher and higher point through their manual work. In addition to this, all through the North and South today the Negro in industry is coming under the influence of a scientific social welfare system that is, in general, working, and in many instances working with great efficiency, toward the same ends as those which Hampton and Tuskegee and the whole system of education they represent are striving for. Moreover, in many cases, these parallel efforts and aims are drawn closer together by the fact that Hampton and Tuskegee graduates are having a large part in such work. . . . The writer was informed by every southerner but one with whom he discussed the problem of the Negro in industry that welfare work of the Tennessee Coal, Iron and Railroad Company . . . is an outstanding example of what can be done to improve the living and social status of the Negro industrial worker. . . . A visit to the beautiful little villages of Ensley, Westfield, Muscoda and Fairfield where the colored employees of this corporation live affords an illustration of the parallel aims just referred to. . . . In this welfare work of the Tennessee Coal, Iron and Railroad Company, two educated Negroes — S. C. Johnson, of Oberlin, and John W. Oveltree of Tuskegee, hold important executive positions: Mr. Oveltree was graduated from Tuskegee in 1893 and has since had a varied experience as principal and superintendent of industries in several large schools. He is now efficiency social agent for the 15,000 Negroes employed by the above company. . . . The DeBardeleben Coal Company of Alabama was the first to admit that the success it has had with its Negro welfare work is largely due to the ability and character of another Tuskegee graduate, Mr. R. W. Taylor, and this, in no small measure, because he is a Negro working for the welfare of his own race. The officials in charge of similar work at the plants of the Tennessee Coal, Iron and Railroad Company also believe that in most cases the welfare executive in direct touch with the Negro worker should himself be a Negro. At Sipsey, Alabama, where Mr. Taylor (Tuskegee,

1890) is principal of the school and executive in charge of welfare work among the employees of the DeBardeleben Coal Company, there has developed a spirit of goodwill and coöperation known even in the North as the "Sipsey Spirit.". . . But perhaps even more significant than any verbal praise which this Tuskegee man can receive from either employer or fellow-worker is the fact that today the Company gives the children of its Sipsey employees two scholarships a year to Tuskegee Institute, and plans to do likewise in its other mining towns in the district. . . . Leadership of their people in this field opens up a new opportunity for Hampton and Tuskegee graduates.[24]

Thus it seems that company unionism, welfare capitalism, and the Hampton-Tuskegee petit bourgeois spirit issue from the same ideological mold. They are unconscious allies in the perpetuation of a universal closed non-union shop in the Alabama coal and iron industry. And the United Mine Workers' defeat in Alabama coupled with its inability to establish effective control in the rest of the southern field, notably West Virginia, account in a large measure for its present status.

The first attempt to unionize West Virginia was made in 1895. Fayette and McDowell Counties were the base of attack. In each of these counties the union gained a substantial hold. Soon after its entrance 40 per cent of the miners in Fayette and 75 per cent in McDowell became affiliated with the organization. The membership was composed chiefly of Negroes some of whom made many sacrifices in order that the organization of the southern counties might prove successful. One Negro miner, Sandy Wooten, is said to have loaned the organization $15,000 for its work in McDowell. It is charged that the leaders of the union in McDowell squandered large sums of money and after being bribed by the operators left the state.[25] After this the attempts to organize McDowell were weak and fruitless.

The United Mine Workers' greatest display of power was between 1910 and 1922. In fact in 1921 the zenith of its

[24] *Southern Workman*, Nov., 1924, pp. 530-36. Compare with Chapter III, pp. 48-52.

[25] Files of the West Virginia Bureau of Negro Welfare and Statistics.

power was reached in the southern counties. Locals were successfully organized in Fayette County, Kanawha County and part of Raleigh in 1910. By 1921 the mines in these counties were almost completely organized. But farther south the highly important county, Logan, stubbornly resisted the encroachments of the union. This was the bailiwick of the notorious Don Chafin, deputy sheriff, the operators' legal bulwark against unionization.

The development of the mines in Logan County did not begin until 1905. And it was the generally accepted policy of the operators to employ at least one-third Negro miners. Although producing something like 10,000,000 tons of coal annually, Logan County has an estimated potential capacity for producing 20,000,000 tons. When the 1919 strike occurred, the mines in both Logan and McDowell Counties worked at full production. The back of the strike was consequently broken. Thus the productive capacity of this new field and the policy of slashing wages in depression and raising them in normal times to a level equal to or above those paid in normal periods by the mines in the central competitive field bred the determination to unionize Logan at all cost. The belief expressed by union miners at this time was that "if Logan falls West Virginia is organized." [26] But Logan, like McDowell and Mingo, was a citadel of non-unionism. And the bitter fight that was made to unionize Logan and Mingo disrupted the United Mine Workers in southern West Virginia.

In the spring of 1920 the union turned its attention to the mines in Mingo County. An effective system of espionage caused the prompt discovery of miners who had joined the union. Discovery of union members led to their discharge, blacklisting, and eviction from company houses. Strikes followed. Miners who refused to give up company houses were forced to do so by Baldwin-Felts detectives whom the operators employed for the purpose. This display of force caused the miners to retaliate in kind. There was street fighting and

[26] *Nation*, May 29, 1920, p. 724.

bloodshed. Many union miners were waylaid, beaten, and imprisoned on false charges and sometimes on no charges at all. Negroes as well as whites were involved. One colored union miner of Mingo, Frank Ingham, was arrested in McDowell while he and his wife were there on business. According to Ingham's testimony the cause of his arrest was never told him. He was released by the sheriff who told him to go with seven men who would take his testimony. Upon reaching a woods some distance from the jail the seven men beat him into insensibility and left him for dead.[27]

The climax came with the fatal shooting of Sid Hatfield of Mingo County. Ten Baldwin-Felts detectives had been killed in the street fighting accompanying the strikes and the evictions. The death of seven was attributed to Hatfield, a leader of the union miners. After his acquittal, he himself was murdered on the courthouse steps in McDowell County where he had gone to answer another indictment. The union miners of Kanawha and Fayette Counties were so aroused by these events that they armed themselves to march into Mingo, release the imprisoned union miners, drive out the Baldwin-Felts detectives, and organize Logan County on the way into Mingo. This was the famous "Armed March" against Logan and Mingo Counties. There were 8,000 or more participants in the march. About one-fourth were Negroes.[28] At the time two Negroes were members of the district executive committee of the United Mine Workers. The march was looked upon by many citizens as an armed insurrection of a ruthless mob bent upon usurping the power of law. The director of the then newly created State Bureau of Negro Welfare and Statistics of West Virginia, who was also joint owner of the McDowell *Times*, a Negro weekly, pronouncedly pro-operator, stated in his annual report to the governor that his office had been instrumental in dissuading 118 Negroes from participating in

---

[27] Testimony of Frank Ingham, Hearings before United States Senate Committee on Education and Labor on West Virginia Coal Fields, 1921, Vol. 1, pp. 27-30 and pp. 469-82. See also *New Republic*, Sept. 21, 1921, pp. 86 and 90.
[28] *Nation*, Sept. 14, 1921, p. 288.

the march. According to this report, "less than 200 Negroes took part in the march, while, on the other hand, more than 500 Negroes in McDowell, Mingo, Mercer and Logan Counties volunteered their services to go to the line of battle and repel the invaders. . . . The majority of Negroes of all classes believe in law and order and the peaceful settlement of all disputes. . . . . They are by nature and training peaceful and will bear many ills before striking a blow for themselves and this splendid attribute has caused the Negro to be severely criticized by radicals and direct actionists, but to many sane, conservative persons of all races it is the . . . salvation of the race." [29]

No doubt the purpose of the march would have been accomplished, but certainly at a bloody cost, had the federal government not interfered. The break-up of the "Armed March" and the failure of the strike spelled the collapse of unionism in southern West Virginia. The whole southern section of the state was completely abandoned when the Borderland Coal Corporation was granted an injunction against the United Mine Workers restraining it from "advising, assisting, encouraging, aiding, or abetting" the unionization or the attempted unionization of the non-union mines in Mingo County, West Virginia, and Pike County, Kentucky.[30] The approval of the Supreme Court of the United States of a permanent injunction granted by a lower court to the Hitchman Coal Company in 1912 served as a precedent in this case.[31]

The opposition of the Hitchman Company was the beginning of the break-up of the union in northern West Virginia. In 1925 sixteen of the leading northern coal companies, protesting their inability to compete with the coal from the

[29] T. Edward Hill, Report of the West Virginia Bureau of Negro Welfare and Statistics, 1921-1922, p. 54.

[30] Gasaway v. Borderland Coal Company, (United States Circuit Court of Appeals, Seventh Circuit, 1921), 278 Fed. 56. The Circuit Court remanded the decree to the District Court for recasting so as to forbid the union from doing only unlawful things. From the union's point of view the decree was substantially the same.

[31] Hitchman Coal and Coke Company v. Mitchell, 1917, 245 U. S. 229.

southern counties because of lower labor costs and richer coal veins, refused to abide by the Baltimore wage agreement which had three years to run. The strike which followed was accompanied by picketing, violence, and restraining orders upon unionization. Negro labor was imported, and largely through its successful employment, the strike was broken, although never officially called off. The 1925 strike marked the union's fatal disaster in West Virginia. And thereupon, District 17, United Mine Workers, began to disintegrate.

It was not alone the intrenched opposition of the West Virginia operators to unionism, but the miners' own antipathy to labor solidarity that made the United Mine Workers' task difficult. In Mercer, McDowell, Mingo, Wayne, Boone, Logan, and Kanawha Counties of West Virginia, and likewise in Johnson, Pike, Harland, and Ball Counties of Kentucky, the population is composed of native mountaineers of American ancestry. Their history is crimsoned with bitter feuds. Like all mountaineers, they are individualistic. They look askance at the "furriners." The operators have capitalized this feeling. It has already been pointed out that the policy of employing native whites, Negroes, and foreigners in varying proportions has been quite generally established in both the southern and northern counties of West Virginia. This policy is likewise becoming characteristic of other coal fields. In their appeal to the West Virginia miner's provincialism, the coal operators have circulated the belief that the operators in the central competitive field and the United Mine Workers have conspired to organize West Virginia for the purpose of creating a general strike for the benefit of those states.[32]

The success of the Ku Klux Klan in West Virginia is an extreme expression of the nativistic psychology. The objects of the Klan's propaganda were Negroes and foreign whites. Wherever Negroes served on the mine committees, opposition

[32] See Gasaway v. Borderland Coal Company, (United States Circuit Court of Appeals, Seventh Circuit, 1921), 278 Fed. 56. Also, A. E. Suffern, *Conciliation and Arbitration in the Coal Industry of America*, p. 68.

to them has been most pronounced. "The West Virginia native white miners dislike serving on committees with 'ignorant niggers who just came from the South.' " Sometimes they refuse to follow orders issued by a colored committeeman.[33] Because of this racial animosity many Negroes had withdrawn from their locals before the 1925 and 1927 strikes. In some places, particularly in the Fairmont district, the Klan's one hundred per cent Americanism produced a defense psychology in the Negro which took the form of adherence to Garveyism, the Negro's Zionism. Although a purely black man's movement, Garveyism was never feared by the union leaders. But the influence of the Klan proved to be so vitiating upon union morale and labor consciousness that the United Mine Workers were forced to outlaw it by constitutional decree.[34]

Another source of opposition to unionism in the West Virginia coal mining industry is to be found in the cultural background of the Negro community and in the character of the local Negro leadership. The reliance of the southern coal operators upon so large a proportion of labor from a single class has meant the rapid advancement of members of this class to such positions as assistant superintendents, foremen, and bosses of varying degrees of minor authority. Perhaps even more important than the mere growth in numbers of Negro miners and their rise to positions of authority — a fact which is often exploited by pro-capitalist Negro leaders to sustain the Negro miners' flagging loyalty to the operators — are the political implications accompanying this growth and its concentration in a few southern counties of the state. Today there are no less than 45,000 Negro miners in the bituminous industry. More than half of all Negroes in the industry are employed in West Virginia mines. And they cluster in the Pocahontas and New River-Kanawha districts. In the mines of Fayette, Kanawha, Logan, McDowell, and Raleigh Counties,

---

[33] *Labor Relations in Fairmont, West Virginia,* United State Department of Labor, Bulletin 361.

[34] Article XIV, Section 2, of the Constitution, United Mine Workers of America, April 1, 1924, p. 34.

there are 17,154 Negro miners.[35] This is more than 70 per
cent of the 23,990 [36] Negroes employed in the entire coal
industry of the state. The degree of concentration of the Negro population of West Virginia in the southern coal producing counties is further indicated by the fact that in 1922, 21
per cent of the entire Negro population of the state lived in
McDowell County, and 67 per cent of it lived in McDowell,
Fayette, Kanawha, Raleigh, Mercer, Logan, Mingo, and
Wyoming Counties.[37] In spite of this high degree of concentration, the Negro population does not outnumber the white
in any county or magisterial district of the state. And yet as
early as 1896 a Negro, Christopher Payne, was elected to the
House of Delegates from Fayette County. From 1896 to
the present Negroes have been elected from time to time
to the House of Delegates from McDowell, Kanawha, and
Fayette Counties, and have held important local political offices. They have been appointed to a relatively large number of
governmental positions inside the state, and one, a former
justice of the peace for almost twenty years in the Adkins district of McDowell County, was appointed recorder of deeds in
the Coolidge administration.[38] The existence of such tax-supported institutions as the West Virginia State College for Negroes, the Bureau of Negro Welfare and Statistics, the Colored
Orphans Home, and many others, all directed and manned by
Negro personnel, is a testimonial to the West Virginia Negro's
political power which in the last analysis is traceable to the
ability of a local race-conscious leadership to corral the votes
of the Negro in the mining centers of the southern counties.
Although, as pointed out above, the Negro voting power constitutes a majority in none of these districts, it holds a balance
in close elections. And as several Negro miners in this district
once said to one of the authors, the miners vote for the man

[35] Report of the West Virginia Bureau of Negro Welfare and Statistics,
1925-1926, p. 22.

[36] Ibid.

[37] Ibid., 1921-1922, p. 12.

[38] Ibid., pp. 62-68.

the operators want elected. In communities where the Negro vote may sometimes hold a balance of power, the Negro politician who, in the miner's words, "doesn't bite the hand that feeds him" has a far greater chance of being elected to office than a white office seeker who concerns himself about employers sharing industrial control with workers. However much these Negro political leaders are lacking in an understanding of the workers' point of view in industrial relations, or are out of sympathy with it, they derive great social prestige and community power from the Negro's belief that his political and civil rights are best protected by a representative of his own race. Thus, the political leaders, the administrators of the various segregated Negro institutions, and the Negroes who are appointed or elected to public office, have become the interlocking guardians of Negro destiny in West Virginia where each of these groups is both the patron and the patronized. They and the members of the professional and business classes are a middle class élite which prides itself on racial loyalty, but which, as elsewhere in the Negro world, is actually divorced in social and philosophic outlook from the economic realities that condition the life of the modern wage earner. Their influence is not confined to the southern part of the state where the majority of Negroes live, but radiates throughout West Virginia Negro life.

By tradition and nurture, Negro leaders are pro-employer in sympathy and outlook. In nearly every important controversy between organized labor and capital in which Negro labor has been involved, the Negro leader has sided with capital. He has approved and often encouraged the use of Negro labor for breaking strikes. He defends his position with the argument that the exclusion of the Negro worker from many trade unions forces him to accept strike breaking as his weapon against the unions and as the only means of obtaining employment in many industries. There is some truth in this defense, but it surely does not justify opposition to unionism per se. Least of all does it justify opposition to the United

Mine Workers which has been more serious about the organization of Negro workers than any other A. F. of L. union, except the International Ladies Garment Workers and the Longshoremen. Many of the United Mine Workers' attempts were successful. But the Negro leader takes the position that, although the official or constitutional policy of the United Mine Workers can not be indicted, unionism thwarts Negro industrial advancement. An expression typical of this attitude is to be found in the 1925 Report of the Bureau of Negro Welfare and Statistics of West Virginia. At the time the report was being written the 1925 strike was in progress in northern West Virginia. "It is stated," reported the director, "that, with few exceptions, white men in strongly organized territory will not permit the employment of Negroes as motormen, brakesmen on motors, head-house operators, machine runners, track layers . . . and other higher waged . . . jobs even though the Negroes are members of the union also. . . . The operators contend that it is to the best interest of the Negro miners to side with them in this controversy because in the state of Indiana, Illinois, Ohio and part of Pennsylvania which are strongly organized by the United Mine Workers . . . very few Negroes are employed, and where operators hire them they are driven from the operations by white union miners; while on the other hand in the non-union fields of West Virginia Negroes are employed in the coal mines in numbers far in excess of the percentage of their race in the whole population." The report further pointed out that the loss of the strike "will result in the employment of more Negroes." [39] In another place the director also pointed out that immediately following the complete unionization of Fayette and Kanawha Counties, the Negroes gradually lost their old influence in public affairs and the higher jobs in the mines — all of which was regained when the union collapsed. [40]

[39] Report of the West Virginia Bureau of Negro Welfare and Statistics, 1925-1926, p. 38.

[40] Unpublished records of the West Virginia Bureau of Negro Welfare and Statistics. Courtesy of T. Edward Hill.

The truth of some of these indictments against the union has been admitted by Negro union miners in the presence of white union members. A Negro miner, formerly of Alabama, but now president of a local in eastern Ohio, complained that the Negro is not given the same opportunity for advancement in the union fields as in the non-union fields of West Virginia and Alabama. Many Negroes who helped to break the strike of 1927 in western Pennsylvania had been members of the United Mine Workers. As some of them passed the union barracks en route to the mines, they would display their cards and say: "You would not work with me before the strike. Now I have your job and I am going to keep it." But the Negro miners of eastern Ohio did not wait for the 1927 strike to repay the white miners for refusing to work with them. On one occasion white members of a local union struck against the employment of Negro miners. The Negro miners appealed to the national executive board of the United Mine Workers, which revoked the charter of the offending white local. Later there was placed in the district constitution the following clause: "Any Local Union that is found guilty of discriminating against a fellow worker on account of creed, color or nationality, said Local Union to be fined not less than $125, for each offense." [41] Of course it is conceivable that many cases of discrimination can not be proven; and that even when they can be proven, it is the business of the individual discriminated against to press the charge. If it happens that he is apathetic he will not press his complaint. In such a case no number of constitutional decrees can remedy the situation. Upon encountering the opposition of white miners, the Negro, it seems, prefers to leave the job rather than protest to his union. A miner who has experienced racial discrimination usually passes the word to others who abstain from seeking employment at what are called "white men's mines." As prevalent as the practice of racial discrimination is claimed to be in union territory,

[41] Article IX, Section 5, of the Constitution of Sub-District 5 of District 6, United Mine Workers of America, April 1, 1925, p. 20.

and as great as the Negro miners' opportunity for advancement is in non-union territory, nearly every interview that the authors had with Negro miners in Cabin Creek emphasized the advantages of unionism over non-unionism.

Cabin Creek, Raleigh County, is in the very heart of the productive non-union counties of southern West Virginia. The interviews were conducted in the fall of 1928 when the strike in the central competitive field was subsiding. The industry in the southern counties was at that time undergoing a depression. Wages had been cut; coal loaders were receiving 44 cents per ton. The wages for machine cutting were 11 cents per ton. In McDowell County where the method of payment was on the basis of cars instead of tonnage, coal loaders were receiving about $1.30 per car in places free of slate, and $2.00 per ton where slate was two feet or more. The miners contended that although the official capacity of the cars was 2 tons, they loaded not less than 3 to 3.5 tons to a car. If the cars held 3 tons the rate was 43 cents per ton which was about the average for coal loading in the southern district. At that very time the wages for coal loading in western Pennsylvania were 25 per cent higher. Of course the miners know the capacity of cars only when they have a representative, the checkweighman, at the tipple. Under non-union conditions they are not given this privilege. The question of wages was aggravated by compulsory dealings at company stores and by the sub-contract system.

A meeting was called by some of the Cabin Creek miners. It was reported to one of the mine superintendents who called in a Negro dentist living in one of the company houses. This dentist, apparently unconscious of the implications in his experience, related it to our party in the presence of some of the Negro miners who had participated in the attempt at unionization. He said that the superintendent reminded him that the company had favored him by renting him a house as his office and residence upon the same terms as it had to its miners. The rent was about $10 per month for four rooms and light.

In return for these favors, as well as the right to practice in the village, which was also company owned, the superintendent requested him to advise the men against any union demonstration. In order to carry out the superintendent's wishes, he called in a Negro political leader who, in turn, addressed the Negro miners in their church, partly supported by the coal company. The theme of his address was "Don't bite the hand that feeds you." When asked for an interpretation of the subject, we were told that the coal operators were very good to their employees. "They furnish the miners with houses at cheap rates; they contribute to the church, and to the school; and they give the miners credit at the company store when times are bad." The operators, it seems, rely upon the tax-supported Bureau of Negro Welfare and Statistics for assistance in making this paternalism effective. According to the report of the director of the bureau:

Each year increasing numbers of coal operators . . . are undertaking activities for the welfare of their employees. . . . Prizes are given for the yards kept cleanest over a period of months. Y. M. C. A's and club houses are provided and maintained . . . bands and baseball teams are encouraged and assisted; good schools are encouraged and frequently the salaries paid teachers by boards of education are supplemented by the company. Funds are donated for . . . playgrounds and many coal companies help finance athletic contests between opposing school teams. . . . The director has been called upon to act as judge in five garden and yard contests, to outline plans for three clean-up campaigns, to judge six debating and three band contests. . . . The bureau has recommended equipment for two coal camp playgrounds and selected books and periodicals for . . . three company club houses. . . . All of these things and more are being constantly done for Negroes and whites by a great number of the coal companies and they are making for improved industrial relations.[42]

Some of the miners place a different construction upon the operators' gestures. If they looked upon welfare as industrial democracy, they certainly would not have attempted to revive

[42] Report of the West Virginia Bureau of Negro Welfare and Statistics, 1925-1926, p. 19.

unionism in a section where it had caused so much warfare. Moreover, the operators' quick discovery of attempts at unionization has created in the aggressive Negro miners a suspicion of company welfare programs, and confirmed them in the conviction that an espionage system had been carefully laid for detecting digressions from company loyalty. Behind bolted doors and drawn curtains they told us that if company officials got wind of our visit in the patches, the persons with whom we had talked would be called on to tell the nature of our conversation. If it became known that we had mentioned unions, the persons who had entertained us would be discharged. Very often the company's welfare man is its spy. Frequently, the spy is self-appointed. Sometimes he is the local Negro preacher who is hired by the company to look after the welfare of its Negro employees. When he is not engaged in performing his religious duties, he is importing labor during a strike or shortage or improving the community life of his charges. Many of these preachers have become so accustomed to the performance of this type of service that they rationalize it as the Negro's "racial salvation." The operators' espionage is made all the more effective by the fact that the mining communities are practically owned by the coal company. The sheriff's salary is often paid by the operators. A Negro miner of Logan County tells of a conversation between himself and the sheriff. "Don Chafin (sheriff) says: 'I want you to go up and get around among them men and find out who is trying to organize and report back to me.' Then he told the others, 'Luther is going to come clean.' And Squire White says, 'If you don't come clean, by God, we will kill you.' I says, 'I come clean, you let me go.' " [43]

The whole program of welfare found in southern West Virginia appears to be more productive of sycophancy than it is of industrial democracy. The same atmosphere was found to be characteristic of the Connellsville Coke and Westmoreland districts, the ancient strongholds of non-unionism in western Penn-

[43] *Nation*, May 29, 1920, p. 725. Also, June 12, 1920, p. 794.

sylvania. Miners with whom we talked in this section admitted their fear of speaking about conditions in the mines lest they be talking to their future betrayers. The submissiveness arose from the consequences of the 1922 strike.

During the 1922 strike the United Mine Workers were joined by the non-union miners of Somerset, Westmoreland, and Fayette Counties. Many of the active participants were Negroes. When the settlement was made it included the central competitive field, but not Somerset, Westmoreland, or Fayette. The non-union miners saved the day for the union, but were left out of the agreement.[44] After remaining on strike for several months, they were finally forced to accept the operators' terms. The leaders, both black and white, of the non-union forces were blacklisted. No other attempts have since been made at unionization. Today when one mentions United Mine Workers to Negroes who participated in the 1922 strike, one merely gets a shrug of shoulders.

The union's desertion of the non-union miners in the 1922 strike caused a revolt within the ranks of the United Mine Workers. Some of the membership saw in this desertion and in the organization's failure to bring West Virginia, Kentucky, and Alabama under control the ultimate loss of control of the central competitive field resulting in the irreparable break-up of the union. The slogan of the revolt was "Save the Union." The test of the United Mine Workers came in 1927 when the operators in the central competitive field broke relations with It. The "Save the Union" faction became more militant in its opposition to the policies of John L. Lewis, president of the United Mine Workers. The opposition was led by John Brophy [45] who had been defeated for president under questionable circumstances. As long as Brophy led, the "Save the Union Committee" was content to remain the official opposition to the Lewis leadership. But during the strike Brophy resigned.

[44] Francis Tyson, *New Republic*, April 25, 1928. Also, the Program of the National Save the Union Conference, April 1, 1928, p. 7.

[45] Interviews with John Brophy. Also *Labor Dynamics* (1928), edited by J. B. S. Hardman, p. 179.

John Watt, Pat Toohey, and Tony Minerich rose to leadership. The communists who had been boring from within the anti-administration forces now came out in the open demanding a dual miner's union. A call issued for a national convention in Pittsburgh, September, 1928, called attention to the backsliding of the United Mine Workers. It said:

The U. M. W. A. was once the most progressive union in the labor movement. It supported the labor party and industrial unionism, and it gave its active aid to every forward cause of the workers. It was an old enemy of the Gompers gang. Its splendid fighting spirit was well known in the American labor movement. But the Lewis machine has choked this progressive spirit. The Lewis program is "coöperation" with the employers, which means surrender to them. He has substituted fake arbitration methods for a real fighting policy. Controlling the union with gangster methods, the Lewis clique, in spite of the progressive attitude of the rank and file, have put the union on record against every progressive measure it ever stood for. They have rejected the old-time labor party policy and officially endorsed the reactionary program of supporting candidates on the tickets of the Republican and Democratic parties. They have flagrantly discriminated against Negroes, foreign-born workers and the youth. With its program of always treating and with close support from coal operators, the Lewis gang has systematically warred against all militancy in the union, ruthlessly expelling thousands of individuals and entire locals, the best fighters among the miners, simply because they dared insist upon a progressive, fighting policy, a real defense of the miners' interests.

The result of the convention was the formation of the National Miners' Union with a Negro miner, William M. Boyce, as vice president. The chief objects of the new union were: (1) the complete organization of the whole coal industry; (2) the organization of Negro miners; (3) the nationalization of the coal industry; and (4) the formation of a labor party. Due to communist control the former discriminations against Negro miners were played up by the National Miners' Union on the theory that this and the election of a Negro to the second highest office in the union would win the Negro miners' allegiance. Immediately after his election Vice President

William M. Boyce issued a ringing appeal to the Negro miners to join the new organization. "Every Negro," he said, "should join the National Miners' Union because it fights vigorously for full economic, political and social equality for them. . . . Lewis and Company did not want the Negro miners. It is a matter of record that U. M. W. A. hoodlums broke up various N. M. U. meetings . . . shouting 'You have niggers with you, yes!' " [46] But such appeals won support from but few Negro miners.

The National Miners' Union never gained a foothold in the industry. It was late in getting under way. The communist group in the anti-Lewis faction of the United Mine Workers had urged the formation of a rival union at the beginning of the strike in 1927, but the Central Executive Committee of the Communist International rejected the idea of "dual unionism." Eleven months later, however, the Committee reversed itself.[47] But by the time the National Miners' Union began to function the strike was already lost and the new union unable to make an effective appeal to the tired and defeated workers passed from the scene before it had a chance to begin its serious work.

It is quite easy to be critical of the United Mine Workers' failures, to hold up for derision the mistaken strategy of the leadership and its shady, if not corrupt politics. But to organize the Negro and native white miners in the southern territory — Alabama, Tennessee, Kentucky, and West Virginia — is more easily said than done. The failure of the United Mine Workers in these sections was in part the result of its incapacity to master subtle community traditions and race psychology and to understand the temperament of the Negro community. Its failure here foreshadowed its defeat and collapse in 1927.

The decline of the United Mine Workers of America, begun by the failure of the strike of 1927-1928 and hastened by

---

[46] *Daily Worker*, January 21, 1930.

[47] Communist International, Sixth World Congress. International Press Correspondence, Aug. 11, 1928, Vol. 8, No. 8, p. 841.

the activities of the left wing and the short-lived National Miners' Union, has been pushed still further along by a new revolt in 1930. This movement, a phase of the general anti-Lewis drive, resulted, in the spring of 1930, in the formation of a new "United Mine Workers," under the presidency of Alexander Howat of Kansas. The chief strength of the Howat organization lies in the well-organized Illinois district.[48]

The whole organization situation in bituminous coal is at present confused and uncertain. The future alone can tell whether the old United Mine Workers will regain its former hold on the organized fields, whether the new union will supercede it, or whether the employers will succeed in imposing an open shop. But one thing seems fairly certain. That is that the Negro will remain an important factor in the industry and that any organization which gains control of the coal fields must be at least as friendly and fair to the Negro miner as the United Mine Workers.

[48] A. J. Muste, "The Crisis in the Miners' Union," *Labor Age*, March, 1930.

PART V

NEGRO LABOR SINCE THE WAR

Chapter XVIII

THE "NEW" NEGRO AND POST-WAR UNREST

THE competition into which Negroes and whites were suddenly thrown as a result of the southern Negro migrations was more direct and on a larger scale than had ever occurred. It was in the nature of a revolution that could not take place without some disaster. The whites resented the intrusion and the underbidding of black labor. But the Negro, too, had his grievances. Although he enjoyed greater economic and industrial opportunity, he found the North less of a haven than he had anticipated. Advancement in industry was not as rapid and as frequent as he had visualized. Residential segregation and high rents, racial discrimination, and social ostracism were found to be characteristic of the North no less than of the South. Yet he had escaped political disfranchisement, illiteracy, and poor schools, and the inhibitions to freedom of thought and expression that Negroes experience in the South. In this atmosphere the Negro imbibed the spirit of race consciousness. He was no less antagonistic to the white worker than the latter was to him. Thus the migration provoked mutual racial antagonism through the competition between Negroes and whites for jobs and threw into relief much of the dissatisfaction and unrest long pent up in the Negro masses. Unrest and racial hostility were intensified by the problem of housing the rapidly expanding Negro population.

The shortage of houses in sections reserved for Negroes forced newcomers to bid for homes in white residential sections. An increase in rents naturally followed, and the effect of high rent was not only felt by the Negro but also by the whites. Because of a belief in the undesirability of Negro neighbors the whites felt impelled to seek houses in other sections of the city where property values, likewise, responded to the pressure of new demand. Very often in these sections, where new real estate developments did not keep pace with the demand or the available houses were insufficient to relieve the pressure of demand, purchase prices and rentals were higher than in the sections abandoned to the Negro. When the whites' retreat from the Negro invasion was temporarily checked by the un-availability of houses elsewhere, and the protest of home owners and tenants' leagues failed to dissuade landlords and real estate agents from plying their lucrative trade among Negroes, violence and intimidation were used. The first victims of the whites' anger were members of the Negro upper classes who were economically able to acquire homes in white neigh-borhoods. But whenever the life or property of a Negro who had moved into a white section was threatened, the Negro masses rose up to protect him. In the Washington, East St. Louis, and Chicago race riots, which were to a large degree caused by competition between Negroes and whites for jobs and houses, the Negro masses demonstrated very clearly that they would meet violence with violence. This determination of the Negro masses to fight back when one of their race was injured or threatened with injury was the expression of a spirit of revolt that accompanied the migrations, the smouldering embers of which were fanned into a militant race conscious-ness by the writings of the younger Negro intellectuals such as Claude McKay [1] and the editors of radical publications like the *Crusader*, the *Messenger*, and the *Challenge*, which loomed into prominence just after the World War.[2]

Typical of the intellectual stimulation given to this surging consciousness of the Negro masses was the following verse:

[1] McKay, the distinguished poet, is known for his adherence to economic radicalism as much as by his poetry and recent novels. He saw in the acceptance of Bolshevism by the white American workers the emancipation of the "black toilers." See his poem, "If We Must Die," which well expresses the belligerent and bitter state of Negro feeling during the post-war period. *The Book of American Negro Poetry*, edited by James Weldon Johnson, 1922.

[2] *The Investigation Activities of the Department of Justice*, Senate Docu-ments, 66th Congress, 1st Session, 1919, Vol. 12, pp. 161-87. Exhibit No. 10.

This must not be!
The time is past when black men
Laggard Sons of Ham,
Shall tamely bow and weakly cringe
In servile manner full of shame.

Lift up your heads!
Be proud! be brave!
Though black, the same red blood
Flows through your veins
As through your paler brothers.

.   .   .   .

Your toil enriched the Southern lands;
Your anguish has made sweet the sugar cane;
Your sweat has moistened the growing corn,
And drops of blood from the cruel master's whip
Has caused the white cotton to burst forth in mute protest.

Demand, come not mock suppliant!
Demand, and if not given — take!
Take what is rightfully yours;
An eye for an eye;
A soul for soul;
Strike, black man, strike!
This shall not be!

This bit of verse, like much of the literature of the period, is not only an expression of race consciousness but also of economic discontent. And it would seem to follow that some of the racial conflict which orginated in economic facts would have been forestalled had organized labor brought Negro and white workers into closer affiliation before the migrations. But organized labor's traditional view of the Negro as a strike breaker and its laissez-faire attitude toward Negro organization as well as toward other important questions rendered it helpless. The Negro was left to himself to make whatever adjustments he could in his new economic environment. The racial movements and philosophies that sprang up among the Negro population during the five years that followed the

World War bore the earmarks of economic unrest and social dissatisfaction for which the inertia of the labor movement and American race psychology were responsible. They were generated by economic competition, racial antagonism, the Negro's awakened self-reliance and race consciousness and his new intellectual freedom. The movements took one of the following forms: economic radicalism, racial self-sufficiency, or Negro Zionism.

The last mentioned movement, Negro Zionism, popularly known as the "Back to Africa Movement," was sponsored by Marcus Garvey, a Jamaican Negro, through his Universal Negro Improvement Association and African Communities (Imperial) League. This was an all-Negro movement built upon pride of race and the exaltation of things black.[3] Negro economic self-sufficiency was a revival of the individualism enunciated by Booker T. Washington. A typical expression of this doctrine in the post-war period was contained in a leaflet circulated by the International Negro Civic Association of New York. The association protested that millionaires were being made in Harlem every five years; that Negroes ought to own Harlem or leave it; that a Negro boy has as much right behind a bank window as a white boy, but that the Negro race had to build banks before this would be possible; and that rents were "murderous" but, owning no houses, the Negro must pay what is asked or be "scrapped."[4] The self-sufficiency movement was closely related to the Garvey movement in that the two of them idealized a sort of self-contained racial economy. One looked to Africa as the place where its dreams were to be realized, while the other hoped to build in America.

The first mentioned movement, economic radicalism, was inaugurated about 1918 by Chandler Owen and Asa Philip Randolph, the editors of the *Messenger*, a magazine of "scientific radicalism." Owen and Randolph had formerly been

[3] For Garvey's philosophy see Chapter VII.

[4] *Revolutionary Radicalism*, a report of the Joint Legislative Committee of the State of New York Investigating Seditious Activities, 1920, Vol. II, Pt. 1, p. 1518.

employed as editors of the *Hotel Messenger*, a journal published by the Headwaiters and Sidewaiters' Society of Greater New York. A rift occurred between the editors and the society when the editors persisted in commenting upon the sidewaiters' inadequate wages and disagreeable working conditions.[5] The ruptured relations led to the founding of the "militant and revolutionary" *Messenger* in 1917. The new magazine avowed itself to be the organ of labor unionism and socialism among Negroes.[6] Associated with Randolph and Owen in the task of intellectually emancipating the workingmen, were W. A. Domingo, editor of the *Emancipator*, whose motto was "to preach deliverance to the slaves," William N. Colson, the Reverend George Frazier Miller, Richard B. Moore, and Cyril Briggs.[7] Later Moore and Briggs withdrew and affiliated with the Communist party of America. These were the vanguard of the "New" Negro whom the *Messenger* editor described as "the product of the same world-wide forces that have brought into being the great liberal and radical movements that are now seizing the reins of political, economic and social power in all the civilized countries of the world." The "New" Negro "unlike the old Negro" was not to be "lulled into a false sense of security with political spoils and

[5] *Messenger*, Nov. 1917, p. 21. Chief among the latter was the rather general practice among headwaiters to compel the sidewaiters to purchase uniforms from them. At this time when employment agencies were just beginning to play an important part in supplying the hotels with labor, the recruiting of waiters for the large hotels at winter and summer resorts was done very largely by the Negro headwaiter. For performing this service the headwaiter levied a revenue upon the sidewaiter and obtained it by means of his monopoly in the sale of waiters' uniforms. A headwaiter would have a shipment of uniforms consigned to him by a wholesaler. He would then compel the waiters whom he had employed to purchase the uniforms at a price often doubling and even trebling the consigned value. The difference between the consigned price, which was never paid to the wholesaler until after sale of the uniforms, and the price at which they retailed was pocketed by the headwaiter as agent's fee or the price of a risk which he never bore. Very little risk entered such transactions, as a waiter usually signed a statement authorizing the hotel management to deduct the price from his pay for delivery to the headwaiter.

[6] *Messenger*, July, 1918, p. 7.

[7] See *Revolutionary Radicalism*, p. 1483.

patronage." He demanded "the full product of his toil." His immediate aim was "more wages, shorter hours and better working conditions." He stood for "absolute social equality, education, physical action in self-defense, freedom of speech, press and assembly, and the right of Russia to self-determination." [8]

The "New" Negroes or economic radicals were the first expression of socialism in the Negro world.[9] They maintained that the Socialist party represented the interests of workingmen and, since 99 per cent of the Negro people were workers, the Negro's logical alignment was with the Socialist party. Furthermore, the Socialist party's advocacy of collective ownership entitled it to the Negro's political support. Under municipal socialism, educated Negroes, it was contended, would have a better chance to obtain the higher positions that are denied them under private ownership.[10]

This type of appeal was, of course, non-Marxian. It was directed toward enlisting the support of the middle-class Negro. At the same time it revealed the racial motivation underlying the *Messenger* radicals' acceptance of socialism. For they attributed race prejudice to capitalism. They held that in an individualistic economic system, competition for jobs and the profitableness of race prejudice to the capitalist class were incentives to race conflict. Therefore the removal of the motive for creating racial strife was conditioned upon the socialization of industry and the nationalization of land, in short, upon the elimination of economic individualism and competition through social revolution.[11]

To have confined their propaganda to the Negro bour-

[8] *Messenger*, Aug., 1920, p. 73.

[9] The Negro radical movement in New York was foreshadowed by Hubert Harrison, a West Indian Negro, whose activity in Revolutionary working-class circles and influence in various intellectual clubs in Harlem laid the foundation for the later propaganda of the *Messenger* editors. See the *Negro Champion*, June 23, 1928, p. 3.

[10] *Messenger*, July, 1918, p. 14.

[11] "The Cause of and Remedy for Race Riots," a *Messenger* editorial quoted in *Revolutionary Radicalism*, Vol. II, Pt. 1, p. 1479.

geoisie would have caused the Negro radicals to compromise with the theories to which they were committed. Their acceptance of the theory of the class struggle and their application of it to the race question caused them to champion labor solidarity between white and black workers. The argument for labor solidarity was the Negro and white workers' identity of economic interest, i e., "the getting of more wages, shorter hours, and better working conditions," and the fact that unorganized workers, whether white or black, are potential scabs upon organized labor. But from the standpoint of socialism, the most potent argument used by the *Messenger* radicals in disseminating the doctrine of labor solidarity was capital's ignoring of color and race in its exploitation of labor.[12] It is therefore not at all singular that the *Messenger* radicals were aided in their espousal of industrial unionism and labor solidarity between white and black workers by such socialistic unions as the Amalgamated Clothing Workers, the International Ladies' Garment Workers, the Brewery Workers, and the Industrial Workers of the World.[13] Whether the anarcho-syndicalist industrialism of the I. W. W., or the socialist-industrial unionism of the Amalgamated was more in accord with the Negro radicals' trade-union philosophy is not clear from their writings. Practical strategy, however, in the organization of all Negro workers in some radical class-conscious union could but lead them to admonish the Negro worker to affiliate with the I. W. W., since the jurisdiction of the Amalgamated Clothing Workers covers only one industry, whereas the I. W. W. looked forward to organizing the workers in all branches of industry. In addition to the I. W. W.'s claim to wider industrial jurisdiction, its liberal attitude on the race question, com-

[12] *Messenger*, July, 1918, p. 14.

[13] Among the organizations enumerated as the financial supporters of the *Messenger* during 1922, were the New York Joint Board of the Amalgamated Clothing Workers, the International Ladies Garment Workers, New York Joint Board of Cloak Makers, the Workingmen's Circle, the Jewish *Daily Forward*, New York District Painters' Council, and the Marine Transport Workers (affiliated with the I. W. W.), *Messenger*, April, 1922, p. 390. See earlier editions for complimentary advertisements of liberal and radical unions.

bined with the *Messenger* radicals' naïve conviction that the world was at that time moving toward industrial unionism, caused them to place their faith in the I. W. W. not only as the embryo of a new social order, but as the possible formidable rival to the American Federation of Labor.[14] And the "proletarian" zeal that had stimulated the insurgency within the labor movement during the nineties, and which now seemed destined to force the rebuilding of unionism on some basis other than that of trade autonomy and the neglect of those workers traditionally viewed as unorganizable, now led the Negro radicals to vent much wrath upon the American Federation of Labor. "The dissolution of the American Federation of Labor," they contended, "would inure to the benefit of the labor movement in this country in particular and the international labor movement in general. It is organized upon unsound principles. It holds that there can be a partnership between labor and capital. . . . It stands for pure and simple unionism as against industrial unionism. . . . The present American Federation of Labor is the most wicked machine for the propagation of race prejudice in the country." [15]

In 1918 when the conference between the Executive Council of the A. F. of L. and the committee [16] of Negro leaders headed by Eugene Kinckle Jones of the National Urban League failed to bring about positive measures for organizing the Negro, the radicals became convinced of the inherent weakness of craft unionism and therefore confirmed in their opposition to the Federation. One cannot be certain, however, as to which of the two elements — the philosophy of class-conscious unionism or militant race psychology — was the determining cause of the opposition. Perhaps one was as basic a motive as the other, since they levelled their criticisms not only against the Federation but against the Negro representatives to the conference. In describing the activity of the Negro representatives they pointed out that:

[14] *Messenger*, May-June, 1919, pp. 6 and 7.
[15] *Ibid.*, p. 7.   [16] See above, pp. 107-11, 142-43.

. . . the dominating influences . . . were Robert Russa Moton, Emmett J. Scott, Eugene Kinckle Jones . . . George E. Haynes and a few other Negroes of similar type. Robert Russa Moton and Emmett Scott came from Tuskegee. On the trustee board of Tuskegee are Rosenwald, Rockefeller, Carnegie, and a long line of similarly wealthy persons. Eugene Kinckle Jones and George Haynes come from the Urban League. On its executive board are William G. Wilcox, E. R. A. Seligman, A. S. Frissell, Paul D. Cravath with such honorary members as William H. Taft, Chas. D. Hillis, Robert Russa Moton, along with John D. Rockefeller as a heavy financial contributor. . . . Such financiers as these and their associates are largely employers of labor. Their object is to get the greatest amount of work out of laborers — white and black — for the lowest possible wages. . . . The point is that Rockefeller, Carnegie, Frissell, and Seligman do not hire people to work against their interests. Nor have they made any mistake in employing the Negro leaders named above. The financial interests that gave us the Ludlow massacre, Bayonne, Bisbee deportations and the like of white men because they had formed labor organizations . . . need to be looked at with suspicion when they begin to accord a helping hand to do for Negro laborers what they import thugs and gunmen to prevent white laborers from doing.[17]

These sentiments contained the sum and substance of the Negro radicals' often expressed dissatisfaction with the older Negro political and intellectual leaders who were either held to be tools of the capitalist class or ignorant as to modern political and economic problems. The logic which dictated their antipathy to the Negro representatives to the conference with A. F. of L. officials in particular, and to Negro leaders in general was an adaptation of Marxian economic determinism — a vulgar version of it, perhaps — to the race question. The use of such logic was the inevitable reaction from the convergence of militant race psychology and the ideology of proletarian class consciousness. And the Negro radicals applied this logic to the race question and to Negro leadership as relentlessly as they applied it to the labor movement.

[17] *Messenger*, July, 1918, p. 20. For Roger Baldwin's criticism of the editor's analysis, see *Messenger*, Aug., 1921, p. 229.

The *Messenger* radicals were not content to remain mere critics of the labor movement or of the intellectuals who pointed the way to Negro economic advancement. They desired to construct the vehicle for reaching the goal. This took the form of several measures for promoting Negro economic welfare and for organizing Negro workers in unions.

Their first actual participation in the labor movement came in the autumn of 1917 when Owen and Randolph organized the United Brotherhood of Elevator and Switchboard Operators. After three weeks, the organization was reported to have had a membership of about 600 out of an approximate total of 10,000 Negro operators in New York.[18] The demands of the organization were the eight-hour day, weekly pay, and a minimum wage of $18 per week. To obtain these demands, Owen and Randolph, as organizers, counseled a strike and a drive for 8,000 members. The effectiveness of the proposed strike was thought to be assured by the general scarcity of labor due to the war, the labor demands of the munition factories, the cessation of immigration, and the fact that the Negro elevator operators held a monopoly of the jobs in New York and Brooklyn.[19] But the strike did not materialize. The *Messenger* radicals soon lost interest. And the operators affiliated with the American Federation of Labor as the Elevator Operators' and Starters' Union, Local 16,030. After this nothing more was heard of the organization. Subsequently Owen and Randolph proclaimed the time "ripe for a great mass movement among Negroes" which should assume the form of "labor unions, farmers' protective unions, coöperative business, and socialism."[20] When the National Brotherhood Workers of America[21] was organized at Washington in the spring of 1919, it seemed that this prophecy was about to be fulfilled. According to one of the originators, R. T. Sims, the Brother-

[18] *Messenger*, Nov., 1917, pp. 14 and 20.

[19] *Ibid.*

[20] *Ibid.*, May-June, 1919, p. 8.

[21] See discussion of the National Brotherhood Workers of America in Chapter VI, pp. 117-19.

hood welcomed the association of the *Messenger* radicals because of a general belief in their intellectual qualifications for dealing with questions affecting labor and race relations. The desirability of their fellowship was further enhanced by the fact that coöperation with some established magazine as a means for quickly popularizing the new organization and, thereby, augmenting its membership was felt to be imperative. Owen and Randolph were elected to the general executive council, and their magazine became the official organ of the Brotherhood Workers. The resolutions adopted by the first convention calling for organization of every Negro into industrial, labor, or trade unions in all skilled and unskilled occupations,[22] are suggestive of the Negro radicals' influence. Other resolutions dealing with Mexican intervention, the Russian blockade, class war prisoners, and the coöperative movement were no doubt initiated by them. But this was the height of their influence. The magazine was never effective in increasing the desired membership. Randolph and Owen were accused of being more interested in the financial support of their magazine than [23] in building an economic organization. Apparently, when the infant organization revealed that its own need for financial succor was greater than its capacity to give it, the *Messenger* editors and the Brotherhood parted company long before the natural death of the organization some time in 1921.

In May, 1920, the radicals launched the Friends of Negro Freedom.[24] This was to be a national organization of local branches throughout the country. The purpose of the Friends was the unionization of the Negro migrant, the protection of Negro tenants, the advancement of coöperation, and the organization of forums for publicly educating the masses.[25] A novel feature of the organization was the plan to fight racial discrimination with the boycott. Only a few isolated locals

22 *Messenger*, Dec., 1919, pp. 17-19.
23 Correspondence with R. T. Sims.
24 *Messenger*, April-May, 1920, p. 4.
25 *Ibid.*, Feb., 1923, p. 529.

were set up, and the Friends enjoyed a paper existence for about three years. About the same time that the Friends of Negro Freedom was initiated, the National Association for the Promotion of Labor Unionism among Negroes was conceived. Owen was president and Randolph, secretary. The advisory board comprised such prominent white labor radicals and intellectuals as Joseph D. Cannon, Joseph Baskin, Charles W. Erwin, Edward F. Cassidy, M. Feinstone, Julius Gerber, Morris Hillquit, James H. Maurer, Andrew Weiners, Max Pine, Joseph Schlossberg, Rose Schneidermann, and A. J. Shiplacoff.[26] From the available records,[27] it seems that the National Association soon ceased to function after Randolph and Owen's futile attempt to organize the Negro laundry workers and a branch of the Journeymen Bakers' and Confectioners' International Union.[28]

Finally, in 1923, the *Messenger* declared that "while out of the unions, Negroes complain against the bar erected by certain unions . . . after they join the unions, they still complain about race prejudice within the unions. Still there is no machinery which can be set in motion either to get the Negroes in the unions . . . or to see that those who are in get justice both from the point of view of getting jobs in their trade and being elected officials in their unions. Thus to the end of creating and stimulating in the Negro worker a larger, more active and substantial interest in the principles, policies, and tactics of the labor movement in general . . . an organization known as the United Negro Trades should be formed. . . ." The United Negro Trades was to function in the Negro's behalf just as the United Hebrew Trades and the Italian Chamber of Labor functioned in behalf of the Jewish and Italian workers, respectively.[29] Obviously, the United Negro Trades was patterned after the National Brotherhood

[26] *Ibid.*, Aug., 1920, p. 62.

[27] The *Messenger* was notoriously irregular in publication. Only incomplete files are available.

[28] *Messenger*, Sept., 1920, p. 95.

[29] *Messenger*, July, 1923, p. 757.

Workers. The only difference between the two organizations was that the United Negro Trades was more ephemeral than the Brotherhood.

Those to whom *Messenger* radicalism had signified a sort of new Negro dispensation [30] were disillusioned when in 1924 the *Messenger*, because of accumulated financial reverses, ceased to function as the organ of "scientific radicalism" and became the "World's Greatest Negro Monthly." But the editors had shown earlier symptoms of retreat. Although Randolph ran for secretary of state of the state of New York on the American Labor party's [31] ticket in 1922, it was evident that economic radicalism was then on the verge of bankruptcy. In the summer of 1922 the *Messenger* had led a fight for the deportation of Marcus Garvey as an undesirable alien. The controversy degenerated into a fight between West Indian and American Negroes, causing William Domingo, himself a West Indian, to resign from the editorial board. Cyril Briggs [32] and Richard Moore, never on the editorial board but supporters of *Messenger* radicalism, had become hostile in view of their affiliation with the Communist party of America. Shortly afterward Owen shifted his scene of activity to Chicago, although he did not relinquish his rights in the magazine. During 1925 and 1926 the Brotherhood of Sleeping Car Porters was formed and Randolph was chosen general organizer. And the *Messenger*, now purged of its radicalism, became, under the "Menckenian" editorship of George Schuyler, the official journal of the porters' union until the organization was no longer financially able to support it. Under the necessity of hewing close to trade-union strategy in organizing the porters, Ran-

[30] See, for example, Mary White Ovington's letter to the editors, *Messenger*, July, 1918, p. 14.

[31] A short-lived coalition of socialists and progressive trade Unionists. See *Messenger*, Oct., 1922, p. 497. Also the *American Labor Year Book*, 1919-1920, p. 2021.

[32] Briggs originated the African Blood Brotherhood before his affiliation with the communists. See Abram L. Harris, "The Negro Problem as Viewed by Negro Leaders," *Current History*, June, 1923.

dolph forgot his social radicalism. The despised American Federation of Labor which the *Messenger* editors had once condemned for its ineptitude, was now courted by Randolph with the hope of having the Federation charter the Brotherhood of Porters as one of its independent national unions. Randolph's indecisive strategy in the organization of the porters and his over-weaning ambition to play the role of scholar, economist, journalist, race leader, and union organizer all in one are suggestive of the shortcomings of economic radicalism five years after its complete abandonment. One is prompted to ask: Were the economic radicals a sport phenomenon, the momentary efflorescence of Negro unrest?[33] Or, were they sincere adherents to the philosophy of class struggle, who, despite their belief in the revolutionary dissolution of capitalism as a prerequisite to complete realization of their ideals, attempted to direct Negro unrest into channels of constructive economic reforms?

The obstacles which economic radicalism had to overcome in order to gain some acceptance in Negro life were: (1) the Negro's orthodox religious traditions; (2) the growing prevalence of Negro middle-class ideology;[34] and (3) racial antagonism between white and black workers.

To overcome the influence of religion was in itself a task of huge proportions. In attacking the question the radicals accused the Negro church of failing to educate the people.

[33] A strong evidence of this unrest and the Negro economic radical's part in it is contained in the Lusk Commission's Report on Seditious Activities, to wit: "The most interesting as well as one of the most important features of radical and revolutionary propaganda is the appeal made to those elements of our population that have a just cause of complaint with the treatment they have received in this country. . . . In recent years opportunity for employment in industry has induced large numbers of Negroes to come to this state [New York] from the South as well as from the West Indies. While in general the Negro in New York State has been treated well, the treatment accorded him in many parts of the country has engendered a spirit of resentment which has been capitalized by agents and agitators of the Socialist Party of America, the I. W. W. and other radical groups." *Revolutionary Radicalism*, Vol. II, Pt. 1, p. 1476.

[34] For discussion, see pp. 50-52, 424-25, 431, 465-67.

They said: "the church must become an open educational forum where problems of hygiene, labor, government, racial relationships, etc., are discussed. . . . The Negro ministry must get education of information instead of education of inspiration. It needs less Bible and more economics, history, sociology and physical science." [35]

Such criticism of the church did not necessarily run counter to the Negro's faith in orthodox religion. As a matter of fact large sections of the Negro population were becoming responsive to this type of attack because of resentment against economic and social disadvantages and because of the complacence of the church in the face of these disadvantages. One can, therefore, easily dismiss the viewpoint advanced by Dr. George E. Haynes [36] that the *Messenger* radicals' attack upon the Negro church and the Negro leaders weakened their influence, especially when similar attacks by Marcus Garvey only served to augment his following. Yet few Negroes were then or are today tolerant of atheism. In an editorial on Thanksgiving the *Messenger* declared: "We do not thank God for anything nor do our thanks include gratitude for which most persons usually give thanks at this period. With us we are thankful for different things and to a different Deity. Our Deity is the toiling masses of the world and the things for which we thank are their achievement." They were thankful for the Russian, German, Austrian, and Bulgarian Revolutions; for world unrest, labor solidarity, the "relegation of trade unionism," and the rise of industrial unionism; for the "New Crowd Negro" who was taking his place in socialist politics; and "for the speedy on-coming of the new order of society in which Thanksgiving will be relieved of its cynicism and hypocrisy — when people may be thankful every day in the year." [37]

The attempt to combine religious radicalism with their

[35] *Messenger*, Oct., 1919, p. 6.
[36] George E. Haynes, *The Trend of the Races* (1922), p. 14, footnote 1.
[37] *Messenger*, Dec., 1919, p. 4.

radical economic philosophy, rather than their mild attack on the social shortcomings of the Negro church was most potent among the factors responsible for their failure, for any Negro movement which rests upon a social theory strongly tinged with atheism is not likely to receive large support from Negroes. While the economic radicals' atheism ran counter to the Negro's religious traditions, their advocacy of proletarian class consciousness and labor solidarity could hardly strike a responsive chord among new industrial workers whose experience seemed to contradict the doctrine of identical interest between themselves and the white workers. As put by W. E. B. Du Bois: "Theoretically we are a part of the world proletariat in the sense that we are mainly an exploited class of cheap laborers; but practically we are not a part of the white proletariat and are not recognized by that proletariat to any great extent. We are the victims of their physical oppression, social ostracism, economic exclusion, and personal hatred; and when in self defense we seek sheer subsistence we are howled down as scabs." [38]

Race prejudice has inhibited effective coöperation of Negroes and whites in the industrial world. To escape economic circumscription imposed by race feeling, the Negro has cultivated the good graces of those in whom the power of the disposal of opportunity lies. The more fortunate among the Negro have entered the professions and self-employment. To-day it is generally assumed that: (1) Negro material welfare rests upon the establishment of business enterprise as the basis of a sort of self-contained economy furnishing jobs to Negroes and erecting a Negro middle-class; (2) the benefactions of wealthy philanthropists will continue; and (3) the Negro masses' traditional allegiance to the employing and financially dominant classes will be maintained. To expect a people who have such a background and who have been chiefly employed in agriculture and domestic service to embrace social radicalism when white workers with older industrial traditions have not,

[38] *Crisis*, Aug., 1921, p. 151.

is to expect the miraculous. Because of economic and political unrest a people inured to conservatism and habituated to servility might willingly adopt a militant and race-conscious leadership dedicated to the acquisition of their political rights and the protection of their civil liberties. They are not likely to give lasting support to a form of leadership which predicates betterment upon the reorganization of industrial society.

Another outstanding weakness of *Messenger* radicalism was the attempt of the leaders to combine socialist propaganda with racial journalism and practical economic reform. It is evident that many of their reforms would have ameliorated some of the Negro's industrial problems. But as reformers they subordinated constructive planning and management to socialist propaganda and racial protest which, though often degenerating into mere vituperation,[39] contained much valid criticism of social politics. Upon the death of one reform they conjured up another. They could initiate movements but lacked the power of sustaining them. This dismayed their friends and convinced their opponents of their instability. This was their undoing.

The fact that the soil necessary to the growth of economic radicalism was lacking among Negro workers, and indeed among white workers as well, seemed never to have occurred to Owen and Randolph. Only one [40] of the economic radicals expressed an appreciation of the resistance that the Negro's cultural background set up against socialism. Owen and Randolph's failure to see it explains their failure to see the futility of Marxian propaganda in Negro life. But this disability was not peculiar to the Negro exponents of socialism. It has been one of the outstanding shortcomings of American socialism in general. American socialists have just begun to realize that their doctrines were foreign importations which did not interpret American conditions.

[39] For example, see attacks on Negro leaders, *Messenger*, Jan., 1918, p. 23; July, 1918, pp. 8 and 28; March, 1919, p. 23; and Sept., 1919, p. 9.

[40] W. A. Domingo. See his "Socialism Imperilled, or the Negro — a Potential Menace to American Radicalism." Quoted in *Revolutionary Radicalism*, Vol. II, Pt. I, p. 1494.

CHAPTER XIX

SOCIALISM, COMMUNISM, AND THE NEGRO

THE Negro economic radicals were related to American socialism both historically and theoretically. But years before the emergence of the *Messenger* radicals, the forerunners of the Socialist party welcomed the Negro workers to their ranks, and attempted to indoctrinate them with "class-struggle" theory. The first communistic clubs formed by German workers in the sixties in New York City welcomed all toilers regardless of race.[1] In 1871 the American Committee of the International Workingmen's Association, in reporting its activity to the general council, described a parade of 20,000 New York trade unionists and noted that for the first time "Negro organizations [participated] in a demonstration got up by English speaking unions (the German Unions having treated them as equals already years ago)." [2] The early socialists had no racial policy. They were oblivious to racial differences. To them post-Civil War competition of Negro labor was not at all a racial question. It was just another facet of the class struggle. The Socialist Labor party took the same position in the nineties. And the Socialist party did likewise during its life as the chief agency of American socialism. The refusal of both the early and latter day socialists to explain racial antipathy except by economic determination, i. e., in terms of the class struggle, has caused them to be indicted as unrealistic. Describing the racial attitude of the early American socialists, Sartorius von Waltershausen [3] pointed out:

[1] See reference to the "labor reformers," Chapter II, pp. 22 ff.

[2] *Documentary History*, Vol. IX, pp. 367-68.

[3] A. Sartorius von Waltershausen, *Die nordamerikanischen Gewerkschaften unter dem Einfluss der fortschreitenden Productionstechnik*, p. 95.

The North American socialists' comprehension of Negro competition is most unrealistic. They wholly misconceive racial antipathy and maintain that race and nationality are artificial barriers which are erected by the unproductive classes in order to divide the workers.

This summary describes the heritage that early socialism bequeathed to its later agencies.

Upon the death of the Social Democracy, led by Eugene V. Debs, the Social Democratic party of the United States was formed in 1898.[4] In the presidential campaign of 1900, the Social Democratic party with Debs as its standard bearer called upon "the wage workers of the United States without distinction of color, race, or sex . . . to organize" under its banner and "wage war upon the exploiting class until the system of wage slavery shall be abolished and the coöperative Commonwealth . . . established."[5] The party further demonstrated its desire to bring the Negro into the fold of radicalism by demanding universal suffrage. It attributed the disfranchisement of Negroes to their lack of property and to their membership in the "lower orders in society."[6] When the Socialist party was formed by the amalgamation of the Social Democratic party and dissatisfied elements in the Socialist Labor party at the famous Unity Convention in 1901, "the presence of three Negroes by no means the least intelligent and earnest of the delegates," observed Hillquit, "attested the fact that socialism had begun to take root among the colored race."[7] The newly created party threw open its doors to all who subscribed to its principles "without distinction of sex, race, color or creed."[8] The convention adopted the following resolution on the Negro question:

[4] For the evolution of the Socialist party, see Morris Hillquit, *History of Socialism in the United States* (1910), Pt. II, Chapter IV.

[5] Platform, Socialist Party of the United States, *Socialist Campaign Book,* 1900.

[6] *Ibid.,* pp. 117-18.

[7] Hillquit, *op. cit.,* p. 309.

[8] Article II, Section 1, of the Constitution of the Socialist party, *Proceedings of the National Socialist Party,* 1904, p. 310.

WHEREAS, The Negroes of the United States because of their long training in slavery and but recent emancipation therefrom, occupy a peculiar position in the working class and in society at large;

WHEREAS, The capitalist class seeks to preserve this peculiar condition, and to foster and increase color prejudice and race hatred between the white worker and the black, so as to make their social and economic interests to appear to be separate and antagonistic, in order that the workers of both races may thereby be more easily and completely exploited;

WHEREAS, Both the old political parties and educational and religious institutions alike betray the Negro in his present helpless struggle against disfranchizement and violence, in order to receive the economic favors of the capitalist class; be it therefore,

Resolved, That we Socialists of America, in national convention assembled, do hereby assure our Negro fellow worker of our sympathy with him in his subjection to lawlessness, and oppression, and also assure him of the fellowship of the workers who suffer from the lawlessness and exploitation of capital in every nation or tribe of the world; be it further

Resolved, That we declare to the Negro worker the identity of his interests and struggles with the interests and struggles of workers of all lands, without regard to race, or color, or sectional lines; that the causes which have made him the victim of social and political inequality are the effects of the long exploitation of his labor power; that all social and race prejudices spring from the ancient economic causes which still endure, to the misery of the whole human family, that the only line of division which exists in fact is that between producers and the owners of the world — between capitalism and labor; and be it further

Resolved, That we, the American Socialist party invite the negro to membership and fellowship with us in the world movement for economic emancipation by which equal liberty and opportunity shall be secured to every man and fraternity become the order of the world.[9]

This appeal contained the essence of socialist philosophy on the Negro's relation to economic radicalism, viz., that the economic interests of white and Negro workers are identical;

[9] Resolution adopted by the Socialist party, National Convention at Indianapolis, Indiana, 1901. Quoted by Charles H. Vail, *Socialism and the Negro Problem* (1902), p. 15, Columbia University pamphlets.

and that since race antagonism is bred by modern capitalism, a new social order of human brotherhood irrespective of race should supplant capitalism. These ideas became the radicals' stock-in-trade approach to the question of racial antipathy in the labor movement. But the party never got far beyond the resolution stage. Its organized effort among the Negro has been transitory and even more ineffectual than among the white workers. And shortly after its formation it discarded the policy of specifically appealing to the Negro masses. This was not revived until after 1912 when the Negro migrations aroused considerable interest in labor circles.

After 1901 the party made no special overtures to the Negro. Nor was anything said directly or by implication on the question in the 1904 and 1908 conventions although Article II, Section 1 of the constitution, relating to racial and sex discrimination, remained unchanged.[10] I. M. Rubinow in his criticisms of the socialists' timidity on the problem complained that "even the model state and municipal platforms presented to the national convention of 1909 . . . avoid this matter." [11] The change in policy was attributed by Rubinow to Debs who insisted that the party repeal the resolution on the Negro question.

"We have nothing special," said Debs, "to offer the Negro, and we cannot make separate appeals to all the races. The Socialist party is the party of the working class, regardless of color — the whole working class of the whole world." [12] Debs' position was based upon his notions of the class struggle. He believed that racial and national lines were obliterated by the common exploitation of all workers by the capitalist class. This attitude, actuated as it no doubt was by lofty idealism, was an escape from the reality of the relations between the white and Negro workers rather than an assault upon race antipathy. The East St. Louis race riot brought about a change

[10] *Proceedings, Ibid.*, 1908, p. 324.
[11] I. M. Rubinow, "The Negro and Socialism," the New York *Call*, May 19, 1912, p. 13.
[12] *Ibid.*

of attitude in Debs and caused the party to pray for class solidarity. This tragedy followed the first great wave of Negro migrations. To Debs the riot was "a foul blot upon the American labor movement." With characteristic feeling he declared that "had the labor unions freely opened their door to the Negro instead of barring him . . . and in alliance with the capitalist class, conspiring to make a pariah of him, and forcing him in spite of himself to become a scab . . . the atrocious crime at East St. Louis would never have blackened the pages of American history." [13] At the convention that followed closely upon the riot, the party protested against the outbreaks between workers of different races, attributing racial antagonism to the profit system which had to be destroyed if the race problem were to be solved.[14]

As long as northern industry remained comparatively free of Negro labor, the Socialist party could well afford to follow the policy advocated by Debs. But the shifting of large numbers of southern Negroes to the industrial centers of the North during 1910-1920 caused trade unionists and socialists to take heed of the implications of the migrations to the labor movement and radicalism.[15] Toward the latter part of 1911, the socialists of New York were raising money to forward propaganda among colored people.[16] And in May, 1912, a series of articles on the relation of socialism to the Negro appeared in the New York *Call*, an official organ of the party. These appeared before the full force of southern Negro migrations was felt in the North. They marked a transition, however, in the Socialist party's racial policy as between 1904 and 1918. Their author, I. M. Rubinow, chastised the party for neglecting the

[13] *Intercollegiate Socialist*, Dec.-Jan., 1918, pp. 7-8.

[14] Socialist party, *Convention Proceedings*, 1919, p. 45.

[15] *Men and Mules*, a pamphlet by W. F. Reis, published in 1907 in Ohio, carried the admonition "The Negro problem looms up dark and threatening and continues to get worse. Though you think the Negro is not your equal mentally, he is physically. . . . All that has been said about Socialism for the whites applies with equal force to the blacks. Socialism will effectually settle the race, the Japanese, and all other oriental problems forever."

[16] *Crisis*, Jan., 1912, p. 97.

Negro. "It is unfortunately true," he said, "that in the North the vast majority of the Socialists are entirely oblivious to the existence of the [Negro] problem, while in the South the socialists' attitude often characterizes him as a southerner rather than a socialist." [17] Mr. Rubinow described the struggle between white and black laborers as suicidal and called upon the party to convince the growing Negro radicals that their only hope in the future lay in joining hands with the socialists for the curtailment and abolition of economic exploitation. He declared that the party must "convince the American labor movement . . . that in resisting the economic and civic growth of the Negro" it obstructs its own development.[18] This the party tried to do but failed.

To carry its message to the Negro at that time, 1900-1916, it would have had to go into the South. There, because of industrial backwardness and race feeling, effective organization was impossible. Any socialist demonstration which by word or deed implied racial equality would have met the same fate as was visited upon the United Mine Workers in its strikes of white and Negro miners in Alabama. In some of the few industrial sections of the South the party had a small number of white members and a smaller number of Negroes. Whites and blacks belonged to different branches. But race feeling was not the only impediment to working-class solidarity. The party's insistence that its functions were primarily political kept it from going into the trade unions to initiate necessary changes in outlook and policy. The party's 1912 resolutions on the trade unions, although avoiding any specific mention of the Negro, had important bearing on his organization. The party called the attention of the labor movement to "the vital importance of . . . organizing the unorganized . . . who will constitute a menace to the progress and welfare of [the] organized if they remain neglected." All labor organizations that had not already done so were urged, "to throw their doors wide

[17] New York *Call*, May 12, 1912, p. 16.
[18] *Ibid.*, May 19, 1912, p. 13.

open to the workers of their respective trades and industries abolishing all onerous conditions of membership and artificial restrictions." [19] The party also spoke disparagingly of the Roosevelt Progressives' stand on the Negro question, and attributed low wages and the lack of strong labor unions in the South to the playing of Negro and white workers against each other by Democratic politicians.[20] With this declaration it stopped, because agitating for the organization of the unorganized was the problem of the trade unions. The party felt its mission to be primarily political. For this reason it had refused to come out for industrial unionism which was advocated at the 1910 convention as the best means of organizing the unorganized. A southern delegate maintained that industrial unionism was the only means of organizing the Negro worker and of carrying socialism to him. He declared that the Negro could be organized industrially but not politically because in the South where most Negroes live the Negro was disfranchised.[21] But the report of the majority prevailed. Although the party desired that socialists bore from within the American Federation of Labor for progressive trade-union reform, it insisted that it had neither the right nor the desire to interfere in controversies in the labor movement over form or methods of organization.[22] What the party desired was that its hegemony as the political expression of the proletariat be accepted by the Federation just as it accepted the Federation's autonomy on the economic front. This compromise with the trade-union leadership was, in the language of those who opposed it, "a betrayal of the cause of the working class." [23] If the present leaders of American socialism were to take an inventory of the causes of its impotence and actual non-existence

[19] Report of the Committee on Labor Organizations, Socialist party, *Convention Proceedings*, 1912, Appendix F, p. 195.

[20] *Socialist Campaign Book*, 1912, pp. 98 and 265.

[21] Speech of Delegate Barnes. Socialist Party, *Convention Proceedings*, 1910, p. 280.

[22] *Ibid.*, p. 277.

[23] See Minority Report. Socialist Party, *Convention Proceedings*, 1910, pp. 278-79.

they would very likely conclude that chief among them was the party's failure to lead the local and national trade unions to a realization of the necessity of organizing the unorganized and the excluded. Because it confined its efforts to the political arena and refused to grapple with trade-union issues, the party made it impossible for its teachings to reach the rank and file of the most articulate sections of the workers. It thereby destroyed its effectiveness even in its chosen field of politics. In spite of its declarations of class solidarity, it could not hope to win the Negro worker politically without first capturing him economically and educating the unions to the necessity of organizing him as chief among the unorganized and excluded. Moreover, so long as socialism was primarily political it could not gain much adherence among Negroes because of their well-nigh unshakeable affection for the Republican party.

In 1907 a delegate to the Third Niagara Movement [24] reported that Negro Florida was subscribing to the principles of socialism. The delegate said, "we are joining hands with white socialists — establishing centers throughout the state. . . . Laboring people — black and white — are closer together than anywhere else." But this was just a momentary defection in the Negro's allegiance to Republicanism. The Negro was not to be so easily pried loose from the party to which he had been bound for a half century. Nor was the white worker, for that matter, any readier to abandon the old parties.

To effect a political alignment between Negro and white workers required more than socialist appeals and resolutions. For the political differences between white and black workers reflected economic interests which in the light of logic were identical, but which in the light of race feeling were antithetical. Rubinow saw this conflict and called it to the attention of his comrades, saying:

[24] Founded by W. E. B. Du Bois. It was the spiritual predecessor of the present National Association for the Advancement of Colored People. Unpublished documents of the Niagara Movement. Courtesy of Dr. W. E. B. Du Bois.

Nothing hurts the negro as much and nothing raises his wrath . . . as does the opposition of white labor to his efforts to obtain a footing in the industrial field or to retain it after having once won it. Granted that you do not want us in your parlor, nor in your cars, theatres, libraries nor on your juries; or in your civil service; and granted that you have decided to keep us out of all political life, surely, you must give us an opportunity to pursue peacefully our trades and to earn a living. . . . This very thing the white workmen, whether organized or not, do deny the Negro laborer, unless he is willing to remain satisfied with the lowest and least remunerative employment.[25]

Another significant observation was made in 1912 by Mr. R. R. Wright on the attitude of the Negro steel worker to socialism.

. . . I found no socialists among them. I discussed the question of socialism with several. One man said it was a pretty good theory; and he noticed that most of the people for it were poor, while the wealthy were as a rule against it. So far as he was concerned, he sympathized with the poor. "Things are bad I know," he said. "The poor people don't get what they ought to." "But," he added, "I am afraid of the poor white men; they don't see that we Negroes have to live as well as they, and they are not willing to give us a chance. So far as I am concerned, I let socialism and all that sort of thing alone; and I stand by the man that stands by me, and that is the rich man every time. . . . No Negro ought to have anything to do with socialism." And this, I found was the general attitude of the Negro workingman who had thought at all on the subject.[26]

The indifference of the Negro steel worker toward socialism is characteristic of the attitude of Negro workers in general toward economic radicalism and progressive social politics. In the I. W. W. the Negro longshoreman was a trade unionist and not a revolutionary syndicalist.[27] In the conventions of the

[25] I. M. Rubinow, New York *Call*, May 19, 1912, p. 13.

[26] Mr. Wright adds that in 1913 the secretary of the Allegheny County Campaign Committee of the Socialist party wrote that he had not been able to discover a single socialist among the colored steel workers in Allegheny County. R. R. Wright, "One Hundred Negro Steel Workers," in *Wage-Earning Pittsburgh*, p. 108.

[27] See Chapter XVI.

American Federation of Labor Negro delegates gave little support to the progressives who sought to transform that body's policies on many issues, including the organization of black labor. Some months after the adjournment of the A. F. of L. convention in 1921, a progressive [28] pointed out that the Negroes consistently voted with the extreme conservatives to their own detriment. He declared that their failure to support the progressives was in no small measure responsible for the Federation's neglect of the interests of Negro workers. This general conservatism of the Negro explains, in part, the failure of the Socialist party to attract the Negro masses. It was only among a small group of militant Negro intellectuals that the party made any headway.

The center of the Socialist party's strength among the Negroes in the United States was the 21st Assembly District of New York City, which includes Harlem. This was especially true from 1917 to about 1924. The chief source of the propaganda was the *Messenger*, a magazine edited by Chandler Owen and A. Philip Randolph. In the 1917 mayoralty campaign Owen and Randolph, as secretary and president, respectively, of the Independent Political Council, campaigned for the Socialist party's candidate, Morris Hillquit.[29] Three years later when Randolph and Owen had earned their spurs in the socialist cause, the former was nominated by the party for comptroller of the state of New York, and the latter was made candidate for assemblyman from the 21st District. The other Negroes included on the ticket were W. B. Williams, candidate for Assembly from the 5th District; Grace Campbell, candidate for Assembly from the 19th District; and Frank Poree, candidate for state senator from the 18th Senatorial District.[30] None of them was elected. The nomination of a Negro ticket was the Socialist party's greatest demonstration of racial equality to the Negro world. It was a dramatic but

[28] Louis Langer, secretary, Joint Board of the Cloak, Skirt and Reefer Makers' Union of Greater New York. *Messenger*, Oct., 1921, p. 267.

[29] *Messenger*, Nov., 1917, p. 28.

[30] *Ibid.*, Nov., 1920, p. 139.

futile gesture. The masses of Negro voters in New York as in other large northern cities have never hesitated to gamble with the two major parties. They have never shown any disposition to jeopardize the jobs and appointments flowing from the support of a major party by "throwing their vote away" on a strange political animal. Even as confirmed a socialist as Dr. W. E. B. Du Bois, editor of the *Crisis*, and radical champion of Negro rights, has consistently urged the political strategy made famous by Samuel Gompers of "rewarding friends and punishing enemies." In the 1929 New York mayoralty campaign, when Norman Thomas was socialist candidate for mayor, Dr. Du Bois served on the Colored Citizens Non-Partisan Committee which advocated the reëlection of James J. Walker, the Democratic incumbent. This committee pointed out that "the administration of Mayor James J. Walker had been three times as valuable to the Negro (as) that of his predecessor and seventeen times more valuable than that of the Republican administration which went out in 1917." [31] As proof of the claim figures were cited showing that in Mr. Walker's administration the number of Negroes holding city jobs increased over 1,200 per cent or from 247 in 1917, drawing salaries totaling $260,844 to 2,275 in 1929, drawing salaries of $3,852,375.

In national politics the Negro's historical allegiance to the Republican party has scarcely ever weakened in the face of the idealism of a third party whether socialist or progressive. But the propaganda of the "Negro comrades" continued until about the end of 1922. The 1924 convention of the Socialist party felicitated them because they "were doing so much to arouse the Negro workers to an interest in socialism." It again adopted resolutions urging the workers to bury their racial differences, and called upon the white workers to encourage the organization of Negroes into trade unions and to break

[31] *New York City and the Colored Citizen*, published by the Colored Citizens Non-Partisan Committee for the Reëlection of Mayor Walker (1929), pp. 12 and 15.

down existing prejudices.[32] The following convention reported the dissemination of propaganda through Negro newspapers. When the Pullman porters organized under the leadership of Philip Randolph, the party pledged its support to the union.[33] If by this token of friendship the party expected to win the Pullman porters to adherence to socialist principles, it was mistaken. In times of stress the union was not at all disinclined to accept financial aid from socialist sources but socialism itself was not to the porters' liking. Conscious of the general conservatism among the porters, the Pullman Company and some Negro leaders used the socialist scare as an easy means of discrediting the union leaders in the eyes of the porters.

Just as the Negro's traditional alignment with the Republican party was a bulwark against political socialism, his newness to modern industry and his cultural heritage made him impervious to socialist economic philosophy. But there were other important considerations which prevented him from embracing socialism. The doctrines of increasing proletarian misery and exploitation and the class struggle never took root among the American white workers. In the first place the race problem, the heterogeneity of the working population, and the absence of fast lines of social cleavage have prevented the development of class consciousness. In the second place the American worker's progressive material comfort and economic opportunity have made him more of an individualist than a socialist. In these respects the Negro is as essentially American as the white worker. The Negro may protest against economic inequality and discrimination, but he has not been persuaded to believe that equality of opportunity and advancement will result from the destruction of capitalism. His leaders almost without exception have steered him away from radicalism. They teach the Negro that his greatest material advancement lies in the preservation of the existing economic order [34]

[32] Minutes of the 1924 Convention, *Socialist World*, p. 11.
[33] Socialist Party, *Convention Proceedings*, 1928, p. 15.
[34] See Chapter VII.

Such of them as Booker T. Washington have counselled him in purely pragmatic fashion to emulate the habits of the white bourgeoisie — thrift, savings, and business enterprise. The few Negro intellectuals who have subscribed to socialism have exerted little influence on the masses. These social forces in Negro life in particular, and in American life in general, were ignored by the Socialist party. And it consequently gained few adherents and little prestige among the working classes of either race.

The World War disrupted international socialism. On the eve of hostilities the Second International, the international confederation of Socialists of which the American Socialist party was a part, was divided into antagonistic factions by nationalist patriotism. After the war the attempts to revive the old Second International or to create a new one met with the opposition of those socialists who wished affiliation with the new Third (Red) International that had been organized by the leaders of Russian communism. On this issue international socialism was divided into opposing camps of lefts and rights, communists and socialists. The lefts or communists favored affiliation with the Third International and the rights or socialists favored the Second International. In the United States the discussion led to withdrawals and expulsions of members of the Socialist party and finally culminated in the formation of the Communist party,[35] which became affiliated with the Third International at Moscow.

The Third International, unlike the Second, was committed to international proletarian revolution. For the "reformism and parliamentarianism" of the Second International it substitutes "revolution and direct action"; and for a loose international association of socialist parties it substitutes a highly centralized and doctrinaire organization which attempts to dictate the course of international revolution. Thus the policies of the American Communist party are determined by

---

[35] For the events leading to the formation of the Workers party, see *The American Labor Year Book*, 1919-1920, pp. 405-21; 1921-1922, pp. 392-93 and 404-5; and 1923-1924, pp. 159-65.

the Third International's right to say what is legitimate communist propaganda and who are its legitimate exponents outside of Russia.[36]

Soon after its formation, the "Comintern," or Communist International, declared that it:

... once forever breaks with the traditions of the Second International which in reality only recognized the white race. The Communist International makes it its task to emancipate the workers of the entire world. The ranks of the Communist International fraternally invite men of all colors: white, yellow, and black toilers of the entire world.[37]

This was not merely a reiteration of the passive theory of "white and black labor solidarity" that had been enunciated by the socialists. The Communist International looks upon the Negro in the United States as an important link in its program of world proletarian revolution. The theory upon which this prospective participation of the American Negro is based is the Leninized version of the doctrine of capitalist self-destruction. According to the new Marxism, propounded by Lenin, the national liberation movements of oppressed peoples are bound up with the proletarian revolution and the downfall of world capitalism. Modern capitalism, the theory runs, rests upon financial imperialism which cannot exist without the exploitation of colonies — without colonial markets for investment of surplus capital and colonial raw materials. On this basis the world becomes divided into the "camp of the civilized nations which comprise no more than a small minority, though they control financial capital and exploit the overwhelming majority of the globe; and the camp of the oppressed and exploited peoples in colonial and dependent lands, far more numerous than their exploiters. The colonial and dependent countries, oppressed and exploited by financial capital, form

[36] See "Democratic Centralism and Party Discipline" in Draft Thesis on Party Organization, *Daily Worker*, Jan. 10, 1929, p. 3. Also note the recent expulsion of famous American communists by the Comintern for so-called reformist tendency. One of the charges was the failure of accomplishment among Negroes. *New York Times*, July 5, 6, and 7, 1929.

[37] *Crisis*, July, 1921, p. 103.

the main field from which imperialism draws its reserve forces." [38] Consequently the hope of colonial people is a revolutionary struggle against imperialism. Such a revolution, it is held, will bring about a crisis in world capitalism by cutting off the colonies as markets for investment and as sources of raw materials, thus leading inevitably to unemployment, and financial crises at home. Lenin maintained, therefore, that:

... the proletarian movement in advanced countries and the nationalist movement for the liberation of the peoples of colonial and dependent lands being both revolutionary movements, or two different aspects of the same great revolutionary movement, it will be to their interest to unite to form a united front against the common enemy — imperialism.[39]

The Sixth World Congress of the Communist International echoed Lenin's theory. It was said that the "class struggle is an attack upon imperialist super-profits"; that "the racial movement is therefore a revolutionary struggle of the poor peasantry and workers against capitalist exploitation"; and that "this question is related to the general question of the Negroes throughout the world." [40] "War," said Bakharin, "arising from the inherent contradictions of the capitalist system will lead to the downfall of capitalism. The Comintern must hold the Negroes and the oppressed colonials until the break comes." [41] The Comintern was therefore called upon to link up the struggles of the Negro as an oppressed minority in the United States with the anti-imperialist struggles in Haiti, Santo Domingo, and Africa.[42] This theorizing culminated in the appointment of a committee to deal with the Negro ques-

[38] Joseph Stalin, *Leninism* (1928), p. 140.

[39] *Ibid.*, p. 140. For a concise application of the essentials of this theory to the "New Capitalism" in the United States, see Scott Nearing's statement in *New Tactics in Social Conflict* (1926), pp. 22-27. Published by League for Industrial Democracy.

[40] Address of James Ford before the Communist International, Sixth World Congress, Moscow, 1928, *International Press Correspondence*, Vol. 8, No. 74, Oct. 25, 1928, p. 1347.

[41] *International Press Correspondence*, Vol. 8, No. 49, Aug. 13, 1928, p. 867.

[42] Gomez, *Ibid.* Oct. 17, 1928.

tion in the United States. The report of the committee as
finally adopted read in part:

The Negro question in the United States must be treated in its
relation to the Negro questions and struggles in other parts of the
World. The Negro race everywhere is an oppressed race. Whether it is
a minority (U. S. A., etc.), majority (South Africa), or inhabits a so-
called independent state (Liberia, etc.), the Negroes are oppressed by
imperialism. Thus, a common tie of interest is established for the revolutionary struggle of race and national liberation from imperialist domination of Negroes in various parts of the world. A strong Negro Revolutionary movement in the U. S. A. will be able to influence and direct
the revolutionary movements in all those parts of the world where the
Negroes are oppressed by imperialism.[43]

Such is the theoretical foundation of the communists' hope
of building a Negro revolutionary movement in the United
States.

The expressed determination of American communism at
its very inception to revolutionize the American labor movement had significance for the Negro workers. Its purpose was
to supplant obsolescent trade unionism with revolutionary industrial unionism and to awaken the unskilled and unorganized, including the "agricultural proletariat," to organization
and action. It held that the problem of organizing the Negro
was closely connected with that of the unorganized and unskilled. But in addition the Negro had a special significance
to communism. He was regarded as the real American proletariat: "The racial expression of the Negro is simply the
expression of his economic bondage and oppression, each inten-
sifying the other. This complicates the . . . problem, but
doesn't alter its proletarian character. The Communist party
will carry on agitation among the Negro workers to unite them
with all class-conscious workers." [44] Beginning with these declarations the party at each of its succeeding conventions has

[43] Communist International, Resolutions on the Negro Question in U. S. A.
Reported in full in *Daily Worker*, New York, Feb. 12, 1929, p. 3.
[44] Platform of the Communist party, *The American Labor Year Book*, 1919-
1920, p. 419.

gone into the problem with increasing precision and attention to the details of organization and propaganda. To a large degree the task of indoctrinating the Negro with communism fell to the lot of such Negro members as Otto Huiswood, Lovett Fort Whiteman, Richard B. Moore, Cyril Briggs, and Otto Hall. All of the foregoing, except Hall, had been members of the Socialist party and supporters of *Messenger* radicalism.

The main features of communist propaganda among the Negroes were as follows: (1) trade unionism and the relation of white and black workers: (2) boring from within existing Negro organizations; (3) the American Negro Labor Congress; and (4) the national liberation movement and self-determination.

With regard to trade unionism, the party takes the position that since the cause of the Negro in the labor movement is an essentially "left wing fight," the communists' duty is to accept it as theirs.

Our party [the 1925 platform reads] must work among the unorganized Negro workers destroying whatever prejudice may exist against trade unions, which is being cultivated by white capitalists . . . [and] the Negro petit bourgeoisie. . . . Our party must make itself the foremost spokesman for the real abolition of all discrimination of the as yet largely unorganized Negro workers in the same union with the white worker on the same basis of equality of membership, equality of right to employment in all branches of work and equality of pay.

The party demanded the inclusion of Negro workers in the existing unions as against racial separation and dual unionism. It declared that it would organize Negroes into separate unions where they were debarred from existing organizations using, separation as a battering ram against Negro exclusion.[45] On the relationship of the Negro and white workers, the party subscribed to full social equality. It advocated the right to vote, the abolition of Jim Crowism in law and custom, including segregation and anti-intermarriage laws. The accom-

[45] Communist Party, *Proceedings of the Fourth National Convention*, p. 119.

plishment of these ends was not a thing in itself. It was the struggle for their accomplishment that was important:

In the course of the struggle with such demands we will demonstrate . . . that these aspirations can be realized only as a result of the successful class struggle against capitalism and with the establishment of the rule of the working class in the Soviet form.[46]

These special demands of the Negro were to be supported by the white workers.

The Negro problem must be part and parcel of all and every campaign conducted by the Party. In the election campaigns, trade union work, the campaigns for the organization of the unorganized . . . the Central Executive Committee must work out plans designed to draw the Negroes into active participation . . . and at the same time to bring the white workers into the struggle on behalf of the Negroes' demands.[47]

How do these pronouncements work out in practice? Before the Communist International held its Sixth Congress, boring from within in contradistinction to dual unionism was the strategy officially approved by Moscow. In keeping with this the American Party "led the Negro fig and date workers' strike in Chicago, the laundry strike in Carteret, New Jersey, the Colored Moving Picture Operators' strike in New York . . . organized the Negro Miners' Relief Committee; and captured the Tenants' League from the Socialists." [48] This work, however, was admitted to have been sporadic and ineffective.[49]

Because communism made little headway by boring from within, the Communist International at its Sixth World Congress held in Moscow in 1928, promulgated the policy of dual unionism. The American "comrades" who had been "boring from within" the "Save-the-Union" Committee, which opposed John L. Lewis' administration of the United Mine Workers,[50] now came into the open and led in the formation

[46] *Ibid.*
[47] *Ibid.*
[48] Cyril Briggs, "Our Negro Work," *Communist*, Sept., 1929.
[49] *Ibid.*
[50] See Chapter XVII.

of the National Miners' Union.[51] Other unions were likewise started. In a recent statement [52] Robert W. Dunn, of the Labor Research Association, stated that 500 Negro miners were members of the new union. Mr. Dunn also stated that approximately 1,500 Negroes were affiliated with recently organized communist leagues and unions, and that about 1,000 were members of district groups not yet separated into national unions. The unions with their Negro memberships were as follows: the National Miners' Union, 500; the Needles Trades Industrial Union, 500; the Marine Workers' League, 300; and the Railroad Workers' Industrial League, 200.

These figures are without doubt exaggerated. There could hardly be 500 Negroes in the National Miners' Union. Ben Gitlow, who was recently expelled [53] from the party along with Jay Lovestone, the former leader of the American communists, states that at the last Party Plenum the total dues-paying membership of the National Miners' Union was 400.[54] He also maintains that the rest of the unions are in a state of collapse.[55] Mr. Gitlow's analysis is perhaps not far wrong. For one of the orthodox leaders has recently asked: "Why in view of the great unemployment in the U. S. A. . . .[and] the

[51] See Report of the Fourth Congress of the Red International Labor Unions, July, 1928, p. 139.

[52] Letter to Ira De A. Reid, director of research, National Urban League, April 24, 1930.

[53] Lovestone, Gitlow and others were expelled from the party for "right heresy." A part of the report of the executive committee of the Communist International which indicted them states: "The ideological lever of the right errors in the American Communist Party was the so-called theory of 'exceptionalism,' which found its clearest exponents in the persons of Comrades Pepper and Lovestone whose conception was as follows: a crisis of capitalism, but not of American capitalism; a swing of the masses to the left, but not in America; the necessity of accentuating the struggle against reformism, but not in America; a necessity of struggling against the right danger but not in the American Communist Party." *The Crisis in the Communist Party*, p. 13, published by Revolutionary Age. This pamphlet was issued by Lovestone in reply to the charges.

[54] Ben Gitlow, "For Genuine Militant Unionism," *Revolutionary Age*, May 21, 1930.

[55] *Ibid.*

complete fascist rôle of the A. F. of L. and its capitulation to the bosses, our revolutionary movement is so weak and so small; [and] why, in view of the great wave of lynching against the Negro workers, and the response of the Negro to our movement in the South . . . we do not have more Negroes in the Trade Union Unity League," [56] the communist federation of trade unions.

It should be remembered that communist trade unions are not designed to function as regular labor organizations, but are intended as schools where workers are prepared to serve the cause of the proletarian revolution. Nevertheless it is hoped that these organizations will somehow acquire sufficient strength either to capture or to supersede the old line labor unions. Should this hope be realized it is difficult to see how, under the present system, the communist unions would differ from the organizations that they displace. It is to improve working conditions rather than to bring about a social revolution that working men have organized. If communist unions are to command the confidence of the rank and file they must deal successfully with the "concrete demands" [57] of labor — hours, wages, and working conditions. In that event their revolutionary character will become submerged. On the other hand if they use the "concrete demands" of labor merely to prove the futility of concessions under capitalism, and thus the necessity for its overthrow, they will lose the support of the proletariat and once more become mere revolutionary minorities.

Divorced from a position of power in the labor movement such revolutionary minorities will be unable to force their ideal of white and black solidarity upon the working classes. Their demands for equal opportunity and equal treatment for all races may catch the Negro's imagination for a time. But to hold his permanent support labor organization must give

[56] James Ford, "Postponement of the R. I. L. U. Congress," *Labor Unity,* June 11, 1930.

[57] Report of the Fourth Congress of the Red International Labor Unions, July, 1928, p. 14.

him tangible results, for the Negro even more than the white worker is interested in immediate economic gains.

The extent to which the party itself, as distinct from its trade unions, is attracting American white and black workers is revealed by its membership. Its paid up membership was 9,642 in 1927.[58] Although party officials place the present membership at 15,005, Mr Lovestone maintains that there are not more than 7,650 members even when liberal allowance is made for "padding" and "manipulation." [59] The increased "radicalization of the masses" of which the leaders boast does not seem to be taking place if we are to gauge it by membership figures. And while we have not succeeded in ascertaining the exact Negro membership in the party, it has been admitted to be extremely small. "It is a shame," said one of the delegates to the Sixth World Congress in 1928, "that we have only fifty or so party members out of thirteen or fourteen million Negroes in America." [60]

The reason for the small Negro membership was explained as follows by one of the American delegates to the Congress:

A comrade remarked that it was necessary for us to establish a new line of work among the Negroes, to adopt a new programme. It is not so much the question of a new programme but of carrying out the programme that was adopted by the Fourth and Fifth Congresses on the question. The central slogan around which we can rally the Negro masses is the slogan of social equality. And the reason why we have not organized the Negroes in America and why we have such a small number of Negroes in our Party is because we have not fought consistently for this principle. And this is due to the fact that we have white chauvinism in our Party.[61]

This "white chauvinism," is indistinguishable from that social attitude known to the bourgeois world as race prejudice. Its manifestations in the party have been as sharp as in many

[58] *The American Labor Year Book*, 1929 Edition, p. 154.

[59] Jay Lovestone, "Stop That Game of Bluff," *Revolutionary Age*, May 21, 1930.

[60] Katayama, before the Communist International, Sixth World Congress, *International Press Correspondence*, Oct. 17, 1928, Vol. 8, No. 72, p. 1313.

[61] *Ibid.*, p. 1393.

groups which lay no claim to radicalism. The Moscow International complained that "in some instances where Communists were called upon to champion and to lead in the most vigorous manner the fight against 'white chauvinism,' they instead yielded to it." [62] A Negro comrade declared that much of the good work done among the Negro masses was destroyed when a convention of the party in New York "went out of its way to repudiate social equality." [63] In Seattle, Washington, several comrades objected to the presence of Negro members at party dances. In Norfolk, Virginia, white communists refused to admit Negroes to their meetings.[64] And in Detroit they drove their Negro comrades from a party social given to aid the miners during the 1928 strike.[65] The Detroit affair occurred at the very time that the communists were attacking the United Mine Workers for racial discrimination and were making special appeals to the Negro miners to join the communist National Miners' Union.

"White chauvinism," according to the Communist International, "is the expression of the ideological influence of American imperialism among the workers." [66] It has called upon the American party to wage a relentless war against it. The party has attempted to fight race prejudice in its ranks by expelling those found guilty of it. It even went so far in one instance as to expel a number of members who voted against the expulsion of comrades charged with "white chauvinism." The International has directed the continuance of these tactics on the grounds that "the Negro masses will not be won for the revolutionary struggle until such time as the most conscious section of the white workers show *by action* that they are fighting with the Negroes against all racial discrimination and persecution." [67]

[62] See Communist International, Resolutions on the Negro Question in the U. S. A., *Daily Worker*, Feb. 12, 1929.

[63] Cyril Briggs, *op. cit.*, p. 497.

[64] *Ibid.*

[65] Communist International, Resolutions, *op. cit.*

[66] *Ibid.*

[67] *Ibid.*

The Communist party in its attempts to capture the rank and file of organized labor for the social revolution has not confined its policy of boring from within to the trade unions. At one time it had hoped that by boring from within Negro reform organizations it would be able to reveal itself to the Negro workers. When this policy was first inaugurated the organizations designated were the National Association for the Advancement of Colored People and Marcus Garvey's now defunct Universal Negro Improvement Association. Although revolutionary communists could not share Garvey's "Back to Africa" vision, they saw in his organization the embodiment of the emotional unrest of the Negro proletariat, militant, agressive, and sympathetic with the world proletariat. In order to guide the Garvey movement away from the shoals of utopianism toward anti-imperialism and the labor movement, it proposed to organize "communist fractions" within the Improvement Association. These proposed "fractions" were to surround themselves with Negro workers and poor farmers and to transform the organization into one fighting for the Negro's class interest.[68] In a like manner, "selected communists" were to enter the conventions of the National Association for the Advancement of Colored People and "make proposals to enlighten the Negro worker under its influence as to the nature and necessity of the class struggle, the identity of their exploiters. . . ."[69]

But the results that the communists got from "boring from within" Negro petit bourgeois organizations were evidently disappointing. For the Comintern in one of its most recent pronouncements on Negro propaganda advised the American party to change its strategy. Work in the Negro reform organizations now became subordinate to "the extension of our influence in the existing working class Negro organizations,[70] such as the Brotherhood of Sleeping Car

[68] Communist party, *Proceedings of the Fourth Convention*, p. 122.
[69] *Ibid.*, p. 123.
[70] Communist International, Resolutions, *op. cit.*

Porters [71] and the Chicago Asphalt Workers." If apathy to the class struggle denotes a bourgeois psychology, the porters are as middle class in their economic orientation as the Association for the Advancement of Colored People is in its bias toward political rights and civil liberties.[72] Anyone but doctrinaire and optimistic apostles of proletarian revolution would soon tire of sowing the seeds of revolution on such stony ground. But the communists are indefatigable. Their persistence results from a self-assurance which causes them to style themselves "the vanguard of the proletarian army." Their resoluteness and abstruse naiveté on the Negro question may lead to an ephemeral movement containing elements of realism like their American Negro Labor Congress, or to the formulation of a fatuous romance like their Negro Socialist Soviet Republic of the United States.

The American Negro Labor Congress was first held at Chicago in October, 1925. Representatives from Negro labor unions, Negro farmers' organizations, fraternal and benefit societies were invited to attend. The purpose of the congress was:

to unify the efforts . . . of all organizations of Negro workers and farmers as well as organizations composed of both Negro and white workers and farmers . . . for the abolition of all discrimination, persecution and exploitation of the Negro race and working people generally; . . . to bring the Negro working people into the trade unions and the general labor movement with the white workers; . . . to remove all bars and discrimination against Negroes and other races in the trade unions; . . . and to aid the general liberation of the darker races and the working people throughout all countries.[73]

The congress was to function through local councils composed of Negro labor unions, trade unions that did not discriminate against Negroes, groups of Negro industrial workers organized for the purpose of obtaining admission into existing

[71] See below, Chapter XX, p. 455.
[72] See below, Chapters XX and XXI.
[73] Constitution and Program of the American Negro Labor Congress (1925), p. 5.

unions, organizations of Negro agricultural workers, and delegates elected by groups of three or more Negroes who worked together in a workshop, factory, or on a farm.

These constructive measures initiated by the congress were never put into operation. Local units were never formed; and the plan of Negro unionization remained a resolution. That the congress was designed as a nucleus of communist agitation rather than a functional body is demonstrated by some of its resolutions, notably that of the Negro workers' relation to the overthrow of capitalist-imperialism. The Negro delegates to the congress evidently suspected communist influence for they soon became apathetic. They were evidently looking for industrial and social reforms, not for a revolution or a promise of the millennium. After two conventions nothing more was heard of the congress, except the Comintern's order that it be revived as the means of "mobilizing the Negro workers under our leadership." [74] And it is doubtful if the American Negro Labor Congress so long as it remains a revolutionary body will succeed any more than the party's proposed Negro Socialist Soviet Republic of the United States.

The plan of establishing a Negro socialist state in the United States is a logical result of the assumptions of official communist theory. One of the postulates of this theory, as has been noticed, stresses the revolutionary implications of national liberation movements. Although these movements are led by "petit bourgeois reformers" whose ideal is "self-determination," the communists see in them the germs of genuine proletarian revolution against the "super-profits of capitalist-imperialism." In this sense the Chinese liberation movement and Indian unrest are thought of as essentially proletarian disturbances. Marcus Garvey's Universal Negro Improvement Association is in the same way looked upon as epitomizing the misdirected revolutionary spirit of the American Negro proletariat. What the communists desire to do with Garvey's Universal Negro Improvement Association is to direct its

[74] Communist International, Resolutions, *op. cit.*

striving for self-determination from Africa to the "black belt" of the South where greater possibilities are believed to exist for a Negro state. The "black belt" has been described by them as a colony within the United States composed of "starving and pauperized" Negro farmers and agricultural workers, the most exploited of the proletariat. From this Negro colony are extracted the "super-profits" so important in the growth of American imperialism.[75] Here in this "black belt" colony the basis for developing a Negro nation is to be found, to wit: a population of 3,000,000 blacks comprising a majority in 219 counties "over a contiguous area"; "semi-feudal conditions"; "complete segregation"; "common traditions of slavery"; and "the development of distinct classes and economic ties."

The Communist International has placed this plan for a Negro Socialist Soviet in the southern part of the United States and, likewise, a similar plan for the natives of South Africa in the forefront of its Negro propaganda. It, therefore, calls upon the Communist party of America to come out "openly and unreservedly for the right of the Negroes to national self-determination in the Southern States. . . ." [76] The American communists, although willing to accept almost anything that emanates from Moscow, are somewhat more acquainted with American conditions than are the omniscient theoreticians of the Communist International. As if to apologize for this fantastic scheme the American communists make it clear that self-determination cannot be realized under capitalism.[77] But postponement of the event gives it the same utopian character as Garvey's "Back to Africa" movement. And it is unlikely that the black agricultural peasants of the South will do much

[75] See John Pepper, "American Negro Problems," *Communist*, Oct., 1928, p. 630.

[76] Communist International, Resolutions, *op. cit.*

[77] *Ibid.* We note as we go to press that the American communists still make "self-determination" their main appeal to Negroes. See *Thesis and Resolutions for the Seventh Convention of the Communist Party of U. S. A.*, p. 24, Central Committee Plenum, March 31-April 4, 1930.

revolting to obtain the Utopia. In his observations on the southern Negro André Siegfried remarks: "They are docile, passive, and accept their subjugation without murmur. A Spartacist revolt is the last thing to be feared, for their efforts are directed rather toward adaptation. Circumstances have developed in them an extraordinary instinct for judging people and knowing what they can get out of them. . . . With the rich they quickly adopt a flattering attitude, but they utterly despise the 'poor whites.' " [78]

It is true that the industrialized Negro has shown considerable resentment in recent years. But this resentment is not the stuff out of which revolutions are made. It is a dissatisfaction growing out of discrimination in such matters as trade-union membership, wages, advancement in industry, and civic and social circumscription. The interest which Negroes first showed in the Negro Labor Congress was caused by a growing realization of the necessity of creating some agency to handle their industrial problems. This practical consideration has found expression in the high court of communism. One delegate to the Sixth World Congress said: "There is no objection on our part to the principle of a Soviet Republic for Negroes in America. . . . The question before the Negroes today is not what will be done with them after the revolution but what measures we are going to take to alleviate their present conditions in America." [79] Language of this sort sounds like a speech at a trade-union convention rather than one at a congress of revolutionary communists. Yet the sentiments expressed are characteristic of the American Negro working class which, like the white, has never shown much inclination toward economic radicalism. Communist logic which deduces revolution from Negro social and economic unrest is as mistaken as *Messenger* radicalism. It overlooks the Negro's cultural background and his very recent attainment of a footing

[78] André Siegfried, *America Comes of Age* (1928), p. 101.

[79] Comrade Jones (U. S. A.) Communist International, Sixth World Congress, *op. cit.*, Oct. 30, 1928, Vol. 8, No. 76, p. 1393.

in modern industry. Failing to heed the factors responsible for the indifference of American workers, white and black, to socialist doctrine and politics, the communists are forced to run from pillar to post, with an eye for any dissatisfaction that can be seized upon for its revolutionary possibilities. Thus they see revolution where there is only conservatism. One might criticize their Negro policy as a Karl Marx, in an address to the German workers, criticized the attitude of his opponents in the Communist League: "Whereas we draw the German worker's attention to the undeveloped condition of the proletariat, you grossly flatter the national sentiment and the class prejudices of the German handicraftsman, which is, of course, far more popular. Just as the democrats have sanctified the word 'people,' so you sanctify the word 'proletariat.' Like the democrat, you subordinate revolutionary development to revolutionary phrase-making." [80]

[80] Karl Marx, *Klassenkampfe in Frankreich*, quoted by Otto Rühle, *Karl Marx* (1929), p. 176.

Chapter XX

THE PULLMAN PORTERS

With the failure of his radical preachings, A. Philip Randolph in 1925 turned his attention to the organization of the Pullman porters. The Pullman porter occupies a strategic place among Negro workers. From the time the Pullman Company began its operations in 1867 the porter's work has been practically a Negro monopoly. Of about 12,000 porters now in the Pullman service all are Negroes except some 400 Mexicans employed on cars running into Mexico and a few dozen Filipinos, Japanese, and Chinese recently placed on club cars. To the general public, the Pullman porter is above all else a Negro. He is in fact the only contact which thousands of white persons have with the race. His doings therefore assume an importance which extends beyond the confines of his own group and makes any organized movement on his part a matter of concern to the whole Negro population.

Though the need for organizing the Pullman porters had been talked about for many years, such talk did not become current until 1913 to 1915 when both the California Railroad Commission and the United States Commission on Industrial Relations were investigating the Pullman Company's labor policy.[1] But no serious attempts at organization were made until the railroads came under federal control. Then the Railway Men's International Benevolent and Industrial Association, under the leadership of Robert L. Mays, brought well over a thousand porters into its ranks, but they left the organization as soon as they won an increase in pay. Several subsequent attempts to form porters' organizations also ended in

[1] See *Crisis*, Jan., 1913, p. 123; Jan., 1914, p. 113; Feb., 1914, p. 166; Nov., 1914, p. 11; Jan., 1915, p. 62.

failure.[2] These efforts, however, were not entirely barren for they caused the idea of organization to take root in the porters' minds. At the same time they taught the Pullman Company that its employees were not an altogether contented lot and forced it to take some steps toward correcting their grievances.

In the summer of 1925 A. Philip Randolph, at the request of several dissatisfied porters, turned his attention to the problems of these workers. He ran a series of articles in the *Messenger* discussing their working conditions and urging the need for organization.[3] His task was no easy one, for in spite of the fact that the porter's grievances were many and serious the feeling persisted that his job was a good one and that the Pullman Company was the Negro's steadfast friend. The porter's contact with the well-to-do traveling public led him to absorb its point of view and to seek to emulate its standards. The porter had all of the familiar middle-class prejudices of the white-collar worker and upper servant. It gave him a thrill to have bankers and captains of industry ride in his car, even though their tips were smaller than they might have been. It made him feel like a captain of industry himself, even if it did not make him affluent or ease the burden of his work. Even a vicarious captain of industry is rather poor trade-union material.

On the other hand there were elements in the situation more favorable than those which labor organizers usually have to face. The porters are a homogeneous group. They work for a single employer with a single labor policy. Aside from the major portion of the two Canadian railway systems and a few lines in the United States which run their own sleeping and parlor cars and employ their own porters, the sleeping and parlor car service of the entire continent is in the hands of the Pullman Company. Consequently, the porters' grievances are comparatively uniform. The nature of the job is such that

[2] See above, Chapter VI, p. 126.
[3] *Messenger*, July, 1925, pp. 254-55; Aug., 1925, p. 289.

the porter can easily be found and approached by organizers without their running the risk of entering the company's reservation. But most important of all was the fact that there was genuine discontent in the porter body. The men had real grievances which Randolph's able pen and winning voice were able to exploit. Their wages were low. They began regular assignments at this time, 1925, at $67.00 a month. Increases at stated intervals brought this to $94.50 after fifteen years of service. It was necessary to depend upon tips from passengers to augment this utterly inadequate pay. Randolph asked a wage of $150 a month so that the "degrading" practice of tipping could be abolished. New porters instead of being assigned to regular runs were used as substitutes or put in charge of extra cars. These so-called "extra" porters, though required to report regularly for service, received no pay unless actually assigned to work. A flat rate of pay was asked for these men. The porters also pointed out that their real wages were reduced by heavy occupational expenses, which included the cost of uniforms for the first ten years of service, shoe polish for patrons, and meals during runs.

Hours of labor were long beyond all comparison with other branches of railroading. Where 240 hours per month was the standard for all train-service employees including Pullman conductors, 11,000 miles of travel, amounting to about 400 hours a month, was the standard for Pullman porters. The porter's paid time was calculated from the hour of the departure to the hour of the arrival of his train. Besides this he was required to report some time before departure to get his car in the yards and make it ready for the journey (preparatory time), and to be on hand in the station some time before departure to receive and assist passengers (terminal time). For all this essential service the porter received no pay. The porters asked in place of the 11,000 mile standard month a 240 hour standard, such as other railway workers enjoyed, the time to be calculated from the hour of reporting for duty to the hour of leaving the car in the yard.

The mileage standard of pay and its long equivalent in hours practically deprived the porter of compensation for overtime for delayed arrivals. The average porter's train might be several hours late at every trip and he would receive no pay for the hours spent on duty beyond his regular schedule because his extra hours would be put in his accumulated mileage column until his total time on the road equalled 400 hours or the equivalent of 11,000 miles. For example, a porter running from New York to Washington, a distance of 227 miles, makes thirteen round trips a month. His total distance traveled back and forth in a month would be 5,902 miles. If he were three hours late each trip or 78 hours late for the month he would still be entitled to no overtime, since 78 times 30 (the mileage rate of his train) equals 2,340 miles, which, plus 5,902, his regular distance traveled, equals only 8,242, or 2,758 miles short of the required 11,000. The Pullman conductor on the same run would receive extra pay for all overtime.

The demand for the 240 hour standard month automatically covered this grievance. It also covered another grievance, the "doubling out" system, one of the most serious of all the porter's complaints. Doubling out means leaving on another trip immediately after arrival from a run, depriving the porter of his rest period and burdening him with extra work when tired. But the worst feature of the doubling out system is that it is compensated at a lower rate than the regular run since the porter is paid on a mileage basis.

Another complaint of the porters, that they were not allowed regular and adequate sleep, led to the demand for a specific time allowance for sleeping of four hours the first night out and six hours the second and third nights.

The porters also asked that they be given conductor's pay when running "in charge" of a car — that is, when required to perform the duties of a Pullman conductor in addition to those of porter. Under the company rules porters running in charge of one car receive ten dollars a month extra for their work, instead of a conductor's minimum salary of $150. While it is true that the company's rules do provide that porters running in charge of two cars receive a conductor's minimum pay, the conductor's union requires the employment of regular conductors whenever two cars are run.

With these grievances as a rallying point, propaganda for a porter's union continued for some weeks and finally culminated in a mass meeting in Harlem, New York City, on August 25, 1925, at which the Brotherhood of Sleeping Car Porters and Maids was formally launched. Randolph became head of the new union with the title of general organizer. No vote was ever taken electing him to this post, but there is no doubt that the rank and file of the porters endorsed his leadership. His paper, the *Messenger*, furnished the new movement with a ready-made organ well known both in the Negro community and in white labor circles. The fact that Randolph had never been in the Pullman service was a talking point for the Pullman Company but in no way affected the confidence of the porters and maids.

The Pullman Company absolutely refused to have anything to do with the new Brotherhood and proceeded to fight it with every weapon at its command. At eight o'clock on the morning following the Harlem mass meeting at which the Brotherhood was organized, a district superintendent in New York called fifty men into his office to ask them why they had attended the meeting. At Pittsburgh the superintendent openly declared that he would fire any man who joined the organization, while at St. Louis the porters were told that if they were fools enough to join the union their places would be taken by Mexicans and Japanese. It was charged by the porters that the company's welfare workers were used for spying and that unofficial individual spying was also encouraged. A supervisory official at the Pennsylvania Station in New York is reported as having told the porters: "If you see anything happening in the homes or on the streets or anything concerning our employees which might interest us, we want you to come right into my office and tell me personally. Your name will not be mentioned." [4]

Through press releases and other publicity the company attacked the union as a dangerous radical movement. The principal leaders were attacked as disgruntled former employees who had been dismissed from the service for good cause. The company claimed that Roy Lancaster, the secretary-treasurer of the organization, was dismissed for drunkenness, an "unpardonable offense" for a railway employee. Lancaster, himself, claimed that he was dismissed on a trumped-up charge because of his activity in behalf of the porters prior to the formation of the Brotherhood. Randolph, who had never been in the Pullman service, was condemned as a professional agitator, a dangerous radical, and an exploiter of his people.

Negro opinion was by no means united behind the new organization. Years of propaganda by the Pullman Company, setting itself up as a great benefactor of the race, led many to oppose the movement.[5] The Negro press was largely hostile, partly because of its middle-class and anti-labor background, partly because it thought it could gain more by supporting the company, and partly because it honestly opposed the policy and tactics of the union even while sympathizing with the porters. Important Negro organs like the *Whip*, the Chicago *Defender*, and the St. Louis *Argus* were bitterly hostile. Negro politicians like Perry Howard of Mississippi and Melville Chisum of Chicago and numerous others took the same stand. On the other hand, the National Association for the Advancement of Colored People and influential Negro papers in such important centers as New York, Chicago, Pittsburgh, and Washington supported the movement. Of all the Brotherhood's champions among the Negro press, the Pittsburgh *Courier*, according to Randolph, was the most militant and uncompromising, giving unlimited space to presenting the por-

[4] *Messenger*, Dec., 1925, p. 395.
[5] See, for example, an article by Henry Pope, Jr., "Lest We Forget" in the Nashville *Globe*, May 25, 1928.

ters' cause.[6] Yet, when the Brotherhood needed support most, at the time when its relations with the company were reaching a crisis in the spring of 1928, Robert L. Vann, the editor of the *Courier*, issued an open letter to the Pullman porters demanding Randolph's resignation as head of the union.[7] He declared that the company had refused to recognize the union because Randolph was a socialist, and that American capital would never deal with an organization headed by a socialist. Randolph refused to resign [8] and the *Courier* became one of the Brotherhood's critics.

The Brotherhood was also endorsed by such influential white labor bodies as the American Federation of Labor, and the four railway brotherhoods. It was favorably received by the metropolitan press. It was favored by the National Urban League, though many of the local Urban Leagues and the Negro Y. M. C. A.'s were far from friendly. The church was also divided. Sometimes it was very helpful but usually it was very hostile.

To the Negro community the porter's Brotherhood was a racial rather than a purely occupational movement, and the differences of opinion which it aroused were mainly differences over racial tactics. Race militancy versus salvation through white philanthropy, and the union of white and black labor against white capital versus a rapprochement between white capital and black labor against the white worker were the policies dividing the Brotherhood's supporters from its opponents. It was well-nigh impossible for a Negro leader to remain neutral toward the union, and the position which he took toward it became a fundamental test.

It was in this atmosphere that the Brotherhood of Sleeping Car Porters and Maids began the serious business of recruiting members and acquainting the public with its grievances and demands. The direct repressive tactics of the company

[6] *Messenger*, Feb., 1927, p. 55.
[7] Pittsburgh *Courier*, April 14, 1928.
[8] "Randolph Replies to Vann," *Messenger*, May-June, 1928, p. 114.

such as threats of discharge and discipline, while never altogether abandoned, gave way for the most part to an attempt to create an unfavorable impression toward the union among the Negro population. News of the company's benevolence and efforts in behalf of the Negro began to flood the Negro press. The new organization was represented as "subversive," "socialistic," "communistic," and "red." It was going to destroy everything the Negro had gained. It was pointed out that the porters already had a union of their own, the company's Plan of Employee Representation, and the new group would merely become the pawn of the white American Federation of Labor which was always hostile to the Negro worker. One paper, the St. Louis *Argus*, carrying a most bitter attack of this character, also prominently displayed a half-page advertisement of the Pullman Company.[9]

One of the company's boldest strokes was to enlist the aid of certain prominent Negro politicians against the union. About three months after the formation of the Brotherhood both the Negro and metropolitan papers carried a story of how agents of the federal government had joined the Pullman Company in an effort to prevent the porters from organizing. The article told of how Perry W. Howard, Negro Republican national committeeman from Mississippi and special assistant to the Attorney General of the United States, was directing a campaign "to defeat the plans of Randolph and others." Howard claimed that he was acting as a special labor representative of the administration to check a movement engineered by communists receiving instructions from Moscow. He declared that the Department of Justice became interested when it found that the Randolph movement was "inspired, fostered, and promoted by the communistic and extremely radical element in the labor world."[10]

The next day the Department of Justice disavowed Howard's action, asserting that he worked for the department on

9 St. Louis *Argus*, Oct., 30 and Nov. 2, 1925.
10 New York *World*, Nov. 18, 1925.

special assignment, and that when not so engaged he practiced law in a private capacity. It also developed that Howard was in the employ of the Pullman Company [11] and that his attacks on the Brotherhood and his appeals to the employees of the Pullman service to keep out of the union and utilize the company's representation machinery [12] were inspired from company sources. Some years later when Howard was tried and acquitted on the charge of selling federal offices in Mississippi, it developed that he had made a bank deposit of $4,000 " 'apparently' from the Pullman Company" in December, 1925, at the very time when his activities against the Brotherhood were at their height.

"What was an employee of the government doing on the payroll of the Pullman Company?" asked Senator McKellar of Tennessee.

"I don't know," answered Mr. Miller E. McGilchrist of the Department of Justice.[13]

The attacks on the Brotherhood commonly appealed to the Negro's prejudice against the American Federation of Labor. Melville Chisum, another Negro politician, issued a warning to the porters, saying:

Probably the most burning question before Black America today is "Should the Pullman porters be organized into the American Federation of Labor?"

The history of the colored worker in his efforts to affiliate himself with the organized unions in this country is one vast tragedy of cracked skulls, broken necks and prison stripes, resulting from the organized colored worker having been used as a cat's paw during the periods of strikes, which are always called as soon as the colored brother gets organized.

It would appear that the more practical thing to do, would be to seek to win the Pullman Company officials to the point where he will be

[11] New York *World*, Nov. 19, 1925.
[12] See *Spokesman*, Nov., 1925. Open Letter to Pullman Porters by Hon. Perry W. Howard, Republican national committeeman and special assistant to U. S. Attorney General.
[13] Washington *Star*, Jan. 30, 1929.

promoted to branches of the service where the work will change the status of the man, but to make a serving porter a directing executive, it cannot be done.

This organization business is probably going to be annoying for quite a time but the men who appreciate their positions had better listen, for none know better than they that it does not require the knowledge of a college professor to do a Pullman bed and they are waiting for the opportunity to try their hand.[14]

In answer to attacks which attempted to play upon the Negro workingman's distrust of the American Federation of Labor, Randolph constantly emphasized the Brotherhood's independence, though he seldom failed to mention that it had the Federation's "moral support." [15]

About the time of the issue of the foregoing appeal this same Melville Chisum called a conference in Washington for the ostensible purpose of fighting segregation. Prominent Negro politicians were well represented though nationally known leaders of the anti-segregation movement were not present, and the National Association for the Advancement of Colored People, which had always stood at the head of the equal rights campaign, was not asked to coöperate. The one act of the conference to attract attention was the publication of a resolution attacking the porters' Brotherhood which was sent out broadcast by the Negro Associated Press. Rienzi B. Lemus, head of the Brotherhood of Dining Car Cooks and Waiters, charged that this published attack was never adopted by the conference but was substituted after adjournment for a resolution on industrial relations which contained no mention of the Pullman porters. The sponsorship of this conference was never made public, though it is commonly believed, as some Negro papers charged, that it was another step in the company's offensive against the union.[16]

The next step in the company's frontal attack was the re-

[14] Louisville *News*, Dec. 26, 1925.
[15] See, for example, *Messenger*, Dec., 1925, p. 381.
[16] *Messenger*, 1925, p. 389.

placement of a number of the Negro porters on club cars by Filipinos. This move was evidently intended merely to serve as a warning, since the policy of replacement which it seemed to foreshadow and which some of the company's spokesmen had threatened never went beyond this gesture.

The Brotherhood protested that the company's action was a violation of the seniority rights of old employees under the agreement between the company and the employees' representatives made at the wage conference of 1923. They claimed that this violation was an example of the inability of the representation machinery to safeguard the porters' interests. But among Negroes outside of the service, existence of such conference machinery together with the corporation's other personnel work were telling arguments against the new union.

The company's personnel activities fall under five heads: (1) general welfare work; (2) the pension plan; (3) the Pullman Porters' Benefit Association of America; (4) the plan of employee stock ownership; and (5) the Plan of Employee Representation. Of all these the last is probably the most important.

The company's general welfare work includes both relief and recreational activities. The former consists of the usual home visiting and advising by a corps of paid welfare workers, usually ex-porters. The latter includes entertainments of various sorts to which the public is frequently invited and at which officials of the company are always present, field days, and the encouragement of bands and choruses, which, according to President Carry, "has had markedly beneficial effect upon the *esprit de corps* of these employees." [17]

The Pullman pension plan which became effective in 1914 provides for the compulsory retirement, with a pension, of all male employees at the age of 70 and female employees at 65 who have served the organization for twenty years. Special provision is made for the retirement of workers suffering permanent disability as a result of accident, under which they are

[17] Report of President Carry of the Pullman Company, 1922.

entitled to a pension regardless of age if they have completed twenty years of service. Pension allowances are paid monthly. They equal one per cent of the average monthly pay during the last ten years of service multiplied by the total number of years in the service, but no pension is less than $15.00 a month. The company is not bound by contract to pay these pensions and may terminate payment at any time and for any reason.

The company also has a death benefit plan under which the dependents of an employee who dies after a year or more in the service receive the equivalent of a year's salary.

In addition to these benefits and pensions the company fosters the Pullman Porters' Benefit Association of America. This is a voluntary organization to which about eight thousand of the eleven to twelve thousand porters in the service belong. Any Negro male person in the Pullman Company's service of good character and in good health and under forty-five years of age is eligible to membership. Persons over forty-five when the Association was founded were entitled to membership with partial benefits if they joined before a given date. The dues are $28.00 a year for those under forty-five and $32.00 for those over that age. Men separated from the service in good standing may continue their membership without voice in the affairs of the Association. Their annual dues are 50 per cent higher than those of active members. The Association pays death benefits up to a maximum of $1,000 and disability benefits of $10.00 per week after the first five days on the sick list. Unless an extension is granted no member may receive disability benefits for more than 12 weeks in a calendar year. The company contributes "a fair portion of the amount necessary" to the administrative expenses of the organization, furnishes legal advice and other assistance to the officers and makes possible the attendance of delegates at meetings.[18]

In December, 1925 the company instituted a plan of employee stock ownership. Ten thousand shares were set

[18] Constitution and By-Laws of the Pullman Porters' Benefit Association of America (amended 1922-1923), pp. 4-5.

aside for purchase by the employees at $140 per share payable in installments of $3.00 a month. Every employee may purchase one share for every $500 earned in salary each year. This makes it impossible for a porter to buy more than about two shares a year.

The most important of the company's personnel activities, the Plan of Employee Representation, was instituted in 1920. The organization consists of a hierarchy of committees topped by a bureau of industrial relations at the general offices of the corporation in Chicago. The primary unit is the local committee consisting of an equal number of representatives of the management and the employees, the latter being elected by the employee body on the basis of one representative for every 200 workers. The committee meets upon the call of the chairman, the request of the management, or the request of a majority of the staff. The next unit in the scale, the zone general committee, also consists of an equal number of staff and management representatives. The former are chosen by the employee representatives on the local committees from their own number. The bureau of industrial relations, the central organ of the Plan of Employee Representation, is headed by a supervisor appointed by the company. Like the lower committees it consists of an equal number of representatives of management and staff. Each category of employees, such as the porters and maids, the repair shop employees, or the clerical force has a representative on the staff side. Although the bureau of industrial relations is to all intents and purposes the court of last resort on matters within the jurisdiction of the Plan, the agreement between the company and its porters and maids signed in 1924 allowed an appeal from the bureau to the United States Railway Labor Board.[19] Subsequent agreements signed in 1926 and 1929 provide for the "right to appeal as provided by law." [20]

[19] Agreement between the Pullman Company and Its Porters and Maids, 1924, p. 9.

[20] Ibid., 1926, p. 10; 1929, p. 11.

The Brotherhood condemned the whole company program. The welfare work, pensions, and entertainments were characterized as "soothing salve." The bands and singing groups were an attempt to "make monkeys" out of the porters and to divert their attention from their real grievances. "If by giving them a band," wrote Randolph, the Brotherhood leader, "the company can get their feet more active in dancing than their heads in thinking, the company will certainly give them bands." [21]

The Pullman Porters Benefit Association was described as purely a benefit society controlled by the company so as to prevent any discussion of employment conditions and to forestall any development toward independence. An illusion of democratic control was maintained by the election in districts of sixty-six porter delegates, while real control was in the hands of seven directors. Originally this board consisted of five porters and two welfare workers, but its personnel was gradually transformed so that all are now instructors or welfare workers getting more than twice the salary of the average porter. In practice no money can be paid out by the association without the consent of the company treasurer.

The sharpest of all the Brotherhood's shafts was leveled against the Plan of Employee Representation, for it was this that the company offered the men as an alternative to the union. The strength of the Brotherhood's case is borne out by the fact that almost every important objection which it raised against the plan has also been made in private by employee members of both local and zone committees.[22] The most telling criticism of the Plan is its ineffectiveness in the handling of major issues. The question of wage revision is specifically excepted from its scope. Other major grievances such as the 400-hour or 11,000-mile monthly working standard, the doubling back system, and the inadequate overtime

[21] *Messenger*, Aug., 1925, p. 290.

[22] Interviews with employee representatives on the Plan committee. These views were volunteered. No attempt was made to draw out opinions.

provisions have never been considered under the Plan despite the fact that employee representatives admit that they are serious causes of unrest. These same employee representatives admit that the Brotherhood arose and grew as a result of these very real grievances.

Nor has the machinery proved much more effective in the handling of minor matters. The employees in general, according to both the Brotherhood and the Plan committeemen, have little confidence in the Plan. Many hesitate to take advantage of it because they distrust the presence of supervisory officials on the committees, and object particularly to the common practice of having the official who makes a charge against an employee sit on the committee which reviews the charge. How extensively the machinery is distrusted may be indicated by the fact that but one appeal was made from the decision of the management, out of twenty-four discharges in one of the New York yards in July, 1928, which, in the opinion of the employee representative, might well have gone before the local committee. The Brotherhood also objected to the fact that in practice the company uses the Plan to save its face. The committees have almost invariably upheld the management. Even when they reversed its decisions they gave the management a clean bill of health and removed the penalties against the employee in the name of mercy rather than justice.[23]

Various guarantees given the employees under the Plan have also proved ineffective. The placing of Filipinos on club cars in violation of seniority rights has already been mentioned. The pledge: "The company will not permit its employees to be discriminated against because of any action taken by them in performing their duties as committeemen" has been flagrantly violated. A local committeeman was discharged as a trouble maker for writing to delegates on the use of the 1926 conference of the Plan calling attention to the "annual opportunity" to discuss wages and working conditions with the

[23] *Messenger*, Sept., 1925, p. 312.

management and urging these delegates to state what their constituents wanted considered at the meeting.[24]

The constitution of the Plan also contained the very important guarantee:

There shall be no discrimination by the Company or by any of its employees on account of membership or non-membership in any fraternal society or union.

This was constantly violated. Porters were questioned as to their union affiliation and threatened with discipline or discharge.[25] The company not only took no notice of such acts of its agents but actually permitted the discharge of a number of employees for organization activity without making any attempt to disguise its motives.[26]

When it became clear during the first year of the Brotherhood's existence that the company's tactics could not stem the growth of the organization, an attempt was made to forestall the Brotherhood's propaganda by calling a special conference to revise wages and working rules. Delegates were chosen through the machinery of the Plan of Employee Representation. The Brotherhood used the calling of the conference to further its cause by publicly urging the delegates to support the program of the union and asking them to refuse to sign the agreement unless its demands were met.

The results of the conference failed even to approximate the union's program. Two changes were made in working rules affecting doubling and overtime for delayed arrivals. The new overtime rule provided that when a train was an hour or more late the porter would receive extra compensation "for the full amount of the delay on the basis of 30 miles per hour of such delay computed at the rate of 60/100 of a cent per mile.[27] This was an improvement over the old rule which pro-

[24] *Ibid.*, Dec., 1925, p. 395.

[25] Pittsburgh *American*, Sept. 11, 1925.

[26] Federated Press Sheet 3, No. 3140, Oct. 20, 1927.

[27] Agreement between the Pullman Company and Its Porters and Maids, 1926, p. 4.

vided that all overtime due to delayed arrivals be put in the porter's accumulated monthly mileage column and that no extra compensation was to be paid until the standard 11,000 miles was reached.

The new rule on doubling actually worked to the disadvantage of the men. Doubling back under the 1924 rule was paid at the rate of sixty cents per hundred miles. Under the new rule, though paid at the same rate, it was "credited at thirty miles per hour from the time required to report until released." Thus a porter doubling back on the Twentieth Century formerly got 60/100 of a cent for each of the 961 miles traveled or $5.76. Under the new rule he got 20 (the time of the trip) x 30 (the mileage ratio) x 60/100 or $3.50. Men on slow trains did not suffer to so great an extent under the new rule, but doubling has always been confined largely to the fast trains.

The most disappointing feature of the whole conference was its handling of the wage question. The scale was increased by 8 per cent, raising the minimum from $67 to $72.50 per month and the maximum from $96.50 to $104. The wage scale under the 1926 agreement was as follows:

TABLE XXVI

Wage Rates of Pullman Porters and Maids under the Agreement of 1926

Length of Service	Standard Sleeping & Parlor Cars	Tourist Cars	Outside Parlor Car Men	Porters in Charge	Private Cars Porter in Charge	Maids
Less than 2 years......	72.50	78.50	84.50	85.00	90.50	70.00
2 to 5 years...............	76.00	84.00	88.50	89.00	95.00	73.50
5 to 15 years............	80.00	86.00	93.00	93.00	99.50	77.00
Over 15 years...........	83.00	89.00	97.00	97.70	104.00	80.50

A study of the service made for the Brotherhood by the Labor Bureau, Inc., of New York City showed that of the 777 men included in its survey only 11 per cent were in the minimum grade; 27 per cent had been in the service from 2 to 5 years; 30 per cent, from 5 to 10 years; 15 per cent, from 10 to 15 years; and 17 per cent, over 15 years.[28]

Under the new scale the average wage in 1926, according to the Labor Bureau's survey, the most reliable source available, was $78.11 a month.[29] The scale completely disregarded the union's demand, "no tips but a living wage," and left the porter as completely dependent upon tips as before. Tips, according to the Labor Bureau, average $7.56 each round trip and $58.15 a month. Two men reported tips of more than $200 a month. Five reported less than $15. Three-quarters of the men keeping records made about $65 a month, while three-quarters of those not keeping records reported between $75 and $80. Ninety per cent of those keeping records made less than $95, and 90 per cent of those not keeping records made less than $100. The reported average earnings from tips of those not keeping records was $59.77, of those keeping records, $56.84." [30] The average income from tips, as stated, was $58.15 a month. This, added to the average monthly wage, brought the porter's income up to $136.26 a month. It is necessary, however, to deduct certain occupational expenses, such as the cost of food and lodging on duty, shoe polish, and uniforms for men in the service less than ten years, etc. These expenses averaged $33.82.[31] It is perhaps questionable as to whether lodging on layovers can legitimately be classed as a necessary occupational expense since the company does furnish quarters free of charge to men away from home. Yet, of the 673 men included in the Labor Bureau's survey but 266 used the company's quarters. The others purchased their own accommodations at an average cost of $1.24 a night.[32] The de-

[28] *The Case of the Pullman Porters* (MS of a survey by the Labor Bureau, Inc., Oct. 20, 1927) p. 75.

[29] See Docket No. 20007 before the Interstate Commerce Commission: Brotherhood of Sleeping Car Porters v. the Pullman Company. Oct. 20, 1927.

[30] Labor Bureau Survey, *op. cit.*, p. 105.

[31] *Ibid.*, p. 117.

[32] *Ibid.*, p. 114.

duction of occupational expenses gives the porter an average
wage of $102.26 a month.

By failing to adjust a single major grievance the 1926 conference increased rather than allayed the discontent. The porter delegates themselves were far from satisfied with the results and two of them refused to sign the agreement.[33] Four
were reported to have signed under protest.

The Brotherhood continued to grow. Within a year after
organization work began its membership passed the 51 per
cent mark. In the fall of 1927 it claimed 7,300 of the 12,000
porters in the service. The Pacific Coast was almost 100 per
cent organized, the North and Middle West more than 80
per cent. In New York about 50 per cent of the 3,500 eligible
in the city carried union cards. Membership in the South, however, was negligible.

All through its first year the Brotherhood pursued a policy
of "watchful waiting." Its tactics, in its own words, were "to
make haste slowly" and to exercise "reasonable caution" but
to hammer away "with unremitting constancy on organization,
agitation, and education." [34] The leaders were strongly urged
to change this policy and take positive steps towards a wage
readjustment even before the meeting of the company's conference. They were urged to take their case before the old
United States Railway Labor Board. There is evidence that
if this step had been taken at least two influential members of
that body would have been favorable toward the Brotherhood's claim.[35]

But Randolph and his colleagues refused to go before the
board. They had some doubts as to whether their union could
muster the vote of 51 per cent of the porters necessary to secure recognition by the board. They maintained this position
even though Negro labor leaders with long experience before

[33] Pittsburgh *Courier*, Feb. 13, 1926.
[34] *Messenger*, June, 1926, p. 185.
[35] Interviews with former Brotherhood supporters and a member of the
Railway Labor Board.

government labor bodies assured them that no union ever failed to secure an overwhelming majority on the Labor Board's ballot because this ballot contained only the name of the union making the appeal. But a far more important reason for the Brotherhood's refusal was the uncertainty of the Labor Board's future. The great transportation brotherhoods favored its abolition. Randolph wanted the support of these organizations and he was afraid that he would not get it in an appeal to a board to whose continuance the brotherhoods were opposed.

The porters' union, instead, put its trust in the Watson-Parker bill, which the four brotherhoods favored. This measure provided that if a dispute between a carrier — sleeping car companies were specifically included in the term — and its employees could not be settled in conference, it was to be referred to an adjustment board "designated by the parties or by either party." If a settlement failed again either party might refer the issue to the Board of Mediation, a permanent body appointed by the President of the United States. If mediation failed the matter was to go to an arbitration board of three or six members, one or two chosen by each side in the dispute and one or two chosen by those already selected. If arbitration failed and if the dispute threatened to deprive any community of essential transportation service the President of the United States was empowered to set up an emergency board to dispose of the case.[36]

The porters' union supported this bill despite the fact that they were urged from many sources to oppose it on the ground that it was designed to aid the powerful and well organized crafts but would be of little help to the minor groups.[37] In answer to this Randolph declared that "examination of the bill did not reveal that it would not serve colored as well as white workers if organized." And besides, it was "bad policy to oppose a bill favored by powerful brotherhoods and rail-

[36] Public Law No. 257, 69th Congress.
[37] See New York *Age*, April 21, 1928.

way companies as a road to industrial peace in the railroad industry." [38]

When the Watson-Parker law was passed Randolph announced that it was the purpose of the Brotherhood "to be the first or among the first" to file its case with the new board. "It will secure for us an unprecedented amount of moral support and valuable publicity."

"It will also," he added, "enable us to secure the active coöperation of the big brotherhoods whose interest it is to see that every union of railway workers gets 100 per cent fair consideration before the board, so that it might serve as a precedent for subsequent actions on the part of other railway organizations." [39]

If the porters' leaders really put their faith to any large extent in the Watson-Parker bill in the hope of securing "the active coöperation of the big brotherhoods," they were acting with lamentable ignorance of the ways of these organizations, which have never been known for their altruism. The "big four" had supported the porters' cause from the start to the extent of giving advice when asked and sending speakers, often prominent officials, to Brotherhood meetings. And that is probably as far as they ever went for any other labor organization. As a matter of fact, a number of other labor unions, particularly the needle trades organizations, were quite as helpful as the "big four."

However, even that much support from the "big four" had publicity value, and publicity for the porters' cause was Randolph's chief aim. He always took great pleasure in listing the supporters of the union. It made little difference whether these supporters were influential and strong or small and insignificant so long as they added to the length of the list. Thus, important groups like the "big four" and the American Federation of Labor went down on the same list as a struggling union of government employees, and a liberal discussion and

[38] *Messenger*, June, 1926, p. 185.
[39] *Ibid.*

dining group, the Civic Club of New York.[40] Further to promote their efforts at publicity the Brotherhood established a "council of strategy" consisting "of the ablest journalists, publicists, and labor men to acquaint every social, civic, and religious organization with the aims and methods of the Brotherhood to get them to pass resolutions endorsing our movement." [41]

The results of these efforts were amazingly successful. Where the doings of powerful labor unions in vital industries got merely perfunctory press notice, the Pullman porters got editorials and columns on the front pages of the leading metropolitan papers.

As soon as the Watson-Parker bill became law the Brotherhood set to work to get the "moral support and valuable publicity" of being one of the first groups to present its case to the new Mediation Board. The board, after examining the books of the Brotherhood, decided that it represented a majority of the porters and was therefore qualified to act as their spokesman. The company, however, steadfastly refused to recognize the Brotherhood and insisted upon dealing with its workers through the Plan of Employee Representation. This, it held, was a more representative organization than the union, having received 85 per cent of the votes of the porters and maids at the election of November, 1926, despite vigorous efforts of the union to keep employees from voting for it. The union claimed that the employees who voted for the Plan did so only as a result of intimidation and coercion by the company and submitted one thousand affidavits to the Mediation Board in proof of its contention.[42]

After four weeks of futile effort the members of the board in charge of the case announced on August 9, 1927, that mediation had failed. The parties were asked to submit their case to arbitration. The Brotherhood immediately consented but

40 *Messenger*, Feb., 1926, p. 62; June, 1926, p. 185; Feb., 1927, p. 56.
41 *Ibid.*, June, 1926, p. 186.
42 *Ibid.*, Sept., 1927, p. 384.

the company refused, claiming that it knew of no dispute between itself and its porters and maids. Its relations with these employees were fixed by contract — the agreement of February, 1926 — and this contract itself provided the way of its alteration. Since arbitration was voluntary, matters were deadlocked.

Meanwhile the Brotherhood attempted to achieve its ends in a somewhat different way. It instituted an action before the Interstate Commerce Commission to put an end to the practice of tipping. It contended that in fixing wages at a rate insufficient to enable porters to remain in the service without tips the company was "inducing payment by passengers for service rendered in excess of the price indicated on the ticket" and was thereby violating the Interstate Commerce Act.[43] By a vote of 8 to 3 the commission rejected the union's plea as a matter beyond its jurisdiction. But the Brotherhood leaders were not dissatisfied. The case had publicity value, and Randolph and his colleagues seemed to feel that this in itself was worth while.

With the disposition of this action the Brotherhood again concentrated upon the prosecution of its claims under the Watson-Parker law. Mediation and efforts to bring about arbitration having failed, its next step under the law was to seek the establishment by the President of the United States of an emergency board to ascertain and report upon the facts of the controversy. But the Mediation Board was authorized to recommend the appointment of such a board only when a substantial interruption of interstate commerce was threatened.

The Brotherhood therefore set out to threaten such interruption by taking a strike vote. "Twice," said Randolph in a newspaper interview, "have we tried to bring the company into the ring to thrash the matter out, but so far the company

[43] Before the Interstate Commerce Commission: Brotherhood of Sleeping Car Porters v. the Pullman Company. Petitioner's Brief on Motion to Dismiss, Docket No. 20007, Oct. 20, 1927, p. 2.

has succeeded in avoiding us. This is the first time we have threatened a strike and we intend to go through with it if our men favor doing so." [44]

Eight days later, however, Randolph was not so sure as to what the union was going to do with the strike vote after it was taken. "A strike vote," he said, "doesn't mean that the porters will necessarily strike. A strike vote is intended to show to what extent the men are committed to their demands, how firmly they believe in their cause, and how many are willing to strike if necessary to achieve their demands." [45]

A week later the union issued another statement to much the same effect. "A strike vote is not a strike. It is a sign of the iron resolution of the men to fight to the finish for their rights. It does not follow that the Pullman porters will strike because they take a strike vote. The telegraphers' union on the Burlington Railroad took a strike vote and did not strike. The United States Mediation Board stepped in and effected a settlement. . . . But the strike vote expresses the strength of the organization which will bring the company around.[46]

Statements of this sort undoubtedly went far towards convincing the porters that a strike vote was a moral gesture entailing no serious responsibilities. By a vote of 6,053 to 17 they therefore placed authority to call a strike in the hands of their executive and continued to go about their business. The company, instead of rushing to surrender to the Brotherhood when the vote was announced, set about to build up machinery to cope with a strike if one were called. Employees in other branches of the services were designated to do porter work. Men on the company's waiting list were asked to be ready to go to work when called. Strike breakers were fed and housed in the yards and stations. Besides, large numbers of letters from Negroes offering their services if they were wanted poured into the company offices.

[44] New York *Evening Journal*, March 15, 1928.
[45] Washington *Eagle*, March 23, 1928.
[46] St. Louis *American*, March 31, 1928.

The Mediation Board failed to make any recommendation regarding an emergency board. News items to the effect that a strike of porters was probably inevitable began to appear in the papers, and finally, early in June, 1928, a strike order was issued. Still the Mediation Board refused to move. It felt that the Pullman service was not a necessity and that no community would be deprived of essential railroad service if not a single Pullman car ran. At the same time word began to come into Brotherhood headquarters from organizers and agents in the field that the men were not going to strike. Too many porters, despite their complaints, thought that their jobs were too good to lose, and they knew too that there were thousands of Negroes outside who would be only too glad to exchange their dirty, sweaty, hard manual jobs for the comparative ease and gentility of a porter's place.

The Brotherhood was in an unenviable position. It had gambled everything and thus far had lost. The government was not going to come to its assistance. It was clearly in no position to force the company to terms. The leaders had to find some way of backing down as gracefully as possible if they wished to save the organization from complete destruction and their supporters from losing their jobs. Mr. Randolph and some of his colleagues went to Washington and conferred with President Greene of the American Federation of Labor. Mr. Greene came to their aid by publicly advising them to "postpone" their strike until they could "arouse public opinion more thoroughly and mobilize the forces of organized labor behind them."

This, of course, fooled no one. The porters already had the "moral support" of the American Federation of Labor and the transportation brotherhoods, and that was the only way in which the "forces of organized labor" ever would "mobilize behind them." And as to public opinion, the Brotherhood had gotten more publicity in and out of the press and had aroused more public interest during its brief career than most unions do in a lifetime.

The communists, who had been attempting unsuccessfully to bore from within the Brotherhood ever since their convention had ordered such a course in 1928, now came out into the open and attacked Randolph's policies in no uncertain terms. In words not very different from those which Randolph had once been in the habit of using [47] they attacked the "prejudiced labor aristocrats of the American Federation of Labor and the narrow craft monopolists of the railroad brotherhoods" and warned the porters against following such leadership. They called upon them instead to "overcome their isolation" by uniting with the "progressive rank and file" of the unions.[48] To all this Randolph replied: "Communist gossip about Mr. Greene being insincere is the veriest nonsense and silliest tommyrot which could only emanate from crack-brained fanatics or low-grade morons." [49]

Frantic efforts were made to make the strike fiasco appear to have been a well considered and carefully planned procedure which added immeasurably to the strength and standing of the union. The strike, it was claimed, was not "called off," but merely "postponed." The company was pictured as being at a complete loss as to what to do next. The union's "strategy" had compelled it to spend a million dollars to break a strike which did not come off, and thus caused almost as much damage as a real walkout. The "strike manoeuvre" gave the union "a million dollars worth of publicity." It brought the "powerful American Federation of Labor" to its side.

Handbills in this vein flooded the Negro districts. The Negro papers were filled with such statements. The confidence of the porters, however, was sadly shaken. Membership fell off rapidly. By the first of January, 1929, only three thousand of the seven thousand who were in the organization at the time of the strike vote remained. The publication of the *Messenger* was suspended for lack of funds, and several organizers were dropped from the union's staff.

[47] See above Chapter XVIII, pp. 424-25.
[48] See *Negro Champion*, Aug. 8, 1928.
[49] Bulletin issued by Randolph in June, 1928.

But worst of all, the united front which the organization had been able to maintain was broken. Where communist attacks and boring from within failed to shake the porters' confidence in Randolph's leadership, internal politics, official incompetence or worse, and general disillusionment almost destroyed the union. Frank Crosswaith, an organizer who had been dropped, preferred charges of misuse of funds against Roy Lancaster, the secretary-treasurer. These charges were carefully sifted by competent accountants and found baseless. The report completely satisfied a committee of well known white and Negro radicals and liberals. Shortly before this Lancaster, himself, had brought charges of misappropriation of funds against another organizer still on the Brotherhood's staff and proved them to the satisfaction of the committee. But when the evidence was presented to Randolph he merely declared "Oh, it's just a little peculation," [50] and made no move whatever to get rid of the organizer, who remained in the Brotherhood's service until May 1, 1930.

Every effort was made to pump life into what was left of the union and to revive the porters' morale. An application for affiliation with the American Federation of Labor which had been pending for some time prior to the strike fiasco was pressed, but the jurisdictional claims of the Hotel and Restaurant Employees International Alliance blocked the granting of an international charter. Instead, a compromise was effected under which separate charters were issued to porters' unions in a number of cities. In September, 1929, there were 13 such unions directly affiliated with the American Federation of Labor. These 13 unions were located in New York, Chicago, St. Louis, Detroit, Kansas City, St. Paul, Oakland, Washington, D. C., New Orleans, Los Angeles, Cleveland, Denver, and Fort Worth. According to Randolph the plan was but a temporary expedient. The jurisdictional dispute with the hotel and restaurant workers would soon be settled and the porters would get their international charter. However, the hotel workers refused

[50] From a member of the committee.

to surrender their claims and the American Federation of Labor convention at Toronto in October, 1929, allowed the compromise to stand.[51] Meanwhile the Brotherhood, instead of paying a per capita of one cent per month required of international unions, is paying 35 cents per month for the privilege of direct local affiliation with that same American Federation of Labor which Randolph's *Messenger* ten years before had condemned as the "most wicked machine for the propagation of race prejudice in the country." [52] Now Randolph is an out-and-out supporter of the Federation and its president, William Greene.

Some months before effecting this expensive affiliation the Brotherhood, in the course of its efforts to show that it was still alive, bought a building in Harlem, New York City, to house its headquarters. "No more effective repudiation could be made to the Pullman propaganda that the Brotherhood is dead," said Randolph, "than that of the union buying its home." [53]

Yet in spite of the dismal outlook late in 1928 the Brotherhood has managed to hold on. Exact membership figures are not available, but even if, as many disappointed supporters claim, the membership on June 1, 1930, did not exceed 2,000 the Brotherhood would still remain one of the largest Negro labor unions in the country. Recently it established a new official organ, the *Black Worker*. This paper reflects little of the *Messenger's* militancy. Its policy in fact seems to be a complete reversal of the *Messenger's*. The latter's militant tone was in the foreground. True, it did make conciliatory overtures to the company now and then but its militancy drowned them out.[54] Now the situation is reversed. The *Black Worker* runs front page articles on "Porter's Duty to Pullman," [55] "The Brotherhood Coöperation with Pullman Man-

[51] American Federation of Labor, *Proceedings*, 1929, pp. 75, 137-39, 384-85.
[52] *Messenger*, May-June, 1919, p. 7.
[53] Chicago *Defender*, Dec. 8, 1928.
[54] See *Messenger*, June, 1927, pp. 239-40.
[55] *Black Worker*, March 1, 1930.

agement," [56] as well as a series by Otto S. Beyer, Jr., on "The Machinery of Coöperation" dealing with the Baltimore and Ohio and Canadian National plans of union-management coöperation in the railroad shops. Only ten years before Randolph had roundly denounced the American Federation of Labor because it stood for the possibility of a partnership between labor and capital.[57]

The Pullman Company goes right on ignoring these gentle hints and continues to deal with the Plan of Employee Representation and to sign agreements with "elected employee delegates." Such an agreement went into effect in June, 1929, and superseded the unsatisfactory agreement of 1926 discussed above. Under the new agreement, doubling and delayed arrivals were compensated at the rate of 25 cents an hour instead of 60/100 cents per mile, credited at the rate of 30 miles per hour. The new rules also provided that porters on one-night lines should "have approximately a three hour rest period during each night where train schedules of station stops and other operation conditions . . . permit." [58] On runs through densely populated districts, such as New York to Washington, this concession is meaningless because of the frequency of train stops. The other changes are an improvement over the 1926 regulations. Aside from these changes and a wage increase which brought the scale to the figures shown in Table XXVII, the 1929 agreement left working conditions as they were.

The increases amount to about five dollars per grade over the previous rates. Although the leaders of the Brotherhood declared these increases, like those of 1926, utterly inadequate, they have since claimed credit for them.[59] But aside from these advances, which bring the entrance wage to about half of what the Brotherhood demanded, all of the major grievances which

[56] *Ibid.*, Feb. 1, 1930.

[57] *Messenger*, May-June, 1919, p. 7.

[58] Agreement between the Pullman Company and Its Porters and Maids, 1929, p. 6.

[59] A. Philip Randolph, "Porters Fight Paternalism," *American Federationist*, June, 1930, p. 668.

TABLE XXVII

WAGE RATES OF PULLMAN PORTERS AND MAIDS UNDER THE
AGREEMENT OF 1929

Length of Service	Standard Sleeping & Parlor Cars	Tourist Cars	Outside Parlor Car men	Porters in Charge	Porters in Charge Private Cars	Maids
Less than 2 years.....	77.50	84	86	90	95.50	75
2 to 5 years................	81	87.50	90.50	93.50	100	78.50
5 to 15 years..............	85	91.50	94	98	105	82
Over 15 years............	88.50	95	98	102	109	85.50

the union organized to correct remain unsatisfied. And the failure of the organization to hold its membership is hardly a portent of their early correction.

The failure of the Brotherhood has been laid at Randolph's door. The extraordinary extent to which he dominated the movement and the insistence with which he kept his personality and name in the foreground of all its activities make such judgment inevitable. Perhaps the most striking shortcoming of Randolph's tactics was his hunger for publicity. He seemed possessed of the notion that publicity was a good in itself which would in some mystical manner win victory for the porters. It seemed never to have occurred to him that if it were his purpose to win recognition and gain concessions from the Pullman Company too much publicity was likely to strengthen the company's determination not to yield, because yielding in the glare of publicity would be a double defeat. His second error was his undue haste for action on a program clearly impossible of early fulfillment. A less theatrical program of patient effort at organization and agitation accompanied by the tackling of solvable grievances might not indeed have made the front pages, but it would also have invited less company opposition and have involved less risk of ruin. But Randolph's greatest mistake was placing his trust in the Watson-Parker law. This law was designed by the "big four" brotherhoods which were in a position to go through with a strike which would cripple the country's railroads. Randolph's failure to realize that the position of his unskilled and easily replaceable porters in a luxury service was very different from that of the trainmen or locomotive engineers was an error of first magnitude. And the error is all the more grievous in view of the fact that Negro railway labor leaders had warned him that the law could only serve the interests of the indispensable and powerful unions willing and able to fight to the finish if they saw fit. The blunder of allowing the Brotherhood to carry its strike threat as far as it did without first finding out how the men really felt about a genuine strike was of a kind which only the most powerful union could withstand.

The great pity of the virtual collapse of the porter's union lies not merely in its effect upon the porters who have grievances which sorely need correction but in its effect upon Negro labor generally. The hope that this movement would become the center and rallying point of Negro labor as a whole is now dead. Of course a substantial nucleus of the Brotherhood still remains intact, and it may be that in another crisis it will again grow into an important movement. The chances are, however, that it will be a long time before Randolph or any other leader of this group will again be presented with opportunities as favorable as those which were missed.

Chapter XXI

THE NEGRO COMMUNITY AND THE LABOR MOVEMENT

THE change in the Negro's relation to industry during the last decade and a half has been so sudden that neither the black nor the white working world has been able to grasp its significance and adjust itself to its circumstances. The essence of this change has been the shifting of the Negro's position from that of a labor reserve to a regular element in the labor force of nearly every basic industry. It has brought the Negro face to face with problems of working conditions, which, though they may contain many special elements, are essentially the same as the problems of other workers. They are consequently problems with which the Negro cannot cope successfully without the coöperation of his white fellow workers. Yet ever since the rise to power of the American Federation of Labor both sides have raised obstacles to the consummation of such coöperation. Of all these obstacles none probably has been greater than the narrow and exclusive craft structure and opportunist philosophy of American trade unionism.

The official American labor movement consists of associations of boilermakers and bricklayers, plumbers and carpenters, machinists and railway switchmen, bookbinders and stationary engineers, each interested in its own particular job, jealously guarding its jurisdiction against all encroachments, and highly suspicious of every brother organization whose field approaches its own. The craft is a sort of exclusive club consisting of those who now belong. The smaller it is kept the higher will be the value of the craftsman's service. It is therefore made as difficult as possible for new members to join. If whole classes, such as Negroes, can be automatically excluded, the problem of keeping the membership down is made that much easier. The organizations may carry the slogan of unity on their banners, but the ideals of labor solidarity and the brotherhood of all industrial workers have little practical bearing on their conduct. All that they want are signed agreements with employers. Collective negotiation upon a business basis is the ideal which really moves their lives. The American Federation of Labor is an agency set up to keep craft separatism from defeating its own ends. Its purpose is to settle disputes among the unions, to handle matters of common concern, particularly where legislation is needed, and to care in some manner for the organization of those workers who might, if not brought into the system in some way, ignore its claims and threaten its continuation. The American Federation of Labor is after all a creature of the trade unions. While it must have some measure of authority over them in order to fulfill its purpose, it can hardly, in view of its nature, rise to higher levels than its dominating elements — the craft internationals.

Although the Negro is but one of the victims of American craft unionism, he is a victim upon whom the burden falls with special weight, for his peculiar situation in American society makes it particularly difficult for him to cross craft barriers. To the white trade unionist the Negro is not merely an outsider trying to get into the union, but a social and racial inferior trying to force the white man to associate with him as an equal. And the Negro knows that the white worker wants to keep him out of the union not merely as a potential competitor but as a member of a race which must not be permitted to rise to the white man's level. For three hundred years the Negro has been kept in a position of social and economic inferiority, and white organized labor, dominated by the hierarchy of the skilled crafts, has no desire to see him emerge from that condition.

The educated leaders of the Negro community see only the racial aspect of this situation. They see that many employers use Negro labor, thereby giving the black man an opportunity to earn a living which the policy of most white trade unionists would deny him. They see white philanthropists and sentimental friends of the black man trying to help him by giving him schools and social-welfare agencies. They are impressed with the stories of the poor folks who become wealthy through thrift and hard work, and with the history of great institutions which sprang from small beginnings. Here, they say, are friends of the Negro who have proved their friendship, and here are ways of success which have been tried and found effective. So the race leaders counsel their people to beware of the white working man and to put their trust in the white upper classes. Labor solidarity to which the white unionist appeals when he needs the black man to serve his selfish ends, or which the radical preaches to increase his tiny following from any possible source is, they say, a very dangerous doctrine. It is far safer to give loyal service to the white man who wants it, and by hard work and saving to amass enough wealth to bring comfort and security.

Negro leadership for the past generation has put its stress on the element of race. Their people's plight, they feel, is the plight of a race. They turn a deaf ear to those who say that the Negro's plight is the plight of the working class in general merely aggravated by certain special features. All of the various schools of Negro thought which have had real influence upon Negro life have had one end in view, the elimination of racial discrimination.

The most intelligent of all this racial leadership, that of the National Association for the Advancement of Colored People, is in this regard fundamentally little different from the rest. It is interested, not mildly but militantly, in civil liberties. It wants to stop lynching and Jim Crowism in all its forms. It demands that the Negro receive decent and equal treatment in all public places and that he be accorded all those constitutional rights, including full suffrage, which certain communities have denied him. If all these disabilities were removed, the N. A. A. C. P., with the exception of a few leaders like Du Bois, would apparently be satisfied with the world as it is. The problems of the Negro worker which are the same as those of the white man are beyond its concern. A striking illustration of this is found in the campaign against the confirmation of Judge Parker's nomination to be a Justice of the Supreme Court of the United States. Parker's appointment was fought principally on two counts: first, his unsympathetic attitude toward organized labor as expressed in his approval of the "yellow dog" contract; second, his unsympathetic attitude toward Negro political aspirations as expressed in certain remarks made ten years earlier in a campaign speech in North Carolina declaring the Negro unfit to participate in politics. The National Association for the Advancement of Colored People bent all of its great energy toward defeating Parker on the second count. The fact that the judge's economic views were of direct concern to thousands of wage-earning Negroes and that the very decision upon which organized labor based its opposition affected many Negro miners in West Virginia was ignored by the association.

The National Association for the Advancement of Colored People has frequently shown its interest in the Negro's relation to labor organizations. It has fought attempts of the plumbers, electricians, railway workers, and others to keep Negroes out of their unions or to force them out of the occupations which those unions attempt to control. But in every case the association has fought for the Negro's admission into the unions on the ground of civil liberty rather than upon the principle of labor solidarity.

Negro administrators of white philanthropy, such as the leaders of the Urban League and the various committees on interracial coöperation scattered throughout the country, have also tried to lift trade-union barriers. They are interested in greater economic opportunity for the colored worker, and they believe that if he can get into the unions he will be able to follow trades which it is almost impossible for him to follow at present. The lifting of trade-union barriers is but one of the methods by which the Urban League and the interracial bodies seek their ends. Their aim is to foster kindly attitudes toward the Negro. Their principal appeal is to employers and the members of the professions. Their efforts to get the Negro into the labor unions have been confined to seeking the coöperation of prominent trade-union officials. Their appeal is an appeal by Negro leaders to the white upper class. It makes no attempt to reach the white or black rank and file.

Historically the most potent influence in the black community has been the evangelical church. It offered the Negro an escape from the economic and social disabilities of this world through salvation in the next. The church won its hold on the race in slave days by giving the slave an emotional outlet for the expression of his earthly misery and heavenly hopes. On the whole the Negro church has either ignored present ills or counselled its communicants to bear with them patiently and to serve their masters, for one should "Render unto Caesar the things that are Caesar's." Such ills as one found in this world were but a preparation for the blessings of the next. The rôle of the church in Negro life is hard to duplicate in the white world. Religion for the Negro has been a matter of everyday concern. The church has been the very center of the community about which Negro social life revolved.

However, the absorption of the Negro into northern industry is gradually shaking the church's hold and a new philosophy, more in keeping with the dominant thought of the white world is rising in its place. Like the philosophy of the militant National Association for the Advancement of Colored People and that of the conciliatory interracial movement, this philosophy is decidely individualistic and middle class in outlook. It has its roots in the doctrines of Booker T. Washington and the Hampton and Tuskegee schools, which preach the gospel of salvation through thrift, enterprise, and industrial efficiency. Its flower is the National Negro Business League whose purpose is the encouragement and promotion of business within the race so that eventually an independent petty black capitalism will rise within the limits of white society.

This movement has caught the imagination of the Negro people in a striking manner. The ideal of an independent black economy within the confines of the white is a living force in every black community in the land. Yet how such an independent economy is to rise and function when the white world outside controls credit, basic industry, and the state is something which the sponsors of the movement prefer to ignore. If such an economy is to rise it will have to do so with the aid of white philanthropy and will have to live upon white sufferance. If the great white banks and insurance companies decide that they want Negro business it is hard to see how the little black institutions can compete successfully against them. The same holds for the chain stores and various retail establishments. They will be able to undersell their Negro competitors if they want to, and the Negro world will not continue indefinitely to pay higher prices for its goods merely out of pride of race. Basic industry will continue to remain in the hands of the white world, for even the most ardent supporters of an independent black economy will admit that there is no prospect of the Negro capitalists amassing enough wealth to establish steel mills, build railroads and pipe lines, and gain control of essential raw materials.

But granted that all seemingly insurmountable difficulties could be overcome it is still hard to see what good this independent economy would do the great majority of Negro workers. The experiences of immigrants working for employers of their own race or nationality would hardly encourage one to believe that Negro workers would receive any more consideration at the hands of Negro employers than at the hands of white. Negro capital at best would offer an escape only to a handful of the abler, shrewder, more enterprising, more unscrupulous, and luckier members of the race. The majority doubtless would still till the soil or work for white employers as they do now.

White capitalists like Rosenwald, Rockefeller, and others, who are the chief supporters of Negro philanthropy, are being implored by the National Negro Business League to under-write a system of Negro chain stores. The supporters of an independent black economy evidently believe that Negro busi-ness enterprise should now take its place alongside of schools, churches, hospitals, day nurseries, Urban Leagues, interracial committees, and Y. M. C. A.'s as a worthy Negro charity. Like the rest, it will strengthen the hold of race separatism and postpone the day of a more thorough understanding be-tween white and black labor.

Such an understanding, in view of both the middle-class and race-conscious attitudes of the Negro leadership and the exclusive craft separatism and job consciousness of the official labor movement, seems remote indeed. The over-sanguine radicals see in the Negro's special racial grievances and his new position in industry the nucleus of a discontented mass movement. But they overlook the fact that the unique social position of the Negro plus the white worker's absence of class consciousness lends force to the separatist preachings of the Negro leaders. It should not be forgotten that the Negro has won his place in industry in the branches in which labor organization has little or no hold and where the white work-er's opposition to his employment has consequently carried least weight. Race leaders have not failed to point this out and to drive home the moral that after all the employer is the black man's best friend. And the white trade unionist, using the same facts, points out his moral, that the Negro is an irredeemable scab who breaks the white man's strikes and tears down his hard won standards, and that the unions must exclude him lest he play the traitor in their midst.

A labor movement built upon the principle of working-class unity would of course take the Negro into its ranks and fight to raise the general standard. Self-protection alone should dictate such a course. But the white worker, sharing the prejudices of the rest of the white world, balks at the bugaboo of "social equality" and persists in relegating the black laborer to a place of permanent inferiority.

But side by side with all these forces are tendencies in other directions which in time may destroy their potency. Most important is the machine, which is rapidly changing the meaning of skill and obliterating old craft lines. The machine, rather than any concept of working-class unity or industrial brotherhood, will compel the official labor movement to change its structure and policy if it is not to generate into a mere social relic. Ultimately this will probably redound to the Negro's benefit, but during transitional stages technical changes which reduce the personnel will hurt him along with other workers. And where, as on the railroads, the white men are organized and the Negro is not, the unions will seek to protect their members by compelling the employers to save their jobs at the expense of the Negro's.

The hope of distinctive minorities, like the Negro, which are prone to become the tools in the industrial struggle first of one side and then of the other, rests to no small extent upon industrial stabilization. Few Negro railway men would deny that they were better off under federal control than ever before or since. There is little question that Negroes in government enterprises like the postal service or in other branches of the public services, despite all sorts of discrimination and inequality in assignments and promotions, are better off than in competitive industry. Steps towards industrial stabilization, which would eliminate those competitive elements in industry that redound to the disadvantage of the employees generally and minorities in particular, require an extension of governmental control. This in turn can be achieved only through political action of a type in which the Negro seems especially unlikely to participate. His loyalty to the Republican party in national politics and his tendency since his recent settlement in the North to align himself locally with the dominant machine in the city where he lives make him a bulwark of political conservatism rather than a promising progressive element.

On the other hand, Negro workers threatened with wholesale elimination from jobs, or brought face to face with industrial problems which demand united action for solution, have shown a tendency to turn to unions of their own. Frail and ineffective as such organizations have been in the past, they show the beginning of Negro labor consciousness. They may in time develop a labor leadership which will help to educate both the Negro workers and the general labor movement to the realization of the need of black and white unity. It is here that the rising Negro middle class and the movement for a self-contained black capitalist economy may strike a snag, for an organized Negro working class will learn in time that the enrichment of a few Negroes will be of little benefit to the black rank and file.

But even if the Negro world should change its outlook and approve of an industrial and political alignment of the working class cutting across race lines, this change alone would not be sufficient to affect the situation. No such alignment could be effected by the will of the outcast minority alone. It must depend upon the will of the controlling majority, and that majority is white.

APPENDICES

Appendix I

THE KNIGHTS OF LABOR

A. Statement by Hon. Frank J. Ferrell

Frank J. Ferrell, of New York, representative from District Assembly, Knights of Labor, 49, in introducing General Master Workman T. V. Powderly, said:

Governor Lee and Gentlemen of the Convention:

It is with much pleasure and gratification I introduce to you Mr. T. V. Powderly, of the State of Pennsylvania, who will reply to the address of welcome of Governor Lee, of this State, which is one of the oldest States in the arena of political influence of our country. He is one of the thoughtful men of the nation, who recognizes the importance of this gathering of the toiling masses in this our growing Republic. As Virginia has led in the aspirations of our country in the past, I look with much confidence that she will lead in the future to the realization of the objects of our noble Order. It is with extreme pleasure that we, the Representatives from every section of our country, receive the welcome of congratulation for our efforts to improve the condition of humanity. One of the objects of our Order is the abolition of those distinctions which are maintained by creed or color. I believe I present to you a man above the superstitions which are involved in these distinctions. My experience with the Noble Order of the Knights of Labor and my training in my District have taught me that we have worked so far successfully toward the extinction of these regrettable distinctions. As we recognize and repose confidence in all men for their worth in society, so can we repose confidence in one of the noblest sons of Labor — T. V. Powderly — whom I now take the pleasure of presenting to you. — Knights of Labor, *Proceedings*, 1886, page 8.

B. Letter from T. V. Powderly

Excerpts from Powderly's letter to the Richmond press on social equality:

When I heard that there was a likelihood of trouble because Mr. Ferrell attended a place of amusement, I asked of him not to subject himself to insult by going where he was not welcome. He told me that he had no intention of again going to that or any other place where his presence would give rise to comment. Until that time I did not know that colored men were denied admittance to theaters in this City. While I have no wish to interfere with the social relations which exist between the races in the South I have a strong desire to see the black man educated. Southern labor, regardless of its color, must learn to read and write. Southern cheap labor is more a menace to the American toiler than the Chinese, and this labor must be educated. Will my critics show me how the laws of social equality will be harmed by educating the black man, so that he may know how to conduct himself as a gentleman? Will they explain how a knowledge of the laws of his country will cause a man to violate the laws of social equality? Will they in a cool, dispassionate manner explain to me whether an education will not elevate the moral standard of the colored man, and will they tell me that such a thing is not necessary? Will it be explained to me whether the black man should continue to work for starvation wages? With so many able-bodied colored men in the South who do not know enough to ask for living wages, it is not hard to guess that while this race continues to increase in numbers and ignorance, prosperity will not even knock at the door, much less enter the home of the Southern laborer, and that country that has an abundance of ill-fed, ill-bred laborers is not or can not be a prosperous one.

— *Public Opinion*. Volume 2, October-April, 1886-1887, page 4.

Appendix II

THE INDUSTRIAL RESERVE IN COAL MINING

Testimony of Mr. John Mitchell, president of the United Mine Workers of America:

Q. (By Mr. Ratchford). Can you inform us fully of the recent trouble in the State of Illinois between the colored and white miners?

A. Colored labor has been and is now being used for the purpose of reducing the wages of workingmen. They are imported in large numbers from the Southern States to Northern States during strikes, lockouts, and labor disturbances, and are put in the mines, frequently working under guard. To prevent this it is my opinion that laws should be enacted making it a criminal offense for employers to induce laboring men to leave their homes and go to other places under misrepresentation. I might say, gentlemen, that the colored laborers have probably been used more to decrease the earnings in the mines of the workers there than in any other industry. The mine owners of the North and of the South, too, go to centers of industry and even into cotton fields; they induced those colored men to go to some other Northern town or mining town to take the places of the men when they are on a strike. They bring them in there in train loads under armed guards, and they unload them into the mines. Those people when they get down into the mines are able to earn about $1.50. It is more than they get picking cotton or doing the ordinary roustabout work they do in the South. They have taken the places of the white miners and necessarily driven them from the towns they developed, where they have been living all their lives. I know of no element that is doing more to create disturbances in mining circles than is the system of importing colored labor to take white men's places and to take colored union men's places. Our organization does not make any distinction between classes; we regard the colored men fully as much entitled to protection as white men; we make no conditions. It is required that our organization shall treat them without discrimination. We have had during the last year many disturbances in which lives have been lost and property destroyed because of the importation of these people from the South to the North. Information reaching us last night tells of the conflict at Pana, Ill., between the colored people and the white people, where the coal companies have imported colored people to take white people's places, and let me say this is done under most peculiar circumstances. — United States Industrial Commission, 1901, Volume 12, pages 51-52.

Appendix III

THE PLUMBERS AND NEGRO EXCLUSION

A. Letter from George G. Jones

From the *Plumbers' Journal*, March 1905, page 16:

Editor Journal:

Dear Sir and Brother —

To all local unions that are intending to make new agreements with their employers and are going to handle the apprenticeship question, I would like to give them the experience of Local Union 91 along this line:

Prior to April 1, 1902, all journeyman plumbers had their helpers. On that date L. U. No. 91 informed the bosses that no more helpers would be allowed to be hired, and the boys working at the trade at this time would be allowed to finish their trade.

All boys were then registered by L. U. No. 91, getting the date that they started at the business. There were between twenty-five and thirty boys registered. Out of this number we have one left. The rest have either become members of the U. A. or left the trade altogether.

From that date on a helper along with you has been a luxury. The same thing was done with the Negro, only he was cut out entirely as a helper. The only tools he now handles with a U. A. member of L. U. No. 91 is his pen and ink (pick and shovel).

This is one thing that U. A. members that are now allowing burr heads to carry their tools around, should stop. If they don't stop it now the next question will be, How shall we get rid of the Negro?

(Signed) Geo. G. Jones,

Birmingham, Alabama.

B. Proposed Virginia Law for Licensing Plumbers

Norfolk, Va., Feb. 12, 1905.

Editor Journal:

Dear Sir and Brother —

Enclosed you will find clipping from Norfolk paper, which I would suggest that you give space in the next issue of the Journal, believing that it will be of interest to the members of U. A., especially of the southern district, as the Negro is a factor in this section, and I believe the enclosed Virginia state plumbing law will entirely eliminate him and the imposter from following our craft and I would suggest to the different locals that if they would devote a little time and money they would be able to secure just as good if not a better law in their own state. Hoping this may be the means of starting a little agitation along this line, and with best wishes, I remain

(Signed) C. H. PERRY, Sec. L. U. 110.

HOUSE BILL No. 287

A Bill:

To promote the public health and to regulate the sanitary construction, house draining, and plumbing, and to secure the registration of plumbers in all cities within the State of Virginia having a population of 8,000 inhabitants, and to provide for a Board of Examination of plumbers therein, and defining their powers and duties, provide for their compensation, and to provide for penalties for the violation of this act, and to repeal all laws inconsistent with the provisions of this act.

SECTION I

Be it enacted by the General Assembly of Virginia, That in all cities in the State of Virginia, having a population of more than eight thousand inhabitants, there shall be a board for the examination of plumbers, of four members, consisting of one member, to be known as the chief health officer of the city, and one member to be known as the plumbing inspector of the city, one journeyman plumber, and one master plumber, all of whom shall be residents of the city in which their duties are to be performed, and the plumbing inspector, journeyman, and master plumbers shall be licensed plumbers. The members of said board shall be selected as the councils of the respective cities may determine, and said councils shall also prescribe the terms of office of the several members of such board, and the method of their removal from office. The terms of office of such chief health officers and plumbing inspectors as may be in office when this act shall go into effect shall not be affected hereby, and they shall be constituted members of their respective boards for the term for which they may have been elected. . . .

SECTION 3

The said board shall have power, and it shall be its duty, to adopt rules and regulations, not inconsistent with the laws of the State or the ordinances of the city for the sanitary construction, alteration, and inspection of plumbing and sewerage connections and drains placed in, or in connection with any and every building in such city, in which it will prescribe the kind and size of material to be used in such plumbing, and the manner in which such work shall be done. . . .

SECTION 5

Any person not already licensed as herein provided, desiring to work at the business of plumbing in any such city shall make written application to the said board for examination for a license, which examination shall be made at the next meeting of the board, or as soon thereafter as practicable, and said board shall examine said applicant as to his practical knowledge of plumbing, house draining and plumbing, ventilation and sanitation, which examination shall be practical as well as theoretical, and if the applicant has shown himself competent, the plumbing board shall cause its chairman and secretary to execute and deliver to the applicant a license authorizing him to do plumbing in such city. . . .

SECTION 8

It shall be unlawful for any person to do any plumbing in any such city of this state unless he be licensed as herein provided. . . .

SECTION 14

Any person violating any provision of this act or of any lawful ordinances, or rules and regulations, authorized by this act, shall be deemed guilty of a misdemeanor, and shall be fined not exceeding fifty nor less than five dollars for each and every violation thereof, and if such persons hold a plumber's license, it may, in the direction of the board, be forfeited, and he shall not be entitled to another plumbers license for the space of one year after such forfeiture is declared against him by the board.

C. LETTER FROM MISS MARY McDOWELL

When Miss Mary McDowell was commissioner of public

welfare of the city of Chicago a Negro contractor who was putting up a large building for a Negro organization wanted to employ all-Negro union labor. Among those whom he wished to hire was an intelligent Negro plumber, a graduate of Tuskegee who had done plumbing for some time. But the white union refused to admit him although he had passed all the examinations and was experienced.

Discussing this case Miss McDowell wrote as follows, under the date of August 24, 1929:

I called a conference of the Plumbers' secretary and the Negro contractor and the Urban League — Secy. Mr. Hill — now in New York City with Natl. Urban League. — I conferred with one of the foremost labor leaders of Chicago, who said "the plumbers won't even take white men in."

The Plumbers' official said he would arrange for another examination of the plumber and his helpers — which he did, but the helpers did not turn up — and the Union said my friend *did not pass*, which of course was nonsense for it is a very simple examination.

(Signed) MARY E. McDOWELL,

Chicago, Ill.

D. Burke's Report on Greenville, S. C.

Report of General Organizer Burke, December 19, 1905:

There is only one shop in town (Greenville, S. C.) that does any work to amount to anything. When the work is particular he will hire a good man. All the other work, jobbing, etc., is done by Negroes. There is another town called Union close by, but Spartansburg has control of it. Bro. Becker and a few of the boys are going to run over to Greenville and make a thorough investigation and try and have these bosses hire white men. It is a wonder to me that there are not more Negroes working at our business from the way our members in a great many places use them as helpers. I registered a few "hicks" all along the line where I have found them helping. — *Plumbers, Gas and Steam Fitters' Official Journal*, (Chicago, Illinois), January, 1905, Volume X, pages 10-11.

E. Report on Danville, Va.

There are about ten Negro skate plumbers working around here (Danville, Va.), doing quite a lot of jobbing and repairing, but owing to the fact of not having an examining board it is impossible to stop them, hence the anxiety of the men here to organize. — *Plumbers, Gas and Steam Fitters Official Journal*, January, 1905, page 10.

Appendix IV

PUBLIC LICENSING AS A METHOD OF ELIMINATING NEGRO LOCOMOTIVE FIREMEN

The justice which has been denied the white firemen of the Georgia Railroad may be secured, not only for them, but for every white fireman in the South, through legislation such as that now pending in the law-making body of the State of Georgia.

The proposed bill fixes generally the limitations and powers of the Board of Examiners, who shall have themselves been firemen of not less than three years' experience, and shall be five in number.

If the act is passed and becomes a law it is expected to have the effect of reducing to a minimum the number of Negro firemen eligible to fill that position on locomtives in the state of Georgia. — *Locomotive Firemen's and Enginemen's Magazine*, August, 1909, page 278.

BIBLIOGRAPHY

BIBLIOGRAPHY OF WORKS CITED

BOOKS

ALEXANDER, DE A. S., Political History of the State of New York, Vol. III (1906).

ASHWORTH, JOHN H., The Helper and American Trade Unions (1915).

BARNES, CHARLES B., The Longshoremen (1915).

BRISSENDEN, PAUL F., The History of the I. W. W. (1920).

COMMONS, JOHN R., Trade Unionism and Labor Problems (1905).

────── AND ASSOCIATES, History of Labor in the United States (1918), 2 vols.

──────, U. B. PHILLIPS, AND J. B. ANDREWS (EDITORS), Documentary History of American Industrial Society (1910), Vols. II, VII, and IX.

DANIELS, JOHN, In Freedom's Birthplace (1914).

DODD, WILLIAM E., The Cotton Kingdom (1919).

DOUGLASS, FREDERICK, Life and Times of Frederick Douglass; an Autobiography (1892).

DU BOIS, W. E. B., Atlanta University Studies (1903-1907), Vols. VIII-XII.

────── The Philadelphia Negro (1895).

────── The Souls of Black Folk (1903).

────── AND AUGUST G. DILL, The Negro American Artisan (1912).

DUNN, ROBERT W., Labor and Automobiles (1929).

EBERT, JUSTUS, The I. W. W. in Theory and Practice (1920).

FINE, NATHAN, Labor and Farmer Parties in the United States (1928).

FITE, E. D., Social and Industrial Conditions in the North during the Civil War (1910).

FOSTER, WILLIAM Z., The Great Steel Strike (1920).

GLOCKER, THEODORE H., The Government of American Trade Unions (1913).

HARDMAN, J. B. S. (EDITOR), Labor Dynamics (1928).

HAYNES, GEORGE E., The Trend of Races (1922).

HAYWOOD, WILLIAM, Bill Haywood's Book, an Autobiography (1929).

HELPER, HINTON ROWEN, The Impending Crisis (1857, edition of 1860).

HILLQUIT, MORRIS, History of Socialism in the United States (1910).

HOXIE, R. F., Trade Unionism in the United States (1921).

HUNT, E. E., F. G. TRYON AND J. H. WILLITS, What the Coal Commission Found (1925).

JACQUES-GARVEY, AMY, Philosophy and Opinions of Marcus Garvey (1926).

JAMES, A. J., The First Convention of the A. F. of L. (Reprinted from *Western Pennsylvania Historical Magazine*, March 3, 1924.)

JOHNSON, JAMES WELDON (EDITOR), The Book of American Negro Poetry (1926).

LEAGUE FOR INDUSTRIAL DEMOCRACY, New Tactics in Social Conflict (1926).

LEWIS, JOHN L., The Miners' Fight for American Standards (1925).

MACDONALD, LOIS, Southern Mill Hills (1928).

MCNEILL, GEORGE E., The Labor Movement (1887).

MCPHERSON, EDWARD C., The Political History of the United States of America during the Period of Reconstruction (1875).

MITCHELL, BROADUS, The Rise of the Cotton Mills of the South (1921).

MONTGOMERY, ROYAL E., Industrial Relations in the Chicago Building Trades (1927).

PERLMAN, SELIG, A Theory of the Labor Movement (1928).

PHILLIPS, ULRICH B., American Negro Slavery (1918).

——— Life and Labor in the Old South (1929).

ROBINSON, JESSE E., The Amalgamated Association of Iron, Steel, and Tin Workers (1920).

RÜHLE, OTTO, Karl Marx (1929).

RUSSELL SAGE FOUNDATION, Wage-Earning Pittsburgh (1914).

SAPOSS, DAVID J., Left Wing Unionism (1926).

——— Readings in Trade Unionism (1925).

SAYRE, FRANCIS B., Cases on Labor Law (1922).

SCHLÜTER, HERMAN, Lincoln, Labor and Slavery (1913).

SIEGFRIED, ANDRÉ, America Comes of Age (1928).

SPERO, STERLING D., The Labor Movement in a Government Industry (1924).

STALEY, EUGENE, History of the Illinois State Federation of Labor (1930).

STALIN, JOSEPH, Leninism (1928).

SUFFERN, ARTHUR E., Conciliation and Arbitration in the Coal Industry of America (1915).

SYLVIS, JAMES C., Life, Speeches, Labors and Essays, of William H. Sylvis (1872).

TAYLOR, A. A., The Negro in the Reconstruction of Virginia (1926).

THOMPSON, HOLLAND, From Cotton Field to Cotton Mill (1906).

TRACY, GEORGE, History of the Typographical Union (1913).

TURNER, E. R., The Negro in Pennsylvania (1911).

WALTERSHAUSEN, AUGUST SARTORIUS, FREIHERR VON, Die Nordamerikanischen Gewerkschaften unter dem Einfluss der fortschreitenden Productionstecknik (1886).

WARE, NORMAN J., The Labor Movement in the United States, 1860-1895 (1929).

WARNE, FRANK JULIAN, History of the United Mine Workers of America (1905).

WASHINGTON, BOOKER T., The Story of the Negro (1909), Vol. II.
———— Up from Slavery (1913).

WESLEY, CHARLES H., Negro Labor in the United States (1927).

WOLFE, F. E., Admission to American Trade Unions (1912).

WOLMAN, LEO, The Growth of American Trade Unions, 1880-1923 (1924).

PAMPHLETS, ARTICLES, AND ESSAYS

ABELL, JOHN B., "Negro in Industry," *Trade Winds*, March, 1924.

ALLEN, GERALD, The Negro Coal Miner in Western Pennsylvania (MS. Master's Essay, University of Pittsburgh, 1927).

BRIGGS, CYRIL, "Our Negro Work," *Communist*, September, 1929.

BUREAU OF RAILWAY ECONOMICS, Arguments for and against Train Crew Legislation (1915).

CLARK, JOHN T., "Negro in Steel," *Opportunity*, March, 1926.

CLARKE, EDNA LOUISE (MRS. E. C. WENTWORTH), History of the Labor Controversy in the Slaughtering and Meat Packing Industry in Chicago (MS Master's Essay, University of Chicago, 1922).

COLORED CITIZENS' NON-PARTISAN COMMITTEE FOR THE REËLECTION OF MAYOR WALKER, New York City and the Colored Citizen (1929).

CONSUMERS' LEAGUE OF EASTERN PENNSYLVANIA, Colored Women as Industrial Workers in Philadelphia (1919-1920).

DABNEY, THOMAS D., "The Conquest of Bread," *Southern Workman,* October, 1928.

—— "Organized Labor's Attitude toward Negro Workers," *Southern Workman,* (August, 1928).

DIECKMANN, ANNETTE M., The Effect of Common Interests on Race Relations in Certain Northern Cities (MS Master's Essay, Columbia University, 1923).

DOMINGO, W. A., "Socialism Imperilled; or, The Negro — a Menace to American Radicalism," *Revolutionary Radicalism* (Report of the Lusk Committee), (1920), Vol. II.

FIES, MILTON A., Industrial Alabama and the Negro (1922).

FITCH, JOHN A., "Unionism in the Iron and Steel Industry," *Political Science Quarterly,* March, 1909.

FORD, JAMES, "Postponement of the R. I. L. U. Congress," *Labor Unity,* June 11, 1930.

FOSTER, WILLIAM Z., "How Life Has Been Brought into the Stockyards," *Life and Labor,* April, 1918.

FRAZIER, E. FRANKLIN, Negro Longshoremen (Essay written in New York School for Social Work, 1921. MS in Library of Russell Sage Foundation).

GITLOW, BENJAMIN, "For Genuine Militant Unionism," *Revolutionary Age,* May 21, 1930.

HARDY, ERIC W., The Relation of the Negro to Trade Unionism (MS Master's Essay, University of Chicago, 1911).

HARRIS, ABRAM L., The New Negro Worker in Pittsburgh (MS Master's Essay, University of Pittsburgh, 1924).

—— The Negro Population in Minneapolis (1926).

—— "The Negro Problem as Viewed by Negro Leaders," *Current History,* June, 1923.

HILL, JOSEPH A., "Recent Northward Migration of the Negro," *Monthly Labor Review,* March, 1924.

HOWARD, PERRY, "Open Letter to Pullman Porters," *Spokesman,* November, 1925.

JOHNSON, CHARLES S., "Negro Workers and the Unions," *Survey,* April 15, 1928.

KELSEY, CARL, "The Evolution of Negro Labor," *Annals of the American Academy of Political and Social Science,* January, 1903.

LEE, H. G., The History of the Negro in Organized Labor to 1872 (MS. Thesis, University of Wisconsin, 1914).

LEVINE, LOUIS, "Federated Labor and Compromise," *New Republic,* December 5, 1914.

LOVESTONE, JAY, The Crisis in the Communist Party (1930).

────── "Stop That Game of Bluff," *Revolutionary Age,* May 21, 1930.

LYNCH, JOHN R., "Some Historical Errors of James Ford Rhodes," *Journal of Negro History,* October, 1917.

MILLER, KELLY, "The Negro as a Workingman," *American Mercury,* November, 1925.

MUSTE, A. J., "The Crisis in the Miners' Union," *Labor Age,* March, 1930.

NORDHOFF, CHARLES, How Slavery Injures the Free Workingman (1865).

OVINGTON, MARY WHITE, "The Negro in the Trades Unions of New York," *Annals of the American Academy of Political and Social Science,* May, 1906.

PEPPER, JOHN, "American Negro Problems," *Communist,* October 1928.

POPE, HENRY, "Lest We Forget," Nashville *Globe,* May 25, 1928.

PROTOKOLL DES KOMMUNISTISCHEN KLUBS IN NEW YORK 1857-1867, (MS in Library, Rand School of Social Science, New York City).

RANDOLPH, A. PHILIP, "Porters Fight Paternalism," *American Federationist,* June, 1930.

REID, IRA DE A., The Negro in the Major Industries and Building Trades of Pittsburgh (MS Master's Essay, University of Pittsburgh, 1925).

REIS, W. F., Men and Mules (1907).

RUBINOW, I. M., "The Negro and Socialism," New York *Call,* May 19, 1912.

SAPOSS, DAVID J., "The Mind of the Immigrant Community," Interchurch World Movement, Commission of Inquiry, *Public Opinion and the Steel Strike* (1921).

STOLBERG, BENJAMIN, "The Stockyards Strike," *Nation,* January 25, 1922.

TRADE UNION EDUCATIONAL LEAGUE OF AMERICA, The Negro Industrial Proletariat (1928).

TUCKER, HELEN A., "Negroes in Pittsburgh," *Charities and The Commons,* January 3, 1909.

VAIL, CHARLES H., Socialism and the Negro Problem (1902).

WASHINGTON, BOOKER T., "The Negro and the Labor Unions," *Atlantic Monthly*, June, 1913.

—— "The National Business League," *World's Work*, October, 1902.

WRIGHT, R. R., "One Hundred Negro Steel Workers," *Wage-earning Pittsburgh* (1914).

—— "The Negro in Times of Industrial Unrest," *Charities*, October 7, 1905.

MAGAZINES

BLACK WORKER, February 1, 1930; March 1, 1930.

CARPENTER, April, 1902; January, 1903; February, 1903.

COOPERS' MONTHLY JOURNAL, September, 1871.

CRISIS, File, 1911-1930.

ELECTRICAL WORKER, April, 1903.

FINCHER'S TRADES' REVIEW, July 11, 1863; November 4, 1865.

INTERCOLLEGIATE SOCIALIST, December-January, 1918.

INTERNATIONAL SOCIALIST REVIEW, August, 1912.

LABOR'S NEWS, November 23, 1929; June 28, 1930.

LABOR UNITY, June 22, 1929.

LAW AND LABOR, February, 1929.

LOCOMOTIVE FIREMEN'S MAGAZINE, May, August, 1899; January, 1901; August, September, 1902; March, 1904; August, 1909; January, 1910; April, May, 1911; September, 1913.

MESSENGER, File, 1917-1928.

MONTHLY LABOR REVIEW, November, 1924.

NATION, May 29, 1920; September 14, 1921.

NATIONAL BROTHERHOOD WORKER, May, 1921.

NEGRO CHAMPION, June 23, 1928; August 8, 1928.

NEW MAJORITY, July 12, 1919; August 9, 1919; March 19, 1921.

NEW REPUBLIC, September 21, 1921; April 25, 1928.

OPPORTUNITY, File, 1923-1930.

OUTLOOK, June 5, 1909.

PLUMBERS' OFFICIAL JOURNAL, March, 1905.

POSTAL ALLIANCE, March, 1929.

POSTAL RECORD, October, 1917; October, 1919; October, 1927.

RAILROAD TRAINMAN, March, 1919; November, 1919.

RAILWAY POST OFFICE, February, 1929.

SOLIDARITY, September 8 and July 20, 1912.

SOUTHERN INDUSTRIAL FRATERNAL REVIEW, September 5, 1925; July-August, 1928.

SOUTHERN WORKMAN, November, 1924.

UNITED MINE WORKERS' JOURNAL, August 25, 1892; September 29, 1892; May 2, 1901; July 25, 1901; October 3, 1901.

NEWSPAPERS

CHARLESTON (N. C.)	*Daily News*, Jan. 5, 6, 7, 9, 1867; Feb., 1868. *News and Courier*, Jan. 26, 1875.
CHICAGO	*Defender*, Dec. 17, 1921; Dec. 8, 1928. *Record-Herald*, July 19, 1894. *Tribune*, July 13, 1894; March 13, 1921. *Whip*, March 29, 1924; May 15, 1926.
LOUISVILLE	*News*, Dec. 26, 1925.
MEMPHIS	*Press*, Jan. 14, 1919. *News-Scimiter*, Jan. 14, 1919.
MILWAUKEE	*Free Press*, Jan. 7, 1906.
NEW YORK	*Age*, April 21, 1928. *Call*, May 12, 1912; May 19, 1912. *Daily Worker*, Jan. 10, 1929; Feb. 12, 1929; Jan. 21, 1930. *Evening Journal*, March 15, 1928. *Times*, July 5, 6, 7, 1929. *Tribune*, Aug. 24, 1893; Aug. 25, 1893; Aug. 5, 1904; Aug. 25, 27, 1904. *World*, Aug. 1, 1921; Nov. 18, 1925; Nov. 19, 1925.
PITTSBURGH	*American*, Sept. 11, 1925. *Courier*, Feb. 13, 1926; April 14, 1928.
ST. LOUIS	*American*, March 31, 1928. *Argus*, Oct. 30, 1925; Nov. 2, 1925.
UNITED STATES DEPARTMENT OF LABOR	Press Releases, July 7, 1923; July 19, 1923; Oct. 24, 1923; Sept. 8, 1928.

WASHINGTON *Eagle*, March 23, 1928.
Daily Morning Chronicle, Jan. 12-16, 1869; July 13, 1869.
Star, Jan. 30, 1929.

BULLETINS, REPORTS, HEARINGS, PROCEEDINGS, ETC.

ALABAMA MINING INSTITUTE, Brief before United States Coal Commission, Aug. 31, 1923.

AMALGAMATED ASSOCIATION OF IRON AND STEEL WORKERS, Proceedings, 1881, 1900, 1905, 1908.

AMALGAMATED CLOTHING WORKERS OF AMERICA, Proceedings, 1920.

AMALGAMATED MEAT CUTTERS AND BUTCHER WORKMEN OF NORTH AMERICA, Proceedings, 1906.

AMERICAN FEDERATION OF LABOR, Proceedings, 1890, 1891, 1896, 1900, 1902, 1916, 1917, 1918, 1919, 1920, 1921, 1922, 1928, 1929.
——— Executive Council, An Open Letter to Ministers of the Gospel (undated, New York Public Library).

AMERICAN MANAGEMENT ASSOCIATION, The Negro in Industry, (Survey Report No. 5, 1923).

BAKERY AND CONFECTIONARY WORKERS' INTERNATIONAL UNION OF AMERICA, Proceedings, Sept., 1920.

BROTHERHOOD OF RAILWAY TRAINMEN, Proceedings, 1899.

CHICAGO COMMISSION ON RACE RELATIONS, Testimony (MS, Aug. 16, 1920).
——— The Negro in Chicago (1922).

COLORED ASSOCIATION OF RAILWAY EMPLOYEES, Statement of Facts from the Grievance Committee, Jan. 17, 1919.

COMMUNIST INTERNATIONAL, Sixth World Congress, International Press Correspondence, Vol. 8, Nos. 49, 72, 74, Aug. 13, Oct. 17 and 25, 1928.

COMMUNIST PARTY OF AMERICA, Proceedings, Fourth Convention, 1925.

FIRST INTERRACIAL CONFERENCE (held under auspices of Commission on Church and Race Relations of Federal Council of Churches and the Commission on Interracial Coöperation, Cincinnati, Ohio), Proceedings (March 25-27, 1925), Toward Interracial Coöperation.

INDUSTRIAL WORKERS OF THE WORLD, Proceedings, First Convention, 1905.

INTERCHURCH WORLD MOVEMENT, Commission of Inquiry, Report on the Steel Strike of 1919 (1920).

INTERNATIONAL ASSOCIATION OF CAR WORKERS, Proceedings (Special Session) 1905.

INTERNATIONAL BROTHERHOOD OF BOILERMAKERS, IRON SHIPBUILDERS AND HELPERS UNION, Proceedings, 1925.

INTERNATIONAL LADIES' GARMENT WORKERS' UNION, Proceedings, 1925.

JOHNSON, CHARLES S., Secretary, Abstracts of the Report of the Research Committee to the National Interracial Conference, Part IV (1928).

KANSAS, BUREAU OF LABOR AND INDUSTRIAL STATISTICS, 14th Annual Report, 1899.

KNIGHTS OF LABOR, Proceedings, 1885, 1886, 1887.

LABOR BUREAU INC., NEW YORK, The Case of the Pullman Porter (1926).

MARINE TRANSPORT WORKERS' INDUSTRIAL UNION No. 8, BRANCH 1, Strike Bulletin, Philadelphia, (June 15, 1920).

NATIONAL ASSOCIATION OF CORPORATION SCHOOLS, 8th Annual Convention, (1920).

NATIONAL BROTHERHOOD WORKERS OF AMERICA, Proceedings, 1920.

NATIONAL CONFERENCE OF SOCIAL WORK, Proceedings, 1919.

NEW YORK STATE DEPARTMENT OF LABOR, Hours and Earnings of Women Employed in Power Laundries in New York State (Special Bulletin No. 153, Aug., 1927).

NEW YORK STATE LEGISLATURE, Report of the Joint Legislative Committee Investigating Seditious Activities (1920), *Revolutionary Radicalism* (Report of the Lusk Committee), Vol. II.

PULLMAN COMPANY, Report of President Carry, 1922.

RAND SCHOOL OF SOCIAL SCIENCE, LABOR RESEARCH DEPARTMENT, American Labor Year Book, 1919-20, 1921-22, 1923-24, 1929.

RED INTERNATIONAL OF LABOR UNIONS, Report of the Fourth Congress, July, 1928.

SOCIALIST PARTY, Campaign Book, 1900, 1912.

――― Proceedings, 1904, 1910, 1912, 1919, 1924, 1928.

THAYER, ALONZO C., The Causes of Labor Turnover among Newly Employed Negro Miners of the Pittsburgh Coal and Pittsburgh Terminal Companies (1928). (MS. with Pittsburgh Urban League).

UNITED MINE WORKERS OF AMERICA, Proceedings, 1902, 1909.

UNITED STATES, ADMINISTRATOR FOR ADJUSTING LABOR DIFFERENCES ARISING IN CERTAIN PACKING HOUSE INDUSTRIES, First Arbitration Proceedings before Judge Alfred Alschuler, Jan.-March, 1918.

UNITED STATES, BITUMINOUS COAL COMMISSION, Award and Recommendations (1920).

UNITED STATES, BUREAU OF LABOR, Sixteenth Annual Report of the Commissioner of Labor, 1901.

—— Influence of Trade Unions on Immigrants (Bulletin No. 56, Jan., 1905).

UNITED STATES, COAL COMMISSION, Report, 1923.

UNITED STATES, CONGRESS, Congressional Record, Vol. 69, (Feb. 2, 1928).

—— Report of the Special Committee Authorized by Congress to Investigate the East St. Louis Riots (65th Congress, 2d Session, House Document No. 1231).

—— SENATE, Hearings before the Committee on Education and Labor (67th Congress, 1st Session, 1921), West Virginia Coal Fields.

—— SENATE, Hearings before the Committee on Interstate Commerce (70th Congress, 1st Session, 1928), Conditions in the Coal Fields of Pennsylvania, West Virginia, and Ohio.

—— SENATE, Hearings before Subcommittee of the Committee on the Judiciary (70th Congress, 1st Session, 1928), Limiting Scope of Injunctions in Labor Disputes.

—— SENATE, The Investigation Activities of the Department of Justice (Senate Documents, Vol. 12, 66th Congress, 1st Session, 1919).

UNITED STATES, DEPARTMENT OF COMMERCE, Fourteenth Census Report, 1920.

UNITED STATES, DEPARTMENT OF LABOR, BUREAU OF LABOR STATISTICS, Handbook of American Trade Unions (1926, 1929).

—— Handbook of Labor Statistics (1924-1926 and 1929).

—— Labor Laws in the United States (1925).

—— Labor Relations in Fairmont, West Virginia, (Bulletin No. 361, July, 1924).

—— Productivity of Labor in Merchant Blast Furnaces (Bulletin 474, 1929).

UNITED STATES, DEPARTMENT OF LABOR, DIVISION OF NEGRO ECONOMICS, The Negro at Work during the World War and during Reconstruction (1921).

UNITED STATES, IMMIGRATION COMMISSION, Report, 1907.

UNITED STATES, INDUSTRIAL COMMISSION, Report, 1901.

UNITED STATES, INTERSTATE COMMERCE COMMISSION, Brotherhood of Sleeping Car Porters *vs.* The Pullman Company, Docket No. 20007, Oct. 20, 1927.

UNITED STATES, RAILROAD ADMINISTRATION, Report of the Director General of Railroads, 1918.

UNITED STATES, RAILWAY LABOR BOARD, Decisions, Vol. II (1921).

VIRGINIA, DEPARTMENT OF LABOR AND INDUSTRY, Report, 1928.

WEST VIRGINIA, BUREAU OF NEGRO WELFARE AND STATISTICS, Annual Report, 1925-1926.

WEST VIRGINIA, DEPARTMENT OF MINES, Annual Report, 1926.

INDUSTRIAL AGREEMENTS, CONSTITUTIONS, RULES

AGREEMENT, Affiliated Dress Manufacturers, Inc., and the International Ladies Garment Workers' Union, New York, Feb., 1930.

―――― Association of Dress Manufacturers, Inc. and the International Ladies Garment Workers' Union, New York, Feb., 1930.

―――― Brotherhood of Railway Trainmen and the Southern Railway Association, January, 1910.

―――― Colored Firemen and the Management of the New Orleans Texas and Mexico Railway Company; the Beaumont, Sour Lake and Western Railway Company; and the New Iberia and Northern Railroad Company (The Gulf Coast Lines), Sept. 1, 1929.

―――― Missouri Pacific Railroad and the Boilermakers, Sheet Metal Workers, Machinists, Carmen, Blacksmiths, Electrical Workers, Painters, Their Helpers and Apprentices, effective Dec. 21, 1918.

―――― Northern West Virginia Coal Operators' Association and District 17 United Mine Workers of America, Feb. 10, 1923.

―――― Pullman Company and Its Porters and Maids, 1924, 1926, 1929.

―――― Six Shop Crafts with the Brotherhood of Firemen and Oilers regarding Negro Shop Craft Helpers (Railway Employees' Department, A. F. of L. File 8-112, April 10, 1924).

―――― United States Shipping Board and Screwmen's Benevolent

Association, Local 412 and Local 237, International Longshoremen's Association, New Orleans (1921).

ARBITRATION AWARD, SOUTHEASTERN RAILROAD, Basic Rates of Pay for Locomotive Firemen, Helpers, Hostlers and Outside Hostler Helpers on Railroads in the United States, May 1, 1927.

CONSTITUTIONS, Amalgamated Sheet Metal Workers' International Alliance, 1918, 1926.

—— American Negro Labor Congress (Constitution and Program), Oct. 25-31, 1925.

—— Bricklayers, Masons and Plasterers (Constitution and By-Laws), 1905, 1922.

—— Colored Railroad Workers' Union affiliated with American Federation of Railway Workers (Constitution and Due Book), 1918.

—— Hotel and Restaurant Employees' International Alliance.

—— Industrial Workers of the World (Preamble and Constitution), 1905.

—— International Brotherhood of Blacksmiths, Drop-Forgers and Helpers (Constitution and By-Laws).

—— Operative Plasterers and Cement Finishers.

—— Pullman Porters Benefit Association of America (Constitution and By-Laws), 1922-1923.

—— United Mine Workers, 1924.

RULES, Brotherhood of Railway Trainmen (Circular of Instructions No. E3, Grand Lodge), Oct., 1919.

—— Missouri Pacific Railroad, Oct. 1, 1920, Nov., 1920.

INDEX

INDEX

STERLING D. SPERO has been a member of the faculty of the Graduate School of Public Administration of New York University since 1939. He participated in the study *Labor and the Government,* conducted under the auspices of the Twentieth Century Fund, which has been credited with greatly influencing the shaping of the Wagner National Labor Relations Act. Dr. Spero is currently engaged in two major studies of unionism and collective bargaining.

ABRAM L. HARRIS taught economics at Howard University and the University of Chicago. Among his publications is the book *Economics and Social Reform.* Professor Harris died in November 1963.